Carl Lumholtz, Rasmus
Bjo

rn Anderson

AMONG CANNIBALS

Carl Lumholtz, Rasmus
Bjo
..
rn Anderson

AMONG CANNIBALS

ISBN/EAN: 9783741124938

Manufactured in Europe, USA, Canada, Australia, Japa

Cover: Foto ©Lupo / pixelio.de

Manufactured and distributed by brebook publishing software
(www.brebook.com)

Carl Lumholtz, Rasmus
Bjo

rn Anderson

AMONG CANNIBALS

AN ACCOUNT OF

FOUR YEARS' TRAVELS IN AUSTRALIA
AND OF CAMP LIFE WITH THE ABORIGINES OF
QUEENSLAND

BY

CARL LUMHOLTZ, M.A.
MEMBER OF THE ROYAL SOCIETY OF SCIENCES OF NORWAY

TRANSLATED BY

RASMUS B. ANDERSON
EX-UNITED STATES MINISTER TO DENMARK

WITH PORTRAIT, MAPS, 4 CHROMO-LITHOGRAPHS, AND WOODCUTS

NEW YORK
CHARLES SCRIBNER'S SONS
1889

TO

Paul B. Du Chaillu,

THE CELEBRATED EXPLORER OF AFRICA

AND

THE GREAT FRIEND OF SCANDINAVIA'S PAST AND PRESENT

AS EVINCED BY

'THE LAND OF THE MIDNIGHT SUN' AND 'THE VIKING AGE'

THIS ENGLISH EDITION IS MOST RESPECTFULLY

DEDICATED

BY

THE AUTHOR

AUTHOR'S PREFACE

IN the year 1880 I undertook an expedition to Australia, partly at the expense of the University of Christiania, with the object of making collections for the zoological and zootomical museums of the University, and of instituting researches into the customs and anthropology of the little-known native tribes which inhabit that continent.

At the commencement of my travels, which occupied four years, I spent some time in the south-eastern colonies, South Australia, Victoria, and New South Wales ; and succeeded in establishing connections with the museums in the cities of Adelaide, Melbourne, and Sydney, and I may add that everywhere I met with the most cordial reception. I am particularly indebted to the distinguished botanist Baron Ferd. von Mueller, of Melbourne ; to Fred. M'Coy, Professor of Zoology and Mineralogy in Melbourne University ; and to Dr. E. P. Ramsay, Director of the Museum in Sydney.

More than ten months from November 1880 to August 1881 were spent by me at the fine station of Gracemere in Central Queensland, belonging to Messrs. Archer and Co. Both here and elsewhere I was indebted to various members of the Archer family for kindnesses, which in many ways aided me in my work. I was placed under similar obligations to Walter J. Scott, Esq., the proprietor of the Valley of Lagoons station in Northern Queensland. To all these gentlemen I desire to express my sincere gratitude.

In August 1881 I entered upon my first journey of discovery, in the course of which I penetrated about 800 miles into Western Queensland, but the results in nowise corresponded to the hardships I had to endure.

I thereupon selected Northern Queensland as the field of my chief exploration, and here I spent fourteen months in constant travel and study. From August 1882 to July 1883 I made my headquarters in the valley of the short but comparatively broad and deep Herbert river, which empties itself into the Pacific Ocean at about 18° S. lat., and there I lived alone among a race of people whose culture—if indeed they can be said to have any culture whatever—must be characterised as the lowest to be found among the whole genus *homo sapiens*. Not only are many of the Australian aborigines cannibals, but most of the tribes have not yet emerged from the Stone Age in the history of their development. Others have studied the ethnographic peculiarities of this race ; but my predecessors have mainly directed their attention to the tribes of the southern part of Australia, which in many respects have attained a higher intellectual development than their northern kinsmen.

From my base on the Herbert river I made expeditions in various directions, extending in some instances to nearly 100 miles. The greater part of the volume now offered to the public is devoted to descriptions of my life in the camps of the northern savages in different districts. It has been my purpose to present a faithful picture, based on my own observations, of the life, manners, and customs of the Australian aborigines from their birth and infancy to their old age and death; and thus to rescue, for the science of ethnography, facts concerning tribes that have never before come into contact with white men, and that within a generation or two will have disappeared from the face of the earth.

While making these anthropological studies I also succeeded in securing a collection of zoological specimens, some of which are new to science, and all of which may be seen in the museums of the Christiania University. The collection consists mainly of vertebrates, including a considerable number of mammals, which have been described by Professor R. Collett in *Zoologischer Jahrbücher*, Jena, 1887. I brought home about 700 specimens of birds, a large number of reptiles and batrachians, numerous fishes, also some insects and lower animals. Among other things I discovered four new mammals, which have been described and named by Professor R. Collett in the *Proceedings of the Zoological Society of London*, 1884. The four new mammals are: *Dendrolagus lumholtzii* (the tree-kangaroo); and three opossums, *Pseudochirus archeri*, *Pseudochirus herbertensis*, and *Pseudochirus lemuroides*.

In conclusion, I desire to express my obligations to the friends who have helped me in carrying on my work, and in writing this record of it—to Professor Robert Collett and Professor Ossian Sars, of Christiania University, who first encouraged me to undertake the journey, and who never have failed to render me valuable aid and advice; to Dr. H. Reusch and Mr. A. M. Hansen, for their co-operation in drawing up a portion of the appendix to this volume; to Professor R. B. Anderson (late United States Minister to Denmark), for his aid in the preparation of the English edition; to Mr. M. R. Oldfield Thomas, for having revised the scientific names in the proofs for me during my absence in America; and to Mr. John Murray jun., for his assistance in the correction and supervision of the whole work while passing through the press.

Most of the illustrations are by Norwegian and French artists from original photographs, sketches, and specimens brought back by me from Australia.

It should be observed that the area marked red on the map as indicating the district explored by me should be extended so as to include Cashmere, Glendhu, the Valley of Lagoons, and all the intervening country.

As a foreigner, I would ask for the kind indulgence of my readers and critics towards any literary shortcomings in this English edition of my work.

CARL LUMHOLTZ.

LONDON, *August* 1889.

CONTENTS

CHAPTER I

CHAPTER II

CHAPTER III

CHAPTER IV

CHAPTER V

CHAPTER VI

CHAPTER VII

CHAPTER VIII

CHAPTER IX

CHAPTER X

CHAPTER XI

CHAPTER XII

CHAPTER XXVII

CHAPTER XXVIII

CHAPTER XXIX

--- ———

APPENDIX

'Ανδροφάγοι δὲ ἀγριώτατα πάντων ἀνθρώπων ἔχουσιν ἤθεα, οὔτε δίκην νομίζοντες οὔτε νόμῳ οὐδενὶ χρεόμενοι· νομάδες δὲ εἰσιν.

HERODOTUS, IV. 106.

ILLUSTRATIONS

b

BLACK SWAN.

CHAPTER I

ON May 24, 1880, I went on board the barque *Einar
Tambarskjelver* bound from Snar Island near Christiania to
Port Adelaide with a cargo of planed lumber. I carried
with me a hunter's outfit, guns, ammunition, and other articles
necessary for the chase, furnished me by the University of
Norway, as well as some northern bird skins in order to
inaugurate exchange with Australian museums. Sailing in
the north-east trade-winds, a sunset in the tropics, or a mild
starlit night on the ocean with a blazing phosphorescent sea,
do not fail to make a strong impression. Then passing the
pacific belt of the ocean, where a dead calm is suddenly
interrupted by the most violent storm, you soon reach,
by the aid of the south-east trades, the region of the
westerly winds. The Southern Cross and the cloud of

Magellan, the gigantic sperm-whale, whose huge head now
and then appeared above the surface of the water, and the
albatross, whose glorious flight we never ceased to admire,
heralded our arrival within the limits of the Southern
Ocean.   Cape-doves, albatrosses, and gulls accompanied us
for weeks together.   The passage had, however, at times
its dark sides.   On August 17, at six o'clock in the
morning, we were overtaken by a most violent gale.   All
the sails, except the close-reefed topsails and foresail, were
taken in.   We shipped many seas.   The stairs to the
quarter-deck were crushed ;   one wave broke through two
doors in the companion-way to the steerage, another set all
the water-casks afloat in the maddest confusion, a third
filled the galley, so that the cook found himself waist-deep
in water.   The fire was extinguished, and the food was
mixed with the salt water.   Several times the seas broke
through our main cabin door, filling my cabin with water,
making boots, socks, books, and other articles swim about
in all directions.

On a long journey one gets tired of the sea, this " desert
of water," as the Arab calls it—and we long to set foot
again on *terra firma*.   According to the calculations of the
captain we were fifty geographical miles from the coast of
Australia, when one morning we perceived for the first time
the smell of land, in this instance a peculiarly bitter but
mildly aromatic odour, as of fragrant resin.   This fragrance,
doubtless, came from the acacias, which at this time were
in full bloom.   For by the aid of the wind these trees,
particularly *Acacia fragrans*, diffuse the fragrance of
their flowers to a great distance, and this morning
there was blowing a fresh, damp breeze directly from the
land.

On the afternoon of August 29 we got sight of land.
In the evening we saw the lighthouse on Kangaroo Island ;
followed by dolphins we navigated through Investigator
Straits, and on the afternoon of the next day we anchored
outside Port Adelaide.   As it was raining, we contented
ourselves with viewing the town from the distance.   Our
eyes involuntarily rested on a number of chimneys, an
evidence of extensive manufactories.

What most interested me here was the Botanical Garden, which I visited the same day. The weather was splendid, the rays of the sun were reflected in large ponds, where the water-fowl were swimming among papyrus and Babylonian weeping-willows. The parrots chattered in their cages, and displayed their brilliant plumage; the birds sang in the cultivated bushes of the garden, and the frogs croaked with that harsh, strong note, which seems especially developed in tropical lands. There was a life, a throng, an assemblage of dazzling colours, which could not but make a deep impression

FLINDERS STREET, ADELAIDE.

on a person whose eyes for a hundred days had seen nothing but sky and water.

This fine garden contains forty-five acres, and is excellently managed by Dr. R. Schomburgk, celebrated for his travels in British Guiana. In the "palm-house," built of glass and iron, are found tropical plants. The most beautiful and most imposing part of the park is the so-called garden of roses, a large square enclosure surrounded by garlands of tastefully-arranged climbing roses. Here is an abundance of varieties, beginning with the tallest rose-bushes and ending with the smallest dwarf-roses, and the colours vary from the most dazzling white to the darkest red or almost black.

Among the trees familiar to me in this park were an alder and a birch. They stood very modestly, just putting forth their leaves in company with grand magnolias in

VIEW NEAR ADELAIDE.

blossom, elegant araucarias, and magnificent weeping-willows. The hot-houses near the superintendent's dwelling were admirable, and presented a wealth of the greatest variety of flowers from all parts of the world, but mainly from Australia.

Some groups of fine bamboo particularly attracted my attention. The park is visited by several thousand people every Sunday afternoon.

Adelaide, containing about 60,000 inhabitants, is a very regularly laid out city. All the streets cross one another at right angles, and are very broad. Along the gutters railings are placed, to which people may hitch their horses. Even servants go to market on horseback with baskets on their arms.

The residences are constructed in a very practical manner, suited to the demands of the climate, with verandahs and beautiful gardens. In many parts of the city there are public reading-rooms, where the latest newspapers may be found. In the forenoon these reading-rooms are always full of people, particularly of the working classes.

The city cannot fail to make a favourable impression upon the traveller. It is cleanly and elegant, corresponding to its feminine name Adelaide. The inhabitants are unusually amiable, and they are renowned for their hospitality, and this is saying a great deal in so hospitable a land as Australia.

From Adelaide to Melbourne is a three days' journey, and early one morning I went on board a steamer bound for this port. Once there we immediately perceive that we have come to a metropolis, for the flags of all nations are unfurled to the breeze in its harbour.

The International Exhibition was to be opened in a few weeks, and in the distance we could already see the great cupola of the building looming up above the rest of the city. Great clouds of dust appeared in the streets, giving us an idea of Melbourne's dry climate. After a slow voyage up the shallow Yarra river, during which we actually stuck in the mud once or twice, we finally landed at the wharf.

Melbourne with its suburbs has only 300,000 inhabitants, but has the appearance of being much larger on account of its broad and straight streets and its numerous parks and magnificent public buildings.

The first building attracting our attention is the Library, a noble structure in classical style, but the first thing the inhabitants want the stranger to notice is the Post Office and

Town Hall. The question is being perpetually asked: "*Have* you seen the Town Hall and the Post Office?" The Assembly Room in the Town Hall contains one of the largest organs in the world; it has 4373 pipes.

The residence of the Governor occupies a commanding height, and is surrounded by a large park, which is directly connected with the Botanical Garden.

The University, which is attended by about 400 students, has, since 1880, been open to women, who are now admitted

THE LIBRARY, MELBOURNE.

to all the courses except medicine! It possesses a large museum, where the animals are in part set up in groups representing scenes from their daily life, a most instructive arrangement. Here can also be seen a fossilised egg of the extinct gigantic bird from Madagascar, the *Æpyornis maximus.*

The city contains a number of magnificent churches, hospitals, and benevolent institutions. The streets are large, wide, and have immense gutters. It has been well said by an author that Melbourne is London seen through the small end of the telescope.

People seem to be very busy, and move through the streets with great rapidity. Melbourne is a city of enjoyments and luxuries, equipped with great elegance and comfort; everything suggests money and the power of wealth. There is no article of luxury which is not to be found here, from Norwegian herring to champagne in every degree of dryness.

THE GOVERNOR'S HOUSE,
MELBOURNE.

Among sports, horse-racing ranks first, and not a week passes without one or more races on the celebrated Flemmington racecourse, near the city, taking place. Every year, in the beginning of November, about 120,000 people come together to witness the great Melbourne Cup race, where fortunes are lost and won.

The whites born in Australia are gradually becoming a distinct race, differing from other Englishmen. They have a more lively temperament, and are slighter in frame, but tall, erect, and muscular. I also observed in Queensland that some of the children had a tendency to the American twang. The Australians pay great attention to travellers visiting their country, and they are very proud of showing its attractions. Thus a stranger may, as a rule, count on getting a free pass on all the railroads. The ladies are free and easy in their manners. They are frank and confiding, and their acquaintance is quickly made. Their friendship, once gained, may be relied on, and they are untiring in their acts of kindness.

In no other place in the world do the labouring classes have as much influence as in Victoria ; for the *working men* in fact govern the colony. As a rule, they are well educated, and keep abreast of the times, but still their administration of affairs has not always been successful. The economical condition of the labouring classes in Melbourne is excellent, but they are rather fond of intoxicating drinks. I am able to give an example, showing how the people of Australia keep themselves informed on public questions. I once spoke to a labourer whom I met on the street in Melbourne, and as he noticed that I was a stranger, he asked me where my home was. When he learned that I came from Norway, he exclaimed : "Oh, we know Norway very well, and *the Norwegian scheme !*" He then explained this to me as best he could. I afterwards learned that Victoria, in 1874, was on the point of adopting a parliament like the Norwegian, with one chamber which divides itself into two bodies (the odelsthing and lagthing), a proposition which was on the point of being carried.

The climate of Melbourne is not particularly warm, though during the summer excessively hot winds from the interior of the continent may blow for a few days, and not infrequently children die from the heat at this time. The sudden changes of temperature, peculiar to the southern part of Australia, also annually demand their victims, though upon the whole the climate must be regarded as very healthy.

Before leaving Melbourne I made several excursions far into the colony. On one of these I visited the celebrated mining town Ballarat, the place which marks the first epoch in the history of Victoria, and of all Australia for that matter, for it was the gold which especially drew the attention of the world to the new continent.

Since 1851 the annual production of gold in Australia has averaged ten million pounds sterling.

No traveller should neglect to view " the highest trees in the world," for it is easy to see them near Melbourne. *Eucalyptus amygdalina* grows, according to the famous botanist Baron F. v. Mueller, to a greater height than the *Wellingtonia sequoia* of California. Trees have been measured more than 450 feet high. Though these gum-trees are without comparison the highest in the world, they must yield the place of honour in regard to beauty and wealth of foliage. They send forth but a couple of solitary branches from their lofty tops. Thus the *Wellingtonia* retains the crown as the king of the vegetable kingdom. F. v. Mueller says of *Eucalyptus amygdalina:* " It is a grand picture to see a mass of enormously tall trees of this kind, with stems of mast-like straightness and clear whiteness, so close together in the forest as to allow them space only toward their summit to send their scanty branches and sparse foliage to the free light."

At a sheep station about 100 miles from Melbourne I made the acquaintance of two of the most common mammals of Australia. One day I went out hunting with a son of the friend that I was visiting. We learned that a koala or native bear (*Phascolarctus cinereus*) was sitting on a tree near the hut of a shepherd. Our way led us through a large but not dense wood of leafless gum-trees. My companion told me that the forest was dead, as a result of " ring-barking." To get the grass to grow better, the settler removes a band of bark near the root of the tree. In a country where cattle-raising is carried on to so great an extent this may be very practical, but it certainly does not beautify the landscape. The trees die at once after this treatment, and it is a sad and repulsive sight to see these withered giants as if in despair stretching their white barkless branches towards the sky. When we came to the spot, we found the bear asleep and perfectly calm on a branch of a tree opposite the shepherd's hut. One

must not suppose that the Australian bear is a dangerous animal. It is called "native bear," but is in nowise
related to the bear family. It is an innocent and peaceful
marsupial, which is active only at night, and sluggishly
climbs the trees, eating leaves and sleeping during the whole
day. As soon as the young has left the pouch, the mother
carries it with her on her back.

NATIVE BEAR WITH ITS YOUNG.

We did not think it worth while to shoot the sleeping
animal, but sent a little boy up in the tree to bring it down.
He hit the bear on the head with a club and pushed it so
that it fell, taking care not to be scratched by its claws,
which are long and powerful.

The Australian bear is found in considerable numbers
throughout the eastern part of the continent, even within
the tropical circle. I discovered a new kind of tape-worm
which, strange to say, is found in this leaf-feeding animal.

HUNTING THE OPOSSUM

One day our dog put up a kangaroo-rat, which fled to a hollow tree lying on the ground. When we examined the tree it was found to contain another animal also, namely an opossum (*Trichosurus vulpecula*). It is one of the most common mammals in Australia, and is of great service to the natives, its flesh being eaten and its skin used for

TREE-FERNS IN VICTORIA.

clothes. The civilised world, too, has begun to appreciate the value of this kind of fur, which is now exported in large quantities to London. The natives kill the animal in the daytime by dragging it out from the hollow trees where it usually resides. Among the colonists the younger generation are very zealous opossum hunters. They hunt them for sport, going out by moonlight and watching the animal as it goes among the trees to seek its food.

I was now about to leave the capital of Victoria, a city which cannot fail to be admired by the stranger. It is indeed a remarkable fact that in the same place where fifty years ago the shriek of the parrot blended with the noise of the camp of the native Australian, an international exhibition should be held in a metropolis. The first house was built in Melbourne in 1835—the "World's Fair" took place in 1880. It is not merely in jest that Melbourne is called "the Queen of the South."

CHAPTER II

My next visit was to Melbourne's mother city, Sydney, the oldest city of Australia.

As is known, it was originally a colony of criminals, but when the wealth of Australia, its gold and its rich pastures, were discovered, the colony got a large accession of all classes of society, and before long transportation ceased. The city is now very aristocratic and has a more antique appearance than Melbourne; the

SYDNEY HARBOUR.

streets are crooked and uneven; but there are several fine buildings, which do not, however, attract the attention they deserve on account of the unevenness of the ground. The Museum is admirably situated, and its magnificent treasures are well worth visiting. To our surprise we found it open on

Sundays, while in the other towns in Australia, even the smallest, the Sabbath is observed as strictly as in England. Scientific investigation flourishes in Sydney, and several natural history collections are owned by private individuals. The museum of Mr. W. M'Leay deserves special mention. It is really wonderful. The city has reason to be proud of its Botanical Garden, which extends down to the harbour, and is for a great part washed by the sea. The climate is sub-tropical, so that plants from the various zones grow side by side. Thus I noticed *Digitalis purpurea* and the elm-tree growing by the side of *Ficus elastica* and other tropical plants. On the yellow water-lilies (*Nuphar luteum*) the sparrows were singing as merrily as if this were their native land.

In Adelaide I was advised to say, when I came to Melbourne, that Adelaide was a hole, and that no city in the southern hemisphere could be compared with Melbourne, the Queen of the South ; but if I desired to keep on good terms with the people of Sydney, I must take care not to praise Melbourne. On the other hand, I was advised to praise Sydney harbour as the finest in the world.

And it is truly a wonderful harbour. It is large enough to hold all the fleets of the world, and its beauty reminds one of the celebrated entrances to Rio and to Naples.

As the hotels of the city are not clean, and are supplied with most impertinent servants, the visitor should try to secure an introduction to one of the clubs, for there he is always sure of being perfectly comfortable.

If a person comes from the busy and lively Melbourne, he may find Sydney sleepy and lazy, but it must not be considered a city of loafers. It is celebrated for its colossal wealth.

The lower class of the inhabitants seemed to me to be inquisitive and greedy ; the cultivated classes, on the other hand, are engaging and hospitable, and make a most favour-able impression.

Between Melbourne and Sydney there is great rivalry. " It is no exaggeration to say that New South Wales and Victoria are no less rivals than Germany and France," said an Australian literary gentleman. How far he was right I cannot say. Meanwhile the following circumstance shows that the jealousy is very great. Immediately after Sydney, in

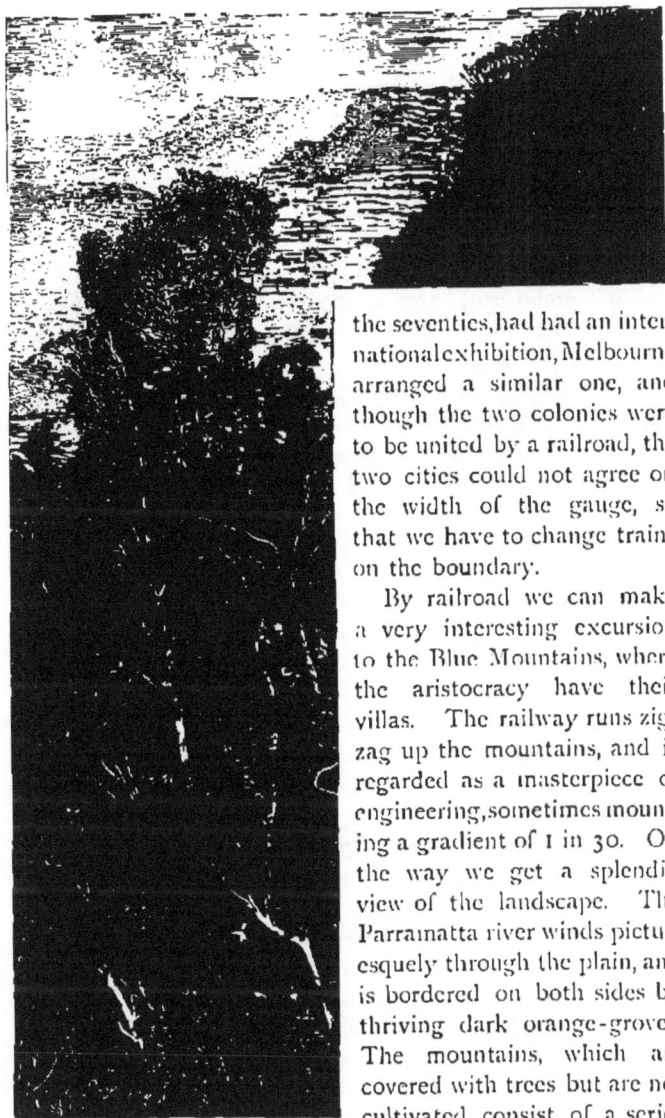

THE BLUE MOUNTAINS.

the seventies, had had an international exhibition, Melbourne arranged a similar one, and though the two colonies were to be united by a railroad, the two cities could not agree on the width of the gauge, so that we have to change trains on the boundary.

By railroad we can make a very interesting excursion to the Blue Mountains, where the aristocracy have their villas. The railway runs zig-zag up the mountains, and is regarded as a masterpiece of engineering, sometimes mounting a gradient of 1 in 30. On the way we get a splendid view of the landscape. The Parramatta river winds picturesquely through the plain, and is bordered on both sides by thriving dark orange-groves. The mountains, which are covered with trees but are not cultivated, consist of a series of parallel ridges of the same height, which are rent by deep ravines. One ridge rises beyond the other until the last is lost in the blue distance.

It is a journey of but little more than two days to Brisbane, the capital of Queensland. Not long after passing the boundaries of New South Wales, the southern entrance of Moreton Bay is reached, a large and shallow body of water not far from the city. When we neared the shore, the sea broke over the long sand bars, which it was very difficult to cross, but we soon afterwards found ourselves in the calm water of the bay. The sun set as a blood-red disc in tropical splendour. Immediately afterwards the full moon rose and shone on the beautiful banks of the Brisbane river, while we steamed slowly up between the forests of mangroves.

We now approached the land in whose solitary regions I was about to spend several years. I stood alone on deck in the sultry night, and my thoughts naturally turned to this strange country. What was I to find in Queensland? Was I perhaps to leave my bones in this land, slain by the blacks, bitten by a snake, or poisoned by malaria?

In Brisbane I met Mr. Archer, the Secretary of the Treasury of Queensland. I had a letter of introduction to him from the zoological professors of the University of Christiania, and was invited by him to make my head-quarters on his estate near Rockhampton.

After a journey of two days we arrived at the mouth of Fitzroy river. Like all the rivers of Queensland, it is very shallow and not navigable for large vessels. This is at present a great drawback to the maritime commerce of the colony; but there are some good harbours, and efforts are continually being made to remove obstacles by dredging.

Passengers and baggage were now transferred to a smaller steamboat, which carried us up the stream. The left bank is flat and uninteresting; while a range of mountains about 1400 feet high rises on the right bank. After a few hours' journey we pass a large establishment for canning meat, in which solder alone for the tin cans amounts to about £300 annually,—and then almost immediately arrive at Rockhampton, the second city in the young colony, containing about 9000 inhabitants. The first thing which attracts attention on arrival is a remarkably fine suspension bridge across the river.

The town itself contains nothing remarkable ; still a fine hospital and a large school-building, both built on a hill just behind the city, may be worthy of mention. Rockhampton consists mainly of one-storied houses with verandahs. The streets, as is the case in almost all Australian towns, have awnings over the side-walks, a very wise provision against the burning heat of the sun. Business is lively in the city, which is of importance as the metropolis of a large extent of territory whose products are marketed and exported here.

THE PARLIAMENT HOUSE, BRISBANE.

This is also the distributing point from which stations in the western part of Queensland are supplied with all sorts of articles of necessity and luxury. A railway extends nearly 300 miles to the west.

Like other Australian cities, Rockhampton of course has its botanical gardens, which in time will be very fine.

We at once drove to Gracemere, Messrs. Archer's cattle station, situated seven miles from the city. The country was flat, monotonous, and swampy, but on approaching the station the ground began to rise. On reaching the highest point a wide view suddenly burst upon us. Before us lay a large lake sparkling in the last rays

C

of the setting sun, hundreds of birds swam on its glassy surface, and on the green shores was feeding a large flock of geese, which hissed and took flight as we passed. On a promontory extending far out into the lake was the station, which was to be my home for some time to come; with its many houses it had the appearance from the distance of a small village.

FROGS (*Hyla cærulea*) ENTERING A WATER-JAR.

We drove along a mighty hedge of cactus to the main building, which lay on the extreme point of the land. The bare timber walls did not impress me very favourably, coming as I did from the luxury of Melbourne and Sydney, but the spacious apartments and cool verandahs gave me a hospitable greeting and looked cheerful and inviting.

When we had taken tea, Mr. Archer brought out his microscope in order to let me examine some insects, thousands of which were swarming about the lamp. But white ants had taken possession of the case, so that the microscope was unfit for use. These insects are a great nuisance throughout Queensland, and precautions must always be taken against them when a house is built. It was a strange life which I now experienced for the first time in the Australian "bush." The summer heat was oppressive in the pitchy darkness of a November evening, though now and then lighted up by flashes of lightning. The insects gathered in great numbers on the ceiling, and blinded by the lamplight they fell in such thick layers on the table that it was not possible to read. Bats fluttered in and out through the open windows and doors. Not only on the floor, but, incredible as it may seem, even in the water-jar, the frogs croaked merrily and often so loudly as to interfere with conversation.

I, however, soon felt perfectly comfortable at the station, where I spent seven pleasant months of summer and winter, busily engaged in my new and rich field of activity. A small house was given me as my working-room, and it was so arranged as to serve as a safe repository for my collections.

My European summer clothes soon became too warm for me, and the first thing I did was to secure the usual Australian dress, which everybody wears who lives in the bush. A light merino-wool shirt, having over this a coloured cotton shirt open in the neck, with sleeves rolled up to the elbows, trousers of heavy white cotton cloth called moleskin, white cotton socks, shoes, a broad-brimmed felt hat with the brim turned down, constitute the dress of the bushmen. This suit of clothes, which can be bought ready-made at a low price anywhere in Australia, is neat and cleanly and very convenient.

The region about Rockhampton is well known for its warm and dry climate, 100° F. being quite frequent during the summer months. Gracemere lies just far enough within the tropical circle to permit us to speak of tropical Australia ; the heat is even greater here than farther north in the more damp sea-climate, where the trade-wind blows. In the winter, hoar-frost is occasionally seen on the ground, and now and then ice may form on a pool of water. Thus it will be seen that the thermometer does not really go very low, but at such times the cold is felt so intensely that it is a comfort to get near a fire.

The sky is almost always clear and cloudless; the air is pure and transparent, especially in winter, when the mountains have a very beautiful deep blue colour. In the clear winter evenings after sunset the heavens often assume a remarkable greenish hue.

It cannot be denied that there is something wearisome and monotonous in a continuous summer—for there is nothing but summer in the greater part of the land—yet

GRACEMERE STATION.

every one who rejoices in sunshine and warmth will be contented in the climate of Queensland; it is doubtless more salubrious than any other in the tropical world.

The principal building at the station, like all the other houses, is almost entirely surrounded by a verandah, which is enclosed in a remarkable manner by creeping fig-trees clinging firmly to the posts. The roof is covered after the Australian fashion with sheets of zinc, and large iron tanks are placed at the corners of the house to catch the rain-water, for this is almost universally used for drinking throughout Australia; it is usually suspended on the verandah in canvas bags, which exposes it to a rapid evaporation and makes it as cold as ice.

Down towards the lake there is a very fine garden, where orange-trees, vines, and the European fig-tree grow side by side with the pine-apple and the mango of the tropical zone. In the winter, stocks, recedas, and asters flourish very well, but the summer is too warm for them. Pelargonium and calladium glow in brilliant colours.

The other most conspicuous trees in the garden are the magnificent Madagascar *Poinciana regia*, tamarind, the Brazilian jacaranda, and several sorts of Australian spruce, especially a beautiful specimen of bunya-bunya (*Araucaria*

THE MAIN BUILDING, GRACEMERE STATION.

bidwillii). This grand tree grows only in a limited territory from Darling Downs north to Burnett river, and is protected by the Government for the sake of the aborigines, who collect the huge cones and use the seeds for food.

Cocoa-nut and date-palms delight the eye, but do not bear good fruit, although the reason is not apparent.

Near the lake the celebrated Egyptian papyrus has been planted in large quantities, and forms a perfect grove. A little singer, the *Acrocephalus australis*, has made his home in this papyrus grove, where several pairs are nesting. It sings in the evening and in the night, and is considered to

be Australia's best song-bird.   The lake, or lagoon as it is
called here, is a little more than a mile long and half a mile
wide, and is the resort of a great number of water-fowls.
In the winter more than 400 pelicans are seen here, but in
the middle of the summer most of them depart.

The pelicans do the most of their fishing in the night,
and together.   The noise they make with the splashing of
their wings while thus occupied sounds something like that
of a paddle-wheel steamer in motion.   Occasionally I could
see them rise, apparently without moving their wings, in a
spiral direction, higher and higher, until they disappeared
from sight.   It seemed as if they did it only for amusement or for the purpose of enjoying the sunshine.   When
they return, they come down so swiftly that a sough is heard
in the air.

A few black swans (*Cygnus atratus*) are seen now and
then.   In November I frequently heard them sing on the
water in the evening.   Ducks and geese abound, and so do
gray and blue cranes, cormorants, and snake-birds (*Plotus*).
Not many years ago Mr. A. Archer counted thirty-seven
kinds of birds on the lagoon.   And still the birds are few
now, both as to numbers and species, as compared with what
they were twenty years ago.   The cattle have eaten the tall
grass and the weeds growing in the shallow water near the
shores of the lake, where thousands of birds found their
homes.   Even black swans made their nests here.   Mr.
Archer believes that a few years ago there were more than
10,000 birds on this lake.   If a gun was fired, the birds
rose with a noise like distant thunder.

The most striking bird on the lagoon is doubtless the
beautiful *Parra gallinacea*, which in Australia is called the
lotus-bird.   It sits on leaves that float on the water,
particularly those of the water-lily.   Blue water-lilies are
found in great numbers along the edge of the lagoon,
and hence the lotus-bird is very common here.   It is somewhat larger than a thrush, and has very long legs, and
particularly highly developed toes, which enable it to walk
about on the floating leaves.   Its food consists chiefly of
snails and insects, which it usually finds by turning the
lily leaf.   Its simple nest is also built on the leaves.

The eggs, which are a beautiful brown with lines and spots, are considered very rare, and are remarkable both on account of their form and colour. They look, says Gould, as though they were drawn by a man who had amused himself by covering the surface with fantastic lines. The young look very funny on account of their long legs and big toes as compared with their small bodies.

The grown bird is not shy, but the young are extremely timid. I had once or twice seen the old birds with young, but as soon as I approached them, the young always disappeared, while the old birds walked about fearlessly, as if there was no danger. It long remained a mystery to me, how they could conceal themselves so well and so long, but one day the problem was solved. An old bird came walking with two young ones near shore. I hid behind a tree and let them come close to me. As I suddenly made my appearance, the small ones dived under the water and held themselves fast to the bottom, while I watched them for a quarter of an hour, before taking them up.

There are large quantities of fish in the lagoon, several varieties of perch, eel, and a kind of pike with a very long snout (the gar-fish). But the fresh-water mullet (*Mugil*) is particularly abundant : it has a remarkable power of leaping out of the water, and in so doing it frequently comes unawares up into the boat and is caught. When the lagoon, on account of long-continued drought, is very low, you can always be sure while bathing of coming in contact with some kind of fish, which sometimes flies over your head.

Gracemere was originally a sheep station, but latterly the sheep have entirely given place to cattle on the whole coast. This change is partly due to the climate, which is too moist, and partly to a nocuous kind of grass, namely the dreaded spear-grass (*Andropogon contortus*), which grows on the coast, and which rendered sheep-raising impossible. It stuck fast in the wool of the sheep, or worked itself into their very bodies and killed them. For this reason Gracemere is now exclusively a cattle station. The sheep were about 350 miles farther west.

As a curiosity it may be mentioned that in the vicinity of Gracemere I saw the *Phragmites communis*, so well known in Norway, probably the only plant which the Norwegian and Queensland floras have in common.

As Messrs. Archer are naturalised Norwegians from Scotland, it may perhaps be interesting to learn that they were the first white men who occupied the spot where Rockhampton now is situated. They have also given Norse names to several localities in the vicinity, as for instance Mount Berserker and Mount Sleipner. The run of their station was at first fifty miles long and twenty miles wide. But gradually, as the country became settled, the " squatters " were not permitted to retain these larger pastures, which they do not themselves own, but occupy by paying rent to the Government. Hence the area of the station very soon became reduced, when the land, owing to the increase of population, was offered for sale. This is usually the case with all new land in Australia. First comes the large sheep and cattle-owner—the squatter—who often lays claim to immense territory. Later he must give place to the smaller selectors, who as a rule cultivate the soil. The squatter is, however, allowed to purchase a certain part of the land for his own possession and use. This the Archers had done. On the run there were at this time only 4000 head of cattle, but they were all of pure pedigree. They had recently brought from Melbourne a bull nine months old for which they had paid £315. It is for the sake of the beef and not for milk that so much stress is laid upon the blood of cattle in Australia.

The vicinity around Rockhampton and Gracemere furnishes considerable variety both of flora and of fauna. The country is hilly, and well watered with small lakes and streams. Along the streams vine-scrubs often abound. The gum-tree (*Eucalyptus*), so characteristic of Australia, also marks the woodlands here, and appears in greater variety than is generally seen in so limited a territory. The gum-trees fit for lumber, *Eucalyptus tereticornis* and *Eucalyptus brachypoda*, are very abundant in swampy places, along with isolated groups of the well-known *Melaleuca leucodendron*, called by the colonists tea-tree, from which is extracted what is known in medicine as cajeput oil. The heights nearest the station are particularly well covered with the tree

IN THE NEIGHBOURHOOD OF ROCKHAMPTON.

To face page 24

familiar to the colonists as blood-wood (*Eucalyptus terminalis*), besides a great many other trees of the same family. A few varieties of acacia, *e.g.*, *A. bidwillii* and *A. salicina*, are found where the hills are drier. On the plains box-tree (*Eucalyptus polyanthemos*) predominates. In a circle of fifteen miles about Rockhampton there are found so many useful trees that the number of species is about one-third of all the useful trees in the colony. Although many of these have great value as strong and solid timber, still they fall far short of being utilised as they deserve. The colonists use the most valuable wood for ordinary purposes, as for building houses and fences. In a tree like *Tristiana suaveolens* may be found a remarkably fine material for work under water, while the *Eucalyptus robusta* furnishes the best mahogany that can be desired.

Various parasites and epiphytes are found in great numbers in the woodlands, as for instance the *Ficus platypoda* and *Ficus cunninghamii*, which grow on the large gum-trees. They send their roots down from giddy heights, enclose the tree, and at last destroy it.

Though the gum-trees usually give the Australian landscape a monotonous appearance, the region about Rockhampton is very beautiful and picturesque. The many little lakes and the changing forms of the hills contribute much to this result. On the lagoons float the beautiful blue water-lilies ; the rare and splendid *Nelumbium speciosum* is also occasionally found.

But the greatest interest centres in the scrubs along the little streams. In contrast with the woodland, where a single kind of tree may prevail, we here find a multitude of families, genera, and species, of which none predominates. All are mixed together, but form more or less a harmonious whole. The average colour of this scrub is usually dark green, but in the edges we find a pleasing change into a lighter green. Here we find the *Bauhinia hookerii*, with its fine light-coloured leaves, and *Capparis nobilis* shines with its large white flowers.

There are only a few ground-flowers, but a number of creeping plants. The trees are festooned with climbing plants such as *Vitis climatidea* and others. Vitis in great abundance and of many varieties are found especially in the scrubs, hence the colonists call this kind of brush *vine-scrub*. The charming *Callistemon lanceolatum*, which is common in the scrubs along the Queensland streams, attracts our attention on account of its rich scarlet flowers, the

LAUGHING JACKASS (*Dacelo gigas*).

more so since the total effect of a scrub is green and very monotonous.

This does not however hinder us from finding beautiful woody scenes along the streams, often indeed so charming that we fancy ourselves transported to an ideal landscape. It is not necessary to be a special lover of nature in order to be captivated by the picturesque arches of the trees over the winding stream, where the silence is broken only by the

VINE-SCRUB NEAR GRACEMERE. *To face page 27.*

shrill cry of the cockatoo or the tittering ha! ha! ha! ha!
of the laughing jackass. Suddenly, as we walk through the
vine-scrub, a lizard will throw itself down into the water with
a great splash to disturb a poor water-hen that has become
absorbed in its own meditations on the strand.

Few of the birds of Australia have pleased me as much
as this curious laughing jackass, though it is both clumsy
and unattractive in colour. Far from deserving its name
jackass, it is on the contrary very wise and also very
courageous. It boldly attacks venomous snakes and large
lizards, and is consequently the friend of the colonist.

The animal life in these woods was of the greatest
interest to me, and every day I added to my collection
during the excursions I made in the vicinity of Gracemere.
In the scrub I shot a *Pitta strepitans*, which is very rare
in these parts, but common in Northern Queensland.

As the region around Rockhampton is comparatively
civilised, I could not look for any large number of mammals,
for they are the first to yield to civilisation. Those that live
in trees were still frequently to be found. The common
opossum abounded, and the hollow trunks of the gum-trees
generally served as abodes of the bandicoot, of the native
cat (*Dasyurus*), and of the kangaroo-rat.

It is very interesting to observe how a kind of "white
ant" make their nests. They build them high up in trees,
constructing tunnels along the stem of the tree to the ground.
If the tree leans, they always build the tunnels on the under
side, to avoid the opossum, which climbs on the upper
side.

My collections consisted chiefly of birds, fishes, and lower
animals, especially *Coleoptera*. I was fortunate enough to
discover a new fresh-water cod, the fish called black-fish by
the colonists. It is so little shy that it would even bite my
leg when I bathed. I at one time had an opportunity of
observing that it can live for nine hours out of water.

One of the largest land-snails of Australia, the *Helix
cunninghamii*, is found on the hills near the station.

My excursions extended not only to the immediate
vicinity of Gracemere, but I made journeys of investigation
to regions 200 miles away. Near Westwood, a little town

about thirty miles from Rockhampton, I found for the first time the so-called bower-birds (*Chlamydodera maculata*), a family that has become celebrated on account of the bowers which they build for their amusement.

These bowers, which must not be confounded with nests, are used, as is well known, exclusively for amusement. They are always found in small brushwood, never in the open field, and in their immediate vicinity the bird collects a mass of different kinds of objects, especially snail-shells, which are laid in two heaps, one at each entrance, the one being much larger than the other. There are frequently hundreds of shells, about three hundred in one heap and fifty in the other. There is also usually a handful of green berries partly inside and partly outside of the bower; but like the empty shells and the other things collected, they are simply for amusement. Besides, these birds doubtless have the sense of beauty, as is indicated by the variegated and glittering objects gathered. This bower-bird has another remarkable quality, in its wonderful power of imitating sounds. When it visits the farms, where it commits great depredations in the gardens, it soon learns to mew like a cat or to crow like a cock.

In the woods here I shot a young cuckoo (*Eudynamis flindersii*), which was fed by four wood-swallows (*Artamus sordidus*). One of the swallows fell to the same shot. The three survivors swooped down toward the young cuckoo several times, but they took no notice whatever of their dead companion. I tried to approach the place, but the bold birds kept flying against me, as if to prevent me from proceeding, or to exhibit their wrath at what had happened. I shot one more, and waited to see what would happen. Both disappeared, but in the course of half an hour they returned accompanied by two others.

On a farm outside the village I saw a large nocuous insect, a moth which sucked the juice out of the oranges in the garden. Every evening a war of extermination had to be made against these animals, which are all the same very beautiful. Farmers have many other foes in tropical Australia. The large fruit-eating bat (*Pteropus*) does great damage to the orchards, and it is no pleasant sight for the industrious farmer to see the devouring swarms of these so-

TRUE AUSTRALIAN SCENERY.

To face page 29.

called flying-foxes advancing on his crops of an evening. Were it not for these enemies, fruit-growing in Queensland would be still more profitable than it is. An orange is no cheaper in Australia than in Norway, and all kinds of fruit are paid for in proportion.

Nor is the European bee, introduced by the colonists, permitted to live in peace in its new home. A kind of moth attacks the larvæ and destroys them.

From Westwood I proceeded to Peak Downs. Outside the village the landscape was enlivened by the rare sight of flowers on the ground, the red blossoms of the *Pimelea hæmatostachya* affording an agreeable change to the eye.

At Peak Downs, situated about 200 miles west of Rockhampton, I received the first impression of genuine native Australian scenery. Large plains, with here and there an isolated gum-tree; extensive scrubs, and now and then low mountain-ridges in the background; sometimes an emu would appear, or a little flock of kangaroos that are suddenly startled—all of which is so characteristic of the country.

I was surprised at the great number of marsupials that had their abode there. They had proved to be so troublesome that several of the squatters had found it necessary to surround their large pastures with fences so high that the animals could not jump over them and consume the grass. One of the sheep-owners told me that in the course of eighteen months he had killed 64,000 of these animals, especially wallabies (*Macropus dorsalis*) and kangaroo-rats (*Lagorchestes conspicillatus*), and also many thousands of the larger kangaroo (*Macropus giganteus*). The bodies of these animals are left to lie and rot, for none but the natives will eat the flesh; and although the skin of the large kangaroo can be tanned into an excellent leather, still it does not pay to skin the animal so far away from the coast. The only part that is used occasionally is the tail, from which a fine soup is produced.

The squatters at Peak Downs took great interest in my work, and my first experience of Australian "bush-life" was particularly agreeable. They placed their men at my disposal, so that I had a splendid opportunity of adding to my collections. At the station where I was a guest, even one of the ladies of the house offered me her assistance, and once or twice she accompanied me when I went after emus and kangaroos, which are easily approached when you are driving in a buggy. My fair companion held the reins while I did the shooting.

Emus are very inquisitive, and can therefore easily be enticed within shooting range. Thus a man at Peak Downs told me that he frequently had attracted their attention by lying on his back and kicking his feet in the air. When the animals came near enough he shot them.

In the winter I made an excursion to Calliungal, where the inhabitants were surprised that I suffered so much from the cold. As a joke they invited their nearest neighbours to come and look at "a Norseman who felt cold in Australia." It was so cold in the nights that the pools were frozen over, while the day was comparatively hot. On account of the cold nigh's I, who was unaccustomed to this climate, found it difficult to get woollen blankets enough for my bed.

In the Dee river, which flows by Calliungal, I observed several times the remarkable Platypus (*Ornithorhynchus anatinus*) swimming rapidly about after the small water insects and vegetable particles which constitute its food. It shows only a part of its back above water, and is so quick in its movements that it frequently dives under water before the shot can reach it.

CHAPTER III

A WOOL-WAGGON.

IN the beginning of July I prepared myself for a long journey
to the west. I first despatched several cases of things
collected to Christiania, and then proceeded on my journey
in company with a man who was to bring provisions to
Minnie Downs, Messrs. Archer's sheep station, about 350
miles west from Rockhampton.

I had long contemplated this journey, as Western Queensland was in my imagination a veritable Eldorado for the
naturalist. So far as I knew, no zoologist had yet studied
the fauna of the far west. With my limited acquaintance
with Australian bush-life I was happy to get a companion ; he had a waggon drawn by three horses, so that
our day's journey was comparatively short, which was a
great advantage to me. I thus had the opportunity of
making many digressions on the way, and of procuring many
animals, while my companion preceded me. The greater
part of the day I was occupied on my own account in
hunting and in preparing my game. In the course of the
afternoon I overtook the waggon, the track of which I was
always able to follow.

At sunset we encamped for the night, and the horses were let loose with their forefeet hobbled. We made a large fire and prepared our supper, which, as is common in the bush, consisted of salt beef and *damper*. The latter is the name of a kind of bread made of wheat flour and water. The dough is shaped into a flat, round cake, which is baked in red-hot ashes. This bread looks very inviting, and

HEAD OF "MORE PORK" (*Podargus cuvierii*).

tastes very good, as long as it is fresh, but it soon becomes hard and dry.

After supper we immediately made up our beds, which consisted simply of a waterproof laid on the ground and some woollen blankets. For the sake of convenience we usually slept under the waggon with the fire before us. Generally there is no other roof for the Australian traveller than the sky, and this is, as a rule, quite sufficient in Western

Queensland, where no dew falls except immediately after the rainy season. On the coast it is, however, necessary to be more prudent; if you do not sleep in a tent, you should at least take care to have something over your head, so as not to inhale the dew. A couple of boughs will often answer—a precaution never taken by the careless bushmen.

How well one feels in this out-of-door life! When we lie down to rest we are lulled to sleep by the melancholy, sleep-inspiring, and not disagreeable voices of the night bird *Podargus*—"more-pork! more-pork!"—and we are awakened in the bracing morning air, before the sun is up, by the wondrous melodious organ-tones of the Australian magpie (*Gymnorhina tibicen*).

At Expedition Range we came to dense scrubs, the so-called Brigalow-scrubs. The motley blending of plants which characterises the scrubs of the sea-board is not found here. The Brigalow (*Acacia harpophylla*) frequently occupies the whole ground for miles around; the air is heavy and oppressive; occasionally the gray monotony is broken by an isolated bottle-tree (p. 55) (*Sterculia rupestris*), which derives its name from the wonderful resemblance of the stem to a bottle. The inner part of this tree is porous and spongy, and therefore absorbs a great deal of moisture, a fact of which the cattle-owner sometimes avails himself during a prolonged drought. In a few places this damp wood, which contains a great deal of starch, is used for fodder.

After journeying two or three days through this gray wilderness, we crossed Comet river. Along its banks my attention was drawn to a number of *Casuarinas*—those leafless, dark trees which always make a sad impression on the traveller; even a casual observer will notice the dull, depressing sigh which comes from a grove of these trees when there is the least breeze. Near Springsure I stopped a day at a station, where I was invited to take part in a kangaroo hunt. There were several of us in the company, all on horseback. Toward sunset we set out, for the animals at that time go out to feed, and it was not long before we caught sight of one of them. Our dogs, which were all fine kangaroo hounds, were now let loose, and we galloped after them as fast as our horses could carry us.

D

The kangaroo jumps as quickly as a galloping horse, but usually it gets tired soon, especially if it is an "old man," as the colonists say. He then places himself with his back against the trunk of a tree and seeks to protect himself from the dogs to the last. Woe be to the dog who comes within reach of his paws! He seizes it with his arms, and rips its belly open with his strong big toe. The dog therefore takes good care not to come too near. Sometimes the kangaroo takes refuge in a pool of water, and if the dog is too intrusive, the kangaroo ducks it instinctively under water, and holds it there till it is dead. The hunt proceeded as rapidly as our fast horses could gallop, but it did not take long before the kangaroo turned on the dogs in the manner I have described. One of the hunters came up, dismounted, and one or two powerful blows from his club put an end to the animal. We killed six of them in this manner.

Not far from Nogoa river I overtook my travelling companion. In this region I shot two specimens of the beautiful parrot *Platycercus pulcherrimus* under the following remarkable circumstances. An hour before sunset I left the camp with my gun, and soon caught sight of a pair of these parrots, a male and a female, that were walking near an ant-hill eating grass-seed. After I had shot the male, the female flew up into a neighbouring tree. I did not at once go to pick up the dead bird—the fine scarlet feathers of the lower part of its belly, which shone in the rays of the setting sun, could easily be seen in the distance. Soon after the female came flying down to her dead mate. With her beak she repeatedly lifted the dead head up from the ground, walked to and fro over the body, as if she would bring it to life again ; then she flew away, but immediately returned with some dry straws of grass in her beak, and laid them before the dead bird, evidently for the purpose of getting him to eat the seed. As this too was in vain, she began again to raise her mate's head and to trample on his body, and finally flew away to a tree just as darkness was coming on. I approached the tree, and a shot put an end to the faithful animal's sorrow.

About 250 miles from the coast we passed the part of the Great Dividing Range, which here forms the watershed

between Eastern and Western Queensland. In this part the watershed consists of a low range. Nevertheless no one can fail to observe the great difference in animal life on the two sides as well as the immediate change in the character and aspect of the country. No sooner is the range passed than we meet with the red-breasted cockatoo (*Cacatua roseicapilla*), which is never found on the eastern side.

From this time we were in Western Queensland, as it is called, the great rich pasturage, where millions of sheep wander about, and we were soon aware that we had come within the confines of the squatters. One can scarcely imagine a more characteristic picture of Australian bush-life than the sight of a wool-waggon approaching from the distance. Eighteen or twenty strong oxen in the scorching heat, their tongues far out of their mouths, laboriously drag a heavy waggon loaded with bales of wool. By the side of the caravan walks the driver, sunburnt and dusty, with his long whip in his hand. Under an awning on the top of the load, which is as high as a house, the driver's family have their quarters, and a few sheep and goats follow behind.

Such a carrier makes his living by transporting wool from stations in the far west to the coast, and also by bringing back supplies. Thus he spends his life on the road from one year's end to another. He is himself the owner of both oxen and waggon. If he has several of such teams and also a wife, she usually drives one, plying her whip as dexterously as any man.

Finally we meet the great flocks of sheep from Minnie Downs, proof that we are now near this station, our goal. The month I spent here gave me an excellent knowledge of station-life. The raising of cattle and sheep, the most important industry of Australia, has more or less influence on all kinds of business in that country. In the older colonies the cattle and sheep farmers are also the owners of the land where their herds and flocks graze, but in the larger part of Queensland the pastures are rented from the Government. These great cattle and sheep farmers are called squatters, and they are the aristocracy of Australia. If the squatter is a sheep-farmer, he not unfrequently has 200,000 sheep upon his station, while the cattle-farmer often owns 15,000 head. He does not hesitate to pay as high as £2000 for a fine bull, or as high as £600 for a ram of choice pedigree.

A station resembles a little village. Besides the main building, which is the residence of the squatter or his superintendent, there are a number of shanties for the workmen, a butcher's shop, a store-house for wool, and a shop where most of the necessaries of life may be bought. A garden of vegetables may usually be found down by the water, for there is always a creek or a water-hole near every station. The garden is generally managed by skilful Chinamen, who are, it is true, hated by all colonists (every Chinaman must pay £30 for permission to settle in Queensland), but at the same time are recognised as the most able gardeners. The secret of their art is chiefly the untiring attention they give to the plants, watering them early and late in sunshine and even in rain.

The stock-yard is an enclosure indispensable to every station. The cattle are driven into it when they are to be captured, but it is usually occupied by the horses, which are lodged there every morning so that the stock-man may select his own animal. Most of the work on a station is done on horseback, and one can hardly conceive of an Australian unable to ride.

There is of course much work to be done on a station having such extensive pasturage. The sheep cause the most trouble. The transportation of the wool to the coast is very expensive, and often costs more than the freight from the coast to England. And yet sheep-raising may often give a profit of as much as thirty per cent. The cattle are sent alive to the cities to be slaughtered. Milk is scarcely used at all in the bush. On a station containing about 10,000 head not more than three or four cows may be milked, as the cattle are half wild and have to be tamed for milking purposes. The chief stress is laid on the beef. What, then, becomes of this immense quantity of beef? The greater part is eaten in Australia, where the consumption is enormous. More recently establishments have been built, in which the beef is either canned or frozen for export. Besides, considerable quantities are used for the production of tallow. In the neighbourhood of Rockhampton there is an establishment where the carcasses of about 100,000 cattle and sheep are annually boiled down and converted into tallow.

In Australia, wherever there are good pastures to be found, the land is quickly taken up for the feeding of large droves of cattle and flocks of sheep. First, the cattle consume the coarse grass, then the sheep are turned into the pastures. Distance is a matter of no consequence. It may require months to bring the stock up to the new station, but no place is so far away that there is any hesitation about forming a station there, provided the pasturage is good. The greatest difficulty with which the squatter has to contend is the climate, for prolonged drought may completely ruin him.

I was now in one of the best grazing districts of Australia, covered for hundreds of miles with the well-known Mitchell-grass (*Astrebla elymoides*), which has a remarkable power of withstanding the drought without losing its nourishing qualities.

In the vicinity of Minnie Downs there still were scrubs, but farther west they became less abundant. These were mainly Brigalow-scrubs, and near the station they occupy large tracts of land. Here we also become acquainted with a new kind of scrub, called by the colonists gidya-scrub, which manifests itself even at a distance by a very characteristic but not agreeable odour, being especially pungent after rain. The Australian inland scrubs give a vivid impression of solitude and desolation, with their gray or brown masses of stiff, often shadeless trees, which like a sea undulate over barren plains and low hills. To ramble in these woods, where all is dry and hot, and silent as the grave, is no pleasure as it would be elsewhere. It is very difficult to discover life in this woody wilderness, and the monotony is rarely broken by the sight of a bird or any other living thing. These scrubs, which sometimes are of immense extent (for instance in South Australia 9000 square miles), are peculiar to Australia, and, as Mr. Wood well says, are just as characteristic of the country as the steppes of Tartary, the prairies of America, and the deserts of Africa are of these respective countries.

In the great gidya and Brigalow-scrubs in the vicinity of

the station I could not therefore expect to find any great
variety of animal life. Nor does it exist to any extent
in the open country generally. The Australian dog (*dingo*)
was formerly very numerous here and in all Western Queensland. But as it is the sworn enemy of the squatters they
have begun to kill it, so that it is now in course of extermination. On the large stations a man is kept whose sole
work it is to lay out poison for the dingo. The black variety
with white breast generally appears in Western Queensland
along with the red.

I frequently had occasion to observe the spiders, and

SPIDER PARALYSED BY A HORNET (natural size).

among them the large woolly *Phrictis crassipes* was found
in great numbers. It makes a hole 18 inches deep, and in
a slanting position, but the entrance is not supplied with
a trap-door, as is the case with the burrows of many other
spiders out here. I once saw a hornet (*Mygnimia australasiæ*)
proceed boldly into one of these holes, which I then immediately closed. I dug to the bottom of the hole from
the side. There I saw the spider paralysed by the plucky
hornet, which was sitting on its back. I was anxious
to test the effect of the poison of this colossal spider,
and once let it bite the snout of a kitten, which thereupon
became very sick and vomited violently, but soon recovered.

Another spider (*Lathrodectus scelio*), which is very common here and everywhere in Queensland, is very dangerous even to men. It is a small black animal, of the size of our house-spider, with a brilliant scarlet mark on its back. A friend of mine was bitten in the leg by one of these dangerous spiders, which is feared like a snake. The pain was violent, and was followed by paralysis which lasted for three days. He was able to feel the venom work its way up the leg, pass through the bowels, and descend down the other leg, whereupon it ascended to the breast. But on the third day he had a cold perspiration, and recovered.

This spider is found especially in old wood and rubbish, but is also fond of staying in houses, keeping itself concealed during the day and coming out at night. On my verandah at Gracemere I could collect as many as I pleased, for they are not at all timid.

I soon began to long for regions farther west, where the fauna is more abundant, and continued my journey alone with only two horses. As a rule there was a path which I could follow. When no path was to be found, I proceeded as best I could, and made my camp wherever night overtook me. Every day I expected new scenes, but I was always disappointed. It was the same over and over again ; large, gray plains covered with dry Mitchell-grass undulated before me ; here and there stood a solitary gum-tree, especially on the banks of the rivers. Dwarf scrubs were the only things that occasionally varied the landscape.

When I arrived at Barcoo river, I discovered to my surprise only a dry river-bed with pools of water here and there, instead of a veritable stream. Yet this is naturally explained by the fact that the river owes its existence exclusively to the rains, which is the case with the majority of the Australian streams.

It seldom rains in Western Queensland ; but during the rainy season the rivers rapidly fill their beds, overflow their banks, and in some places become several miles wide. The water, however, soon disappears again, and the high temperature reduces the mighty stream to isolated water-holes. Water is therefore a precious article in the Australian bush. To furnish drink for the cattle the squatter must build large dams, especially across the rivers, and thus gather a supply which may protect him against irreparable losses. In recent years water has been obtained by boring very deep wells. I may here mention the fact that, at the end of 1887, water was found in Barcaldine at a depth of 691 feet by an artesian boring. It was clear as crystal and perfectly fresh, but very warm, the temperature being 101° F. Through a pipe 10 inches in diameter it rose with such force that it formed a fountain above the ground, and carried to the surface stones of the size of emu eggs. The amount of water from this artesian well is about 176,000 gallons per day.[1]

The soil consists, as a rule, of a fertile, deep, and chocolate-coloured deposit. Water is all that is wanted to make a great deal of Western Queensland a large wheat-growing country, and I feel sure, owing to the great success artesian borings of late have had, that such a future is really in store for this country. In the present circumstances it is difficult to keep garden flowers alive.

In Western Queensland nobody is surprised if a drop of rain does not fall for eight or ten months together. Nevertheless, cattle and sheep keep fat all the year, for the grass retains its nutriment even though it looks dry and gray, and a shower will make these dry stalks green.

On the way to Thompson river I spent a night with an Irish shepherd, who lived far away from any neighbour, occupied wholly with his sheep. As a peculiar and pedantic hermit, he preferred this solitary life, to which he had accustomed himself for many years. He could not bear any interruption in his habits, and with Australian straightforwardness he did not hesitate to make it apparent that all things in his neat little cottage must be kept in their places. But if one adapted oneself to his habits, it was not difficult to get on with him. He was, in fact, a type of those old Australian shepherds who are rapidly being relegated to the domain of history. Though his

[1] The artesian well at Blackall last year struck water at the depth of 1666 feet and gives 300,000 gallons per day, at a temperature of 119°. In other places several borings have been successful at a slight depth.

hair had turned gray in the bush, he had not forgotten his Irish descent. "England is too powerful," said he; "her fate will be like that of Rome in ancient times."

After supper he spread some sacks on the floor, and these were to be my bed. But I was not yet ready to retire, so I went out in the starry night, where the moon and the Southern Cross shone cold on the lonely landscape. The pure, clear winter air was chill on the gray plains and dark green trees, while in the cottage the fire blazed high on the hearth and shed a ray of light out through the small windows.

I opened the door and was deeply touched to find the hermit kneeling before his bed. Here the old man lived alone with his God in the desolate Australian bush.

On the banks of the Thompson river I observed the well-known nardu (*Marsilea*). The seed of this plant is crushed and ground by the natives, and used for food. Nardu has become painfully celebrated, for it was on this seed that the famous travellers Burke and Wills subsisted until they finally perished from starvation.

At Westlands station I had the good fortune to witness a *korroboree*, that is, a festive dance by the natives in the neighbourhood. The melody sung to this dance was genuine Australian, but the text was mixed with English words. The air was as follows:—

Tempo di Valse.
Allegro.

La - la - la - la - la   La - la - la - la - la

La - la - la - la - la   La - la - la - la - la

La - la - la - la - la   La - la - la - la - la

La - la - la - la - la   La - la - la - la - la

La - la - la - la - la   all to - ge - ther

yarn a - way   all to - ge - ther   yarn a -

way   all to - ge - ther   yarn a - way. Bahl

bood'gry Bo - ran - do   Bahl bood'gry Bo - ran - do.

The water we are obliged to drink in the interior of Queensland is wellnigh intolerable. Frequently it is so thick with mud that it has to be boiled, after which the dirt is allowed to sink to the bottom. Very often it is white, mixed with chalk, or it may be coloured black from decayed leaves. When the bushman wants a drink of water he does not hesitate to drink it as it is, and I have even seen these careless people drink from a dam in which there lay a couple of putrid sheep. That people do not oftener fall ill is doubtless due to the circumstance that the water is almost universally drunk boiled with tea. Though the water is not always as unhealthy as its appearance would indicate, I seldom omitted to boil it; but as I often found it inconvenient to dismount and make a fire, I accustomed myself to do without it all day long. I made up for the want, however, in the evening, when I was lucky enough to encamp near good water. At one station I emptied two large pitchers in the course of an hour.

Though one perspires freely in this climate, still the moisture evaporates so rapidly that one keeps perfectly dry while riding beneath the perpendicular rays of the sun.

About a month after my departure from Minnie Downs I reached Windex station, 650 miles from Rockhampton, where I found the same hospitable reception always accorded a stranger in the Australian bush. I was invited to remain for a while to explore the vicinity. The owner was himself interested in zoology, and he believed it would pay me to stop ; he was right, for the animal life was interesting even if it were not rich in species. I here added to my collection Australia's smallest marsupial animal, the beautiful *Phasco-logale minutissima*. A cat playing with something that looked like a mouse led to the capture of this specimen, for on closer examination it appeared that it was not an animal of the mouse family, but this little marsupial. It had no less than nine young in the pouch. From Windex I made an excursion for a few days to a mountain region about thirty miles distant. Here I shot the beautiful white species of kite (*Elanus axillaris*), and a couple of specimens of the charming Diamantina-pigeon. These beautiful little birds are very numerous here, and so tame that the stock-men can easily kill them with their whips.

On the broad sandy heights in the vicinity the so-called spinifex is found in great abundance. This grass (*Triodia irritans*) is the traveller's torment, and makes the plains, which it sometimes covers for hundreds of miles, almost impassable. Its blades, which have points as sharp as needles, often prick the horses' legs till they bleed, and it is generally regarded simply as a nocuous grass; still, the horses will eat the tender blades of the young plant.

The district in which I now found myself had a year before been visited by a plague of rats. They came from the north-west and proceeded, *via* Winton, on their wander-ings towards the east. A man in Ayrshire Downs told me that they appeared in countless numbers—during the day they kept concealed, but in the evening the ground seemed to be alive with them, so numerous were they. One night for amusement he laid a piece of meat on his threshold, and killed with a stick 400 of these animals which came up to eat the meat. An occasional straggler was left behind, but the main body disappeared in a short time. Afterwards I learned that an army of rats had also passed Westwood, doubtless the same clan, but greatly reduced in number, and probably but few of them reached the coast. I have been informed that the small marsupials (*Phascologale minutissima*) before mentioned make similar periodical migrations.

From Ayrshire Downs I proceeded south to Elderslie, a station in process of construction. It was so difficult to get building timber in the vicinity that it had been found expedient to use stone for building. The station lies near the confluence of the Diamantina and Western rivers. I here met two men who were looking for opals in the mountains east of the Diamantina river. Not far north of Elderslie lies a very rich copper-bearing district called Cloncurry, which is said to surpass even the celebrated Lake Superior mines in North America. Moreover, gold and actual mountains of pure iron ore abound here, but on account of the difficulty of transportation this enormous wealth is not yet available. Queensland will, it is said, become a centre for the production of precious metals. Besides great wealth of gold, silver, tin, and other metals, the land, according to recent investigations, has so vast an amount of coal that its coast is destined in time to become the most important emporium of coal on the southern hemisphere.

The natives near Diamantina river astonished me by their bodily structure ; neither before nor since have I seen them so tall and upon the whole so well nourished as in the tribe near Elderslie. Some of the women were even monstrously large ; their hair was generally straight. Their food consisted chiefly of fish, snakes, rats, and clams.

A conspicuous trait in the character of the Australian native is treachery, and the colonists are wont to give the stranger the warning, " Never have a black-fellow behind you." Nor should one, as a rule, rely on them. How difficult it is for them to lay aside their uncivilised habits may be seen from the following incident, which happened at

Dawson river. A squatter was walking in the bush in company with his black boy, hunting brush-turkey (*Talegalla*). As they sauntered forth, the black boy touched him on the shoulder from behind and said, "Let me go ahead." When the squatter asked why he wished to go before him, the boy answered, "I feel such an inclination to kill you." The black boy had been on the station for several years, where he had served as shepherd and had proved himself very capable.

I observed an interesting fact among the natives of this locality. In cases of murder they administer justice in a peculiar manner, as the following instance will illustrate. A black boy at Connemara station was sent on an errand to Diamantina gates. On his way home he fell in with an old man and his two wives, all of whom belonged to the same tribe as the boy. In the course of the journey the boy killed the old man and took possession of the two young wives. Meanwhile, one of them escaped and reported what had happened to the tribe, which caused universal indignation. Fourteen men with spears and other weapons then proceeded to Connemara to punish the murderer. The boy concealed himself, and the white people on the station would not surrender him, for he was a good servant. They even fired one or two shots at the blacks in order to frighten them away. Three or four days passed, and the boy believed that all danger was over. As he went out one morning to take in a horse, he was killed by his tribal kinsmen only half a mile from the station.

From Peak Downs I have heard similar stories. A black man who was to be punished, probably for murder, was pursued to the very station. When the white folk got sight of him he was so covered with spears that he looked like a porcupine.

In the new main building at Elderslie station the fleas had already made their appearance. They usually live in the ground, and as soon as you step on the soil they creep by the dozen up your legs. In Europe I have never felt a bite of these insects, but the Australian representatives were genuine blood-suckers. As I could not abstain from scratching, I broke my skin, and thus produced a series of bad and irritable sores which would not heal. At last I felt so uncomfortable when I moved, that to my great annoyance I was obliged to keep still for a week. When the week was over, this sitting still became unbearable. Besides, I had received an invitation to take part in an expedition down the Diamantina river.

An inspector of the native police, whose barracks were down by the river, was going to make a tour of inspection

QUEENSLAND NATIVE MOUNTED POLICE.

southward, and I was to go with him. In spite of my wounds I started for the barracks, which were situated about thirty miles south; but when I got there I was so ill that I was obliged to give up my intention of joining the expedition. As soon as I stirred, and especially when I rode, swellings arose on various parts of my body, which, however, disappeared whenever I lay down. There was accordingly nothing else to do but to remain idle, lying on the verandah of the policemen's bark hut. The native police, in whose quarters I now was, is a body organised by the

Government of Queensland for the protection of the settlers. They are stationed in those parts of the colony where the natives appear to be dangerous. Such a corps of police consists of natives from other parts of Australia, and consequently they are the natural enemies of the blacks against whom they are employed. They are commanded by a white officer, the so-called sub-inspector, and by a sergeant. The force is in uniform, armed with rifles, and consists of splendid horsemen. From the barracks, which are generally some low bark huts, the police several times a year make tours of inspection through the large districts under their charge. When the natives kill a white man, the police punish them, and if they prey upon the cattle of the squatter, the latter sends word to the police barracks and demands that the blacks be "dispersed." As Queensland becomes colonised, the native police force is being gradually reduced in numbers, and at the present time there are but few barracks in the northern and western part of the colony.

During my sojourn here I had the good luck to obtain a valuable flint knife (p. 48) which the natives of Georgina river use for the peculiar mika-operation [1] to prevent the

[1] This remarkable custom, by which the natives produce hypospadi artificially, belongs especially to the tribes west of the Diamantina river, and west and north of the Gulf of Carpentaria, and does not, as might be supposed, originate in lack of means of sustenance, since the districts in question are full of rats, fish, and such vegetables as nardu, pigweed, and the like. In a few tribes the children are operated on, only about five per cent being spared. In other tribes it is the husband who, after becoming the father of one or two children, must submit to the requirements of the law, as it is said, amid certain festivities (as for example trees are cut down and stuck into the ground in a circle around the place of operation). A man about twenty years old from Georgina river, whom I examined, explained to me that the reason for the operation was, that the blacks "did not like to hear children cry in the camp," and that they do not care to have many children. This person had not been operated on himself, as he had not yet been the father of a child. According to the information I gathered, the cut, which is about an inch long, extends almost to the scrotum. The surface of the wound is first burnt with hot stones, whereupon the wound is kept apart by little sticks which are inserted, and in this manner an opening is formed, through which the sperma is emitted. The natives of these tribes are fat and in good physical condition. Mr. White, a squatter from Rocklands in North-western Queensland, and an excellent observer of the blacks, noticed for the first time in 1876 near Boulya that some of them had been injured in some way, and found that they had been operated on in the manner described. Later he saw a number of cases, and they all explained to him that the reason was that they did not care to be burdened with too many children. (See in regard to this custom also two articles by Baron N. von Miklucho-Maclay in *Zeitschrift für Ethnologie*. Berlin, 1880 and 1882.)

increase of population.   It has a very sharp point and three
sides, two of which are very sharp, so that the blade is in
fact two-edged.   The handle is made of a lump of resin
(probably from a eucalyptus), and is in reality black, but
is painted with reddish-brown ochre.   The knife is stuck
into this handle, the resin having been softened over the
fire.   On the other end of the handle a flat piece of wood
is fastened, painted with chalk figures.   To the knife belongs
a sheath of the bark of the tea-tree.   The pieces of bark

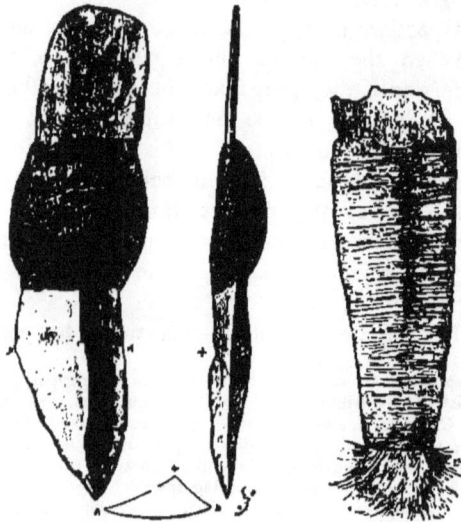

FLINT KNIFE FROM GEORGINA RIVER WITH ITS SHEATH
($\frac{1}{2}$ size).

are placed side by side and bound together by a kind of
string, which is probably spun from the hair of the opossum.

The outer side of the sheath is whitened with chalk, and at
the small end of it is a tuft of red cockatoo down.   The
natives procure the knife by making a fire on the flint rock
and then pouring water on it.   Thus it splits, and very nice
pieces can easily be selected.   This flint knife is the finest
Australian implement I have seen.   One would hardly think
that it was made by an Australian native, so much labour
has been bestowed upon it.

I obtained the little pouch represented below on the same occasion. It is a torpedo-shaped network made of plant fibre, and is used exclusively for carrying the leaves of a tree called pituri (*Duboisia hopwoodii*). The leaves contain a stimulant which possesses qualities similar to those of tobacco and opium, and are chewed by several tribes in the

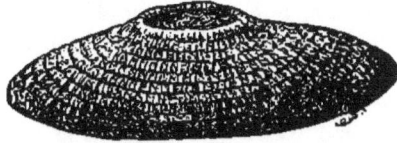

POUCH FOR THE CARRYING OF PITURI
(¼ size).

interior of Australia. Pituri is highly valued as a stimulant, and is taken for barter far and wide ; the habitat of the tree is, however, probably not so limited as has been supposed. The pituri pouch obtained by me was secured from natives about 200 miles west of Diamantina river, and was knitted with great skill in about two hours.

When the native police are at home at their barracks they have not much to do. The troopers are fond of roaming about in the woods, and they devote themselves to the athletics peculiar to their race, usually undressing themselves so as to be more free in their movements. In cool evenings they often amuse themselves with throwing the boomerang, and their matchless skill invariably commanded my admiration. It is strange that so primitive a people as the Australian natives should have invented this weapon, which, as we know, has the peculiarity of returning to the thrower, provided it does not meet with any obstacle on the way. The boomerang is a curved, somewhat flat and slender weapon made from a hard and heavy wood, Briga-low (*Acacia excelsa*) or myall (*A. pendula*), but the best one I found was made of a lighter kind of wood. The curving of the boomerang, which often approaches a right angle, must be natural and lie in the wood itself. One side is perfectly flat and the other slightly rounded. The ends are pointed. The peculiarity of the boomerang, viz. that it returns of itself to the thrower, depends on the fact that it is twisted so that the ends are bent in opposite directions ; the twisting is accomplished by putting it in water, then heating it in ashes, and finally bending it, but this warp must occasionally be renewed, for it sometimes disappears, especially if the weapon is made of light wood. Upon the whole, there is no striking irregularity in the plan of the boomerang ; this warped boomerang is, as a rule, used only as a toy.

In Western Queensland, as elsewhere in Australia, numerous boomerangs which are not twisted are used, but these, which are only for war and hunting, do not return when thrown. They are thrown with killing effect into flocks of pigeons and ducks.

When an Australian is throwing a boomerang, he seizes one end, which is usually made rough in order to afford a better grip, and holds it backward in such a manner that the concave side of the weapon turns forward. Grasping it firmly, he runs a couple of paces forward, and then throws his boomerang in a straight line before him. The moment it leaves his hand it turns into a horizontal position, and starts off, buzzing like a spinning-wheel. While going with great speed, it revolves round its own axis, and in this manner takes a slanting direction upward through the air. It does not return the same way as it went, but curves toward the left, and thus describes an ellipse. Gradually it loses its momentum and so falls slowly, sometimes only a couple of paces from its starting-point.

Dexterity rather than strength is needed to throw the boomerang with success. Above all, it is important to hold it firmly until it is suddenly let loose. It cannot fail to astonish everybody to see how far and at the same time how gracefully this weapon can whirl through the air. I was never tired of witnessing this amusement, which is so highly prized by the blacks, and also learned to throw the boomerang myself, but did not acquire the skill of the natives. It is very difficult to throw this weapon well, and it requires considerable practice. All the blacks are by no means perfect in its use, and very few white people acquire the art.

The natives frequently make the boomerang touch the ground ten or twelve paces from where it is thrown ; but this, far from diminishing the speed, gives it on the contrary increased velocity. It may even touch the ground a second time, and then whirl off in the above-described circle from the right to the left. It is impossible to aim accurately with the returning boomerang : with the plain one, which does not return, it is much easier to do so, and the mark is not missed. A man is rarely killed by a boomerang. An acquaintance of mine told me that he once in a skirmish was hit in the thigh ; the wound was only about an inch and a half deep,

BOOMERANGS FROM QUEENSLAND (⅓ size).

a, b, c, plain ones from Central Queensland (Coomooboolaroo).
d, a returning one from Herbert river.[1]

and was soon cured. His horse was hit in several places, without receiving any harm worth mentioning.

It has been asserted that the Egyptians and Assyrians used the boomerang, and from this the conclusion has been drawn that the Australian natives are descended from a race that have had a higher degree of development than

[1] On the Herbert river I never saw boomerangs ornamented with engraved lines like those farther south and west in Queensland.

they now possess. But, according to Mr. B. Smyth, it is extremely doubtful whether the Dravidic or Egyptian boomerang is identical with the Australian, since the former could not have had the quality of returning. Moreover, we find in Australia intermediate forms of this remarkable weapon, which show a development towards, rather than a retrogression from, the present boomerang.

It is a remarkable fact, which is asserted by several persons, that the boomerang is also used in South-eastern India ; detailed accounts are, however, lacking. This weapon reminds us of the myth about Thor's hammer, Mjolner, which also returned to the hands of the thrower.

To explain the origin of the boomerang, which is found as far north as Herbert river, would be difficult. But we can conceive it to have been invented by accident. A twig or a piece of wood which was on the ground may have become warped by rain and sunshine, and thereby assumed a form which revealed the striking quality of returning when it was thrown. In the forests the natives generally lay hold of any piece of wood for the purpose of killing a small animal. It is more probable, however, that the idea was discovered in their games. The native Australian seems to amuse himself with everything that comes in his way. Thus I have frequently seen them fold the leaf of a common palm into a square, give the two corners a little twist, one to each side, and throw it into the air, making it skim round and return. A white man told me that his black boys, while round the camp fire, used frequently to amuse themselves with the leaves of the Brigalow-acacia, which have a striking resemblance to the boomerang. They gave them a flick with the finger, causing the leaves to start off, but to return in the same manner as the boomerang. This seems to me to be the most reasonable explanation of the matter. The blacks may also have received a suggestion from the whirling movements described by the winged fruit of the gum-trees as it falls to the ground.

CHAPTER IV

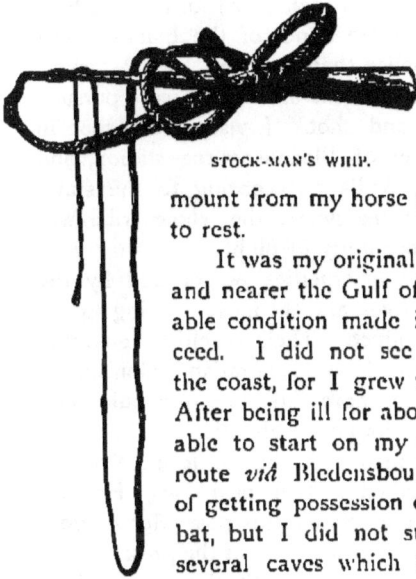

STOCK-MAN'S WHIP.

AFTER staying eight days at the barracks, I felt so well that I was able to ride back to Elderslie. But on the way I became ill again, and repeatedly had to dismount from my horse and lie down on the ground to rest.

It was my original intention to go farther west and nearer the Gulf of Carpentaria, but my miserable condition made it impossible for me to proceed. I did not see how I was to get back to the coast, for I grew worse and worse every day. After being ill for about a month, I was at length able to start on my way back. I now laid my route *via* Bledensbourne, chiefly for the purpose of getting possession of a large, white, fruit-eating bat, but I did not succeed, although I searched several caves which these animals were said to frequent. The large lizards, commonly called iguana, here attain so great a size that they possibly may be a new species.

In the vicinity of Bledensbourne I was shown a large number of skulls of natives who had been shot by the black police in the following circumstances :—A couple of teams with provisions for the far west, conducted by two white men, had encamped near the blacks. The latter were lying

in ambush, and meant to make an assault, as two black women
had been ravished by the white men. Instead of defending
themselves with their weapons, the white men were cowardly
enough to take flight, leaving all their provisions, oxen, tent,
and all their other things in the hands of the blacks. The
fugitives reported to the police that they had been attacked,
and so the "criminals" a few weeks afterwards were pursued
far into a narrow valley and shot. I visited the spot in
company with the manager of Bledensbourne station, and
saw seven or eight of the skulls. According to the statement made by several persons, nearly the whole tribe was
killed, as there was no opportunity of flight.

This is one of the many cruelties perpetrated by the
native police against the natives, and the most thrilling stories
could be told of their conduct. Their cruelties constitute
the black page in the annals of Australian colonisation.
This police force has become more and more unpopular, and
voices have been raised for its entire abolition. The police
inspector often left it to his men to do the murdering, " to dis-
perse the blacks," as it is called, at their own risk. He thus
shirked the responsibility and retained his post ; for he does
not dare kill the blacks openly, at least not at the present time.

It is not strange that such an institution is hated by
the blacks, or that they take every opportunity of revenge.
During my sojourn here an inspector was killed by a spear
hurled by the blacks, while he was treating with the savages,
and a year later they killed another inspector in his own
camp at night.

The summer heat had now set in, as it was already late
in November. The sun was at its zenith, and poured down
its scorching rays day by day, unrelieved by a cooling breath
of air or by any refreshing lake or prattling brook—only
mocking *fata morgana*. There was no animal life to be
seen ; all living things sought refuge from the burning heat
of the sun. 104° to 105° F. in the shade was the average
heat. The highest temperature I observed was 116° F., and
the heat was then so great that it seemed oppressive even to
sit still. The wind that blew was as hot as if it came from
an oven, and the thermometer rose and fell with the wind.
Still, the climate was more tolerable here than on the banks

of the Diamantina river, where the thermometer rose to 126°
F. in three consecutive days, a perfectly exceptional heat,
even in tropical Australia. The trees which are to be found

REST UNDER A BOTTLE-TREE (*Sterculia*).

furnish but little protection against the beams of the sun, for
their foliage generally hangs vertically from the branches, and
consequently gives but little shade. When I rested at noon,
I could find shade nowhere except under the horse. As a

rule I do not suffer from heat, and am able to ride all day long beneath the perpendicular rays of the sun ; but at this time I was weak from my illness, and the hot weather was too much for me. Many times in a day I had to lie down in the burning rays of the sun and rest my weary limbs.

The coolness of the night, however, makes the people in general feel comfortable. As soon as the sun sets the air is cooled, as it is not moist enough to retain much of the heat. The thermometer would sink 40° F., so that I needed a woollen blanket to keep myself warm during the night. To my other troubles was added the annoyance of the flies, which at some stations were so bad that it was necessary to eat under mosquito-nets. These nuisances are especially troublesome to the eyes, which when bitten by the flies first smart and then swell up, so that they sometimes cannot be opened for several hours. To keep the flies away from the eyes, we wore nets over our faces, and even the horses were protected in this manner.

" Life in Western Queensland during the summer is simply a struggle with the flies " ; " When I am about to sign a draft, I must have a man to fan the flies away and watch the inkstand," are expressions which I still remember to have heard in that country.

The specimens I had collected were kept in a number of pasteboard boxes, which had to be loaded and unloaded every morning and evening. I had to dismount many times a day to straighten them, for they soon became disordered, and galled the back of the horse by not being evenly balanced. Once I nearly lost all, as my active packhorse got loose and galloped away, kicking up all sorts of pranks and nearly getting the whole load under his belly. Gradually my horses became so lean and poor from the long journey that I scarcely believed they would live till I reached my destination. In spite of every care taken, the back of my pack-horse became galled, and this was another reason why I had to travel slowly.

Both at Winton and at Thompson I found an old acquaintance from Europe, the greenshank (*Totanus glottis*), but both times I saw but one bird, and it was exceedingly shy. Animal life awakes and makes its appearance only about sunset, and is observed chiefly near the water-holes. There are many varieties of birds, but as a rule there are but few of each kind ; generally they are scattered over a large territory, though some of them are strangely confined to a very limited territory. The cockatoos and hawks are comparatively numerous, and the kites and the beautiful black falcons (*Falco subniger*) are particularly noticeable.

After many difficulties I finally came to a hut, in which there lived a boundary-rider. I now began to approach more densely-populated regions, and the next day I arrived tired, with my exhausted horses, at Isis Downs station, where I for several days enjoyed much-needed rest and obtained milk, which is a great rarity in Western Queensland.

Christmas Eve I returned to Minnie Downs in terribly hot weather. It was so hot that even under cover at the station we had to seek relief in wet towels wound about the head. In such weather, when the air seems to vibrate, we shrink from going out, just as much as we do at home in Norway when it is bitterly cold. As a rule people in Australia pay no attention to the heat. The work goes on regularly at the station, and singularly enough, the heat is felt much less out of doors when one is hard at work than when sitting still doing nothing in the house. Those who drink to excess are most troubled by it In Rockhampton, for instance, nine drunkards died in one week. But, with all this, the climate of Queensland is healthier than that of any other country in the same degree of latitude. It is not necessary here, as in many other tropical lands, to send the children to colder climes to be reared. They grow strong, and are the pictures of health. Of course there is fever, but almost exclusively in new-settled districts, where the soil is yet uncultivated. Though sometimes fatal, it is generally of a far milder type here than in other tropical lands. A man who had lived for two years in a fever locality without perceiving any symptoms of the disease, had his first attack after taking cold. As the soil gradually becomes cultivated, the fever disappears.

Another illness which troubles the colonists is sandy blight, a very severe disease of the eye, which sometimes ends in blindness. In Western Queensland people are also subject to bad sores on the hand, called *Barcoo-rot;* a traveller will be struck by the fact that nearly everybody wears a bandage about his hands, because the most insignificant scratch develops into a large sore which may last for months. *Beliander* is also a common disease in Queensland ; without the slightest apparent cause, a person is suddenly seized with vomiting, but is relieved just as suddenly. These diseases doubtless have their origin in the

BUSHMEN.

climatic conditions, and the colonists have therefore acquired the habit of blaming the climate whenever they are ill.

It cannot but surprise us how people keep in tolerably good health who take as little care of themselves as the bushman does. He gets up before sunrise, eats, saddles his horse and rides to his work. As a rule, he is out all day until sunset. He sleeps in rainy weather under the open sky ; he eats whenever it happens to be convenient, if he has the time—if not he waits until he finds time ; he lives on salt beef and damper every day ; he drinks muddy water or alcohol : such is the bushman's mode of life.

Externally there is no difference between the squatter

and his workmen.   All are dressed alike, and do the same
work ; no kind of work is dishonourable.   I have seen
young gentlemen beneath a scorching sun do work that the
common labourer in Norway would regard as below his
dignity.   The long, short-handled whip, which the bushman
uses for horses and cattle, is his chief implement, and this
he handles with great dexterity.

When the day's work is done, the squatter retires in the
evening to the main building, where he usually takes a bath
previous to his dinner, which is of a solid kind, frequently

A SQUATTER'S HOMESTEAD.

with vegetables, but without much variety.   At the same
time the working man goes to his more modest hut, where
he drinks his tea with damper and salt beef.   Jams are not
uncommon as articles of luxury, and are eaten with the
bread.

Women are but seldom seen at the stations.   The
squatter is usually a married man, at least in the most
civilised districts, but the hands rarely have wives.   Hence
the women who venture into this far west country soon find
their fortunes, for in Queensland there are 142 men to every
100 women.

During my stay at Winton I had an opportunity of

observing how quickly the chains of matrimony are forged in Western Queensland. An Irish girl who had recently arrived was standing over the wash-tub, and soon attracted the attention of a bushman. He entered into conversation with her, and after half an hour they agreed to get married; she wiped the soap off her arms, and so both proceeded without making any further toilet to the magistrate to have the ceremony performed.

In the long run the station life becomes very monotonous. The squatter therefore makes a trip to Melbourne, to Sydney, or even to Europe, while the labourer amuses himself as best he can where he is. Twice a year races are got up. The men are very fond of horses, and they take a deep interest in the races in the cities, betting heavily on the different events. Newspapers, which are extensively read everywhere in Australia, also find their way to the bush, as the Government provides for the carrying of mails to nearly every station.

The bushman has but few wants, and consequently saves nearly all his wages; but after a year or two he naturally feels the need of change, and so goes to the squatter to ask for a cheque—for ready money is not used in the bush. It frequently amounts to £100, and then he makes up his mind to have some sport. He takes his horses, rides off, dismounts in the first little village and "has a good time"—that is to say, he drinks every kind of liquor that is to be had. He hands his cheque or draft to his host, and from this time forward he lives in a perpetual state of intoxication as long as he has a penny left, and all who approach him drink his health at his expense—live and let live! Nervous and prostrated, he finally comes back to the bush, works a year or two more, and again returns to the village as a man of means to repeat the old story. The liquors he consumes are of course manufactured according to the receipt of the keeper of the dram-shop; they are poor and adulterated—simple poison. This shameful business is chiefly carried on on the borders of civilisation, and there are many stories about dram-shop keepers who have accumulated fortunes by vending this awful stuff. A few years ago there was a terrible report about such a liquor-dealer in Isisford. He

had a special burial-place for all those who were not strong
enough to survive his treatment.

Towards the end of January 1882 I bade farewell to
Western Queensland, and left Minnie Downs. From Tambo
I travelled for a time in the coach of the well-known
stage company, Cobb and Co., but as there was no place for
my dog, I had to walk the last twenty-seven miles before I
reached the railroad station, and from there I had a long
day's journey by rail to Rockhampton. During the last
fourteen days the heat was very oppressive ; black clouds
gathered in the rainy season ; and I reached Gracemere just
in the right time, for the following day the rain began to
pour down in the greater part of Central Queensland, and
it rained so violently that large districts were flooded. A
mail-carrier from Aramac had to stay for three days in a
tree to escape the flood. These terrible inundations are
thought to be periodical. Mr. C. Russel tries to show that
they occur every nineteenth year in the Darling river
district.

It seemed refreshing to be once more in a moist coast
climate. The results of my journey did not correspond to
my exertions, although I had found some very interesting
objects. Amid many privations I had traversed 1700 miles,
and was now merely gathering strength for a journey to
Northern Queensland.

Before I leave Gracemere I must relate a snake story
connected with it. One forenoon I was asked to come
down to the garden to kill a snake. As I approached the
place I was greatly astonished to find the reptile hanging
dead down a stone wall. At the same time I noticed
the head of another snake concealed farther up the wall,
which had seized the dead serpent by the middle, so that
the head and tail of the latter touched the ground. As it
was difficult for the victor to swallow his prey in the above-
described position, he dropped it to the ground and crept
down after it. Meanwhile I had stepped back, and from my
place of concealment I could now watch and see what it
was going to do. They were both of about the same size.
The serpent laid itself conveniently opposite its victim, and
began to swallow it. Its jaws were opened wide, wild with

desire ; the head of the dead serpent disappeared past its greedy teeth, and the rest of it soon slipped down.

I allowed it to swallow about one-third of the dead serpent ; then I stepped forward and gave it a blow across the back. It now tried with all its might to get rid of its prey, but the head stuck fast in its throat, and it soon had to succumb to my blows. In this condition they were put in spirits, as they could not be separated except by force. The greedy animal was a brown snake (*Hoplocephalus*), one of the most venomous in Australia. Its prey was a harmless kind, the so-called brown tree-snake (*Dipsas fusca*). The venomous one measured 4 feet 2 inches, and the other 4 feet 7 inches.

Snakes were numerous in this vicinity, as everywhere in Australia. At Waverley station, not far from Gracemere, one man in two days killed 203. The country was flat, and stood under water in the rainy season. The snakes found their way up to his hut, which was situated on high ground, so that he could do nothing for two days but defend himself, as they literally besieged his house.

CHAPTER V

IN May 1882 I was at length able to set out on my journey to Northern Queensland. Early one morning at four

ELEPHANT SUGAR-CANE, MACKAY.

o'clock I arrived by the steamer at Mackay, where I put up at the city hotel. Everything was open ; there was nobody to receive you, nor would anybody get up for the purpose. I had to look for my room myself, and at last I succeeded in finding one.

Mackay is a small town, owing its existence to the production of sugar, and the vicinity, celebrated for its fertility, is at the present time the most important sugar-producing district of the colony. Queensland has been found to be upon the whole especially adapted to the cultivation of the sugar-cane, and the colonists have learned how to overcome all the disadvantages of the climate, so that the sugar-cane is raised not only in the tropical regions in the north, but also as far south as the vicinity of Brisbane. The work on these plantations has in a great measure been done by the natives of the South Sea Islands, who in Australia are called Kanakas — a capable and intelligent race, especially suited to this kind of work, for they are strong, and endure the tropical heat far better than the whites. They contract to stay three years, and are paid £18, and get a free passage both ways. As a rule they are well treated on the plantations, and it frequently happens that they settle in the land. They are well liked, because they are willing to work; but they are hated by the white workmen, who look upon them as competitors. Many abuses have crept in through the introduction of the Kanakas, and the Government, earnestly supported by the white working men, has to a great extent prohibited their importation. The result is that it has become necessary to limit the cultivation of sugar in many places, which is very unfortunate, for the Queensland sugar is strong and of an excellent quality. There is an abundance of fertile lands, so that the production of sugar must in time become one of the most important industries of the colony.

During my sojourn in Mackay my dog, a fine Gordon setter, was exposed to great danger at a station near the town. She suddenly stopped in the high grass, and as I cautiously drew near I discovered in front of her a splendid specimen of the black snake (*Pseudechis*), whose head had assumed the flat form which is peculiar to venomous snakes when they become excited. The hot weather had made it still more angry. With the head slightly raised from the ground, it lay just ready to give my dog a fatal bite if the latter made the slightest motion. I hastily called the dog back, broke off a branch from a tree, and killed the treacherous

MY GORDON SETTER POINTING A BLACK SNAKE.

enemy, the most venomous snake of Australia. It was glistening black with a reddish belly, and longer than myself when I held it up.

. . . . . .

In July I embarked in a coasting steamer which was to take me farther north, and after a journey of two days we reached Townsville. The steam-launch met us out in the bay in order to bring us ashore, for the harbour is so shallow that large ships cannot lie alongside the wharf. Townsville is situated on Cleveland Bay, partly along a little river and partly on the slope of a mountain which rises to the elevation of 900 feet above the town. The latter accordingly has a very fine situation. The locality now occupied by Townsville was first discovered in 1864. The town is growing so rapidly that it is already regarded as the chief metropolis of Northern Queensland, and there is no doubt that it will take the first rank when this part of Queensland is divided from the south as a separate colony.

The value of land in this city, which now contains about 7000 inhabitants, has risen so enormously that it borders on the phenomenal, even in a newly settled land like this. Thus it has not unfrequently happened that a lot in the course of two or three years has doubled in value several times.

Townsville is the terminal station of the northern railway, and were it not for the shallow harbour it might safely be predicted that it would become one of the principal cities of Australia, both on account of its extensive shipping and of the rich soil of the interior. The chief industry in the vicinity is cattle and sheep raising, and wool is the principal article of export. Nor is the town without importance in relation to the rich gold beds at Charters Towers. As Townsville has an agreeable climate, the squatters in the arid west are accustomed to come to the comfortable Queen's Hotel, which is situated by the seaside, in order to seek recreation after all their hard work and privations. I also put up at the Queen's, which in spite of its northern situation is undoubtedly the best hotel in Queensland ; but this is, after all, not saying very much in its favour.

My destination was Herbert Vale, a deserted cattle

F

station on Herbert river. My first intention was to get there by way of Cardwell, a little coast town north of the mouth of Herbert river, from which the distance to Herbert Vale would be only twenty miles, while from Dungeness, which is situated at the mouth, it was at least forty miles up the river.

Meanwhile I learned that there were many obstacles in the way of reaching Herbert Vale from Cardwell. On the other hand, I was strongly advised to go to Dungeness and thence up the river by boat to some sugar plantations, where I should have more chance of obtaining the necessary horses than at Cardwell. Besides, I had a letter of introduction to one of the largest plantation-owners there, and knowing from experience how valuable such an introduction might be in uncivilised districts, I decided to go by way of Dungeness.

In the afternoon, one or two hours before the departure of the little coast steamer, I went down to the captain to buy a ticket for Dungeness. All my baggage had already been sent on board marked "Cardwell." I requested the captain to look after it and have it sent ashore, and showed him where it stood. But no sooner did he see that it was marked "Cardwell" than he began to insist that I was obliged to go to Cardwell. In vain did I strive to maintain my right to go where I pleased. The captain insisted that I must go to Cardwell, and not to Dungeness. He was one of those rough fellows whom we occasionally meet on the borders of civilisation, and it was the first time that I made the acquaintance of a specimen of that amiable race of Northern Queensland—the rough northern men, as they are called.

I of course realised that every argument was superfluous; and therefore made no objections, thinking matters would right themselves in due time. The captain went down into his cabin, and I was on the point of going ashore, wondering how so small and modest a boat really could contain so mighty a man, when my eyes fell upon one of the crew, who looked more accommodating than the others. I told him who I was, and that I was bound for Herbert Vale, where I was to collect specimens of natural history for the Christiania University. In proof of my statement I pointed to my red-

painted spirit cans which were marked, " University of Christiania, Norway."

"Why, are you Norwegian ? " asked he with the usual
coolness of a sailor ; " I am also from Christiania, and the
captain yonder is from Horten," he added, in a genuine,
broad Christiania dialect, pointing to a little steam-ferry
which lay moored by our side.

I expressed my surprise at meeting Norwegians so far up
in the tropical north, and in the name of our common country
I asked him to help me. He had heard my loud conversation
with the captain, and exclaiming in a very disrespectful
tone that what the captain had said was a matter of no
moment, he at once began to have my baggage properly
placed for my destination, Dungeness. In the evening
we weighed anchor and started for the north. The captain
came on deck intoxicated, as we were about to start, and so
the crew took command. The next day we arrived safely at
Dungeness at the mouth of Herbert river.

Hinchinbrook Island, a rocky isle rising to an elevation
of about 2500 feet above the level of the sea and nearly always
enveloped in fog, attracts the attention of the traveller. The
few white people who heretofore have visited it were cedar-
cutters. The valuable red cedar (*Cedrela*) grows in the dense
scrubs along the rivers in Northern Queensland, and the timber
is floated down the streams in the rainy season. Unlike the
Australian spruce, which soon decays, the cedar log may lie a
whole year in the woods before it is floated. The wood is as
beautiful as mahogany, but not quite so firm and solid. It
has been in such great demand that whole forests have been
entirely exterminated in the most accessible places ; it is the
only wood exported from Queensland.

I at once proceeded in a boat up the river, whose banks
for several miles are covered with mangrove forests. The
landscape gradually widens into a broad and flat valley,
with excellent sugar land, which is now thoroughly cultivated ;
a steam-plough even having recently been brought here. I
was well received, but wholly failed to obtain horses, as I
had expected. There was none to be hired, nor could any
be purchased ; hardly a saddle could be procured in this
comparatively uncivilised district.

One day I went down to the mangrove swamps to shoot a small gray heron, which I had seen on my arrival. On my way back I passed a farm, which belonged to a country-man of mine. Fastening my boat to the river bank, I

A NATIVE MAN FROM CENTRAL QUEENSLAND, NEAR ROCKHAMPTON.

went ashore to pay him a visit. The place gave me the impression of wealth and comfort. A corn-field extended up to the house, and on the verandah was a large heap of corn-husks. The farmer was married to a Norwegian woman, but both had nearly forgotten their mother tongue. They had several children, and the whole family, having been afflicted with the malarial fever, looked pale ; yet they were well and happy.   The husband had begun life in Australia as a carpenter on the first sugar plantation in the district.

A NATIVE WOMAN FROM CENTRAL QUEENSLAND, NEAR ROCKHAMPTON.

Mechanics are usually the most successful among Australian immigrants.   Here, where the climate was unhealthy, they were especially well paid.   He therefore accumulated a considerable sum of money in a short time, and bought land. Fortunately for him his property soon rose in value, for the land along the whole river proved to be excellent for sugar-growing. A large plantation was established farther up the stream, and there being a good harbour on his property, he sold a piece of land for a large price, and was now worth about £10,000. Ten years ago he came here penniless.

The banks of the river consist of rich soil, and on the higher ground are extensive plains covered with mighty gum-trees, which were continually being felled, while the ground was being ploughed for sugar-cane. Down by the river there are scrubs, the favourite of all farmers on account of the fertility of the soil, and they are more dense and thrive better than those in Mackay. The country is, upon the whole, decidedly tropical. A great part of these woods had been cleared, and large waving fields of sugar-cane with some patches of corn had taken their place. The cultivated fields were being extended with great industry, neither capital nor labour being spared, and it made me almost sad to see the field of the naturalist daily disappearing. The large flocks of pigeons had difficulty in finding the high quandang-trees, in which they are wont to light. The magnificent "weaver-birds" flew about homeless in large flocks, for the great trees in which the colony had their numerous nests were felled. The cassowary became more and more rare; still I could see its footprints in the sand. The only animal which was not disturbed by the restless work of man was the crocodile, which was not even affected by the traffic on the river. It frequently happens that both blacks and whites disappear, for the crocodile is no less bold in its own element than it is timid on land. Thus a Kanaka was one day standing near the plantation washing his clothes in the river. His companions suddenly shouted to him to warn him, but he thought they were making fun, for he was standing scarcely up to his knees in the water, and consequently gave no heed to the warning. The crocodile approached noiselessly, pulled the unhappy man out into the river, and the waves closed over them. Only a stream of blood indicated where he had disappeared.

Having learned that a man who took an interest in natural history lived in the neighbourhood, I one day paid him a visit. His name was Gardiner, and he kindly invited

me to stop at his house.   Here I made my first acquaintance
with the blacks of Northern Queensland.   A large number
of them, both men and women, all entirely naked, had their
camp on his land.

The first thing which attracted my attention was Mr.
Gardiner's treatment of these people.   In the uncivilised
districts the relations between the whites and the blacks are
as bad as possible.   In the remote districts the natives are
treated almost like brutes.   Still there are persons who take
an interest in them (the " protectors of the blacks "), and Mr.
Gardiner was one of them.   He always had work for them
on his farm, he furnished them with tools, and frequently
went with them, cutting down trees, building fences, and the
like.   He had a remarkable faculty for getting the slow and
lazy people to work, but he was certainly a great worker
himself.   By way of salary he gave them large quantities of flour, sugar, and tea, and especially tobacco ; when
he killed cattle, he also gave them meat.

He not only abundantly supplied the men who worked,
but also furnished the women with every necessity ; in short,
the whole camp lived at his expense.   No wonder then that
the blacks were fond of him ; they, however, did not forget
their nomadic nature.   Now and then they had to return to
their native woods, but others would come in their places, so
that Mr. Gardiner always had a camp of blacks on his farm.

They had gradually learned to make damper from their
flour, and they made it as well as any white person.   They
prepared their own food in the camp, where they had cooking
utensils which Mr. Gardiner had provided them with.   They
could be seen everywhere, even in the kitchen, where they
always tried to keep on good terms with the cook, but they
were not allowed to enter the sitting-room.

Mr. Gardiner liked to have these savages about him, still
it was no easy matter to manage them.   When he was with
them, one would not think that he had much heart, for he
addressed them in a harsh tone, and scolded them terribly
when they had done anything wrong.   If the camp became
too unruly, he sometimes had to go out in the night and
frighten them with a rifle shot.   This was quite necessary in
order to maintain discipline, though he was in reality good-

ness itself; he even protected their women against the white working men on the neighbouring plantation.

It cannot be denied that he was too liberal toward the blacks. They were quite spoiled, and did not appreciate his disinterestedness; the result was that they became bold and aggressive. He told me himself that they would steal from him whenever they got a chance, and everything had to be kept under lock and key; he could never let the axes and knives which they used lie out of doors, and once a black man even broke in and stole. That, however, was an uncommon occurrence.

Upon the whole their civilisation was of a rather low order. Eleven days before my arrival they had killed and eaten a man of another tribe on some hills near the farm. They returned triumphant, and boasted of their inhuman act. When they were abused for having eaten a man, they gradually became silent, and understood that it was something which the whites did not do and which accordingly was not right. This is always the habit of the Australian natives: as long as they remain in their native condition they make no secret of their cannibalism, but continued intercourse with the whites teaches them to regard it as something which is not *comme il faut*. Yet they keep up this infamous custom in secret before abandoning it altogether.

I was continually with the natives, both during the day and in the evening, hunting animals, and I was very much amused by the companionship of these children of nature. The blacks of Herbert river gave me from the very beginning an increased interest in the Australian race.

The boomerang was rare in these regions, for in the large scrubs there is no use for it. On the other hand I frequently saw another weapon, the " nolla-nolla " or club, the warlike weapon of the Australian native most commonly in use. It is a piece of hard and heavy wood sharpened to a point at both ends. One end is thick, and tapers gradually to the other end, which is made rough in order to give the hand a more secure hold; in using the weapon the heavy end is thrown back before it is hurled.

No great pains are taken in the making of these clubs.

The majority of them are about two feet long. At a distance of ten to twelve yards the native will hit an object with a tolerable degree of certainty, but only small animals can be killed with this weapon.

As a weapon for hunting, the club is also of great service in another way. The small end is used for digging up the ground and loosening it when the native wants to bring out bandicoots, rats, roots, and similar things. With it he searches for eggs in the remarkable mounds of the talegalla. With his nolla-nolla he pounds at the trees to learn whether they are sound, and picks out the larvæ from the decayed trunks.

One day an egg of a cassowary was brought to me ; this bird, although it is nearly akin to the ostrich and emu, does not, like the latter, frequent the open plains, but the thick brushwood. The Australian cassowary is found in Northern Queensland, from Herbert river northwards, in all the large vine-scrubs on the banks of the rivers and on the high mountains of the coasts.

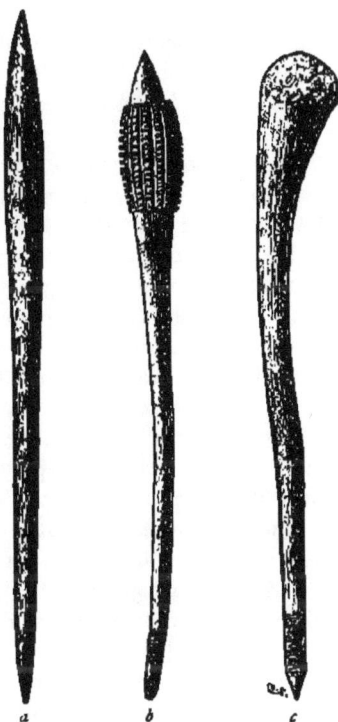

"NOLLA-NOLLAS," CLUBS (¼ size).

a, *c*, from Central Queensland, near Rockhampton ; *b*, from Northern Queensland, Herbert Vale. The thickest end of that marked *c* is usually stained dark brown.

For some time I made daily visits to the river bank and caught the beautiful green and blue *Orthoptera*, which from ten to eleven o'clock in the morning were found flitting among the trees and bushes.

In the vicinity of Mr. Gardiner's farm there were both coffee and tobacco plantations, where the plants throve very

well. According to the owner's idea, however, the proper
varieties had not yet been found. He had a tobacco factory
near the plantation, but the tobacco produced here was so
inferior in quality that the more fastidious even of the blacks
disdained it. Tobacco thrives very well everywhere in
Northern Queensland, and like cinchona, quinine, arrow-
root, rice, and cotton, which wherever planted have thriven
well, its cultivation is doubtless destined to become an important industry. It is only necessary to find the variety adapted
to the climate. It requires great care, and the owner told
me that he was obliged to look after every plant daily.

Although my visit to Mr. Gardiner's farm was both
interesting and agreeable, I longed to get to my destination.
Originally I intended to go there on foot and get some of
the blacks to carry my baggage, but Mr. Gardiner surprised
me one day by offering me an old horse (Kassik) which he
had kept in pasture for a year and a half on the other side
of the river. I was permitted to keep him as a pack-horse
as long as I pleased. He likewise placed a saddle-horse at
my disposal for a limited time. I felt very grateful for this
liberal offer, which I accepted with pleasure, as it would
relieve me from many difficulties.

Cheerful and happy, I started on my journey in beautiful,.
sunny spring weather, following the river upwards. All about
me was fresh and green. Light green patches of grass and
thriving vine-scrubs, by the side of brooks and streams, which
crossed my path on their course down to the river, passed
in pleasing succession. The dark green vine-scrubs which
extended along the banks on both sides of the river gave the
landscape its most conspicuous character, and contrasted well
with the light green spots. The bottom of the valley was
flat and fertile. Before me I saw continually the scrub-clad
hills, the foot of which I knew to be my destination. It
was on these mountains that I based so many hopes. It is
true that Mr. Scott, the owner of this deserted cattle station,
which he had kindly invited me to use as my headquarters,
had warned me that I was coming to a poor place, where
I must renounce every comfort. I was well aware of
this, but was prepared to submit to various kinds of
privation if I could but get the opportunity of living amid

this instructive Nature, where I anticipated such great results.
It was impossible to be melancholy in the midst of such
wonderful surroundings ! All was bright and inspiring.

On the evening of the second day, as I was approaching
Herbert Vale, I constantly heard a peculiar whistling sound
in the grass, which I could not comprehend. On dismounting,
I found that it came from an infinite number of small grasshoppers which were not yet fully developed. They retreated
before my horses, and were so numerous that the blades of
grass literally bent under their weight. Herbert river is
sometimes visited by vast swarms of grasshoppers, which do
considerable damage to the young sugar-cane.

Darkness set in, but I continued to ride three-quarters of
an hour after sunset. Several times I was obliged to dismount
in order to look for the direction of the path. When at
length I could no longer find my way in the darkness of
the night, I suddenly scented smoke, and after going a few
steps in that direction I discovered that the grass had been
recently burnt. Far away, the stumps of trees still shone
with fresh embers. Fortunately I came across a camp
of blacks near the river's bank. To the great terror of the
natives I entered their camp, but quieted them immediately
by showing them tobacco, for two pieces of which currency
I induced one of them to be my guide to Herbert Vale.

CHAPTER VI

ARRIVING at the entrance to the yard, I met a white object, which proved to be a Kanaka in his Sunday clothes. He took my horses under his care and called the superintendent of the station, who was an old white man. A bureau, a couple of wooden chairs, and a camp-bed constituted the entire furniture of my room. The bed, in which I slept exceedingly well, possessed the unexampled luxury of two thick canvas sheets, and I had been prudent enough to bring with me a heavy double woollen blanket. At breakfast I asked the old man to introduce me to some of the blacks, whose assistance I needed, for I could accomplish nothing without them. I therefore also inquired whether there were any "civilised" ones among them. The answer was, that for the last two years he had permitted them to come to the station, and consequently some of them might have the right to this title. To know that they will be killed if they murder a white man, to be fond of wearing the garments and ornaments of white people, and to smoke tobacco, is all that is required in order to be styled "civilised" among the Australian blacks, though sometimes they do learn a little more than that. These so-called "civilised" blacks look upon their savage brethren with more or less contempt, and call them *myall*.[1]

---

[1] A tree (*Acacia pendula*) which grows extensively in the less civilised districts is called by the Europeans *myall*. This word was soon applied by the whites as a term for the wild blacks who frequented these large remote *myall* woods. Strange to say, the blacks soon adopted this term themselves and used it as an epithet of abuse, and hence it soon came to mean a person of no culture.

We had not finished our breakfast when we saw their heads peeping through the gate;—all were men armed with spears, as they were just going out to hunt the wallaby. Most of them were slender and tolerably well built, though on the average small. Their height varied greatly. One of them, a lean and slender fellow, called by the old man Tommy, who I afterwards learned had five wives, was distinguished for his stature ; but he was scarcely over 5 feet 8 inches in height. Their faces varied conspicuously, some having longer noses than I had observed before among the Australian natives, but very flat ; all were entirely naked. Some of them wore about their necks a sort of yellow band made of hollow straws cut into small pieces. This band was wound several times round the neck.

PECULIAR POSITION OF NATIVES
WHEN RESTING.

The old superintendent pointed out one of these blacks, called Jacky, who knew a few English words. He was a square-built, well-proportioned man, in good physical condition, with a cunning but good-natured face. As he was considered the most civilised person of the lot, I tried to make him explain to the others that I desired to obtain all things creeping on the ground or flying in the air, and that I would give them tobacco for what they brought me. I also wanted one of them to go with me and find *tshukki-tshukki*. This word is used to the civilised blacks to indicate birds. Jacky said he would "belong to me" to-morrow, but now they were all going out hunting ; he added that they would bring me something when they returned in the evening. Jacky was the only one with whom I could talk; the others were silent.

I observed that some rested in a most peculiar position, a habit which I have often noticed since then. They stood on one foot, and placed the sole of the other on the inside of the thigh a little above the knee. The whole person was easily supported by a spear (p. 77).[1]

The blacks left us, and I took this opportunity of studying my surroundings. Herbert Vale, which belongs to the Scott Brothers, had been abandoned as a cattle station, because the soil along the lower part of the river proved to be so excellent for sugar-growing that it rose in value and became too expensive for cattle-raising. The English-man always knows how to make himself comfortable, so the station had comparatively good houses, and for this reason the owners had left an old white man in charge of the property. His chief duty was to keep the blacks from setting fire to the houses when they burned the grass while hunting.

Around the whole property there was a natural hedge of sharp thorns. Passing through a little gate we came to a two-storied wooden house painted red, the first floor of which was used for kitchen and dining-room. The kitchen was quite primitive, having neither floor nor door. The main building, a low one-storied house, stood a few steps farther to the west nearer the river.

On the side facing Herbert river I had access from my room to a spacious verandah, from which there was a fine view far up the river. Besides these two buildings, a large store-house, in which the superintendent kept a supply of flour, sugar, tea, and tobacco, gave the impression of wealth.

Mr. Scott had made a large garden, which now unfortunately was in an entirely dilapidated condition, as the old superintendent made no use of it; the only thing he cultivated being some sweet-potatoes (*Batatas edulis*). The only care which the garden received was that the grass was mown now and then when it became too high, in order to keep it from smothering the trees. In spite of the miserable

---

[1] This custom also prevails among the inhabitants of the Soudan and the White Nile district. See James's *Soudan*.

condition of the garden it was a pleasure to see that even
in these uncivilised regions there existed a taste for the
beauties and comforts of life, and not simply a love of money.
The cheerful houses among the thriving trees could not fail
to gladden the traveller, whose eyes in this part of the
country rarely witness other than primitive cabins of bark.
In Northern Queensland it is even more rare to find things
done simply for comfort than it is farther south ; farther
west and north the country becomes still more wild and
uncivilised. The desire to earn money seems to monopolise
everything, and there is no time to think of such a luxury as
a garden. Of course occasionally a bed of cabbage, carrots,
sweet-potatoes, and the like, might be found, but fruit or
shady trees are looked for in vain.

In the middle of the garden stood a bread-tree, but it
did not thrive ; this was also the case with a few cocoanut-
palms. Conquat, loquat, and guava-trees, on the other hand,
bear excellent fruit. A granadilla, which twined itself gracefully round an old fig-tree, furnished us for Christmas with
a small amount of palatable fruit. A part of the garden
might be called an orange-orchard, which bore oranges in
abundance, but, alas, they were, chiefly from want of care,
too sour to be eaten. The mango-tree yielded the best fruit
to be found in the whole garden.

Herbert Vale lies about forty miles above the mouth
of Herbert river, 18° S. lat. ; its rainfall is about ninety
inches annually. The locality is exceedingly beautiful,
occupying a high plain on the eastern bank of the river where
the latter makes a bend. The bottom of the river valley
is very flat, and dotted with grass and brushwood. In the
distance in almost every direction appear mountainous
uplands covered to the very horizon with dense scrubs,
now and then broken by an opening, through which picturesque waterfalls may be seen dashing down the hillside,
greatly enlivening the sombre groves. The streams which
form these waterfalls often unite and empty into Herbert
river, and along their whole course they are bordered with
scrub on both sides. The mountains are the same as those
extending hundreds of miles northward to Cape York.

In the afternoon the natives returned, but, alas, it was a

disagreeable surprise to find what they had brought for me—the thigh and tail of a kangaroo—in their estimation the most valuable thing they could procure. It was always difficult to make them understand what I wanted. I succeeded better after I had coaxed them to tell me what animals they knew and what they called them. Notwithstanding the fact that they knew they would be well paid for what they might bring, they rarely found anything of interest; they were too lazy and too stupid to care for anything beyond the present moment. If my efforts were to produce any result, I would have to go with them myself, and stay with them early and late, well supplied with tobacco, a small amount of which will induce them to do anything in their power. For some time I succeeded in keeping one man, who accompanied me on all my tours. Thus I made excursions in the neighbourhood of Herbert Vale until towards the close of October, always attended by the blacks.

I was deeply interested in the study of the Australian natives, who are supposed to be the lowest order of the human race. I went with them on their excursions through the dense scrubs; I admired their skill in climbing the tall gum-trees; and wondered at their keen and trained senses, by which they discovered animals in the most surprising manner. We hunted the cassowary or dug out from the earth bandicoots and *Dasyuridæ*—not a day passed on which we did not go out on some hunting expedition; in short, I was constantly with them, and frequently spent the evenings in their camp, which, as a rule, was pitched near the station. As I gradually became able to make myself understood, my interest in this remarkable and most primitive race of people increased.

Mr. Scott's keeper at the station was a peevish, conceited old man, who spent most of his time sleeping on a sort of cot which he had placed on the verandah. He had left the care of the house entirely to a Kanaka. This latter had purchased from the tribe in the neighbourhood of Herbert Vale a girl, Nelly, for his wife, and the main burden of housekeeping was put upon her. The only thing that the Kanaka did himself was to milk the cow in the morning, bake the damper, and chop the fuel for the kitchen. There

was not much variety in our bill of fare: salt beef and damper, damper and salt beef, were the standing dishes at all three meals. On two occasions a chicken was killed, which was prepared in the plainest manner; the head being chopped off, it was stripped of its feathers, and at once put into the kettle to boil. For a time we also had sweet-potatoes, which Nelly placed on the table for breakfast, dinner, and supper as long as they lasted. No care was bestowed on our hens, however; they laid many eggs, which Nelly, our skilful cook, invariably did her best to serve in an almost petrified condition.

The old man delighted in a numerous family of cats; for, in his opinion, after a woman, a cat was the chief source of domestic comfort. As soon as they heard the sound of kettle and plates, they gathered in large numbers from all quarters. As a rule a couple of them could be seen in the forenoon sleeping among the washed plates on the kitchen table, while the fowls wandered about everywhere. The cock crowed on the dining-room table, and the hens laid their eggs on the hearthstone. It was indeed strange to see how little pains the old man took to make himself comfortable. How nice he could have made it here if he only had taken some interest in the affairs of the household! Besides the chickens, he had, as we have seen, a cow, and at times fresh meat, for there were several cattle for slaughter left on the deserted station.

In the long run salt beef and damper make rather un-wholesome food, and though I therefore repeatedly tried to give Nelly lessons in cooking, my efforts were fruitless. I wanted her to fry the beef, but she used such a quantity of fat that it took away all my appetite. Too old to make any progress in the art of cooking, Nelly clung to her former habits, and preferred to boil salt beef and sweet-potatoes, if she had any. However, I must confess that she had great talent for making the fire burn. Sometimes the fat caught fire, and in this manner I got rid of the detestable fluid; but then the meat was burnt to a cinder.

The fact that the old man evidently did not like me to meddle with the kitchen affairs made it all the more difficult to bring about any reformation in the culinary

G

department; he preferred to keep matters in the old groove and could not bear any interference on the part of an epicure. Nelly had a high opinion of her own ability. When with a pipe in her mouth, she was washing plates and knives, satisfaction beamed from her dark brown face. Her appetite was marvellous; she not only devoured incredible quantities in the kitchen, but also constantly secured food by bartering with her black friends, for she appeared not to have lost her appetite for their plain messes even after her elevation as the white man's cook. She always had a supply of baskets filled with various kinds of vegetable provisions of the plainest sort hanging in the kitchen.

The highest ideal of these natives' existence is to have plenty to eat, and Nelly ate most of the time. When she was not engaged in this her favourite occupation, she smoked tobacco, and when she neither ate nor smoked she slept. Thus her existence was a happy one, marred only by an occasional flogging from her husband. In her domestic troubles she was as a rule the wronged party, but being the weaker of the two she of course could never claim the victory, which was determined by fisticuffs.

Old Walters, the keeper, had forbidden the black men to come within the enclosure, but the women had free admittance. In course of time the most courageous ones ventured not only to pass through the gate but even to steal into the kitchen. They tried to keep on good terms with Nelly, who now and then would save a bite of food for them, especially if they aided her with the work, which of course served them as a convenient pretext. They took every opportunity of helping themselves to tallow and meat, the women doing the stealing by day and the men by night.

I cannot deny that it annoyed me to know that the food was prepared by the blacks; for the women who washed the dishes were naked, and filthy in the extreme, and moreover the natives were troubled with skin diseases, so that both the old man and myself were liable to catch the infection. Such diseases, the faithful attendants of civilisation, have also found their way to the natives of the Herbert river region. Fortunately but few were sufficiently advanced in civilisation. Nor were there very many who ventured into the kitchen, at least at first ; but as they gradually became acquainted with

JACKY, A "CIVILISED" BLACK-FELLOW.

the place their number increased in the same proportion as their respect for the keeper diminished.

The external mark of civilisation among the Australian natives is usually a European shirt which has been white, but which, on account of age and want of washing, has assumed a colour thoroughly in harmony with the complexion of its owner. Nor is a common English clay pipe ever wanting to complete the impression of being a "gentleman" among his colleagues, to say nothing of a felt hat, which in the eyes of the Australian native is the chief mark of distinction between a white and a black man. They usually ask the white man for a civilised name, and if this request is granted they are constantly called by it among their comrades.

The natives on Herbert river near my headquarters had just begun to enter this state of civilisation, but very few of them had succeeded in obtaining a shirt or an old hat. The fact of their incipient civilisation was at least of one advantage to me—they were less afraid of the white man.

Whenever a bullock was killed they regularly congregated in large numbers at the station, for at such times there was always something to get. The meat was salted in the usual manner, and the head, the hide, the bones, and all the entrails were given to the blacks. A slaughter day was a real festival at Herbert Vale. It was usually found out several days in advance, was reported from one tribe to another, and was a topic of conversation far away in the mountains among those who did not dare to approach the station.

It amused me very much to watch the blacks in the slaughter-yard, an enclosure about 150 yards from the main building. When the time approached for the old keeper to appear with his rifle to shoot the bullock—*tombbero*, as the blacks call both the animal and the beef—they came up from their camp, but were not allowed to stand near the enclosure. As the Australian cattle are used to see men only on horseback, they become very frightened at the sight of people on foot, and especially of the blacks, not only because they are on foot, but because the poor beasts occasionally have made the acquaintance of their spears.

First, the blacks had to keep themselves concealed from the sight of the bullock, for fear it should get frightened and run to and fro in the yard, and thus make it impossible for the old man to shoot it. The keeper would then get so angry that he would hurl empty threats at their heads. They however gradually became so accustomed to this that they did not mind it. Upon the whole his authority was not much respected by them, and the fact that he often missed his mark when he shot at the bullock materially increased their contempt for him, for the blacks expect a man to hit the object at which he aims.

As soon as the animal falls, which is easy for them to observe from their ambush, they rush forth from all parts of the wood and stand around the enclosure—men, women, and children—all alike eager to get their share of the slaughtered animal.

First, the throat of the bullock is pierced with a long knife that the blood may run out. Some old women are then permitted to come within the yard, and with both hands they scoop up from the ground the coagulated blood into their baskets. Next the flaying begins, and several men are allowed to come in and help. None of them seems much inclined to assist in the work, but they all like to get inside the yard, for then they are sure of securing some of the spoils. Some of them hold the beast by the feet or tail while others remove the hide with the old keeper's knives. As soon as the animal is cut open it is important to be at hand ready to lay hold of the largest pieces of the entrails, all of which fall to the lot of the blacks. At this point men, women, and children all rush into the yard.

Amid deafening noise and clamour a regular fight for the intestines commences ; they pull them into pieces in their tussle for them, each one trying to secure the longest piece. The worthiest among them, that is to say the strongest and those who have the most wives, have agreed beforehand who is to have such delicate parts as the liver, the lungs, and the heart. There is also a great struggle for the tail, to say nothing of the hide, which is always an object of lively competition.

A number of blacks gather round it and hold it up between them, but it is no easy matter to divide an ox hide, for it cannot be torn into pieces. Iron implements are needed, and so the axe and large knives are borrowed. One begins to cut out a large piece with the axe, while others who have succeeded in getting knives pay no respect to an equitable division of the booty, but cut out as large pieces as possible. Those who have failed to secure any knife stand crestfallen, impatiently watching the proceedings, and expecting every moment that the piece will be cut out; but to their despair the sharp weapon continually plunges farther into the hide. At length the cutting is finished, and only miserable portions of the large hide remain. All that is now left to be done is to divide the head between the two who have taken possession of it, and who have agreed in advance to share it equally.

When the blacks have taken all they can, the whole crowd return to the camp, where they gorge themselves not only with the entrails but also with the hide. The intestines and the stomach have already been emptied and are ready to be prepared for eating, the stomach having been turned and the intestines emptied by drawing them between the fingers; washing them is out of the question. They are torn into smaller pieces and laid on the coals, and after being turned once or twice with a wooden stick, are fished out of the fire and eaten. The hide is treated in the same way.

The old man now has the carcass left and the butchering is done. For dinner, which is to be eaten in about half an hour, he lays aside the most tender parts—the diaphragm, the kidneys, and the pancreas. This is all prepared by Nelly, who on such solemn occasions is particularly proud of her skill as cook. The meat floats on an ocean of fat, while she now and then licks the point of the knife with delight. At such times she can brook no joking, having a sublime sense of her own importance, and being thoroughly convinced that she is indispensable. This important task finished, the delicate viands are placed on a plate in a pyramidal heap.

One gets accustomed to everything in Australia, and as when people are hungry they will eat almost anything, so the inhabitants of Northern Queensland are willing to live like pigs if they can only make money. The man who can "work well" is most respected, and to this there can be no objection; but the idea of a "good worker" implies that he is rough, and does not care what he eats. They do not understand that it is possible to work and eat in a decent manner at the same time. I remember a proprietor in Northern Queensland speaking of this matter in a very characteristic manner. His workmen had requested him to buy for them a little butter and some pickles to eat with their plain food, a luxury they could well afford, as they earned two pounds a week each. But the fact that they could think of such a thing offended him to such a degree that he said to me : " I really think it would be better for people to spend all their money on liquor than to eat it up in this fashion."

The only extra trouble Nelly had from a butchering, which occurred once every three weeks, was that she had to make tallow for lighting, and for greasing the boots. The tallow was placed in a tin cup in which a rag torn from an old pair of corduroy breeches served as wick ; that was our lamp. Usually the tallow soon gave out ; for it stood in a kettle on the hearth, and here the fowls, in competition with the blacks, consumed it. As we shall see later on, the blacks have a great predilection for fat.

We had now finished our dinner, which, in addition to the fresh beef, consisted, as usual, of damper and sweet-potatoes. Making beef-tea or soup from any part of the beef was utterly out of the question.

In the afternoon all the beef is to be salted, and this is old Walters's task. When he has eaten his dinner, he and Nelly and the Kanaka proceed to the slaughter-house. Meanwhile the natives have returned from their camp, and are sitting patiently waiting for the bones which fall to their lot after the meat has been cut off. The large joints are roasted and then gnawed most thoroughly, the cartilage, hoofs, and the softer parts of the bone disappearing into their strong stomachs.

Nelly is wholly occupied with the great event of the day. Her movements indicate unusual solemnity and earnestness. Conscious that something important is going on to-day, she feels her own superiority as compared with the other natives. The idea of belonging to the old man who has such mountains of food ! How grand she must appear to the other blacks !

To-night they expect bits of meat, which she steals from the kitchen and divides among them.   Nor does she neglect herself, but is continually chewing something or other.

Soon after sunset all is over, and the blacks have retired to their camp satiated and happy.   They have to-day eaten *komorbory*, *i.e.* very much, and consequently from their point of view have experienced the greatest enjoyment that life can afford.

Such was a slaughter day at Herbert Vale.   Now and then a sick animal was shot and given to the blacks.   I remember that an old cow which was so lean and miserable from pleuro-pneumonia that it could scarcely walk, was driven into the yard to be killed for the natives.   Pleuro-pneumonia causes great destruction of cattle in some parts of Australia. Many cattle are saved by inoculating the virus near the upper end of the tail, but the disease is contagious, and when an animal cannot be cured it is best to kill it.   The old cow fell at the first shot, and the natives were permitted to do as they pleased with it.   They borrowed an axe with which they chopped it in two along the back to get at the kidneys and the fat around them, for these parts they like best. There was a little fat about the kidneys, but none elsewhere ; scarcely any meat could be found on the bones, and the lungs were consumed and had a horrible smell.   The natives do not like anything which smells bad, but to reject other than the damaged parts was out of the question.   The rest was eaten, and no one was taken ill after this disgusting meal.

It must be admitted that my headquarters could hardly be called comfortable ; but if we understand the art of adapting ourselves to circumstances, we may at all times make things more bearable than they seem to be.   In a new country like Northern Queensland, where people live so far apart, and where each one thinks only of himself, it is easy to see what a great advantage it must be to have a place where one can find shelter.   Besides, it was a real comfort to know that I was not likely to die of starvation, thanks to Nelly's damper and salt beef.   During a short period there was also fruit in the garden, but, after all, my greatest treat when I came down from the mountains was milk.   Every one who has travelled in the tropics knows what a luxury this is.

CLIMBING WITH THE AID OF KĀMIN. *To face page 89.*

CHAPTER VII

A FEW days after my arrival at Herbert Vale, the natives
were to undertake a hunt of the wallaby, and with two black
companions I presented myself at the place where the hunt
was to begin. We left home in the morning. The forenoon
was devoted to hunting for small mammals, which during
the daytime keep themselves concealed in the high trees.
With kind words and tobacco I induced my blacks to climb
up one immense gum-tree after the other.

The Australian black on the Herbert river was more skilful
in climbing than any of the other natives I had seen up to this
time. If he has to climb a high tree, he first goes into the
scrub to fetch a piece of the Australian calamus (*Calamus
australis*), which he partly bites, partly breaks off; he first
bites on one side and breaks it down, then on the other side
and breaks it upwards—one, two, three, and this tough whip
is severed. At one end of it he makes a knot, the other he
leaves as it is. This implement, which is usually sixteen to
eighteen feet long, is called a kämin.

After wiping his hands in the grass so as to remove
all moisture from perspiration, he takes the knot in his left
hand, throws the kämin around the big tree-trunk, and tries
to catch the other end with his right hand. When, after a
couple of abortive efforts, he has succeeded in this, he winds
this end a few times around the right arm and thus gets
a secure hold. The right foot is planted against the tree,
the arms are extended directly in front of him, the body is

bent back, so that it is kept as far as possible away from the tree, and then the ascent begins. He keeps throwing the kāmin up the tree, and at the same time he himself ascends about as easily as a sailor uses an accommodation ladder, but as climbing by means of the kāmin is of course much harder work, he is compelled to stop every few moments to take breath. When he has reached the branches of the tree he hangs the kāmin on one of them, while he examines the holes in the trunk.

It seemed to me that he placed his kāmin so carelessly that it might easily fall down while he was engaged in the hunt for animals in the tree. If this should happen, I hardly know how he could get down those high and smooth trees. But with the aid of the kāmin it is easy enough. He walks down backwards very rapidly. If it is a very large tree, and the bark very smooth, he chops niches in it for his big toe. He takes his tomahawk in his mouth, and when he wants to use it removes the kāmin from his right arm and winds it around his right thigh, whereupon with his free hand he cuts the next niche or two in the bark of the tree.

Thus we see the importance of having a knot in one end of the kamin and none in the other. This arrangement has also another advantage, that the kāmin can be used in a tree of unequal thickness, and in different trees; for the native usually carries this implement with him and uses it in a number of trees. Instead of rolling it together, or winding it into a coil, he draws it behind him, simply holding on to the knotted end. Strange to say, this is the most practical way of carrying it, for the kāmin is hard and smooth, so that it never sticks fast in the brushwood. Rolled into a ring it would doubtless be a great source of trouble in the dense scrub. No tree is too high or too smooth for the Australian native to climb, provided its circumference is not too great.

But my blacks climbed the high gum-trees in vain. They did not succeed in discovering a single opossum, flying-squirrel,[1] or any other nocturnal animal that hides in tree-trunks. The reason for this, in the opinion of the blacks, was

[1] The marsupial flying-phalanger is so called by the Australians.

a circumstance unknown to me, viz. that both the opossum and the flying-squirrel disappear in the summer time and do not return before the rainy season, at which time they are abundant. At first I had grave doubts in regard to this explanation, and made my natives climb a number of trees, but as I did not find a single specimen, I came to the conclusion that they were right. The opossum (*Trichosurus vulpecula*) and the flying-squirrel leave the bottom of the valley in the summer. I do not know what becomes of the former, but I found *Petauroides volans* and several species of *Petaurus* in the middle of the summer on the open grass plains in the mountain regions near Herbert Vale. In the rainy season the opossum and the flying-squirrels were very numerous about the station.

Late in the afternoon I arrived with my companions at the spot where the wallaby hunt was to take place. It was a large plain, surrounded on all sides by scrub and overgrown with high dense grass. The wallabies (*Macropus agilis*) are very numerous in the Herbert river bottoms, but keep themselves concealed during the day. The usual way of hunting these animals is by setting fire to the grass ; this starts them up and they try to escape. The natives stand on guard ready to attack the flying animals, and try to kill them with spears while they, fleet as the wind, run by. As a rule the hunt is postponed until the afternoon, for there is so much dew in the morning that the grass looks as if there had been a shower of rain ; but after noon it is quite dry again.

I looked in vain for my black hunting companions, but soon discovered that they were just crossing the river, which flowed among the scrubs below the plain. I rode to the bank and discovered one group after the other coming into view behind the trees on the other side, the women peeping curiously from behind the bushes to catch a glimpse of the white man. They looked timid, and deemed it safest to cross the river higher up, where they came over each with her children on her shoulders and a basket on her back. Some of them had fire with them, carrying burning sticks in their hands. The men waded across at the place where I stood. It interested me to watch them in their natural nakedness as they gradually gathered around me on the bank of the river, but as usual it was necessary to be watchful of the long spears which they bore.

They soon separated, some of them stationing themselves on the outside of the field, while the rest remained to set fire to the grass. Jacky, one of my blacks, indicated to me that for the sake of the horse I had better remain where I was. He himself went with the other men, and took his station on the side of the field. Soon those who had remained behind spread themselves out, set fire to the grass simultaneously at different points, and then quickly joined the rest. The dry grass rapidly blazed up, tongues of fire licked the air, dense clouds of smoke rose, and the whole landscape was soon enveloped as in a fog.

I fastened up my horse and went into this semi-darkness, watching the blacks, who ran about like shadows, casting their spears after the animals that fled from the flames. But though many spears whizzed through the air, and though a large field was burned, not a single wallaby was slain.

The Australians have the reputation of being able to hurl the spear skilfully; they do much damage to the white man's cattle, and many a white man is killed by this weapon; but, strange to say, I have never observed any remarkable skill in its use among the blacks of Herbert river. This may be explained by the fact that in a great measure they find their food in the scrubs, where spears cannot be used. Of course it is difficult to hit an animal running at full speed, but I have often seen them miss sitting shots. On the other hand, it sometimes happens that they kill three or four during a hunt.

This time all the booty consisted of a few bandicoots (*Peramelidæ*), which were dug out of the ground between the roots of a large gum-tree. While the men were busy doing this the women stood ready to receive the game and take it home. The bandicoots are good eating even for Europeans, and in my opinion are the only Australian mammals fit to eat. They resemble pigs, and the flesh tastes somewhat like pork.

During the whole chase the women took the greatest delight in watching the sport of the men. At the same time

WALLABY HUNT.

T. Jun. July 92.

they were busily occupied in pulling up the roots of acacias, inside which a larva (*Eurynassa australis*) is concealed, which is eagerly sought after, and is regarded by the natives as a most delicate morsel. The larva when found was immediately roasted in the red-hot ashes lying everywhere on the ground, and was at once devoured.

On grassy plains the hunt of the wallaby, which is the sport most dear to the men, is always carried on in the manner above described, that is, by burning the grass or simply by wandering about hunting for the sleeping animals. The wallabies have excellent ears, and start at the least noise. They may sit for a few moments moving their large ears to catch any suspicious sound ; but, as a rule, even the catlike steps of the blacks are too noisy to enable them to approach sufficiently near the wallaby. When it rains they do not hear so well, and it is then easier to kill them.

These wallabies, the large kangaroos, and the white man's cattle are the only animals which the blacks near Herbert Vale kill with their spears, though the latter are their most important weapons. The spear, usually eight to ten feet long, consists of two parts—the front, which is sharp-pointed, made of a heavy hard kind of wood, and the butt end, which is usually the longer of the two, of *Xanthorrhœa* or a similar light material. These two parts are joined and bound together with wood fibres, or with sinews of the kangaroo's tail, and beeswax heated over the fire. The point is never envenomed, as they know little or nothing about poison. Nor is there any flint point attached, as is often the case in Australia. In Northern Queensland I have occasionally seen the point of the spear furnished with a barb of fish bones for a length of one or two feet up the spear. Such javelins were thicker and shorter than the common ones and were used only for fishing.

The spear is thrown with the help of a throwing stick, which is equal to a quarter or a fifth part of the whole length of the weapon, and has a hook at one end made of wood, likewise fastened with beeswax and fibres of wood or the sinews of the kangaroo's tail. This hook is attached to the butt end of the spear, which has a socket fitting the hook. Thus the stick lies along the under side of the spear. When the latter is to be thrown, the stick and the weapon itself are seized with the first three fingers. Both are carried back as far as possible, and the spear is thrown with the force of a sling.

In the wallaby chase the blacks on Herbert river also use nets with large meshes, placing them in a line between posts to which they are fastened. Such a net is fifteen to twenty feet long, and the meshes are about four inches each way.

The chase took place in the so-called open country on Herbert river, which, to the superficial observer, does not differ in any striking manner from that of Southern Queensland. The high gum-trees are found here, but the country is more fertile, and the grass is so high that it is difficult to get through it. On this moist soil grow whole forests of the screw-palm (*Pandanus*, p. 95). The country altogether does not look so dry as farther south ; small swamps exist here and there, and brooks often cross one's path.

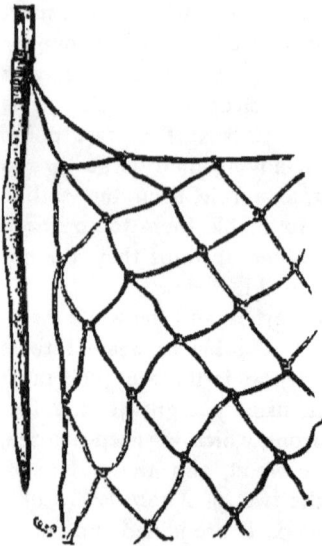

WALLABY NET FROM HERBERT RIVER (⅛ size).

I found fewer birds in this open country than I used to see elsewhere in Australia. Nor did I ever meet in the bottoms of Herbert river valley with those birds which seem to belong inseparably to an Australian forest landscape, such as the piping crow (*Gymnorhina tibicen*), the butcher-bird (*Cracticus nigrogularis*), or the Australian wagtail (*Grallina picata*). Parrots were also scarce, but in the scrubs up the mountains I saw plenty of them. The bird *Centropus*, which is common in all Queensland, is found here in great numbers. Although it really is a cuckoo, the colonists call it the "swamp-pheasant," because it has a tail like a pheasant. It is a very remarkable bird, with stiff feathers, and flies with difficulty on account of its small wings. The "swamp-pheasant" has not the family weakness of the cuckoo, for it does not lay its eggs in the nests of other birds. It has a peculiar clucking voice, which reminds one of the sound produced when water is poured from a bottle—a sound familiar to all who have camped beneath the gum-trees of Australia.

The open country was therefore not the best territory for me, for there was but little game. On the other hand I

THE SCREW-PALM (*Pandanus*).

reaped a more abundant harvest in the scrubs, where there is a greater variety of animal life; and to wander with the blacks in these almost impenetrable jungles in the wide river valley was very interesting. Nothing escapes their notice. On one occasion, in the middle of September, when I made an excursion with one of them, he made me understand that he wished to go away for a moment to look for something. Time passed, and I became impatient, but when I began to shout for him I was not a little surprised to hear his response coming from the far distance above. Approaching, I discovered him in the top of an immensely high tree. He threw down to me two large young of the gigantic wader

Jabiru (*Mycteria australis*). Quickly, and with the dexterity of an acrobat, he descended, laying hold with his hands of the twining plants which hung like natural ropes down the trunk of the tree.

It is not easy to penetrate this scrub, which is so dense that one has scarcely elbow-room ; but along the rivers there is more breathing space. Here beautiful landscapes are often disclosed to view ; the most varied trees vie with each other for a place along the quiet stream ; while creeping and twining plants hang in beautiful festoons over the water.

On first entering the scrub, the solemn quiet and solitude which reign there are striking. You work your way through it by the sweat of your brow ; you startle a bird, which at once disappears, and your prevailing impression is that there is no life. But if you come there in the early morning or towards evening, and sit down quietly, it is surprising to see the birds approaching gently, as if they had been called, and disappearing as noiselessly as they came. Silence as a rule reigns in the scrubs, and the song of birds is rarely heard ; though the doves coo in the evening, and sometimes the melancholy note of the jungle-hen is to be heard, or even, if you are lucky, the thundering voice of the cassowary.

One of the first birds you notice is the cat-bird (*Æluroedus maculosus*), which makes its appearance towards evening, and has a voice strikingly like the mewing of a cat. The elegant metallic-looking "glossy starlings" (*Callornis metallica*) greedily swoop with a horrible shriek upon the fruit of the Australian cardamom [1] tree. The ingenious nests of this bird were found in the scrubs near Herbert Vale—a great many in the same tree. Although this bird is a starling, the colonists call it "weaver-bird."

There are few birds that look better in the green tree-tops than the Torres Strait pigeons (*Carpophaga spilorrhoa*), which is white, like a ptarmigan in winter dress, with the exception of its wings and tail, which are black. In November a pair of them built their nest in a high tree near

---

[1] This is a fictitious name, as are the names of many Australian plants and animals. The tree belongs to the nutmeg family, and its real name is *Myristica insipida*. The name owes its existence to the similarity of the fruit to the real cardamom. But the fruit of the *myristica* has not so strong and pleasant an odour as the real cardamom, and hence the tree is called *insipida*.

the, scrub, and like several other varieties of birds, had just arrived from the northernmost part of Queensland and New Guinea; for it was now spring, and all the birds that migrate northward in the winter had returned, such as the celebrated Australian giant cuckoos (*Scythrops nova-hollandiæ*), whose terrible shrieks are heard at a great distance when in scores they gorge themselves in the large fig-trees. On the banks of a stream I shot a specimen of the very small kingfisher (*Ceyx pusilla*), which belongs to New Guinea and Northern Australia. It was the only specimen I saw on Herbert river. The racket-tail kingfisher (*Tanysiptera*) has also been shot in the scrubs here.

But what especially gives life and character to these woods are the jungle-hens (mound-builders), which I have already mentioned. The weird, melancholy cry of these birds once heard is not easily forgotten; at sunset and in the twilight of the evening it is in perfect harmony with the stillness and repose of nature. The bird is of a brownish hue, with yellow legs and immensely large feet; hence its name *Megapodius*. It is very shy, and therefore it is not easy to get a glimpse of it, but its remarkable nests, which are formed of large heaps of earth and decayed leaves, like those of the talegalla, are frequently to be found in the scrubs. From my own experience I venture to assert that the mounds of the jungle-hen are larger than those of the talegalla. For many years they were thought to be the burying-grounds of the natives, says Mr. Eden, who mentions one which was sixteen feet high and sixty-two feet in circumference at the base. One would hardly think that birds could build so large a mound.

In these scrubs the proud cassowary, the stateliest bird of Australia, is also to be found. I had already made several vain attempts to secure a specimen of this beautiful and comparatively rare creature. We had frequently seen traces of it under the large fig-trees, the fruit of which it eats. The excrement of the cassowary looks more like that of a horse than of a bird, and I saw large heaps under the fig-trees. We often approached without seeing it, for it is exceedingly shy and departs on the slightest noise, consequently it is very difficult to get a shot.

On October 6 the natives brought me two eggs
and a young bird just hatched. I at once requested
one of them to guide me to the nest, whither I took
it, hoping thereby to attract the old bird. Near the nest,
which was formed of a not very soft bed of loose leaves

YOUNG CASSOWARY.

massed together, we placed the young one and then stepped
aside to see what would happen. It first began to run after
us, but as it soon lost sight of us, commenced to cry violently.
After a lapse of about ten minutes we suddenly heard the
voice of the cassowary, which usually sounds like thunder
in the distance, but now, when calling its young, it reminded

us of the lowing of a cow to its calf. The sound came nearer and nearer, and soon the beautiful blue and red neck of the bird appeared among the trees, and its black body became visible. It stopped and scanned its surroundings carefully in the dense scrub, but a charge of No. 3 shot, fired from a distance of fifteen paces, laid it low.

My black companion gave a shout of victory, and ran back to the camp to get some men to carry the precious burden home. Six natives took turns in carrying it to the station, where I at once set to work skinning it. The blacks made a feast of its flesh, and the skin formed a valuable addition to my collection. It was an unusually fine specimen of a male, who thus appears to care for the young, at least in the early stage. The eggs, three[1] in number, are frequently laid at long intervals. In this instance there was a bird just hatched, an egg almost hatched, and another egg the contents of which could easily be blown out. Thus we see that the young are not hatched at the same time, and that the male must therefore care for them while the female is busy brooding. After the third egg is hatched, the male and female probably share the burden of supporting the family.

The first specimen of this variety of cassowary (*Casuarius australis*) was shot in these same scrubs near the close of the sixties.

Its eyes, which cannot fail to be admired, form the most beautiful feature of the cassowary. Their expression is defiant and proud, as that of the eagle's eyes. The natives hunt the bird with the aid of their dingoes, which are able to kill the half-grown and sometimes even the old birds. The flesh tastes very much like beef, and is very fat. In the rainy season the cassowary is sometimes compelled to take to the water, and proves itself to be a good swimmer.

The blacks claim that their hands become white if washed in the contents of its stomach at the season of the year when it mainly feeds on a fruit which they call *tobola*. I give this for what it is worth ; but I have seen natives having on their hands white spots which they insisted were produced in this manner ; no doubt these spots were nothing more than *vitiligo* or *leucopathia acquisita*, found among all races of men.

[1] The colour, which is a light green, varies in shade in the three eggs.

CHAPTER VIII

No person can spend many days with the Australian natives
before finding out that one of their chief traits is their never-
ceasing begging. If you give one thing to a black man,
he finds ten other things to ask for, and he is not ashamed
to ask for all that you have, and more too. He is never
satisfied. Gratitude does not exist in his breast, and friendship he is unable to appreciate. An Australian native can
betray anybody, and confidence can rarely be placed in him.
You should never let him walk behind you, but always in
front. There is not one among them who will not lie if it is
to his advantage. Though it is their nature to be lazy, and
though they have no inclination whatever for work, yet they
can on a hunt develop remarkable energy and endurance.

The women are the humble servants or rather slaves of
the native. He does only what pleases himself, and leaves
all work to his wives ; therefore the more wives he has the
richer he is.

The Australian aborigines do not cultivate the soil, and
their only domestic animal is the dingo (dog). Living from
hand to mouth on vegetables or animal flesh, they are constantly flitting from place to place to find their subsistence,
and have no permanent abodes. Their character is like their
mode of life ; they are the children of the moment—capricious ;
a resolution is quickly formed and as quickly abandoned.
They are humorous by nature, have a keen sense of what
is comical, and a cheerful disposition ; though free from care,

they are never without a secret fear of being attacked by
other tribes, for the tribes are each other's mortal foes.

What they lack in personal courage they make up by
craft and cunning. If they can kill their enemies by a
treacherous attack, they do so without hesitation. The
attacked party takes to flight, each one thinking of his own
safety alone, for self-preservation is their only law.

The Australians are cannibals. A fallen foe, be it man,
woman, or child, is eaten as the choicest delicacy ; they know
no greater luxury than the flesh of a black man. There are
superstitious notions connected with cannibalism, and though
they have no idols and no form of divine worship, they
seem to fear an evil being who seeks to haunt them, but
of whom their notions are very vague. Of a supreme good
being they have no conception whatever, nor do they believe
in any existence after death. Such are in brief the main
characteristics of the Australian native as I came to know
him on the Herbert river.

During my association with these savages I learned that
on the summit of the Coast Mountains, before mentioned,
there lived two varieties of mammals which seemed to me
to be unknown to science ; but I had much difficulty in
acquiring this knowledge. One of the animals they called
yarri. From their description I conceived it to be a
marsupial tiger. It was said to be about the size of a
dingo, though its legs were shorter and its tail long,
and it was described by the blacks as being very savage.
If pursued it climbed up the trees, where the natives
did not dare follow it, and by gestures they explained
to me how at such times it would growl and bite their
hands. Rocky retreats were its most favourite habitat,
and its principal food was said to be a little brown variety
of wallaby common in Northern Queensland scrubs. Its
flesh was not particularly appreciated by the blacks, and
if they accidentally killed a yarri they gave it to their old
women. In Western Queensland I heard much about an
animal which seemed to me to be identical with the yarri
here described, and a specimen was once nearly shot by an
officer of the black police in the regions I was now visiting.

The other animal also lived in the trees, but fed exclusively on leaves. According to the statement of the blacks, it was a kangaroo which lived in the highest trees on the summit of the Coast Mountains. It had a very long tail, and was as large as a medium-sized dog, climbed the trees in the same manner as the natives themselves, and was called *boongāry*. I was sure that it could be none other than a tree-kangaroo (*Dendrolagus*). Tree-kangaroos were known to exist in New Guinea, but none had yet been found on the Australian continent.

As is well known, the Great Dividing Range stretches along the coast of Australia at a distance of from fifty to some three hundred miles inland. This range forms in general the watershed between the eastern and western waters, but there are chains of mountains visible from the coast that are often of greater elevation than this range, such as the Blue Mountains, where the streams break through the mountain masses in picturesque chasms on their way to the Pacific. The Dividing Range is sometimes not easily traced, and the spurs coming from it, as well as detached mountains near the coast, are often much higher and are frequently taken for the main range. The whole body of mountains from south to north is spoken of as the Great Dividing Range, and forms, as it were, the Australian Cordilleras. On the extreme south-east the mountains attain an elevation of 5000 to 6000 feet; going north, they diminish rapidly and considerably. In the south part of Queensland they are low, but in Northern Queensland they again rise to a height of 2000 to 4000 feet (the Bellenden Kerr Hills are even 5400 feet high), then they once more diminish, and gradually disappear into the low-lying country of Cape York. The moist monsoons blow over these mountains and are converted into rain, which, together with the warm climate, produces a luxuriant tropical vegetation. Hence these mountains from base to top are extensively covered with scrubs.

On Herbert river and northward the Coast Mountains are difficult of access. Perpendicular chasms and tracts covered with loose stone abound; but wherever a root could take hold large trees and bushes have grown, while creeping and twining plants form a carpet on the ground. There are hilly but less stony parts, where the vegetation is so dense that a person can hardly penetrate it without being so torn and pricked that blood flows from the wounds.

In the mountain scrubs there grows a very luxuriant kind of palm (*Calamus australis*), whose stem, of a finger's thickness, like the East Indian Rotang-palm, creeps through the woods for hundreds of feet, twining round trees in its path, and at times forming so dense a wattle that it is impossible to get through it. The stem and leaves are studded with the sharpest thorns, which continually cling to you and draw blood, hence its not very polite name of *lawyer-palm*.

In the lower regions the common Australian palm and the fan-palm (*Livistonia*) are found. There is also the beautiful banana-palm, with its bright green, and towards the summit magnificent tree-ferns spread their splendid leaves over the rivers in the humid vales, blending with the endless mass of other trees and bushes. Rivers and streams everywhere tumble down the mountain sides, and frequently form beautiful waterfalls surrounded

PALM FOREST IN NORTHERN QUEENSLAND.

by luxuriant scrubs. Here, in the shadow of dense trees hiding the sun from sight, the water is cool and clear as crystal.

The real scrubs once left behind, and the summit reached, you come to a more open country, Leichhardt's basaltic table-land. At first there are hills and dales with the same kind of scrubs as below, but not so dense, for the lawyer-palm is here more rare.

In these picturesque but very inaccessible scrubs the natives live in large numbers undisturbed by the white man, for there is no gold or other treasure to tempt him to subject himself to all the inconveniences connected with the effort to penetrate into these regions.

After having studied the neighbourhood of the station for some time, I soon discovered that I must abandon Herbert Vale as my night quarters and go farther up into the wild woods of the Coast Mountains, where there was much to entice me. Here I was to find the natives in their original condition, uninfluenced by intercourse with the white man. I had long desired to study these savages—the Australian aborigines, the lowest of the human race—in their actual conditions of existence ; for the ethnological student no phase of human life is so interesting as the most primitive one. It also seemed clear at the outset that new species of animal life must be found there, and that I might secure them with the aid of the blacks. Having heard them speak of the two remarkable mammals, I resolved to do all in my power to get into these regions. But I could not think of going by myself; I needed help to carry my baggage, and not having any white servant, I was obliged to select black attendants, the only ones of course who could be of any real service to me in the scrubs. It would, moreover, be very difficult to find a capable white man willing to accompany me. In all probability he would not understand how to treat the savages, and this might soon result in death for both of us. It is difficult for a white man to find his way in these pathless regions ; besides, it is not likely he would be able to trace the wild animals without the aid of the natives who have their hunting grounds here. My only choice was to secure natives, and make them my

friends and comrades, if I wished to attain my purpose ; and
so I resolved to live surrounded by them alone.

My first object was to find persons willing to go with me ;
no easy task, for the "civilised" natives on Herbert river
were very lazy, and did not care to go up into these mountain
regions ; besides, they were but poorly acquainted with them.
I therefore had to address myself to more remote tribes
living nearer the regions which were my goal.   From the
civilised blacks I had become tolerably well acquainted with
the natives.   I knew a little of their language, and having
had some experience of the manner in which to treat them in
order to make them useful to me, I felt comparatively safe ;
but I must confess to considerable curiosity as to what the
result would be.

It was a new experience to a white man this camping
with Australian natives, who dwell in miserable huts made of
leaves, who have no domestic animals, and are ignorant of
agriculture, as well as savage and treacherous.   A human
life has so little value for them that they think no more of
killing a man than we of breaking a glass ; provided they
feel sufficiently safe, they will kill a white man for a piece
of tobacco or a shirt.   But on picturing to myself the
very interesting life in store for me, my doubts and hesi-
tations were overcome.   I was now to have a splendid
opportunity of studying these natives.   I was to be with
them in sunshine and in rain in their own forests ; to
see them uninfluenced by any form of civilisation, and in
their company to make many interesting discoveries and
observations.

.   .   .   .   .   .

In the course of this and the following year I made
many expeditions in company with the blacks.   I began
with the nearest tribes and worked my way up through these
to the more remote ones, until at last I lived in huts with
natives of Australia who never come into contact with the
white man.

My supplies on these expeditions usually consisted of
from ten to twelve pieces of salt beef in a bag, about thirty
pounds of wheat flour for baking damper, and a small sack of
sugar.   Instead of tea I drank simply sugar-water.   It is a

cooling pleasant drink, especially when the water is as clear and good as in Northern Queensland.

When my provisions were consumed—and they never lasted very long, for the natives liked them too well—I lived on their fare, which was anything but savoury. If I had been obliged to depend on their vegetable food I should soon have starved to death, but fortunately the large lizards, snakes, larvæ, eggs, etc., and what I shot for myself, to some extent took the place of civilised food. The worst was when the sugar gave out, for the plain dishes on which I had to depend went down much more easily with sweet water. I had no canned food, and of stimulants, which as a rule I consider superfluous in the tropics, I had only a bottle of whisky. I never carried salt, and, like the natives, I experienced no inconvenience from the want of it when eating eggs, lizards, fish, game, etc.

As money I used tobacco; my provisions served the same purpose, and these were swallowed by the natives, no matter how satiated they might be with other food. When I ran short of tobacco I was always obliged to go back to the station. Even such things as a shirt or a handkerchief so fell in value when tobacco was wanting as to be almost worthless.

The natives along Herbert river, who do not come in contact with white people, have but few wants. They never wear clothes either winter or summer, and consequently money has no value. Their only drink is water or water mixed with honey. The blacks of Herbert river have no stimulants, and this is the secret of the influence of tobacco, which they value so highly that they sometimes wrap a small piece of about three to four inches long in grass, in order to enjoy it later with allied tribes with whom they are on a friendly footing, or they may send it in exchange for other advantages to another tribe. In this manner the use of tobacco may be known among tribes who have never seen a white man. The tobacco is not chewed, but only smoked, and they believe that it is good for everybody; I have even seen a mother put a pipe into the mouth of her babe, which was sitting on her shoulder, and the little one apparently enjoyed a whiff.

Besides tobacco, which I continually dealt out in small quantities to maintain its value, I had to take with me clay pipes, for the blacks cannot even make such things as these. Still, it was more easy to satisfy them with pipes, for

A WOMAN FROM NORTHERN QUEENSLAND, NEAR TOWNSVILLE.

the whole camp was usually content with one or two, which were passed from mouth to mouth.

Of kitchen utensils I took with me only a tin pail to fetch and keep water in, and a knife, for I soon learned from the natives how to prepare my food in a less elaborate

manner than that adopted in a civilised kitchen, so that
I easily got on without kettle or frying-pan, hunger and
fatigue making sauce and spices superfluous.   In addition to the necessary chemicals for preserving specimens, I
carried with me a small flask of quinine, two bottles containing medicine for the stomach, and one containing
ammonia as an antidote to serpent bites ; this and a small
amount of lunar caustic constituted my whole drug store.
A light merino shirt, a coloured shirt, a pair of corduroy
trousers, two pairs of cotton socks, and a pair of shoes, constituted my whole wardrobe.   For the night I had a large,
double, white woollen blanket in which to wrap myself, and a
piece of mackintosh about two yards square, which I spread
out on the ground to lie upon.   I also always took with me
an overcoat, which I put on when it rained.   For my toilet
I had a tooth-brush, a piece of soap, and a towel.   I let my
hair grow until I came to the station, where the keeper, who
had been a sheep-shearer, plied the shears as a haircutter
with all his accustomed skill.

My watch and compass were left at Herbert Vale, for it
was important to be as unencumbered as possible.   With the
natives I learned to determine time by the sun, and what
was lacking in my ability to find my bearings was supplied by the remarkable instinct of the blacks for finding
their way everywhere.   A double-barrelled gun and an
excellent American revolver were of course the most important parts of my whole equipment, which, as has been
shown, was plain, but I was obliged to limit my necessities
as much as possible.   The natives, who dislike to carry
anything, looked upon everything save provisions and
tobacco as luxuries.

The gun and revolver had even more power over them
than the tobacco.   The Australian aborigines are in great
fear of firearms, for they themselves do not even use bows
and arrows, except in the outlying parts of Cape York,
where they have some clumsy weapons of this kind.   But
you must be careful not to miss your mark in their presence.
You must hit all you aim at, or they will lose their respect
for you.   It makes no difference whether the object you
shoot at is in motion or not ; they are as much surprised

when an opossum is brought down from his tree as when the swiftest bird is shot on the wing. When I was not quite sure of my shot, I took good care not to use the revolver, for it is difficult, as everybody knows, to hit the mark with this weapon. They had great respect for the baby of the gun, as they called the revolver, believing that it never ceased shooting, and I need not add that I allowed them to retain this belief. As a rule they were so afraid of the baby that they did not care to touch it. It was in my belt day and night.

It was exceedingly difficult to secure men among the lazy natives for these expeditions; at first my friend Jacky assisted me. On account of his strength and cunning he was highly respected, and looked upon as the first man in his tribe, and he supported me with his influence. First, it was necessary to get him to tell me who were the best hunters, and then, by promising him tobacco, I either got him to go with me to the tribe in question or to find another person willing to do so.

It sometimes took several days to find these people and treat with them. Frequently they changed their minds, and as they were continually moving from place to place I had to give Jacky more tobacco and take a fresh start to find them. At last I would get my people together. As a rule I was attended by five or six young men, sometimes by more, sometimes by less; occasionally women and children, even the whole tribe, went with me. The natives led the way, the one immediately before me leading the pack-horse, while I followed on horseback.

On the first expeditions it only took us a day or two to get to the base of the mountain range. Here we selected a convenient spot for a camp; a place where there was plenty of grass and water for the two horses, which could not go with us into the large dense scrubs. Their forefeet were hobbled, and they were left to themselves during our absence.

The next morning we were ready to proceed on our journey, the saddles and bridles were hung up in the trees in order that they might not be consumed by wild dogs, my baggage was divided among the natives, and the ascent of the scrub-clad mountain began.

As it is easier to get through the scrubs along a river-bed, over stones and crevasses, than it is to crawl through the dense brushwood and be pricked by thorns and sharp branches, we as a rule followed a mountain stream to reach the summit, where were my real hunting grounds. We frequently made long journeys across the table-land, but every expedition was of course not precisely like the one above described. As a rule we went as far as possible on horseback, then we would penetrate the scrubs and gain the table-lands, where the scrubs, as above indicated, appear in patches of various sizes, partly as isolated groves and partly as a continuation of the forests which cover the ridges next to the ocean.

Every evening I pitched my camp and slept in a hut of leaves built exactly like those of the natives, except that it was a little more tightly put together, so that it usually afforded me protection from the rain. It was put up very hastily just before sundown. A few branches were stuck in the ground and their tops united, and this framework was covered with large leaves of the banana or other palms, or with long grass. A door was out of the question; there was simply an opening large enough for me to crawl through, for the whole hut was not higher than my shoulders.

Such is also the *mitta*, the abode of the natives, which is intended only for a short stay, and adapted to the nomadic life of these people. I took care to have my hut made long enough to enable me to lie straight, and to see that my bed was perfectly horizontal, a matter of no importance to the blacks. It makes no difference to them whether the feet lie higher or lower than the head. My people were on either side of the entrance to my hut, where they built flimsy roofs of trees and grass; if there was promise of fine weather for the night, they simply cut down a tree and laid themselves by the side of it. In the centre a fire was kept burning.

Every evening, before going to sleep, I went outside my hut and fired my revolver to remind my companions of the existence of this terrible weapon, and in case we were on the territory of strange tribes, to keep them from attacking us. This precaution was my way of saying good-night to my men. I may add that I never had exactly the

same companions on these various expeditions, because it is
necessary that the blacks should not become too well acquainted with you : as long as they respect the white man
it is less dangerous to camp with them ; but as soon as they
become familiar with his customs and find out that there is
no danger in associating with him, he is liable at any moment
to a treacherous assault.

That I was not killed by my men (a circumstance which
white people whom I have met have wondered at), I owed
to the fact that they never wholly lost their respect for my
firearms.   At first, at least, I was regarded by them as something inexplicable—as a sort of mysterious being who could
travel from land to land without being eaten, and whose
chief interest lay in things which, in their eyes, were utterly
useless, such as the skins and bones of slain animals.

There was a peculiar protection to me in the fortunate
circumstance that they imagined that I did not sleep, and
I think this was the chief reason why they did not attack me
in the night.   During the winter, when there was a great
difference between the temperature of the night and that of
the day, the cold was very trying to me, and I awoke regularly
once or twice in the night when our large camp fire had
gone out.   All my men lay entirely naked around the extinguished fire ; some sleeping, others cold and half awake, who,
however, thought it too much of an effort to go after fuel,
I then usually called one of them, and by promising tobacco
—and I had made them accustomed to have entire confidence in my words—induced him to go out in the dark
night and procure more fuel.

By being thus perpetually disturbed they acquired the
idea that the " white man " was always on the alert and had
the " baby of the gun " ready.

CHAPTER IX

THE first black man recommended to me by Jacky was named Morbŏra. He belonged to a remote tribe on friendly terms with the blacks of Herbert river, and was regarded as an excellent hunter. Both he and his brother Mangŏran declared themselves willing to accompany me. Morbora was a strong, muscular, square-built man hardly twenty years old, with a remarkably low forehead. He was unable to speak a word of English, and trembled with fear when Jacky introduced him to me. I did all in my power to quiet this young black, and took more than usual interest in him, though I soon noticed that he, like all his black brethren, sought to take advantage of my friendliness; still he was very useful to me.

Mangoran was lean and slender in comparison with his brother, and he looked more like a brute than a human being. His mouth was large, extending almost from one ear to the other. When he talked he rubbed his belly with complacency, as if the sight of me made his mouth water, and he gave me an impression that he would like to devour me on the spot. He always wore a smiling face, a mask behind which all the natives conceal their treacherous nature. Besides these two I secured a young lad, whom we called Pickle-bottle. He was to some extent "civilised," and had learned a few English words; the other two were *myall*.

When we set out we were joined by Mangoran's wife, a tolerably good-looking woman. The first night we en-

camped near a brook under a newly-fallen tree; we cut
down some small trees, laid them sloping on both sides of
the tree-trunk, and made a roof of grass.

Outside this cabin, of which I took possession, my blacks
encamped in the shelter of some bushes which they had
procured for the night, for the weather was very fine. I let
the horses loose, tied bells on to their necks, and fetched
some water in a big tin pail which I had brought with me on
this trip to boil the meat in. A large fire was built, as we
had to bake bread and needed plenty of ashes. After these
preparations, and when I had been to the brook and taken
my usual bath, I had to prepare supper. I sent one of the
blacks to the nearest large gum-tree to chop off a piece of
bark, on which, with the skill of a bushman, I kneaded the
dough of wheat flour and water into the regular round cake.
This damper was then baked in the ashes, while the beef was
slowly boiling in the tin pail.

My companions were impatient for their supper, for the
white man's food is a delicacy wellnigh equal to human flesh.
I distributed beef and damper equally among them, but I
noticed to my surprise that they all gave Mangoran a
part of their share, Morbora being particularly generous.
The cause of this generosity was not then clear to me; for
Mangoran was a very poor hunter and not very strong,
neither did he possess more than one wife, so that his
authority could not rest on those qualifications, which usually
carry influence among allied tribes. I afterwards learned
that he was a cunning fellow, and was successful in procuring human flesh, and there is nothing else that ensures
respect among the Australian aborigines in so high a degree.
In regard to the relation between the two brothers, I
afterwards discovered that Mangoran was simply a black
Alphonse. Without much physical strength, and very lazy,
he preferred to live in idleness, and he left it to his brother
to furnish the *ménage à trois* with the necessities of the
day.

The food quickly disappeared into the greedy stomachs,
and then they all called for tobacco (*suttungo*) and pipes
(*pipo*). I gave them a piece each. They minced up
the tobacco with their nails, rolled it between their hands,

I

put it into their pipes, and gave themselves up to the highest enjoyment.

The night was dark, but radiant with stars. The blacks were lying on their backs round the fire smoking their pipes, which now and then went out, for the tobacco was fresh and damp. The smoker rises a little, supports himself on his elbow, and tries to suck fire into his pipe again ; then he lays himself down once more and revels in existence. But tobacco makes a man thirsty, especially if he spits a great deal, and now they want water, and their gestures and a few words indicate to me that they want to borrow my tin pail. One gets up and takes the pail, another plucks a handful of grass and twists it around a piece of dry wood or bark. This torch is lit, and a similar one is taken to light the way back. This is done, not so much to find the way, as for the reason that they are afraid to leave the camp in the dark. They are partly afraid of their devil, who is supposed to be prowling about at night, and partly they fear attacks from other tribes. All day long the native is cheerful and happy, but when the sun begins to set he becomes restless from the thoughts of the evil spirits of the night, and especially from remembering his strange neighbours, who may kill and eat him.

The blacks now kept quiet round the fire. All was still ; not a sound was heard except the solitary melancholy bell which indicated where the horses were grazing. The natives usually lie on their backs when they sleep, and sometimes on their sides, but they never have anything under their heads, nor do they use any covering in the night. They therefore frequently waken from the cold, and then turn the other side to the fire. As a rule, they lie two or three huddled together in order to keep each other warm.

Early the next morning Morbora and I went out into the scrubs which covered a rocky hill close by. He thoroughly examined the trees, and looked carefully among the orchids and ferns, which grew as parasites far up the tree stems, for rats and pouched mice (*Phascologale*), and among the fallen leaves he searched for the rare yopolo (*Hypsiprymnodon moschatus*). According to the uniform custom of the natives when they ramble through the woods, he frequently took a

handful of dirt or rubbish out of a crevice in the rock, or
from a cleft in a tree, and smelt it to see if any animal
had passed over it.   The Australian has, upon the whole, a
highly developed sense of smell.   Of him the Scandinavian
phrase is literally true, that he " sticks his finger in the ground
and smells what land he is in."   When he, for instance, digs
a pouched mouse out of its hole, he now and then smells a
handful of the earth to see whether the animal is at home or
not.   In this way he perceives whether he is approaching it.
Although I know the smell peculiar to this animal, I was
never able to discover it in the ground.

Morbora's skill in climbing trees was truly wonderful.
He ascended them with about the same ease as we climb a
flight of stairs, and everywhere all his senses were on the
alert.

As there was no lawyer-palm near from which he could
get a kāmin to assist him in climbing, he had to manage in
some other way.   He broke a few branches from a little
tree, made them all the same size, and laid them side by
side, leaving the leaves on them.   But as the branches were
not so long as a kāmin, he could not climb in the same
manner as with the latter.   The leaves furnished a hold
and prevented his hands from slipping, thus compensating
for the knot and greater length of the kāmin ; but in order
to climb the tree he had to draw his heels right up to his
body, which gave him a striking resemblance to a frog
jumping up.   If the tree was not too large in circumference,
he simply embraced it with his arms without using the
improvised kāmin ; he folded his hands and leaped up in
the same curious attitude.   If the tree leaned, it never
occurred to him to climb with his knees as a white man
would do, but he crawled up in the same manner as
an ape would, on all fours, perfectly secure and well
balanced.

Although the Australian natives are exceptionally skilful in climbing, still it would be an exaggeration to compare
them in this respect to the apes.   I also know white people
in Australia who from childhood have practised climbing
trees, and who have attained the same skill as the blacks.

After a day's march we came to a valley which extended

to the summit of the Coast Mountains. We were to encamp near the foot of the mountain range, but the air in the bottom of the valley being surcharged with the fragrance of flowers, very hot, damp, and malarial, I determined to pitch our camp higher up, where the air was more pure, a thing utterly incomprehensible to the blacks. I followed my old rule and made my camp on high ground, to escape the miasma which produces fever and is found only in the bottoms. We had hard work to make our way up the slope in order to find a suitable place for encampment. It was dark before I released the horses, which disappeared in the tall grass.

As usual we awoke a little before sunrise ; but it took the natives some time to rub the sleep out of their eyes. When a black is roused he does not at once recover his senses, and he needs more time than the uneducated whites to pull himself together. It was always difficult for my men to find their bearings in the morning, and they always had much to do before they were ready to begin the day. They lazily stretch and rub their limbs, and then sit down by the fire and light their pipes. When they at length are entirely awake they go to work and make a sort of toilet. They clean out their noses in a manner more peculiar than graceful. This morning I took particular notice of Morbora, who took a little round stick and put it up his nose horizontally, at the same time twirling it between his fingers, whereupon the contents disappeared in the same manner as among the apes in zoological gardens. The natives hardly ever wash themselves. In the heat of the summer, it is true, they throw themselves into every pool of water they come to, just like a dog ; but this is done only in order to cool themselves, and not for the sake of cleanliness. In the winter, when it is cold, they never bathe. If they have soiled their hands with honey or blood they usually wipe them on the grass, or even sometimes wash them in their own water.

In the morning, or when they sit round the fire, they are usually occupied in pulling their beards and the hair from their bodies. It is also a common thing to see even the women take a fire-brand and scorch the hairs off. The hair

on the head is never pulled out, but at rare intervals, when
it grows too long, is burned off with a fire-brand or
cut away with a sharp clam-shell or a stone.   When they
come in contact with civilisation they generally use pieces
of glass for this purpose, and I have even seen a black
cut his hair off with a blunt axe which he had borrowed
from a white man.   This is all the care which their hair
and beard receive, except that it is now and then freed
from vermin, a feature of the toilet which must be regarded
as a gastronomic enjoyment.   The blacks are not troubled
with fleas, but they are full of lice, which are rather large,
of a dark colour, and quite different from the common
Pediculus capitis; they frequently went astray and came
into my quarters, but fortunately they did not there find
the necessaries of life.   Some of the natives are free from
them, but the majority constantly betray their disagreeable
presence by scratching their heads with both hands.   These
animals are also found upon the body, and their possessor
may be constantly seen hunting them, an occupation which
is at the same time a veritable enjoyment to him, for to
speak plainly—he eats them.   The blacks also practise this
sport on each other for mutual gratification, and the operation
is evidence of friendship and politeness.

Morbora and I again went out to look for yarri, and we
followed the valley to the summit of the mountain range
It was a difficult march, over large heaps of debris covered
with carpets of creeping plants.   Every now and then he
would exclaim : "Now we will soon come to yarri!" for
during the daytime the yarri sleeps in this sort of stony
place, and Morbora examined with the greatest care every
rocky cave in our path.   He stated positively that we would
find many yarri (*Komórbory yarri*) when we had ascended
farther.   But when we finally, with the greatest difficulty,
had toiled our way to the summit, he proposed that we
should go down again, saying, *Maja yarri*—that is, No yarri.
The fact was that Morbora did not know the district.   I
became angry, and expressed my dissatisfaction in pretty
strong terms, which made such an impression upon him that
he showed a disposition to run away.   The expression of his
countenance and his whole manner were suddenly changed,

and I was obliged to alter the tone of my voice at once. Had I spoken more angrily than I did, he doubtless would have disappeared and abandoned me to my fate.

Several times we saw some small black ants which lay their eggs in trees. Morbora struck the trunk of the tree with my tomahawk while I held my hands out below to receive them. Several handfuls came down, and I winnowed them in the same manner as my companion did—that is, by throwing them up in the air and at the same time blowing at them. In this manner the fragments of bark were separated from the eggs, which remained in my hands, and were refreshing and tasted like nuts.

When we returned to the camp we found the others lying round the fire waiting for something to eat. They had brought me nothing useful, as they were simply interested in filling their stomachs. The only things they had for me were some miserable remnants of honey and some white larvæ, delicacies with which they had been gorging themselves all day. We removed our camp to another part of the valley, and made excursions in this region for a couple of days. But it soon appeared that Morbora, who was known as a skilful huntsman, could find nothing and was a stranger in this land, while the others cared only for my provisions and for eating honey and larvæ, so I concluded that it would be a waste of time to stay here. Mangoran, who was a great glutton, always smelt of honey, of which the natives are so fond that they can live on it exclusively for several days at a time. He was lazy and most unreliable, and simply a parasite whom I had to tolerate for the sake of his brother; he only did me harm by demoralising my other people. On one occasion Pickle-bottle stated that there were no boongary to be found here, but that in another "land" he had seen the marks of their claws on the tree-trunks as distinct as if they had been cut with a knife. This was another reason for my leaving as soon as possible. The main result of this, my first expedition, was therefore some valuable experience. I returned to the station and remained there a couple of days, preparing myself for a new expedition to another "land," where the natives said that yarri and boongary were found in abundance.

A great *borboby* was to take place three miles from
Herbert Vale. A borboby is a meeting for contest, where
the blacks assemble from many "lands" in order to decide
their disputes by combat. As I felt a desire to witness this
assembly, I asked Jacky if I could accompany him and those
who were going with him, and no objection was made.

In the afternoon we all started from Herbert Vale, I on
horseback and taking my gun with me. We crossed Herbert
river three times, and as we gradually approached the
fighting-ground we met more and more small tribes who had
been lying the whole day in the cool scrubs along the river to
gather strength for the impending conflict. All of them,
even the women and the children, joined us, except a small
company of the former who remained near the river. I
learned that these women were not permitted to be present
because they had menses. As far as I know, the Australians
everywhere regard their women as unclean in such circumstances. In some parts of the continent they are isolated
in huts by themselves, and no one will touch a dish which
they use; among other tribes a woman in this condition is
not permitted to walk over the net which the men are
making.

All were in their best toilet, for when the blacks are to
go to dance or to borboby they decorate themselves as best
they can. The preparations take several days, spent in
seeking earth colours and wax, which are kept by the most
prominent members of the tribe until the day of the contest.

On the forenoon of the borboby day they remain in camp
and do not go out hunting, for they are then occupied in
decorating themselves. They rub themselves partially or
wholly with the red or yellow earth paint; sometimes they
besmear their whole body with a mixture of crushed charcoal
and fat—as if they were not already black enough! As a
rule, they do not mind whether the whole body is painted
or not, if only the face has been thoroughly coloured.

Not only do the men but the women also, though in a
less degree, paint grotesque figures of red earth and charcoal
across their faces. But one of the most important considera-
tions on these solemn occasions is the dressing of the hair. It
is filled with beeswax, so that it stands out in large tufts, or at

times it has the appearance of a single large cake. They also frequently stick feathers into it. The wax remains there for weeks, until it finally disappears from wear or bathing. This waxed headgear shines and glistens in the sun, and gives them a sort of "polished" exterior. Some of the most "civilised" natives may wear a shirt or a hat. On this occasion two of them were fortunate enough to own old shirts, two others had hats on their heads, while the variegated colour of the body was a substitute for the rest of their attire.

Jacky was the best dressed fellow of the lot. His suit consisted of a white and, strange to say, clean body of a dress that had previously belonged to a woman.

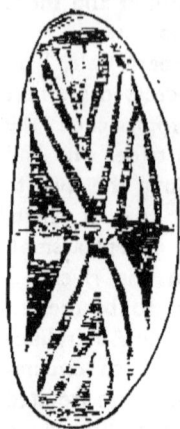

WOODEN SHIELDS FROM NORTHERN QUEENSLAND.

How he had obtained it in this part of the country was a mystery to me. As he was stoutly built, this product of civilisation looked like a strait-waistcoat, and threatened every moment to burst in the back. He strutted about among his comrades majestically, with a sense of being far removed above the "*myall*" (the mob). Two of the natives distinguished themselves by being painted yellow over the whole body except the hair. This was thought to be a very imposing attire, especially calculated to inspire fear.

All the natives were armed. They had quantities of spears, whole bundles of nolla-nollas and boomerangs, besides their large wooden shields and wooden swords. The shield, which reaches to a man's hip and is about half as wide as it is long, is made of a kind of light fig-tree wood. It is oval, massive, and slightly convex. In the centre, on the front side, there is a sort of shield-boss, the inner side being nearly flat. When the native holds this shield in his left hand before him, the greater part of his body is protected. The front is painted in a grotesque and effective manner with red, white, and yellow earth colours, and is divided into fields which, wonderfully enough, differ in each man's shield, and thus constitute his coat of arms.

The wooden sword, the necessary companion of the shield, is about five inches wide up to the point, which is slightly rounded, and usually reaches from the foot to the shoulder. It is made of hard wood, with a short handle for only one hand, and is so heavy that any one not used to it can scarcely balance it perpendicularly with half-extended arm—the position always adopted before the battle begins.

A couple of hours before sunset we crossed Herbert river for the third time, and landed near a high bank, which it was

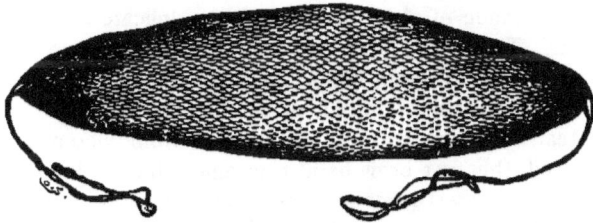

FILLET OR BROW-BAND FROM NORTHERN QUEENSLAND (⅓ size).

very difficult for the horse to climb. Here I was surprised to find a very large grassy plain, made, as it were, expressly for a tournament. Immediately in front of me was a tolerably open forest of large gum-trees with white trunks, then a large open space, and beyond it another grove of gum-trees. On the west side of the plain was Herbert river, and farther to the west, on the other side of the river, was Sea-View Range, behind the summits of which the sun was soon to set. The battlefield was bounded on the east by a high hill clad from base to top with dark green scrubs, which, in the twilight, looked almost black by the side of the fresh bright green of the grass and the white gum-trees. Near the edge of the woods Jacky's men and the savages who had joined us on the road made a brief pause. One of those who had last arrived began to run round in a challenging manner like a man in a rage. He was very tall (about 6 feet 4 inches), and like some of the natives in this neighbourhood, his hair bore a strong resemblance to that of the Papuans, being about a foot and a half long, closely matted together, and standing out in all directions. Shaking this heavy head of hair like a madman, with head and shoulders thrown back, he made long jumps and wild leaps, holding his large wooden sword perpendicularly in front of him in his right hand, and the shield in his left.

When he had run enough to cool his savage warlike ardour he stopped near me. He was so hot that perspiration streamed from him, and the red paint ran in long streaks down his face. Around his head he wore a very beautiful brow-band, for which I offered him a stick of tobacco, and he immediately untied it and gave it to me. It was an extraordinarily neat piece of work, like the finest net, four inches wide, and made of plant fibre forming a delicate and regular texture. The whole was painted red. I saw two others who sold me their brow-bands for tobacco, so that I secured three of these valuable pieces of handiwork (p. 121).

Meanwhile the enthusiastic warrior from whom I had purchased the first brow-band was again busy taking great leaps ; gradually the conversation became more lively, the warlike ardour increased, and all held their weapons in readiness.

Suddenly an old man uttered a terrible war-cry, and swung his bundle of spears over his head. This acted, as it were, like an electric shock on all of them ; they at once gathered together, shouted with all their might, and raised their shields with their left hands, swinging swords, spears, boomerangs, and nolla-nollas in the air. Then they all rushed with a savage war-cry through the grove of gum-trees and marched by a zigzag route against their enemies, who were standing far away on the other side of the plain. At every new turn they stopped and were silent for a moment, then with a terrific howl started afresh, until at the third turn they stood in the middle of the plain directly opposite their opponents, where they remained.

I fastened up my horse at some distance and followed them as quickly as I could ; the women and children also hastened to the scene of conflict.

A WARRIOR IN GREAT EXCITEMENT JUST BEFORE BORBODY COMMENCES.
To face page 122.

The strange tribes on the other side stood in a group in front of their huts, which were picturesquely situated near the edge of the forest, at the foot of the scrub-clad hill. As soon as our men had halted, three men from the hostile ranks came forward in a threatening manner with shields in their left hands and swords held perpendicularly in their right. Their heads were covered with the elegant yellow and white topknots of the white cockatoos. Each man wore at least forty of these, which were fastened in his hair with beeswax, and gave the head the appearance of a large aster. The three men approached ours very rapidly, running forward with long elastic leaps. Now and then they jumped high in the air like cats, and fell down behind their shields, so well concealed that we saw but little of them above the high grass. This manœuvre was repeated until they came within about twenty yards from our men ; then they halted in an erect position, the large shields before them and the points of their swords resting on the ground, ready for the fight. The large crowd of strange tribes followed them slowly.

Now the duels were to begin ; three men came forward from our side and accepted the challenge, the rest remaining quiet for the present.

The common position for challenging is as follows : the shield is held in the left hand, and the sword perpendicularly in the right. But, owing to the weight of the sword, it must be used almost like a blacksmith's sledgehammer in order to hit the shield of the opponent with full force ; the combatant is therefore obliged to let the weapon rest in front on the ground a few moments before the duel begins, when he swings it back and past his head against his opponent. When one of them has made his blow, it, is his opponent's turn, and thus they exchange blows until one of them gets tired and gives up, or his shield is cloven, in which case he is regarded as unfit for the fight.

While the first three pairs were fighting, others began to exchange blows. There was no regularity in the fight. The duel usually began with spears, then they came nearer to each other and took to their swords. Sometimes the matter was decided at a distance, boomerangs, nolla-nollas, and spears being thrown against the shields. The natives are exceedingly skilful in parrying, so that they are seldom wounded by the first two kinds of weapons. On the other hand, the spears easily penetrate the shields, and sometimes injure the bearer, who is then regarded as disqualified and must declare himself beaten. There were always some combatants in the field, frequently seven or eight pairs at a time ; but the duellists were continually changing.

The women gather up the weapons, and when a warrior has to engage in several duels, his wives continually supply him with weapons. The other women stand and look on, watching the conflict with the greatest attention, for they have much at stake. Many a one changes husbands on that night. As the natives frequently rob each other of their wives, the conflicts arising from this cause are settled by borboby, the victor retaining the woman.

The old women also take part in the fray. They stand behind the combatants with the same kind of sticks as those used for digging up roots. They hold the stick with both hands, beat the ground hard with it, and jump up and down in a state of wild excitement. They cry to the men, egging and urging them on, four or five frequently surrounding one man, and acting as if perfectly mad. The men become more and more excited, perspiration pours from them, and they exert themselves to the utmost.

If one of the men is conquered, the old women gather around him and protect him with their sticks, parrying the sword blows of his opponent, constantly shouting, " Do not kill him, do not kill him ! "

In order that the natives might not suspect me of hostile purposes I had, in the presence of all, put my gun against the trunk of a gum-tree hard by, thus at the same time showing them that I was not unarmed. I went to the fighting-ground and took my place among the spectators, consisting chiefly of women. The Kanaka, being a foreigner, felt insecure, and thought it wisest to stay near me. He had borrowed one of Mr. Walters' revolvers at the station, hoping thereby to inspire the blacks with respect ; but as it was so rusty and worn that it usually missed fire, he had finally lost all faith in its virtue as a weapon of terror.

A BOROBDY.

To face page 124.

With the greatest attention I watched the interesting duels, which lasted only about three-quarters of an hour, but which entertained me more than any performance I ever witnessed. Where the conflict was hottest my friend Jacky stood cool and dignified, and was more than ever conscious of his civilised superiority. The old white body evidently inspired the multitude with awe. Boomerangs and nolla-nollas whizzed

OLD WOMEN PROTECTING A FALLEN WARRIOR.

about our ears, without however hindering me from watching with interest the passion of these wild children of nature—the desperate exertions of the men, the zeal of the young women, and the foolish rage of the old women, whose discordant voices blended with the din of the weapons, with the dull blows of the swords, with the clang of the nolla-nollas, and with the flight of the boomerangs whizzing through the air. Here all disputes and legal conflicts were settled, not only between tribes but also between individuals. That the lowest races of men do not try to settle their disputes in a more parliamentary manner need not cause any surprise, but it may appear strange to us that aged women take so active a part in the issue of these conflicts.

With the exception of the murder of a member of the same tribe, the aboriginal Australian knows only one crime, and that is theft, and the punishment for violating the right of possession is not inflicted by the community, but by the individual wronged. The thief is challenged by his victim to a duel with wooden swords and shields ; and the matter is settled sometimes privately the relatives of both parties serving as witnesses, sometimes publicly at the borboby, where two hundred to three hundred meet from various tribes to decide all their disputes. The victor in the duel wins in the dispute.

The robbery of women, who also among these savages are regarded as a man's most valuable property, is both the grossest and the most common theft ; for it is the usual way of getting a wife. Hence woman is the chief cause of disputes. Inchastity, which is called *gramma*, *i.e.* to steal, also falls under the head of theft.

The theft of weapons, implements, and food is rarely the cause of a duel. I do not remember a single instance of weapons being stolen. If an inconsiderable amount of food or some other trifle has been stolen, it frequently happens that the victim, instead of challenging the thief, simply plays the part of an offended person, especially if he considers himself inferior in strength and in the use of weapons. In cases where the food has not been eaten but is returned, then the victim is satisfied with compensation, in the form of tobacco, food, or weapons, and thus friendship is at once re-established.

Even when the thief regards himself as superior in strength, he does not care to have a duel in prospect, for these savages shrink from every inconvenience. The idea of having to fight with his victim is a greater punishment for the thief than one would think, even though bloodshed is rare.

In these duels the issue does not depend wholly on physical strength, as the relatives play a conspicuous part in the matter. The possession of many strong men on his side is a great moral support to the combatant. He knows that his opponent, through fear of his relatives, will not carry the conflict to the extreme ; he is also certain that, if necessary, they will interfere and prevent his getting wounded. The relatives and friends are of great importance in the decision of conflicts among the natives, though physical strength, of course, is the first consideration.

After such a conflict the reader possibly expects a description of fallen warriors swimming in blood ; but relatives and friends take care that none of the combatants are injured. Mortal wounds are extremely rare. Mangoran had received a slight wound in the arm above the elbow from a boomerang, and was therefore pitied by everybody. In the next borboby one person happened to be pierced by a spear, which, being barbed, could not be removed. His tribe carried him about with them for three days before he died.

As soon as the sun had set the conflict ceased. The people separated, each one going to his own camp, all deeply interested in the events of the day. There was not much sleep that night, and conversation was lively round the small camp fires. As a result of the borboby several family revolutions had already taken place, men had lost their wives and women had acquired new husbands. In the cool morning of the next day the duels were continued for an hour ; then the crowds scattered, each tribe returning to its own "land." While I remained at Herbert river four borbobies occurred with three to four weeks intervening between each, in the months of November, December, January, and February—that is, in the hottest season of the year. During the winter no borboby is held.

CHAPTER X

THE natural conditions varying in different parts of Australia, a fact not to be wondered at in so large a continent, the natives also vary in physical and mental development. Mr. B. Smyth is of opinion that the natives in the different parts of the country are as unlike each other in physical structure and colour of skin as the inhabitants of England, Germany, France, and Italy. The following description applies mainly to the natives on the Herbert river.

The southern part of Australia is, both as regards natural condition and climate, so unlike the tropical north that the mode of life of the natives is materially modified. Thus in the south-eastern part the natives live mainly on animal food, while in the tropical north they subsist chiefly on vegetables. This has no slight influence on their physical development. Those that live near bodies of water, and have an opportunity of securing fish in addition to game and other animal food, are more vigorous physically than those who have to be satisfied with snakes, lizards, and indigestible vegetables—the latter affording but little nourishment. I found the strongest and healthiest blacks in the interior of Queensland, on Diamantina river, where even the women are tall and muscular. According to trustworthy reports the same is true of the natives on Boulya and Georgina rivers, farther west. In the coast districts of Queensland they seem to me to be smaller of stature and to have more slender limbs. It is, however, asserted by other writers

PHIL KA.

A WOMAN FROM MARYBOROUGH, CENTRAL QUEENSLAND.

To face page 129.

that the most powerful natives are to be found on the coast.

Farther south in Australia the climate is cool, and hence the natives have to protect themselves with blankets made of opossum skin, things not needed in the northern part of the continent, where they roam about naked both winter and summer. Upon the whole the struggle for existence is more severe in the south, but as a compensation the natives there attain a higher intellectual development.

The natives in one part of Australia have words for numbers up to four or five, while in other parts they have no terms beyond three. The natives along Herbert river have very crude and confused religious notions, but it is claimed that even an idea of the Trinity, strikingly like that of the Christian religion, has been discovered among tribes in the south-eastern part of the continent ; idolatry exists nowhere in Australia. The blacks in the north-western part of the continent are praised for their honesty and industry, and are employed by the colonists in all kinds of work at the stations. In the rest of Australia the natives are treacherous and indolent.

According to the investigations of Dr. Topinard there are two different types of men among the natives of Australia. Those of the lower type are small and black, have curly hair, weak muscles, and prominent cheek-bones. The higher type, on the other hand, are taller, have smooth hair, and a less dolichocephalous form of head. This also agrees with the reports of travellers ; at all events, there is no doubt that the tribes of Northern Queensland are inferior to those found in the southern part of the continent, and a theory has been presented that the higher race living mainly in the southern part of Australia has been a race of conquerors who have subjugated the weaker and driven them to the north.

In New South Wales the average size of the tribes is tolerably high, and equals that of Europeans (5 ft. 2 in. to 5 ft. 6 in.) At Murrumbidgee the natives are of medium height. Round Lake Torrens they attain, according to Stuart, a height of only 3 ft. 8 in., while the average height in the interior is 5 ft. 11 in. During my sojourn on the Diamantina river I heard of a black at Mullagan (twenty-five miles

K

west of Georgina) who was about 7 ft. high. He was well known at the stations out there, and died just before my arrival. In the coast districts along the eastern side of Queensland they are small, while along Herbert river their size was surprisingly irregular; few of them could be called corpulent, a large number were in good condition and well formed though their necks were somewhat short, while others were lean and slender.

The most characteristic feature of an Australian's face is the low receding forehead and the prominence of the part immediately above the eyes. The latter might indicate keen perception, and in this they are not lacking. Their eyes are expressive, dark brown, frequently with a tinge of deep blue. The white of the eye is of a dirty yellow colour and very much bloodshot, which gives them a savage look. The nose is flat and triangular, and narrow at the top, thus bringing the eyes near together. The partition between the two nostrils is very large and conspicuous. Many of the natives pierce it and put a yellow stick into it as an ornament. My men, who of course had neither pockets nor pipe-cases, frequently put their pipes into these holes in their noses as a convenient place to keep them, and fancied that their noses looked all the better for it. Now and then I met men whose noses were almost Roman, and there were all the transitional forms between these and the flat triangular noses. I have also heard of high aquiline noses among the natives of New South Wales. I think it probable that the large noses sometimes found in Northern Queensland may be attributed to a mixture with Papuans, whose noses are known to be their pride. The irregular size of their bodies is evidence in the same direction.

The Australian aborigines have high cheek-bones and large, open, ugly-looking mouths. But the blacks on Herbert river usually keep their mouths shut, which improves their looks, and they are, upon the whole, a better looking race than the natives in the south. Their lips are a reddish-blue, and they have small receding chins. Their muscular development is usually slight and their legs and arms are particularly slender; still I have seen many exceptions to this rule. The women are always knock-kneed, and this is often

CALIKA.

A YOUNG GIRL FROM MARYBOROUGH, CENTRAL QUEENSLAND.

To face page 130.

the case with the men, although with them it is not nearly
so marked, their legs being almost straight. They are
seldom bow-legged to any great extent. The feet, which as
a rule are large, leave footprints that are either straight or
show the toes slightly turned outward. They have great
skill in seizing spears and similar objects with their toes, and
in this way they avoid stooping to pick up things.

Though the natives are slender, they have a remarkable
control over their bodies. They bear themselves as if
conscious that they are the lords of creation, and one
might envy them the dignity and ease of their movements.
The women carry themselves in a dignified manner, and do
not look so savage as the men.

The hair and beard, which are as black as pitch, are
slightly curly, but not woolly, like those of the African negro
I seldom saw straight hair on the blacks near Herbert river
(I should say not over five per cent had straight hair), but it
is quite common in the rest of Australia, especially in the
interior. Men and women wear hair of the same length.
I only once saw a man with his hair standing out in all
directions, like that of the Papuans. There is generally
little hair on the rest of the body. Some of the old men
near Herbert river had a heavy growth of hair on their
breasts and partly on their backs and arms, a fact I have
never observed among the women. The natives along Herbert river had but little beard, and they constantly pulled
out what little they had. In the rest of Australia men are
frequently met with who have fine beards, but they do not
themselves regard the beard as an ornament. In New South
Wales even women are found with a heavy growth of beard.
The hair and beard of the Australian are not coarse,
and would be bright and beautiful if he were more cleanly.
On Balonne river in Queensland there is a family (not
a tribe) of persons who are perfectly hairless. Old individuals sometimes have snow-white hair, but, so far as I
know, albinos have never been discovered in Australia.

The natives of Australia are called blacks, but as a rule
they are chocolate brown; this colour is particularly conspicuous when they are under water while bathing. Their
complexion manifestly changes with their emotions ; they turn

pale from fear—that is to say, the skin assumes a grayish colour. I have even seen young persons, whose skin is thin and transparent, blush. Infants are a light yellow or brown, but at the age of two years they have already assumed the hue of their parents.

The race must be characterised as ugly-looking, though the expression of the countenance is not, as a rule, disagree-able, especially when their attention is awak-ened. Occasionally handsome individuals may be found, particu-larly among the men, who as a rule are better shaped than the women. The latter have more slender limbs; the ab-domen is prominent, and they have hang-ing breasts, mainly the result of hard work, un-healthy vegetable food, and early marriage. I

AN OLD MAN FROM HERBERT RIVER.

have on two occasions seen what might be called beauties among the women of Western Queensland. Their hands were small, their feet neat and well shaped, with so high an instep that one asked oneself involuntarily where in the world they had acquired this aristocratic mark of beauty. Their figure was above criticism, and their skin, as is usually the case among the young women, was as soft as velvet. When these black daughters of Eve smiled and showed their beautiful white teeth, and when their eyes peeped coquet-tishly from beneath the curly hair which hung in quite the modern fashion down over their foreheads, it is not difficult to understand that even here women are not quite deprived of that influence ascribed by Goethe to the fair sex generally. On the Herbert river I never saw a beautiful girl, but about seventy miles west from there, on the table-land, I met a young woman who had a good figure and a remark-ably symmetrical face, beautiful eyes, and a well-shaped nose, the lower part of which was narrower than is usual, and consequently the triangular form was less conspicuous.   I

A GROUP OF NATIVES FROM HERBERT RIVER.

must confess, however, that I have never seen uglier specimens of human beings than the old women are as they sit crouching round the fire scratching their lean limbs.

They have hardly any muscles left. Their abdomen is large, the skin wrinkled, the hair gray and thin, and the face most repulsive, especially as the eyes are hardly visible. The women fade early, and on account of the hard life they live do not attain the age of the men, the latter living a little more than fifty years. It has been thought that the men in some parts of the interior of Queensland attain an age of even seventy to eighty years, but in the northernmost part of the country few are said to live more than forty years. On Herbert river the women are more numerous than the men ; this is also the case among the tribes south-west of the Carpentarian Gulf and elsewhere. But according to accurate observations the opposite is the case in a large part of Australia. The women bear their first children at the age of eighteen to twenty years, sometimes later, and seldom have more than three or four. Twins are very rare.

The birth of a child does not seem to give the mother much trouble. She goes a short distance from the camp, together with an old woman, and when the interesting event has taken place and the child has been washed in the brook, she returns as if nothing had happened, and no one takes the slightest notice of the occurrence. For a long time afterwards she must keep away from her husband. A woman is proud of being with child, and I am able to state as a curiosity that the tribes around the Carpentarian Gulf think they are able to predict the sex of the babe a few months before birth by counting the number of rings on the *papillæ mammæ* of the mother.

On account of the unhealthy food of the blacks the children are weaned late, and it even happens that a child is nursed at its mother's breast with the next older brother or sister.

Instances of death from childbearing are very rare. The advent of a baby is not always regarded with favour, and infanticide is therefore common in Australia, especially when there is a scarcity of food, as under such circumstances they even eat the child. In their nomadic life children are a burden to them, and the men particularly do not like to see the women, who work hard and procure

much food, troubled with many children.   In some parts of
Australia the *papillæ mammæ* are cut off to hinder the women
from nursing children.

The strong smell of the blacks is quite different from
that of an unclean white man.   Nor can it be doubted that
the blacks have a peculiar smell which dis-
turbs cattle, dogs, and horses when they
approach the natives, even if the latter are
not seen ; this, no doubt, has frequently
saved the lives of travellers.
This strong odour, moreover, is
mixed with the smell of dirt,
smoke, paint, and other things
with which they
constantly smear
themselves.

The voice of
the Australian is
melodious, though
sometimes hoarse,
and gives evidence
of musical propen-
sity. Both men and
women have a high
tone of voice ; bass
and falsetto voices
are rare.

The natives are
as fond of decorat-
ing their bodies as
a sailor is, but they

A YOUNG BOY FROM HERBERT RIVER,
SHOWING ORNAMENTAL SCARS.

do it clumsily with a sharp stone or a clam-shell, with
which primitive instruments they cut parallel lines across
the breast and stomach.   To keep the wounds from
healing they put charcoal or ashes in them for a month or
two until they swell up into rough ridges.   Sometimes they
gain the same result by letting ants walk about in the
wounds.   The shoulders are cut in the same manner, with
lines running down three or four inches, making them look as
if they had epaulets.   In course of time these peculiar lines,

which in young men are conspicuous and as thick as one's little finger, become indistinct, so that on old men they are scarcely visible. They always indicate a certain rank, determined by age. Young boys below a certain age are not decorated, but in course of time they get a few lines across the breast and stomach. Gradually the number of lines is increased, and at last when the lad is full grown, crescents are cut round the papillæ of the breast, the horns of the crescent turning outward, thus : ·) (· . This external evidence that the boy is of age is given to him with certain ceremonies, and the strips of skin, which gradually fall off from the wounds as they heal, are gathered in a little basket, which he subsequently carries for some time about his neck until he finally throws its contents out in the woods—gives it to the "devil" as it is called. This is the only trace of a cult that I observed among the blacks of Herbert river, and they doubtless regard it as a sort of sacrifice to avert the wrath of evil spirits. From this time the young man is permitted to eat whatever he pleases, but previously he has been obliged to abstain from certain things, such as eels, large lizards, etc. The transition from boyhood to manhood is not here, as it is in many other parts of Australia, marked by the extraction of one of the front teeth.[1]

SMALL BASKET CARRIED ABOUT THE NECK, HERBERT RIVER.

In addition to these marks of dignity, a man also gets other lines, which are intended as an ornament and are found chiefly on the arms. They are straight, short, parallel lines

[1] A gentleman well known to me told me the following about the Rockhampton blacks : I one day made two or three of those buzzing things, formed by cutting notches in a thin piece of wood with a hole at one end, through which a piece of string is tied ; this instrument is whirled quickly round and round one's head, producing a great noise. I gave these to some black children near my station to play with ; directly the noise began the women covered their heads at the command of their men ; some of the blacks bolted into the scrub, while two ran up and seized the things from the boys, whom they sent off to the camp. They then told me that in old times these boys would have been killed for seeing those things, which were used only at their " Bora " (transition from boyhood to manhood) ceremonies. I told them that such pieces of wood were common playthings in my country, nevertheless they burnt them in the scrub shortly after.

made in groups across the arm, and the wounds are permitted to heal, so that the lines do not become too
prominent. A deep cut here and there is also made on the
back or on the shoulder-blade. I never saw the face ornamented by incisions.

The men alone receive the above-described marks of
dignity on their chests, stomachs, and shoulders. It is
their privilege to be decorated with lines and marks cut in
the flesh, and it is not considered proper for women to pay
much attention to ornaments. The greatest ornament that
a woman ever has is a few clumsy marks across the chest
(frequently across the breasts), arms, and back. She is very
fond of the ornaments granted her, and the sensitiveness
which usually characterises the natives is entirely wanting
when they are about to be adorned in this way. I once
saw two women engaged in cutting marks on each other's
arms with a piece of glass. These marks consisted of
short parallel lines down the arms like those worn by
the men, but the operation did not seem to give them
the least pain, for they smoked their pipes the whole
time.

Tattooing in the strictest sense of the word—that is,
pricking the skin with a sharp instrument—does not exist
among the Australians, but only the above-described custom
of cutting wounds in the flesh.

On the same morning that the borboby ended I started
on my new expedition, taking this opportunity of securing companions, there being so many blacks assembled. In
addition to those who accompanied me on my first expedition I secured three new men. We were to go to another
"land," where yarri and boongary were abundant. Tired
from the exertions of the previous day, and consequently
more lazy than usual, the blacks repeatedly urged me to
encamp, although we had travelled only a few miles. We
ascended along a mountain stream and passed on our way
one of the deserted camps of the blacks, where Pickle-
bottle was determined to stop. I called his attention to the
fact that the "sun was yet large" (still early in the day), and
that neither yarri nor boongary were to be found here; but

he replied that there were plenty of them in this locality, and that this was a good place to eat.

He, of course, sulked when I did not yield to his lazy desires, still he continued the march, leading my pack-horse, as he was the most civilised and was best acquainted with the country. Instead of proceeding up the eastern mountain slope, which seemed to be most accessible, he guided us along the foaming stream, of which the bed became more contracted and the banks more steep as we advanced. Still I depended upon Pickle-bottle as our guide, until the path at length became so narrow that progress was impossible. I now understood that he wanted to force me to submit to his will and get me to encamp in the place which he had proposed. I had no other choice but to return by the same way as we had come, until we could find a convenient place for the ascent. With great difficulty the horses were turned, but being angry on account of the delay, I now led the way myself and gave the blacks orders to follow me.

Now and then I looked back to assure myself that I had them all near me. But to my great surprise I discovered at a turn of the way Pickle-bottle and the pack-horse high up the slope, not far from the place where our progress had been blocked. When he saw that I was determined to advance, he wanted to save part of the road, and had resolved to climb with the horse straight over the high and steep precipice. He believed, like most of the blacks, that a horse can go wherever a man can pass. He was just at the point of bringing the horse over the summit—its forefeet were already planted on the top—when it lost its foothold and its balance among the loose stones, and came rolling slowly down the steep slope like a heavy sack of flour. Greatly excited, I expected every moment that it would stop. But it rolled on and on until it came to the edge of the river, where it fortunately stopped.

Pickle-bottle and the other blacks vanished. When they saw that I was becoming angry they were afraid that I would shoot them, so they hid in the scrubs. Calling to them in a friendly tone of voice, I at once began to loosen the pack from the fallen horse. They cautiously peeped at me from behind the trees to see in what mood I

was, then they took courage and came out. I now found
to my great satisfaction and surprise that the horse, barring
a few unimportant scratches, was not injured and had not
broken a bone. When we had raised him on to his feet again
and washed him in the river, he shook himself, snorted, and
seemed to feel as well as ever after his unsuccessful effort to
climb the mountain.

We continued the journey, and Pickle-bottle was hence-
forth less obstinate. "No tobacco to-day, Pickle-bottle," I
said to him, a threat which made him very thoughtful. He
now easily found the right ascent, and for an hour or two we
followed the paths of the blacks up the ridges. The scrubs
were very dense on all sides, and the mountains came
closer and closer together, until suddenly the landscape
expanded into a broad, high valley with grassy plains in the
bottom surrounded by scrub-clad hills. Here we encamped
on the bank of the river. There was plenty of grass for
the horses, for the soil was fertile and the ground had never
been used for pasture.

This camp was made the starting-point of many excursions into the surrounding scrubs. One day the blacks
showed me traces of boongary on the trunk of a tree. I was
now certain of the existence of the animal, and resolved not
to give up till I had a specimen in my possession. I did
not realise how many annoyances were in store for me, and
that I was to wander about for three months before I should
succeed in securing it. The traces were old, but still so
distinct as to be unmistakable.   ,

On one of these excursions on the top of the mountain
I heard in the dense scrubs the loud and unceasing voice of a
bird. I carefully approached it as it sat on the ground,
and shot it. It was one of the bower-birds already
mentioned (*Scenopœus dentirostris*), with a gray and very
modest plumage, and of the size of a thrush.

As I picked up the bird my attention was drawn to a
fresh covering of green leaves on the black soil. This was
the bird's place of amusement, which beneath the dense scrubs
formed a square about one yard each way, the ground having
been cleared of leaves and rubbish. On this neatly cleared
spot the bird had laid large fresh leaves, one by the

side of the other, with considerable regularity, and close by he sat singing, apparently extremely happy over his work. As soon as the leaves decay they are replaced by new ones. On this excursion I saw three such places of amusement, all near one another, and all had fresh leaves from the same kind of trees, while a large heap of dry withered leaves was lying close by. It seems that the bird scrapes away the mould every time it changes the leaves, so as to have a dark background, against which the green leaves make a better appearance. Can any one doubt that this bird has the sense of beauty?

The bird was quite common. Later on I frequently found it on the summit of the Coast Mountains in the large scrubs, which it never abandons. The natives call it *gramma*— that is, the thief—because it steals the leaves which it uses to play with.

During the summer there is much rain in the mountains. You are never sure of dry weather, and nearly every night it pours. One day we were overtaken by a heavy shower. The mountain brook grew fast into a torrent, down which we waded to get home, preferring this road to the scrubs, which in rain are impassable and dripping wet and dark.

The natives, who under such circumstances are much more susceptible than Europeans, do not like this sort of weather. When it rained I could never persuade them to accompany me, and they have such a dread of rain that in the wet season they prefer to starve for several days rather than leave their huts in quest of food. They shrugged their shoulders, and shivering with cold, hastened down the brook so fast that I could scarcely keep up with them. On the way we found a place where the mountain formed a shelter, and here the blacks soon discovered with their keen sight that a fire could be built, and so they halted. I could not understand where they would find dry faggots, as everything was dripping wet. It did not take long, however, before the shivering fellows found handfuls of dry rubbish from hollow trees and bundles of leaves from the lawyer-palm. A little fire was soon blazing, and the natives crept round it like kittens, wafting the smoke on to themselves with their hands in order to get warm more quickly.

When my men had to make a fire, I usually gave them matches, which they were so delighted to use that they always asked for them to light their pipes with, even when a large fire was burning. They called them *mardshe*, after the English "matches," a word which I gradually taught them. As a rule, they produce fire with two pieces of light wood from eight to fifteen inches long, either cork-tree (*Erythrina vespertilio*) or black fig. One piece, which is half of a split branch, is laid on the ground with the flat side up, the other, a round straight stick, is placed perpendicularly on the former, and is twirled rapidly between the hands, so that it is bored into the lower piece, the wood of which is usually of a softer kind. After a few seconds they

MAKING FIRE.

begin to smoke, and soon there fall out of the bore-hole red-hot sparks which kindle the dry leaves laid around. The man assists by blowing at the sparks. Twigs and branches, which are now quickly collected, are not broken in the manner usual with us—across the knees—but always across their hard skull, the bone of which is so thick that they can easily break branches one and a half to two inches in diameter. The natives usually carry with them the two pieces of wood for kindling fire as long as they are serviceable. I tried to use them, but succeeded only in producing smoke.

Whenever the Australians rest they build a fire, though it be ever so warm, and at all times of the day, partly for comfort, partly in order to roast the provisions which they may have found. On short expeditions they usually make the women carry a fire-brand with them, finding this more convenient than to use the apparatus above described. They always have fire in front of their huts, but usually a small one, no doubt to avoid attracting the attention of hostile tribes.

As we were encamped round the fire I, feeling icy cold in my wet clothes, could not help envying the naked blacks who, independent of garments, became warm and good-

humoured in a few minutes.   But in a short time they were
as cold as ever, for we had to proceed on our journey in the
ceaseless rain.   Now and then they exclaimed with a sigh,
Takolgöro ngipa !—that is, Poor me!—and we had to halt,
so that they might warm themselves again, and soon they
were once more merry and happy.

The rain had ceased when, late in the evening, we returned
to our camp.   The natives were hungry, and were determined
to hinder me from taking my usual bath, striking their
stomachs impatiently, and crying, *Ammeri! ammeri!*—that is,
Hungry! hungry!   I threatened them with my revolver, as
I did not wish to be cheated out of my only pleasure for
the day, so they became quiet, and I took a refreshing
bath in the clear water of a mountain brook.

I always began the day before sunrise, and after making
the necessary preparations for the excursion, I rambled
about with the blacks all day long, frequently without eating.
Marching through the dense scrubs is very exhausting, the
hot climate makes one weak, and it requires much effort to
maintain one's good-humour and courage and at the same
time to stimulate the indolent natives to do their work.
Add to this that it is constantly necessary to be on one's
guard against attacks, and it will be evident that I needed a
few moments' respite ; and in order to preserve my health
and vigour I availed myself of the opportunity of taking a
bath in the nearest pond or brook.

After refreshing myself in this manner I had to be cook
both for myself and my greedy companions.   Fortunately
I did not that evening have to prepare the animals I had
shot, for the weather was so cool after the rain that they
would keep overnight.

On the way home to Herbert Vale we passed the forests
of gum-trees which clothe the base of the mountain range.
Here is the favourite resort of the bees, and my blacks at
once began to look for their hives, for honey is a highly
valued food of the natives, and is eaten in great quantities.
Strange to say, they refuse the larvæ, however hungry they
may be.   The wax is used as a glue in the making of various
implements, and also serves as a pomade for dressing the
hair for their dances and festivals.   The Australian bee is

not so large as our house-fly, and deposits its honey in
hollow trees, the hives sometimes being high up. While
passing through the woods the blacks, whose eyes are very
keen, can discover the little bees in the clear air as the latter
are flying thirty yards high to and from the little hole which
leads into their storehouse. When the natives ramble about
in the woods they continually pay attention to the bees,
and when I met blacks in the forests they were as a rule
gazing up in the trees. Although my eyesight, according to
the statement of an oculist, is twice as keen as that of a
normal eye, it was usually impossible for me to discover the
bees, even after the blacks had indicated to me where they
were. The blacks also have a great advantage over the
white man, owing to the fact that the sun does not dazzle
their eyes to so great an extent. One day I discovered
a small swarm about four yards up from the ground, and
thereby greatly astonished my men. One expressed his joy
by rolling in the grass, the others shouted aloud their surprise
that a white man could find honey.

It is an amusing sight to observe the natives gathering
honey. One of them will climb the tree and cut a hole
large enough to put his arm through, whereupon he takes
out one piece after another of the honeycombs, and as a
rule does not neglect to put a morsel or two of the sweet
food into his mouth. He drops the pieces down to his
comrades, who stand below and catch them in their hands.
At the same time the bees swarm round him like a black
cloud, but without annoying him to any great extent, for
these bees do not sting, they only bite a little.

Most of the honey is consumed on the spot, but
part of it is taken to the camp, being transported in
baskets specially made for this purpose. These baskets are
of the same form as the other baskets made by the natives, but
more solid and smaller in size; they are made of bark, so
closely joined with wax that they will hold water. Sometimes the honey is carried a short distance on a piece of
bark, a border of fine chewed grass being laid round the
edges in order to keep it from running off. Sometimes
also a palm leaf is used, which is folded and tied at both
ends, so that it looks like a trough. It is the same kind of

trough as the natives use for carrying water, and can be
made in a few minutes.

In almost every hive some old honey is to be found
which has fermented and become sour, because these bees,
which have only rudimentary stings, are not in possession
of any poison to preserve it with.   It must also be noted
as a remarkable fact that this honey yielded by the poison-
less bees never quite agreed with me ; it used to give me,
nay even the natives, diarrhœa, while on the other hand I
can enjoy any quantity of European honey with perfect
comfort.   The old honey, which the bees do not eat themselves, looks like soft yellow cheese, and the civilised blacks
call it old-man-sugar-bag.   The blacks do not reject it,
but mix it with fresh honey and water in the troughs
just described.   Fresh honey is also sometimes mixed with
water.

This mixture of honey and water is not drunk, as one
would suppose, but is consumed in a peculiar manner.   The
blacks take a little fine grass and chew it, thus making a
tuft which they dip in the trough and from which they suck
the honey as from a sponge.   While they eat they sit
crouching round the trough, and as each one tries to get as
much as possible, the contents quickly disappear.   Where
spoons are wanting this would seem a natural and practical
invention, and is surely calculated to secure an equitable
division of the honey, as in this way it is difficult for any
one person to get more than his share.   After the meal the
tufts are placed in the basket, where they are carried as long
as they are fit for use.

The Australian wild honey, which is of a dark brown
colour, is hardly equal to the best European.   Its aroma is
too pungent, and its flavour is not so delicate.   In the
trunks of the trees it keeps cool even when the weather is
very hot, and supplies a healthy, pleasant food ; but I could
not, like the natives, make a meal of it.   I soon grew tired of
it, although it now and then formed an agreeable change in
my simple bill of fare, and was to some extent a substitute
for sugar.   In the large scrubs we never found honey.

When I reached Herbert Vale the mail had just arrived.
It was a real festival when the postman, twice a month,

passed the station and brought us news from the outside world. He was in the habit of spending the night here on his way up to the table-land, where there were some stations. Armed with a revolver or a rifle, a postman must often ride 300 miles to deliver the mail.

Sometimes in an evening the Kanaka and I would sit together at the hearth and listen to the postman's stories and news from the civilised world. He was a man of varied experience, and a fine specimen of the so-called rough men, who are not, however, always so repulsive as the name would imply. The horse was not to be found that he could not ride ; or, as he expressed himself, " I can ride any beast that has got hair on." He was a reckless fellow, utterly indifferent, always cool and self-possessed, and he shrank from nothing. He cared not what he ate so that he got food, and whether it rained or shone was a matter of supreme indifference to him.

Born in Victoria, he had been obliged to leave that colony on account of some of his youthful exploits, and had come to these uncivilised regions of the north, but ere long his admiration for the fair sex was transferred to the sable beauties of the forest, and for this very reason he had accepted employment in these wilds of the blacks. Upon the whole he was a good-natured fellow, and a type of the working class among the white men of Australia. They are reliable, correct in their habits, and attentive to their duties, open-handed, but reckless and unrestrained in their associations. " I care for nobody, and nobody cares for me " is their motto.

At the station I met another " rough man," less chivalrous than the postman, and his revolver rested less firmly in his belt. He had encamped close by, and expected to make money by catching living cassowary young for the zoological gardens. He also looked for a kind of palm, which he claimed would make splendid billiard cues. Supplied with tobacco and coloured handkerchiefs as a means of paying the blacks, he made a number of fruitless excursions.

I happened to tell him that I had been present at a borboby, and this aroused his desire to witness the next one, which was to take place in a few days. He did not want me to be the only white man who had seen such a contest,

L

and got the Kanaka to show him the way up there. But both were obliged to save their lives by flight, the blacks having surrounded them, shouting, *Talgŏro, talgŏro !*—that is, Human flesh, human flesh !

Willy, one of the blacks who sometimes came to the station, had noticed that I had both meat and tobacco, and one day expressed a desire to accompany me. He said, "Go with me to my land, and you shall get both yarri and boongary." Willy's land is not far from Herbert Vale, and his mountain tribe was on friendly terms with many of the blacks of Herbert river ; but still, being a border tribe, it was on an unfriendly footing with others. As I was fairly well acquainted with Willy, and had some confidence in him, I resolved to visit this region which he praised in such high terms.

CHAPTER XI

I WAS now to make an expedition to Willy's much-lauded country, taking both him and his friend Chinaman into my service, and retaining some of my previous companions. On account of the recent borboby, several of my men were supplied with swords and spears. As they would have no use for them, they hid them in the course of the day under a bush for some other occasion. I never heard of such things being stolen from them. They always left them in the fullest confidence that they would find them again. The contrary is the case with provisions, which they sometimes conceal in this manner; every man will take what food he can lay his hands on. There is, however, considerable respect for the right of property, and they do not steal from one another to any great extent.

If, for instance, a native finds a hive of honey in a tree, but has not an immediate opportunity of chopping it out, he can safely leave it till some other day; the discoverer owns it, and nobody else will touch it if he has either given an account of it or marked the tree, as is the custom in some parts of Western Queensland. If they hunt they will not take another person's game, all the members of the same tribe having apparently full confidence in each other. Thus the right of property is to a certain extent respected; but least of all, as has before been pointed out, when it concerns their dearest possession—the women. But it is, of course, solely among members of the same tribe that there is so

great a difference between mine and thine ; strange tribes
look upon each other as wild beasts.

The road was very difficult. We climbed hills and
marched through deep valleys, and sometimes had to fell the
trees in order to get through.   I was surprised to see how
quickly the blacks cut down the trees with their tomahawks.
Though I was stronger than they, still they brought a tree
down more rapidly, because they understood how to give the
axe more force. After riding for some time up a grassy
slope, which at length became perfectly level, we suddenly
caught sight of a broad and long scrub-grown mountain
valley, through which there flowed a river, which now foamed
in rapid currents and now fell over high precipices, forming
magnificent waterfalls.   The roar of the waters and the dark
green vegetation clothing the hills on both sides of the valley
from base to top made me cheerful, and awakened in me
hopes of interesting finds. Against the dark green background the palms stood out in strong contrast among the
lower parts of the scrub.   There were great numbers of these
stately trees, with their bright, glittering crowns towering far
above the rest of the forest.

An air of indescribable freshness seemed to breathe
upon us as we entered the last grassy plateau. Willy
proposed that we should build our huts in a different manner
from what we had done before.   His motive was, of course,
laziness, for he wanted to avoid fetching palm leaves from
the scrub, but his proposition was a fortunate one, for I
thereby obtained a more solid hut than I should otherwise
have had.   He hewed the stems of some slender trees, and
made four short fork-shaped stakes, the lower ends of which
were sharpened so as to be easily driven into the ground.
The stakes were put in a square, and were scarcely a yard
high.   In the forks long branches were laid, and over these
the roof was made with more branches and long dry grass.
I made myself a very comfortable bed of leaves and grass,
spreading a mackintosh over the latter, and using some of
the things I carried with me for a pillow ; among these was
my dearest treasure—the tobacco. By my side was my
gun, which was always my faithful bedfellow.

While we were occupied in making the huts, Chinaman

had disappeared. He soon returned with a large number of
jungle-hens or *grauan* (*Megapodius tumulus*), a name applied
by the natives both to the bird and to its eggs. This was
Chinaman's own "land," and so he knew every spot in the
forest, and particularly all the mounds in which jungle-hens'
eggs were to be found. November was just the time for the
grauan, which is found in great abundance in the lower part

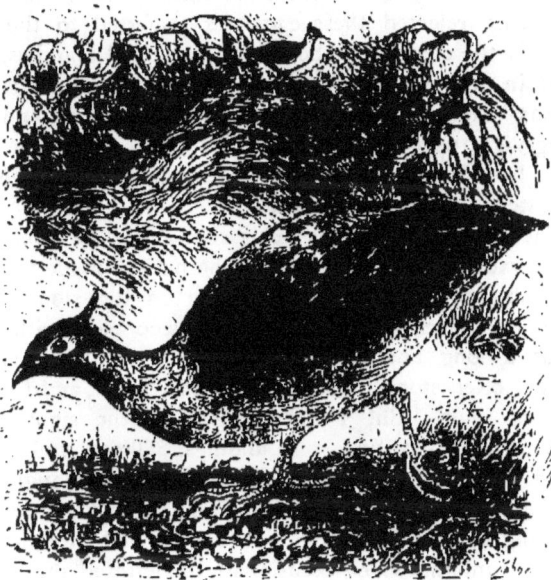

JUNGLE-HEN (*Megapodius tumulus*).

of the scrubs, but not higher up, where the *cootjari* (*Talegalla*)
takes its place.

The eggs are about four times the size of hens' eggs, and
are prepared and eaten in the following original manner :
The blacks, having first made a hole on one side of the egg,
place it on the hot ashes, and after a minute or two the
contents begin to boil. Two objects are gained by making
a hole in the egg—in the first place it does not break
easily, and in the second place it can be eaten while lying
boiling in the ashes. They dip into the egg the end of a

cane that has been chewed so as to form a brush, and use this as a spoon.

As is well known, the jungle-hen, like the brush-turkey (*Talegalla*), hatches her eggs by the aid of artificial heat. She lays the eggs in a large mound, which she constructs herself from earth and all sorts of vegetable debris ; and the heat generated in the mound by the fermenting of the decaying vegetable matter is sufficient for hatching the eggs. Several females use the same mound, and the eggs being laid at long intervals, they are, of course, in different stages of development. As a rule there are chickens in them, but far from being rejected these eggs are preferred to the fresh ones. If the chicken is about half developed and lies, so to speak, in its own sauce, the natives first eat with their " spoons " the white and what remains of the yolk, and then the egg is crushed and the chicken taken out. The down having been removed, the chicken is laid on the coals, and then eaten—head, claws, and all.

The next day we made our ascent along the river. We had to wade most of the time. The natives made the most remarkable progress, stepping lightly on the stones, while I with my shoes on could scarcely keep pace with them. It was a long and difficult road to travel. Weary and thirsty, I often stooped to drink the cool water, and to bathe my head in it. But I was cheered by the sight of the luxuriant and beautiful surroundings. Trees and bushes formed a wall along the mountain stream, overhanging the babbling water. In the woods all was dark and damp, but on gazing upward I saw the tree-tops flooded with the most brilliant sunlight, which occasionally penetrated through the branches, and above us was spread the sky in an infinite expanse of azure blue. Occasionally among the trees I caught a glimpse of the hills, rising on both sides in a mass of green of the most varied shades and tints. Here and there could be seen the tall slender stem of the common Australian palm, or of the fan-palm with its large glistening leaves.

Now and then we startle from its branch the beautiful little indigo blue and red kingfisher (*Alcyone azurea*), which with quick wing-strokes flies before us up the stream. Among

the tree-tops the large brilliant blue or green butterflies
(*Ornithoptera*) flutter. In the water pools were seen numerous
crawfish, which the natives are fond of spearing with a stiff
palm branch sharpened at one end, which they thrust down
to the creature, at the same time uttering a low babbling
sound to attract its attention. The crawfish takes hold of
the stake ; a quick thrust with the nimble hand of the black
man, and it is pierced by the point.

As we ascend, the landscape gradually grows wilder
and more picturesque. The river gorge becomes narrower,
the amount of water diminishes, and no more kingfishers are
seen. The palms are replaced by gigantic tree-ferns, which
here, in the damp rocky clefts, spread their mighty leaves in
all their splendour over trickling brooks, which frequently
disappear in little waterfalls down steep precipices. To form
an idea of the size of these ferns I broke off one of the
secondary leaves, and found that it reached up to my chin,
but I saw several that were much larger. The effects of
light and shade are magnificent here, the scenery is simply
overwhelming in its splendour, and yet there is no one to
admire all this beauty save the blacks, who do not comprehend it ! ·

Thus approaching the end of our day's march, and making
our way up among the rocks, Willy, who led the way, suddenly
stopped, and gave me to understand that I must come to him
quickly with my gun. But before I got half way the animal had
disappeared. It was a young yarri, which he had frightened
up from its lair only a few steps away. Willy might have
killed it with his tomahawk, but neglected to do so, as he
had contracted the habit of thinking that everything must
be shot with the gun, in whose fatal and unerring influence
my blacks had acquired great confidence, and for this reason
they usually left it to me to kill the game we happened to
find. On account of Willy's stupidity we this time failed to
secure this rare animal. Then we had a difficult march over
debris of round stones or in thorny scrubs. Among these
thick masses of stony debris there grew tall, slender, foliferous
trees, and here it was that my blacks expected to find boongary ; for the leaves of these trees are their principal food.
Where no trees grew, creeping plants covered the debris like

a carpet, which made walking dangerous, for the stones
would roll away, while our feet stuck fast in this net of
climbing plants.

On the summit we also meet with scenes of a wholly
different character. Here is the real home of the lawyer-
palm, which grows on small hills, where the soil consists of a
deep black mould, and consequently is so fertile that it produces everything in the greatest abundance. Progress is
difficult here, because this palm grows into immense heaps
twenty to twenty-eight feet high, one by the side of the
other, and often firmly woven together. In this way large
connected masses are formed, appearing like an impenetrable
wall. But the native usually finds a narrow passage, through
which he can crawl, but not without getting badly scratched.

In this dense and pathless forest the boongary has his
home, and we found many traces of the animal, some of them
quite recent, both on the high slender stems and on the
smaller trees of the scrub.

Working our way up the side of the mountain near the
summit, the natives called my attention to an animal the
size of a cat, which ran about in the branches of a tree.
They called it toollah. It was late in the afternoon when I
killed this animal, which proved to be a kind of opossum
now known in zoology by the name of *Pseudochirus archeri;*
it has a peculiar greenish-yellow colour with a few indistinct
stripes of black or white, and thus looks very much like a
moss-grown tree-trunk. Though it is a night animal, it also
comes out about three or four o'clock in the afternoon, and is
the only one of the family which appears in the daytime.

One of the greatest annoyances in this almost inaccessible
region is the poisonous nettle, the stinging-tree (*Laportea
moroides*). It is so poisonous that if its beautiful heart-
shaped leaves are only put in motion they cause you to sneeze.
The fruit resembles raspberries in appearance, the leaves are
covered with nettles on both sides, and a sting from them
gives great pain. It will make a dog howl with all his
might; but it has an especially violent effect on horses.
They roll themselves as if mad from pain, and if they do
not at once receive attention they will in this way kill themselves, as frequently happens in Northern Queensland. The

natives greatly dread being stung by this nettle, and always avoid it. If you are stung in the hand you soon feel a pricking pain up the whole arm, and finally in the lymphatic glands of the armpit. You sleep restlessly the first night. The pain gradually leaves the arm, but for two to three weeks you have a sense of having burned your hand if the latter comes in contact with water, for then the pain at once returns where you were stung by the nettle.

Still, I found the fear of this nettle to be exaggerated. If you at once put on some of the juice of the plant called *Colocasia macrorhiza*, which resembles an *arum*, and which is always found growing near the nettle, the pain is soothed and the effect of the poison neutralised. This sharp white juice, which is itself poisonous, produces a violent smarting pain where the skin is thin, as for instance on the lips.

It is a remarkable fact that the antidote to this poisonous nettle always grows in its immediate vicinity, and I cannot help thinking of a parallel case, viz. *kusso* and *kamala*, the best remedies for tape-worm, which are found in Abyssinia, the home of the tape-worm.

One night we spent in a cave near the brook. I had some hesitation at first in spending the night in these scrubs, where the air is unhealthy and apt to produce fever. Four white men died in one week in the scrubs along Johnston river. But I assumed that I, being by this time used to the climate, could sleep there as well as the blacks, who did so without injury. Besides, the lower scrubs are surely much more unhealthy than those farther up the mountains, and I had never suffered any harm from stopping in them overnight. The cave was not large, and was low, cold, and damp, and thus not very inviting. We had but its naked stones for a couch, for there was of course no grass to be found in the scrub. A big fire was kindled ; outside it was pitch dark.

My blacks had found in a large fallen tree some larvæ of beetles (*Coleoptera*), on which we feasted. There are several varieties of these edible larvæ, and all have a different taste. The best one is glittering white, of the thickness of a finger, and is found in the acacia-trees. The others live in the scrubs, and are smaller, and not equal to the former in flavour. The blacks are so fond of them that they even eat them alive while they pick them out of the decayed trunk of a tree—a not very attractive spectacle. The larvæ were usually collected in baskets and so taken to the camp. The Australian does not as a rule eat raw animal food ; the only exception I know of being these coleoptera larvæ.

The large fire crackled lustily in the cave while we sat round it preparing the larvæ. We simply placed them in the red-hot ashes, where they at once became brown and crisp, and the fat fairly bubbled in them while they were being thus prepared. After being turned once or twice they were thrown

EDIBLE BEETLE (*Eurynassa australis*)
(natural size).

LARVA OF SAME
(natural size).

out from the ashes with a stick, and were ready to be eaten. Strange to say, these larvæ were the best food the natives were able to offer me, and the only kind which I really enjoyed. If such a larva is broken in two, it will be found to consist of a yellow and tolerably compact mass rather like an omelette. In taste it resembles an egg, but it seemed to me that the best kind, namely the acacia larva, which has the flavour of nuts, tasted even better than a European omelette. The natives always consumed the entire larva, while I usually bit off the head and threw aside the skin, but my men always consumed my leavings with great gusto. They also ate the beetles as greedily as the larvæ, simply removing the hard wings before roasting them. The natives are also fond of eating the larger species of wood-beetles. Some crawfish, moreover, were roasted, and had as fine a flavour as those in Europe; unfortunately there were not many of them.

In the strong light from the fire my eyes discovered on the roof of the cave some figures made by the blacks who frequented these regions : these figures represented a man and a woman with a baby. The drawing consisted merely of a few lines scratched with charcoal and red paint, and the figures had large spreading fingers and toes. They were upon the whole very imperfect, still not without symmetry ; the left side was precisely like the right, but apart from this the figures were very irregular. The natives can draw pictures only of the crudest kind. I once showed them my photograph, but they had no idea of what it was meant to represent, or of how it was to be held ; they turned it upside down and every other way, but the Kanaka, who was present, at once knew what it was. The civilised blacks, on the other hand, have a clearer notion of pictures, and easily recognise a person from a photograph.

In the morning we were roused by the lively singing of birds. Most prominent was the monotonous and persistent sound of a bird which the blacks call towdala, on account of its unceasing chattering. Its breast is reddish-brown ; it is about as large as a quail, is very shy, and usually stays on the ground, moving very rapidly. This morning one was sitting on the other side of the river singing so persistently and so loudly that it irritated one of the natives, who tried to drive it away, throwing stones at it. The bird (*Orthonyx spaldingii*) is inseparably connected with the scrubs, and keeps up a lively song morning and evening. Though its song is monotonous, I always liked to hear its jubilant and happy voice.

In the sand along the stream the common " water-iguana " had laid its eggs, which are so well concealed that it is almost impossible to find them, but nothing escapes the keen eyes of the natives. Every now and then they dig out the eggs, which are not, however, very numerous in any one place.

They also occasionally succeed in capturing the lizard itself, or in killing it by throwing sticks at it. It usually lies resting near the stream, but is very shy, and on being disturbed disappears into the water with a great splash. Both the lizard, which tastes like a chicken, and its eggs are eagerly eaten by the natives.

We spent several nights at our headquarters in this beautiful and invigorating mountain region. When we had eaten our supper and put all things to rights we laid ourselves round the fire, feeling very comfortable after the fatiguing journeys of the day. One of the natives then usually sang a song while lying on his back, accompanying himself with two wooden sticks. The song was, as usual, a ceaseless repetition of a couple of strophes, each one of which ended in a long monotonous series of deep tones by which the strophe was repeated. To be able to hold the last tone very long is a sign of ability to sing well. If a song has been known a long time in a tribe, it gradually loses its popularity, and gives place to a new composition, which is either original or borrowed from a neighbouring tribe. But they do not often have the opportunity of learning new songs, and consequently their repertoire is very limited. The song in vogue at this time, and which was sung repeatedly, was as follows:—

Tempo di marcia.

Mol-le-mom-bâ va-ri-nâ   (â) mombâ   va-ri - nâ

Kat-su-bu - râ   in-dan-gô   gân-go-

ril - la   mol-le-mom - bâ   va - ri - nâ   mom-bâ

va - ri - nâ   kat-su-bu - râ   in - dan - go gan - go-

ril - la   mol - le - mom - bâ va - ri - nâ mom - bâ

va - ri - nâ   kat - su - bu - râ   in - dan - gô gan - go-

ril - la

It is a remarkable fact that they themselves sometimes do not understand the words which they sing, the song having been learned from a tribe which speaks another dialect. Thus a good song will travel from tribe to tribe. I heard the above-quoted song sung by "civilised" blacks near Rockhampton, 500 miles due south of Herbert Vale. Doubtless it originated in the vicinity of Rockhampton, and accordingly it must have travelled through "many lands" before it came to the savages in the mountains on Herbert river, where it was sung without being understood.

They rarely sing without accompaniment. The singer produces this by beating a boomerang against a nolla-nolla, the former hitting the latter with both ends, but not quite simultaneously. When weapons are wanting, pieces of wood are used. Sometimes they also have their own musical instrument. It is a somewhat thick piece of hard wood in the form of a club. But this, their only musical instrument, is rare, and I only saw it once on Herbert river.

The natives have a better ear for rhythm than for melody. Still I learned from them a few tolerably melodious songs, as for instance the one above quoted. They took no interest whatever in my songs. There was but one of them that they could appreciate at all, and this only when strongly accentuated, namely, Erik Bögh's : " I have sailed around the world, and I have walked many a mile." But I did not often attempt to entertain so unappreciative an audience.

Their voices are hoarse, but never seem to give out. The singer in the camp usually sits with his legs crossed before the fire. As a rule only one, but sometimes two, sing at a time, accompanying themselves, but they never sing in chorus. A black man rambling among the trees alone may at times be heard making the woods echo with his joyful song. He feels free and happy in his native hunting-grounds. The following war-song, which celebrates the knob on the throwing-stick, I used to hear in the woods on Herbert river :—

Andante.

Wom - bon ma - ræ - ry !   Wom - bon ma-

ræ - ry ! mo - ri - dan   ko - by bee - bon bindalgoh !

The women are also sometimes heard singing in the woods, but hardly ever in the camp.

The Australian natives are gay and happy, but their song is rather melancholy, and in excellent harmony with the sombre nature of Australia. It awakened feelings of sadness in me when I heard it from the solemn gum-tree forest, accompanied by the monotonous clatter of the two wooden weapons.

My men were in good spirits on this expedition, and they sang nearly every night of their own accord. The sole cause of their happiness was that they received plenty of the white man's food. I had taken with me an abundance of provisions, and I distributed them liberally, on the false assumption that the more I gave them the better they would work. Though I had long been careful to give them nothing gratis, and always to demand work for what I bestowed, I had not yet learned to give them *only* fair compensation, for the more they get the more they want. To be liberal is simply dangerous, for they assume that the gift is bestowed out of fear, and they look upon the giver as a person easy to kill. Too great liberality demoralises them. They become exacting and disobedient, and finally treacherously assault the giver.

As long as they understand that they can have advantages from a white man, they let him live. The one thing which keeps them from killing him is fear.

After having received all the food they wanted they became lazy, and demanded a fuller compensation for their work. Their demands increased day by day, and were no longer limited to food, but gradually included the most unreasonable things, such as the clothes I wore, not to mention my weapons and the whole supply of tobacco.

One morning when Willy and I went out to get the horses, he boldly demanded the trousers I was wearing. When I positively refused to give them to him, he wanted to borrow them to protect himself from the dew on the grass, which he said annoyed him.

No matter how much they had eaten, they never said no when I, in excessive liberality, offered them more food. They laid by what they did not eat, but I did not scold them, for I was anxious to keep them in my service. It soon became plain to me, however, that I must take a different course if I wished to save my life.

CHAPTER XII

THE wives of Willy and Chinaman had kept far in the rear of the expedition all the time, as they, in company with other women of the tribe, were in search of fruits and larvæ. Among the blacks it is the women who daily provide food, and they frequently make long excursions to collect things to eat. The position of woman here, as elsewhere among savages, is a very subordinate one.

She must do all the hard work, go out with her basket and her stick to gather fruits, dig roots, or chop larvæ out of the tree-stems. She finds the fruits partly within her reach, partly in the trees, which she climbs, though less skilfully than the men. The stick in question, the woman's only implement, is indispensable to her on her expeditions after food. It is made of hard tough wood four or five feet long, and has a sharp point at one end made by alternately burning it in the fire and rubbing it with a stone. Even at dances and festivals the married women carry this stick as an emblem of dignity, as the provider of the family.

The woman is often obliged to carry her little child on her shoulders during the whole day, only setting it down when she has to dig in the ground or climb trees.

When she comes home again, she usually has to make great preparations for beating, roasting, and soaking the fruits, which are very often poisonous. It is also the woman's duty to make a hut and gather the materials for the purpose.

Her husband assists her in cutting down the four or five slender trees for the frame, but the woman herself has to carry the large armfuls of palm leaves or grass to the camp, and level the ground for the hut, removing with her stick and her fingers all inequalities. She also provides water and fuel.

When they travel from place to place the woman has to carry all the baggage. The husband is therefore always seen in advance with no burden save a few light weapons, such as spears, clubs, or boomerangs, while his wives follow laden like pack-horses with even as many as five baskets containing provisions. There is frequently a little child in one of the baskets, and a larger child may also be carried on the shoulders.

The husband's contribution to the household is chiefly honey, but occasionally he provides eggs, game, lizards, and the like. He very often, however, keeps the animal food for himself, while the woman has to depend principally upon vegetables for herself and her child. The husband hunts more for sport than to supply the family with necessaries, a matter that does not really concern him. Upon the whole he feels no responsibility as the father of a family, but lives a thoroughly selfish life, waiting in the morning until the grass is dry before he goes out, and often returning to the camp with empty hands, having consumed his game where he caught it.

He treats his wife with but little consideration, and is often very cruel ; he may take her life if he desires. In cold rainy nights she is obliged to go out to fetch water and fuel. If in the evening I requested one of my blacks to do this, he usually transferred the order to one of his wives, who went at once ; as a rule he had no regard for her age. During one night which I passed on a farm not far from Mackay, I heard a terrible cry in a camp of civilised blacks near by. On going down there the next morning we found one of the young women in a pitiful condition, bathed in blood and weeping ; two of her fingers were broken. She said that her husband had flogged her during the night. I asked him why he had done so, and he answered that it had been very cold in the night, and that this wretch of a woman

M

had not been willing to go at once and fetch fuel for the camp fire.   He was an unusually capable black, who, on one occasion, had accompanied a Catholic missionary across the continent to the Gulf of Carpentaria.   But with all his good qualities he had not yet learned to treat his wife otherwise than his black brethren, who do not regard her as a human being like themselves.

The worst crime a woman can commit is, of course, to run away from her husband, whose slave she in reality is. She is oppressed, but is as a rule contented with slavery, having no knowledge of a freer condition.   She has no will of her own, and she knows that her husband will not brook opposition.   But, however subject to the will of her husband she may appear to be, and however oppressed she has been for generations, many instances are still to be found where she has refused to submit to her fate and has taken flight. She may also have some one whom she adores, and a woman frequently runs away to a person she loves, although she risks punishment ; she may even be maimed by her husband if he ever gets hold of her again.   In such cases he usually gives her one or two blows on the back with his tomahawk, which the blacks call "marking" the woman.   Frequently the woman is killed, particularly if she tries to run away a second time.

When a wife is punished for other errors, the husband usually gives her a rap on the head with the first object he can lay his hands on.   As a result of this treatment the women are often marked or scarred from blows received from their cruel husbands.   The punishments are quite informal, and are inflicted in the excitement of the moment, no matter whether others are present or not.

As the women perform all the labour, they are the most important part of the property of an Australian native, who is rich in proportion to the number of wives he possesses.

They usually have two, frequently three, sometimes four wives, and I saw one man who had six.   All the wives live in the same hut with their husband.   He who has many is envied by the others.   "No one should have more than two wives," said my men to me, who had only one wife apiece, and whose highest ambition it was to double the number.   The

black man usually has a favourite wife, whom he prefers to the others and treats better.   Still, polygamy does not give rise to as many family troubles as one would think, though there may be discord enough among the men on account of the women.   As a rule, man and wife apparently get on very well, and the women are not constantly being flogged.   I have even seen instances where the husband was governed by his wife, and was scolded and corrected by her, and I have also seen husbands ask their wives for advice ; but such cases as these are, of course, very rare.

It must be admitted that sometimes the Australian treats his wives well, even in cases where the husband is the *boss*, and two of the men who were with me on this expedition were exceptions of this kind.

It was an unusually fine trait in the characters of Willy and Chinaman that they saved part of the provisions which they received from me for their wives.   One afternoon, when they wanted to go and see their wives, they asked me to lend them a bag, and soon afterwards I saw them starting off with a large amount of provisions which they had saved. This consideration did not imply any self-denial on their part, for I had given them more than they could eat, but I have since learned that they sometimes did make sacrifices for their wives, and in this instance it may be said to their credit that they gave them what they themselves might have consumed at a later time.

Willy and Chinaman's wives were very young, one of them being a little girl of about twelve years.   As long as the wives are so young I think they receive better treatment than they do later on.

Thus even Australian women may have their honey-moon.   These two men were proud of their young wives, because it is, as a rule, difficult for young men to marry before they are thirty years old.   The old men have the youngest and best looking wives, while a young man must consider himself fortunate if he can get an old woman.

A woman is delivered over to her husband when she is about nine or ten years old.   It is simply ridiculous to see a man with a wife whom one would take to be his young daughter.   She lives with her husband, who may be said to rear her, the two being at the same time really married. In this respect the custom existing among the more southern tribes, as, for instance, near Rockhampton, where the woman is not married before she has reached maturity, differs from that on Herbert river; even here, however, some respect is paid to her age, for a twelve-year-old wife is not expected to provide as much as a grown woman. "She runs about too much when she is so little," said Willy and Chinaman, meaning that she was not as capable as the older ones of finding food. I invariably observed that the grown woman performed her work in an earnest and careful manner, and did not permit herself to be disturbed. It is not uncommon for an Australian to inherit a wife; the custom being that a widow falls to the lot of the brother of the deceased husband. But the commonest way of getting a wife is by giving a sister or a daughter in exchange. Marriage may be either exogamous or endogamous. I have previously stated that it is usual to steal one another's wives; but it should be added that this, as a rule, occurs among the smaller families or sub-tribes, and but rarely among the larger tribes. A beautiful girl from another tribe was maltreated and killed not far from my headquarters. When I asked why they did not keep her rather than take her life in this manner, they said that they feared the strange tribe, to whose attacks they would continually be exposed if they kept the woman alive. Killing her would give less cause for resentment.

Willy and Chinaman always took into consideration the youth of their wives, and did not make them carry the large burdens usually laid upon women. Of course they had to fetch leaves and grass for the hut, run after water, and find larvæ and fruits, and go on errands in general, but upon the whole they had an easy time of it, and their husbands gave them a considerable amount of food. Surely when they received the bag of food I mentioned before, their husbands must have been prompted by higher motives than simply the idea that the food would make them stronger, and therefore capable of doing more work.

In the evening, when Willy and Chinaman came back from their wives, they brought a basket of fruit from the poisonous palm *Cycas media*, which is called by the natives

kadjĕra. When the nut is cracked, the kernel is subjected
to an elaborate process of pounding, roasting, and soaking,
until all is changed into a white porridge. Although my
men were very fond of my fare, which I shared with them
plentifully, still they felt a need of their own food. *Kadjĕra*
constitutes during this season of the year, from October to
December, the principal food of the blacks, *tobŏla* and
koraddan, other fruits, being what they live chiefly upon from
January to March. When the time comes for harvesting
these fruits, the women set out together to gather and prepare them, and they are frequently absent from the camp
for several days.

We had now exerted ourselves a long time, and suffered
much fatigue from trying to secure a specimen of boongary,
when all the men one day suddenly declared that nothing
would induce them to hunt the boongary without a dog, and
that there was no use in continuing the expedition. Though
this was a great disappointment to me, there was nothing
else to do but to return to my headquarters to get a dingo
and more provisions.

On my arrival at Herbert Vale I also secured some new
men. Among them Jimmy was especially noteworthy. He
was a square-built, athletic fellow with a short neck and
broad shoulders. There was a sinister expression in his face,
and he was a man of few words. I also enlisted in my
service another native, Mangola-Maggi, a smooth-haired
young man who, in spite of his youth, was highly respected
among the blacks on account of his ability to procure *talgoro*
—that is, human flesh. This was certainly not the particular
qualification that I sought. What I wanted was good hunters,
and in choosing my men I had to pay special attention to
this point without regard to other less desirable qualities.

I suggested that they should take their wives with them,
and they were the more easily persuaded to do so as the
women were going in the same direction to gather fruits, and
the latter received orders to keep a sharp look-out for
boongary, which during the day sleep in the high trees.

On our journey across the open country Willy and I
led the way. In the afternoon some of my people remained
behind to dig out a bandicoot, among them Lucy, Willy's

wife. She had stayed without her husband's consent, and
for this she must be punished. When, after about an hour,
she overtook us, Willy, greatly enraged, asked her why she
had remained behind, and at the same time picked up a
large piece of wood and hurled it past her face. She did
not dare to stir or hardly to blink with her eyes, and made
no effort to ward off the projectile, knowing that her husband
would become only more angry and try the more to hit her.
As it was, he only threw the piece of wood several times to
frighten her.

The bandicoot, which had given rise to this domestic
scene between Willy and Lucy, I wanted for my collection ;
but Chinaman would not give it up. He was, on the whole,
very selfish, passionate, and greedy. He twice told me that
he liked the flesh of little children better than that of grown-
up people, because the former were " so fat." When we had
slain an animal the thought of eating was uppermost in his
mind, and I often failed to secure rare specimens which he
and his comrades had killed and eaten before I could claim
them. It was therefore necessary not only to find and kill
the animals, but also to save them from disappearing into
the hungry stomachs of the blacks. Even though they
knew that they would get tobacco for the animal, moment-
ary enjoyment so predominated in their minds that they
had no time to think of the tobacco.

We rose at sunrise the next morning, and continued the
ascent. I had so distributed my baggage among the natives
that the women carried the provisions and the men the gun
and ammunition and the thighs of a wallaby, which I had
taken as a lure for yarri. Saturated with strychnine, the flesh
of the wallaby was exposed in various places along the river,
particularly where brooks emptied into the latter, for here,
according to the statements of the natives, the yarri were apt
to be found during the night.

We worked our way up over large stones and among
creeping vines, and toward noon approached the goal of
our day's march, about 600 ft. below the level of the
mountain summit. Before us we still had a very steep and
difficult country to traverse, and we now halted near the
confluence of two mountain brooks to get something to eat.

I had so planned that the women were to go for several days by themselves in another direction in order to search the scrubs, and at the same time gather fruits, while we were to follow the brook and make our camp on the summit of the mountain. The woods are so dense that a man cannot make a long journey in a day, and as it was of importance to investigate as large a region as possible, I hoped that the women would in this way be of great use to us. The men were, however, unwilling to agree to this plan, and they suggested instead not to send the women out until the next day, but to send them on now with the provisions and baggage to the proposed camping-place, while they and I were to make a digression to the south in order to look for boongary. We were to meet again on the top of the mountain. Their proposition seemed to me excellent, for in this way we might make a better use of our time, and so we set out, without any suspicion on my part of their treacherous intentions. As usual, it was not long before I was some distance behind my people, who during such ascents were wont to proceed much more rapidly than I did; my boots making it difficult for me to keep pace with them. Certainly I thought they were in a greater hurry than usual, but I paid no particular attention to this fact. Finally, I had only Chinaman and his dog before me. Our course along a little brook was very steep, and so narrow that we frequently had to creep on our hands and knees under the enormous fern-trees, in order to get through.

Presently Chinaman also disappeared in the scrub, and I suddenly found myself all alone with my dog " Donna." I shouted, but heard no answer, and it now dawned upon my mind that I was the victim of a plot. In order to get possession of my provisions, they had, of course, agreed on a place where they were to join the women, or perhaps they intended to meet at the place fixed upon for a camp, in order to feast on my food. I knew that they would not rob and eat everything, for like children who help themselves to sweets, they imagine that nothing will be discovered if only something is left, be it ever so little. There was danger, however, that my provisions would be consumed to such a degree as to make it impossible to continue the expedition. I had been careless enough to leave the food in two open bags, but had looked better after the tobacco, the latter being well packed in the centre of my baggage.

After a short time I heard them in the distance giving signals to the women. The only thing for me to do was to make an effort to proceed alone. I knew pretty nearly where we were to encamp, but it was not so easy to find the way through the scrub, where nothing is to be seen to guide the traveller.

I was several hours in reaching the summit. Meanwhile it had begun to rain, sunset was drawing on, and it was high time that I found the camp. At length I heard the blacks talking on the top of a little hill near by, and I soon found the place, a little opening in the dense scrub scarcely eight yards square, where they had already built their huts. It was a very convenient place for a camp, and I could see that it had frequently been used for this purpose, for on all sides there were large heaps of fruit husks.

I at once commanded them to produce the provision bags, and discovered to my satisfaction that they had consumed less of the contents than I feared. When I asked them why they had abandoned me in order to steal the provisions, they answered that they had been very much afraid that the white man would get lost, but added, in an ingratiating manner, that they were now going to make him a good hut. The only way to punish them which was left me was to shoot one of them, and I therefore let the matter drop, but gave them to understand that if the offence was repeated I should use the revolver. I then ordered them to build a hut, as it was already night and the rain was increasing. From this incident it is clear that it is not true, as many maintain, that the Australian native is guided wholly by his instincts. I am willing to admit that his reasoning powers are but slightly developed, as he is unable to concentrate his thoughts for any length of time on one subject, but he can come to a logical conclusion, a fact which has been denied.[1]

In a few minutes my hut was ready. It made me feel depressed to be alone with the savages in such a stormy

[1] See, for example, *Transactions of Royal Society of New South Wales* for January 1883.

night.   The fog was dense, and it was so dark that we could
not see our hands before our eyes.   As my hut stood in the
centre of those of the natives, I had built a fire on either side,
and in order to keep close watch of them I made two
entrances.   I was tired, and soon fell asleep.

Later in the night a most violent shower of rain suddenly
fell upon us ; the water poured through the roofs of our huts
and put out the fires.   I awoke in inky darkness and
heard the natives groaning in their disgust at this unexpected shower-bath on their naked bodies.   I got up and
drew my woollen blanket close around me and waited for
the dawn of day.

Long before daybreak the natives began making fresh
fires, and with their remarkable skill in this respect they soon
had a fire kindled in front of each hut.   By constructing a
sort of shed of palm leaves they succeeded in keeping
them alive through the night.   Every now and then they
had to go out into the scrubs and gather pieces of bark or
dry rubbish from hollow trees.   Our huts became united, as
it were, by these little sheds under one roof, and the result
was that we were considerably troubled by smoke.

It is most delightful to be able to stretch one's wet and
tired limbs by the fire even in the hut of a savage, and to be
warm and cosy while the rain pours down outside.   To the
Australian the fire is, of course, of great importance, for
with him it takes the place of clothes in cold weather.   On
Herbert river the natives, as before stated, go naked all the
year round.   The women, and particularly the older ones, may
occasionally be seen covered with a mat made from the
inner bark of the tea-tree, and this mat was also sometimes
used on the floor of the hut.   They wear it over their
shoulders, but it scarcely does more than cover their shoulder-
blades, like a lady's cape.   The skins of animals are never
used as mats or clothes.

During the two or three days that we stayed here the blacks
spent most of the time in sleeping and eating.   The women
mended the fires and repaired the roofs where they leaked.   I
was busy much of the time drying my clothes.   I hung them
in front of the fire, and in the course of a day they were sufficiently dry to put on.   As exercise in the open air was out of

the question, I had to spend these days in my hut either in a reclining or a sitting position, and, like the blacks, tried to pass the time by sleeping. The unceasing rain soon destroyed the roofs of our huts, so that both the men and the women had to repair to the scrub and get more palm leaves. They also made a little trench round each hut to carry the water away, but they were usually idle. When they did not sleep they continually demanded food and tobacco ; the men had some right to do so, but the women had no claim on me, for it was originally agreed that they were to accompany me at their own expense. They had also brought with them their own food, consisting of the usual unpalatable plants and fruits.

My people had noticed that I took my meals—breakfast, dinner, and supper—regularly, and this had given rise to their habit of asking for food at the same time and of applying civilised names to the meals. Savages live irregularly, and eat when they are hungry. It was curious to hear them demand "breakfast," "dinner," and "supper," even if they had just been gorging themselves with their own food. During these days I scarcely heard any other words from their lips.

I was astonished to see the men on this occasion give the women a part of their rations, and what particularly surprised me was that they gave them more than they kept themselves. The native likes to assume a liberal air, sometimes even towards his wife ; for a person bestowing gifts right and left is looked upon as a great man. Thus it is the custom for a man who has slain a wild animal to eat but little of it himself, and to distribute it freely among his comrades, whom he watches with satisfaction while they prepare and consume his game. This chivalry towards the fair sex was an annoyance to me, for my provisions were not over abundant.

As the rain continued some days longer, I was obliged to call the attention of the blacks to the fact that my provisions were nearly consumed, so that they must look for their own food. Two of them did go out, and soon returned with a few larvæ and some young shoots of the palm-tree. This was all the effort considered necessary to supply them-

selves with food for a whole day.   These shoots consisted of
the fresh buddings of the *Ptychosperma cunninghamii*.   It
was roasted in the ashes, but is usually eaten raw.   I could
not eat it, for it has an insipid and revolting taste even
when boiled in water.

One day, as I went outside the hut to stretch my cramped
legs, I discovered in the fog a bird which acted in a singular

RIFLE-BIRD (*Ptiloris victoriæ*).

manner.   While sitting on a branch it raised its wings, twisting its body to either side, in which position it looked like
a cormorant drying its wings.   I shot it, and the blacks
fetched it to me out of the scrub.   It was an Australian
bird of paradise, the celebrated Rifle-bird (*Ptiloris victoriæ*),
which, according to Gould, has the most brilliant plumage of
all Australian birds.   It is difficult to determine its colour,
as its velvet-like plumage assumes the most varied tints
according as the light falls upon it.

CHAPTER XIII

THE following day the rain had entirely ceased, but the natives refused to continue the journey because the scrub was so wet. Still I had determined to raise the disagreeable quarantine, even though I should expose myself to still greater discomfiture. After an hour or two I actually succeeded in getting them to start, in spite of Willy's assurances that it was impossible to get into the other valley for which I was making. Jimmy went alone upon some hills to find *mongan*, a mammal which the natives had mentioned to me, but which I had not yet seen. The women were excused from gathering fruits in the scrub, which was now scarcely accessible, and instead they were to go down to the grassy plain and examine the poisoned meat which we had laid there as lures for the yarri. The men accompanied me to a neighbouring valley, where the women declared they had seen boongary on one of their expeditions to gather fruit.

The long incessant rain had formed countless brooks, which, with their clear and sparkling water, frequently crossed our path to vanish in the dense scrub. The sky was now clear and cloudless, and the wet, dense forest lay bathed in the bright glittering sunshine, which produced an intense heat, while warm vapours rising from the ground and from the trees made the air so damp and oppressive that we became very much exhausted.

We often found large coils of the lawyer-palm obstructing our passage. Willy repeatedly called my attention to the fact that he had been right in urging that the scrub

was impassable, but still we managed to get on, partly by going round, partly by creeping under the obstructions.

When we got out of the scrub we went along the side of a steep heap of debris overgrown with creeping plants, a difficult road, for the stones were continually loosened under our feet and rolled down with a tremendous crash. We saw nothing but old traces of boongary; on the other hand, I shot a specimen of the toollah (*Pseudochirus archeri*) described above. The dogs proved useless, my Gordon setter was, of course, too heavy to work in the scrub, to which she was not accustomed, and Chinaman's dog also disappointed my expectations, for it refused to range at all, thereby making its master so angry that he pelted it with sticks. We had agreed to meet the women and Jimmy at the foot of the mountains, and when we reached the camp at dusk we found them already there; they had inspected all the poisoned meat lures, but none of them had been touched. Jimmy, however, had, to my great delight, found mongan (*Pseudochirus herbertensis*), a new and very pretty mammal, whose habitat is exclusively the highest tops of the scrubs in the Coast Mountains (see coloured plate).

Willy and Chinaman persisted in having the toollah which I had shot, and as our provisions were giving out, I was obliged to surrender it, much to my chagrin. I tried to keep the skin, but they eagerly objected that the animal would lose its flavour if roasted without it. In order to satisfy their hunger, I was therefore obliged to give them both the skin and the body.

They now threw the animal on the fire, in order to singe the hair off. Then they cut its belly open with a sharp piece of wood, placed it on the coals, and as soon as it was half roasted it was torn into several pieces and distributed, whereupon each one roasted his share. In this way the Australian prepares and roasts all small mammals. He does not like to eat the meat raw, but has not the patience to wait until it is thoroughly done. As soon as a crust is formed on the meat, he takes it from the coals and gnaws off the roasted part; he then puts it back to roast the rest.

The women returned from their expedition with a lot of fruit rather like red peas, called by the natives *koraddan*.

It grows on a climbing plant found in abundance in the scrub, but as a rule cannot be reached from the ground, hence the women must climb the trees to gather it. The koraddan is roasted between grass and hot stones, and has a comparatively good flavour, smelling and tasting like boiled peas.

I had much trouble in getting the natives to look after the strychnine lures, in the effect of which they had no

YARRI (*Dasyurus maculatus*).

faith, as they are not in possession of any kind of poison. I promised them tobacco if they could bring me the animal I wanted. At last they started, and one day, to my great surprise, they brought me a yarri. The natives having a superstition that "a great water will rise" if a young man picks up a dead yarri, Jimmy, who was the oldest, had to carry the animal, and at the head of the others he brought it in triumph to the camp, holding it carefully by the tail high in the air. Had he not been present, I doubt whether I should have obtained the animal.

I concealed my joy, and in order to test them insisted
that it was not a yarri that they had caught, but they
shouted wildly *Yarri, yarri, yarri!* declaring, however, that
it was a young one. The skin was hardly three feet long
from the snout to the end of the tail. It was of a yellowish-
gray colour, with whitish round spots. It proved to be a
Dasyurus maculatus, yarri being a name applied to the whole
family of *Dasyuridæ.* I am, however, convinced that there
exists a large animal of this kind that has not yet been
discovered. The one which the natives particularly call
yarri I shall have occasion to mention farther on.

I was sorry to find that the specimen now brought to
me had been lying so long that it had already become
greenish on the under side, and had a bad smell. As my
knives were rather blunt, it was no pleasant task to flay the
animal, whose skin is very tough. Unfortunately my knife
slipped and cut a deep gash in my thumb. To prevent
blood-poisoning I applied caustic and carbolic acid, and continued my work with a bandage on my thumb.

One day I secured a specimen of the wonderful *Hypsiprymnodon moschatus,* which forms the connecting link
between the kangaroos and the phalangers. This animal,
called by the natives *yopólo,* is not very rare in the lower
part of the scrubs, but is difficult to kill, as it haunts the
banks of the rivers and is never seen on the grassy plain.
When we walked along a river in the scrubs my blacks
would often make a smacking sound that causes the animal,
which is very curious, to come forth and thus be discovered.
The yopolo is brown, and about the size of a stoat. Its lair
is formed like a globular nest from fallen leaves near the
root of a tree, but it is only to be discovered among the
leaves and grass by the keen eyes of the blacks. The natives
frequently succeed in catching the animal by placing their
feet quickly on the lair, but as a rule the yopolo is hunted
with a dingo.

The last evening but one of this expedition a very
curious event happened. While we were eating supper we
suddenly heard a terrible cry from the women, who had a
camp by themselves farther down the river. After a
moment's reflection the men ran down and soon brought

the women up to our camp. A ston   been thrown
against a rock close by, nearly hittin[of them, and
this made them afraid of camping down ti.. alone. They
assumed that the stone had been thrown by strange natives,
and they requested me to "shoot the land" to frighten
them. When I had fired four or five times they thought
they would be able to "sleep first-rate."

The next morning I went down to the deserted camp,
and they at once pointed out to me where the stone had hit
the rock with great force. Close by we also found all the
pieces, which together formed a heavy stone about the size of
a potato, and was, no doubt, a meteorite. The women had
made a false alarm, and there was no danger on this occasion.
But as a rule they have every reason for being on their
guard, for the neighbouring tribes are continually on a war-
footing, and they are always in danger of attacks.

Individuals belonging to the same tribe are usually on
the best of terms, but the different tribes are each other's
mortal enemies. Woe therefore to the stranger who dares
trespass on the land of another tribe! He is pursued like a
wild beast and slain and eaten. In connection with this it
should, however, be stated that the small subdivisions of the
tribes that live nearest the border are on amicable terms
with their neighbours, and that accordingly the borders
between the tribes are frequently very indistinct. The
family tribes have well-defined limits, and as a rule they
are on friendly terms with each other. I am hardly able
to state the extent of a tribe. The one living around Herbert Vale owned an area of land which I should estimate
to be about forty miles long and thirty miles wide. It was
divided into many sub-tribes or family tribes, which lived
within their own well-defined limits, the country within
which was well known to them. Outside their borders they
had no acquaintance with the country. This was one of
the difficulties I had to contend with, as I soon found that
a native outside his own "land" was of little or no service
to me, for he there felt very insecure. The case was still
worse when he entered the domain of another tribe; there
he was utterly restless and timid.

In a family tribe there may be about twenty to

twenty-five individuals, often less. How many such small divisions it takes to make a tribe it is impossible to say, as there exists no sort of organisation. They do not even have chiefs, and in this respect they differ from the natives in other parts of Australia, where there are sometimes even two chiefs in one tribe, usually an old man and a young man. It is probably not far from the truth to estimate a tribe at two hundred to two hundred and fifty individuals. On important occasions the old men's advice is sought, and their counsel is mostly taken by the whole tribe, but there is no restraint put on the liberty of the individual. When a camp is broken up, those who wish to follow, do so; those who prefer to go somewhere else or to remain, take their choice. In most cases, however, there is a wonderful consonance between them. The natives on Herbert river have not much use for a chief, as the tribes do not, as in Western Queensland, carry on open warfare with each other, but simply seek to diminish the number of their enemies by treacherous attacks.

The Australian rambles about in his woods all day long, free from care, though he always feels a secret fear of strange blacks. But when "the sun is near the mountains" (*vi molle mongan*), he is filled with anxiety and restlessness at the thought of the dangers which threaten him after darkness falls upon the earth. The least sound makes him suspicious; he shudders and listens, and whispers timidly to his comrades, *Kolle! mal!*—that is, Hush! man! When he has assured himself that the fear is unfounded, he soon recovers his balance, to be again frightened by the next suspicious sound. During the daytime a torn-off leaf or a footprint which he does not understand at once awakens his mistrust.

N

CHAPTER XIV

IT was a pleasure to return to Herbert Vale and meet once more Nelly's smiling face at the gate. She asked with deep interest what kind of animals I had secured, and seemed delighted when I showed her the skins I had brought. My first visit was to the kitchen cupboard, where I took possession of a bowl of fresh milk. Into it I broke a piece of fresh-made damper and sprinkled on it a lot of sugar, making a dish which, under the circumstances, tasted better to me than a dinner at Bignon's.

In the middle of the night both the superintendent and myself were roused by a terrible howl from Nelly, who was being flogged by her husband, the Kanaka, up in the loft of the storehouse. Old Walters had to go up there with his cane, which he always kept near the door, but he did not succeed in getting the Kanaka to respect his authority.

The next morning I at once set out to find a dingo suitable for my next expedition ; this was a very difficult matter, for the dingoes are much more rare here than farther south in Australia, where natives can be seen followed by ten or twelve dogs, which are of different breeds, for the dingoes of the natives quickly mix with the shepherd-dogs, greyhounds, and terriers of the colonists. On Herbert river there are rarely more than one or two dingoes in each tribe, and as a rule they are of pure blood. The natives find them as puppies in the hollow trunks of trees, and rear them with greater care than they bestow on their own children. The dingo is an important member of the family ; it sleeps in the huts and gets plenty to eat, not only of meat, but also of fruit.   Its master never strikes, but merely threatens it. He caresses it like a child, eats the fleas off it, and then kisses it on the snout.

Though the dingo is treated so well it often runs away, especially in the pairing season, and at such times it never returns.   Thus it never becomes perfectly domesticated, still is very useful to the natives, for it has a keen scent

DINGO.

and traces every kind of game ; it never barks, and hunts less wildly than our dogs, but very rapidly, frequently capturing the game on the run.   Sometimes it refuses to go any farther, and its owner has then to carry it on his shoulders, a luxury of which it is very fond.   The dingo will follow nobody else but its owner ; this materially increased my difficulties in finding a dog, for it was useless unless the owner could be persuaded to go with me ; besides, but few of the dingoes understand hunting the boongary, for which they have to be specially trained from the beginning.

In company with four men I rode across Sea-View Range. On its summit a tribe was said to be encamped owning a very good dog, which I had heard much talked of. I sent two of my men to the camp with a supply of tobacco, in order to borrow the dog, but they returned in the evening minus both dog and tobacco, for the dog had followed its owner to another camp, and still they had, with their usual liberality, distributed the tobacco right and left.

On the way I shot a kangaroo, which I wanted to use as a lure. Kangaroos are very hard to kill, and once one of these animals hopped ninety paces after it had been shot by an express rifle, the exploding ball of which had torn its heart into pieces. According to my experience they die most speedily when they are hit in the breast with a charge of large shot, which, if the distance is not too great, generally makes them fall on the spot. In such a case the quick death of the kangaroo made so deep an impression upon my natives that the event was the topic of their conversation for several days, accustomed, as they are, to see kangaroos run away pierced with several spears.

In the evening, as we approached the tribe said to have the dog, I sent two of my men in advance to inform the natives of my coming, otherwise they would be afraid of the white man and take to their heels. We encamped close by on a plat of grass extending into the scrubs. Gongola, the owner of the dog, and two other men came to me when they had learned the object of our visit. Gongola was a large stout fellow, and very friendly. In order to get on the right side of him I at once gave him a piece of tobacco, which he appropriated and then went away.

Before long he returned with two mound-builder's eggs, which he presented to me. This liberality surprised me, for it is rare among the blacks, except among themselves. I suppose he wanted to show me that I was welcome. My experience is, on the whole, that uncivilised blacks are much more friendly and unpretentious than those who have been in contact with the white men. Gongola's friendliness was all the more praiseworthy, since my gift was of no value to him; for he did not like tobacco. It is rare to meet natives who are not fond of tobacco; I only saw one other besides

Gongola. I invited him to have supper with us, and he
took his meals with us as long as we remained here.

Late in the evening my men heard the flying-squirrel
(*Petauroides*) climbing the tall gum-trees above our heads, and
the next day the blacks hunted these animals. Some of the
men climbed the trees with the aid of their kāmins, in order
to frighten them out from their abodes. Like chimney-sweeps
they pulled the kāmins up and down in the hollow tree-
trunks, at the same time shouting *Po-pò! po-pò!* in imitation
of a night bird, and this *po-pò* was repeated by all those who
stood below. The natives think that in this manner they
can give the flying-squirrels the impression that it is night,
and thus more easily coax them out. As a rule, they
come forth quite suddenly, stretch their fliers, and fly
slowly and elegantly into another tree, and while climbing
the stem of this tree they are killed with sticks thrown at
them.

They soon succeeded in frightening one of these animals
out of a tree, and although the sun was shining in all its
splendour, the squirrel landed with remarkable accuracy at
the foot of a gum-tree eighty paces distant. While ascending
the trunk I shot it.

The natives here, particularly the women, looked wretched,
being both poor and filthy. Some of them had a sickly,
pale complexion and dry skin, and many of the children were
covered with eruptions. My impression is that there was
too little variety in their food, as they lived chiefly on
vegetables. The Australian is usually sound and healthy,
and not much troubled with illness. But for the skin
diseases, which he gets from the white men, he is usually a
healthy individual. It is very rare to see any one with a
bodily defect, though an old warrior with one hand was well
known near Rockhampton.

In Central Queensland, about 300 miles west of
Rockhampton, an epidemic of erysipelas is said to have
raged about fifty years ago. The manager of a station in
that district told me that there were caves on the property
in which there were hundreds of skeletons, indicating that
there must have been an epidemic among the natives. The
blacks had informed him that a great many had died at the

same time, being "sick in their mouths and noses." Small-pox has also been known among the Australian natives, for example, near Murrumbidgee in New South Wales, as reported by Beveridge.

I did not think lung diseases possible among the savages of Australia before I saw these pale faces on Sea-View Range. They certainly looked as if they had consumption. But as I had no other symptoms to go by than their exterior, my assumption is not of course of much value.

Strange to say, the natives on Herbert river never complained of rheumatism. They were to some extent troubled with venereal diseases, against which they know no remedy; but these diseases do not appear in their most violent forms in Australia. The blacks who came in to Herbert Vale used to rub their wounds with tar, which they procured at the station. Apart from this, they let the disease run its course.

When the Australian becomes "civilised" and begins to wear clothes he becomes more subject to disease. He regards clothes simply as ornaments that he may wear or not as he pleases. He will perspire during the whole day in a woollen jacket, but in the evening, when he really might need it on account of the cool temperature, he is sure to take it off and sleep in his old-fashioned way. On a hunt he lays aside all clothes for the sake of convenience, no matter how "civilised" he may be, for he wants to be naked when he climbs trees and pursues animals. But this thoughtless way of wearing clothes brings on colds, and as a result rheumatic fevers and lung diseases. I never found fever and ague among the Australian savages, except in the solitary case of a well-dressed civilised black on Herbert river.

As the hard and tough vegetables eaten by the blacks are a severe tax on their teeth, which they also constantly use for making their implements, the older members of the tribe have their fore-teeth worn down to the gums, which therefore become very tender. I have also seen blacks troubled with toothache. In such cases they make one of their comrades suck the cheek until the blood flows, very much as we use leeches. Toothache in one of the front teeth is sometimes radically cured by placing a stick against the tooth, whereupon the "dentist" with a violent blow knocks the tooth into the mouth.

The Herbert river blacks have no medicines. The only remedies used are to suck out the blood over the spot where the pain is felt, or to rub the sore place with saliva. The sick are treated by the "doctor," who as a rule is the most cunning man in the tribe and a great humbug. When he has sucked blood from a spot where the patient feels pain, he usually shows to the latter a piece of bone or a little stone, which he pretends he has sucked out, and which he declares to be the cause of the illness. In other parts of Australia, where diseases must be more common, the blacks are said to know healing herbs, and in many places they have peculiar ways of treating diseases.

On Herbert river no remedy is known against snake bites. The victim simply lays himself down to die. In New South Wales, on the other hand, snake bites are cured in a very interesting manner. The wound is squeezed between the thumb nails until the blood flows; then a piece of warm opossum skin is laid on the wound, which is sucked as soon as the skin becomes cold. The opossum is warmed a second time, and the process is repeated until the patient is out of danger. The operation usually lasts about forty-five minutes. It is a remarkable fact that the Herbert river natives attribute a healing virtue to the sweat of the arm-pits, to which they attach supernatural qualities, putting it under the nose of the patient to make him well.

Wounds and scratches on the blacks heal with remarkable rapidity. Two natives near a station, having borrowed knives from white men, fought. One cut numerous gashes in his opponent's back, while the other continually inflicted wounds right down to the hip-bone of the former. The combatants were separated and brought into the camp in a miserable condition. All their comrades did was to strew ashes in the wounds, and after three weeks' time the victims were perfectly restored.

The natives are very kind and sympathetic towards those who are ill, and they carry them from camp to camp. This is the only noble trait that I discovered in the Australian natives.

After having borrowed Gongola's dog in return for a large piece of damper, I rambled about for a few days before I returned to Herbert Vale. The chief result of the hunt was a kind of bandicoot (*Perameles nasuta*), which utters a peculiar sound which the natives imitate in order to coax it out.

The next evening I was requested by the young men of the tribe to lead an attack on a neighbouring tribe. The purpose was to steal women. They represented to me what beautiful women there were in the other tribe, and how easy it would be to make an assault with a gun. To tempt me still further they held out a promise of the first choice in the division of the spoils. They also called my attention to the fact that we would find a number of yarri. I declined all their tempting offers, but they continued to urge on me their plans for this "Rape of the Sabines"; as they were unable to persuade me, and consequently failed to get the valuable support of the gun, they finally desisted from their purpose.

The majority of the young men wait a long time before they get wives, partly for the reason that they have not the courage to fight the requisite duel for one with an older man. They therefore prefer to wait until they can get a wife in exchange or by inheritance. It is rare, however, for a man to die unmarried, and as the majority of men have at least two wives, the women are more numerous on Herbert river than the men. The same observation is made by the excellent observer Mr. White of Western Queensland, but so far as I know the opposite is true of a large portion of Australia.

After spending the night at Herbert Vale, where I secured more men, I started on a new expedition. I was supplied with provisions for a long time, had an excellent dog and several capable hunters, one of whom was well acquainted with the regions I intended to visit. I started early the next morning in the finest of summer weather. A heavy dew had fallen in the night, running like rain from the roofs of the station houses, and the wet grass glistened in the bright sunshine. There was every promise of a success-ful expedition. At noon the natives were determined to turn northward, as they wanted to go to the "land" that I had visited on my last expedition, urging that we would there find many boongary.   Their real reason was no doubt that, as they knew the country, they would have an easy time of it consuming my provisions, and thus escape the long difficult journey to the strange "land."   I became angry, and called their attention to the fact that they had agreed to accompany me to this more distant region, and I gave them distinct orders to proceed.

Slowly and lazily they started on the journey, and continually presented new difficulties.   They frequently stopped in order to prove to me that it was impossible to progress. We came to a river with steep banks, which it was necessary to cross, but I could not possibly get the blacks to show me the fording-place, and so was obliged to search up and down the river in order to find a place myself where it was possible to get to the other side.

Chinaman, who was our guide and the only person acquainted with the country, proved himself to be a perfect rascal, and was the leading spirit in all these intrigues.   He preferred my food and his own comfort to the fatigues of the journey, but as I firmly opposed all his pretexts, he finally declared that he was unwilling to toil any longer among these rocks and scrubs!   It was impossible to attempt to cross that night, for the sun was already setting behind the mountains.

We experienced some difficulty in finding materials for our huts on this grassy plain.   A few trees were cut down and made into a shed, open on one side.   This was all the shelter we had, and I made a pillar of brushwood, which at the same time formed a partition wall between me and the blacks.   Two of my companions, who had a fancy to imitate the white man, laid claim to the opposite side of my pillow. Although I was not particularly pleased at having them so close, I was too tired to make any objections.

I felt Ganindali's waxed hair against my head, and knew that it was inhabited by those small black animals which give so much trouble to the natives ; but as they thrive only on the blacks, I felt no uneasiness about going to sleep.   Now and then my bedfellows roused me by scratching their heads to get at the uninvited guests, of which process my head not unfrequently had to pay the penalty. When, under these disagreeable circumstances, I was aroused from my sleep, I noticed a horrible smell, which I could not understand.

Finally the odour became so strong that I could not sleep, and not until I had ordered the blacks away did I get peace for the rest of the night. In the morning I discovered that the terrible smell came from a large sore on Ganindali. His comrades told me that he had had it from childhood, and that he had got it from the devil. It cannot be denied that it was very disagreeable to have such a fellow in our company, but the dog would follow no one else, and so he was indispensable.

To my great annoyance Chinaman had disappeared, having deserted during the night; I hoped he would come back, and waited for him until noon, but he did not put in an appearance. We then proceeded without him, and succeeded in finding a good place to cross the river. In the evening we encamped at the foot of the mountains. My people were very willing to do all in their power, but it proved to be utterly impossible to accomplish anything in this unknown country without a guide.

There was therefore nothing else to be done except to accommodate myself to the circumstances and to return to Herbert Vale to make preparations for an expedition in some other direction. I started on my way back in low spirits, my thoughts dwelling on the folly of mankind. As a warning to the others, I threatened to shoot Chinaman if he ever came near me.

The heat was intense; the ground was gray, the grass withered and scorched by the sun; everything had a wintry look. The appearance of Herbert Vale at this time therefore was not inviting. Large swarms of grasshoppers filled the air, greedily attacking the few green shoots to be found at the bottom of the dry grass. They produced a peculiar buzzing sound when in dense swarms they flew up from the ground, and as I stood among them I could not help thinking of a snowstorm. Black lads amused themselves by running round and frightening the grasshoppers. The women gathered large quantities of them in their baskets. In one place a number of natives sat round a fire eating them. First, the contents of the baskets are thrown into the fire in order to burn off the wings and legs, whereupon each grasshopper is roasted separately; they taste like nuts, but there is of course very little to eat on them.

I ordered my blacks to encamp near the station, and at once began to get ready for a new expedition, but as it was difficult to secure more men in a hurry, they became impatient and disappeared with the dog, and thus all my plans were frustrated for the present.

Finally, having secured the aid of a few men, I rode off as soon as possible to capture the fugitives, and after a couple of days succeeded in finding Ganindali and some other blacks out hunting, but they had already delivered the dog to its owner, Gongola. They came to me rejoicing, and told me that it had recently captured a large yarri. It had chased the animal up into a tree, and the natives had themselves killed it with clubs. I asked very eagerly where the animal was, but alas! the old women had already eaten it, they said. The poor comfort I received was that next time they would give the yarri to me.

From Gongola's tribe I had frequently heard that there were many boongaries in a "land" very far away.

They pointed up Herbert river valley to some mountains in the far distance, and thither I now resolved to make my next expedition.

CHAPTER XV

IT was more difficult than ever to secure men. The country we were to visit was situated so far away that the blacks I approached made all sorts of objections. They did not care to run the risk of being eaten. My friends also advised me most positively not to undertake the expedition. Both Willy and Jacky shook their heads, saying, *Komórbŏry talgoro*—that is, Much human flesh. The people there were all *myall*, they said, and would eat both us and our horses, but I comforted myself with the fact that I had in my company a man who belonged to a family tribe living near the boundary of the land we were to visit. Ganindali was also acquainted with one of the neighbouring tribes. Besides, I had with me a " civilised " black, on whom I could place considerable reliance.

On leaving Herbert Vale in the morning the old women took leave of us in a horrible manner, crying and groaning because their friends were going to a dangerous land ; there is, however, an old saying that you must not take evil omens from old women.

We followed Herbert river in a north-western direction, and at noon rested on the river bank. Just as we were ready to continue our journey, we were overtaken by a violent thunder-storm. Before the rainy season begins thunder-showers are frequent, and come on very suddenly, sometimes attended by terrific winds. Flashes of lightning and peals of thunder came almost simultaneously. My men at once

START FOR AN EXPEDITION.

To face page 188

sought shelter under the trees, and they could not comprehend why I stood in the open field and got wet. Strange to say, the natives have no fear of thunder and lightning, which they say are very angry with the trees but do not kill the blacks. Though many trees are seen splintered by lightning, they do not understand that it is dangerous for them to seek shelter under them in a thunder-storm.

We went up along the river as far as it was possible to ride, and crossed it three times. In some places it was a raging torrent, while in others it flowed quietly, but the large stones on the bottom always made the crossing difficult, and twice I had to unload the baggage and let the natives carry it. For the sake of convenience I was lightly clad, wearing simply a shirt, shoes, and round my waist a belt in which I carried my revolver. I also tried to go barefooted like the natives, but I had to give it up, for the stones, heated by the sun, burned my feet. Sometimes the river formed large basins, in which the water was deep, dark, and still, as in a pond. These the crocodiles like to frequent.

The farther we ascended the narrower the valley became, and at last it was impassable for horses. So we made a camp, where we left the horses, distributing the baggage among the natives. Our aim now was to find a little tribe with which Ganindali was acquainted, and which I hoped would be of service to us in hunting the boongary.

I observed with interest how my men acted in order to discover these people. They sought out every trace to be found, took notice of broken branches and bark, or of stones that were turned, or of a little moss that had been rubbed off; in short, of everything that would escape a white man's attention, and which he hardly would understand if his attention were drawn to it.

The keen ability of the Australian to find and follow traces seems to be unique, and doubtless surpasses even that of the North American Indians. The white population has been greatly benefited by this sleuth-hound talent of theirs, which has rendered valuable service in the discovery of murderers. A black tracker of the native police can pursue a trace at full gallop.

The first day we did not succeed in finding the above tribe, but we saw several of their deserted camps. The natives do not destroy their primitive huts when they change their abode, but outside the camp they leave a palm leaf to indicate to their friends in what direction they have gone. By the aid of these signals we finally got on the sure track of the strange tribe. At one of these camps we also found a dingo that had run away from its owner. As it might prove useful to us, we fed it, and thus persuaded it to go with us.

BASKET FROM NORTH QUEENSLAND.

Not until the afternoon of the third day did we approach the little tribe. The natives showed me smoke not far away. As usual, I sent a couple of men in advance to announce our arrival. The strangers were reserved and silent, as they usually are the first time they come in contact with the white man. Some tribes are less cautious on such occasions, and they are in the habit of feeling him all over his body to assure themselves that he is a human being.

On entering the camp I noticed a few women, who sat beating fruits, while two or three of the older men were busy plaiting baskets. The young men were lying down doing nothing.

As soon as the natives became acquainted with my purpose, they were so polite that they sent a message to an old man who lived in the neighbourhood, and had the reputation of being a most skilful boongary hunter. We had to wait for the old man about a day, and this time I spent in the camp with these children of nature. Here they lived uninfluenced by any form of civilisation, uncontaminated by the corruption which always manifests itself when the natives have had intercourse with white men. It was nature in her pristine state, and it is this kind of savage which it is most profitable to study. Nor are these blacks as dangerous as those who have become familiar with the white man's customs and character.

The men sleep late in the morning, for they do not care to go out before ten or eleven o'clock, when the dew has left the grass. The first task of the women in the morning is to kindle a fire, which is always built at the entrance to the hut, where the family gradually assemble. They seat themselves in the ashes, stretch themselves a long time, and spend half an hour in scraping and scratching their bodies, a favourite occupation when they sit round the fire. When the men are thoroughly awake they reach out for the baskets, which are filled with tobola, kadjera, or perchance with the remnants of a roasted wallaby. What the blacks are unable to eat on the spot is put away, and may be kept for one or two days. Meat is slightly roasted for this purpose, or it may be preserved in water. Then the women and the children go out to gather fruits, while the men proceed on some hunting expedition or to look for honey. Every day, when it does not rain, the Australian must have his hunt; even the natives who are sufficiently civilised to be employed in the native police force feel this necessity so strongly that they occasionally take off their clothes and make an expedition with the tomahawk. When they return in the afternoon the inevitable fires are at once built; some of them lie down to sleep, while others chat a little and wait for the women to come back with fruits. Some one of the old men may go to work at a basket on which he is engaged.

The women come home late in the afternoon, and then have their hands full preparing the poisonous plants, but they never work late in the evening. If they have brought much they leave it until the next day. All now enjoy a *dolce far niente* after the more or less fatiguing work of the day. There is nothing to tax their brains, and they have no cares. They have no concern about the morrow or for the future in general. But few words are spoken. They feel somewhat anxious for their lives when night drops her curtain upon the camp, but gradually the whole family falls asleep, and nothing is heard save the melancholy buzzing of insects in the profound silence of the scrubs.

A little before sundown the next day the old man arrived, accompanied by his two good-looking, well-fed wives. He was one of the oldest men in the tribe and was highly respected. As soon as they entered the camp they seated themselves with crossed legs, but said nothing. When they had rested a while the old man ordered out his wives to find palm leaves for a hut, which was built in a few minutes. To show us that we were welcome, they sent a present, consisting of two large baskets, to our camp, which we had made close by. It was an act of politeness which my blacks expected, and had mentioned to me in advance. The baskets were very nice, in fact admirable specimens of native handiwork (see p. 190).

In this strange tribe there were two little boys who pleased me particularly. They took a deep interest in me and my camp, and they were not afraid to approach me. They were also very accommodating. I was astonished to find them so obliging and kind, but I have since seen other instances of a similar kind. The black children are not, upon the whole, as bad as one might suppose, considering their education, in which their wills are never resisted. The mother is always fond of her child, and I have often admired her patience with it. She constantly carries it with her at first in a basket, but later on, when it is big enough, on her shoulders, where either she supports it with her hand or else the child holds itself fast by its mother's head. Thus she carries it with her till it is several years old. If the child cries she may perhaps get angry, but she will never allow herself to strike it. The children are never chastised either by the father or the mother.

An acquaintance of mine, who had associated extensively with the blacks, once gave a naughty child a box on the ear, at which the mother became very much excited, and said, " There was no use in striking the child. He was only a little fellow, not big enough."

Before the children are big enough to hold a pipe in their mouth they are permitted to smoke, and the mother will share her pipe with the nursing babe.

The children always belong to the tribe of their father, but are fonder of their mother than of their father. When grown up they rarely mention him, in fact oftentimes do not know who he is ; for the women frequently change husbands. The father may also be good to the child, and he frequently carries it, takes it in his lap, pats it, searches its hair, plays with it, and makes little boomerangs which he teaches it to throw. He however, prefers boys to girls, and does not pay much attention to the latter. The children play all day long, build mounds, draw figures in the sand, throw boomerangs, etc.

Thus they grow up in perfect freedom, and are never punished. As soon as they can walk they acquire the manners and habits of their elders, but the boys are not permitted to go hunting with their fathers before they are nine years old. Little boys are treated like grown men, or to speak more correctly, the Australian never becomes a man, the father being in thought and deed as much a child as the son.

When the men are in camp their chief occupation, providing they do not sleep, is to make weapons, and particularly to plait baskets. It was interesting to observe their marvellous skill in this work. Only the men plait baskets—the women never—and they are proud of exhibiting the most beautiful specimens of their handiwork.

The basket varies in size, but the shape is usually the same, more or less oval, narrow at the top and broad at the bottom. The material consists almost exclusively of the branches of the lawyer-palm, which are split with the aid of the teeth into thin slender strings, and these

O

are scraped smooth and even with clam-shells and stones. The baskets are made wonderfully fine and strong, and are often painted with red, yellow, or white ochre, and sometimes with stripes or dots of human blood, which the maker takes from his own arm. The basket is carried by a handle made of the same material, and hangs down the back. The handle is placed against the forehead, so that the weight of the basket rests on the head of the person carrying it, as the blacks do not like to carry anything in their hands.

A BASKET MADE OF SOFT MATERIALS (GRASS) FROM HERBERT RIVER (⅓ size).

We arose early in the morning to hunt the boongary; for we had a long day's march before us to the place where this animal was said to be found in great numbers. I did not expect anybody but the old man and one or two of the blacks to accompany me, but we were joined by the whole tribe, so that we were a large party as we proceeded across the table-land. At noon we discovered in the distance a series of scrub-clad hills rising one above the other, and these we were to reach in the evening. The men and I then took a circuitous route through a scrub, while the women, carrying the provisions and the men's weapons, went directly to the place where we were to pitch our camp for the night. On their journeys the natives seldom carry their provisions with them, but depend for their subsistence on what they can find on the way. They therefore take different routes, not very wide apart, and assemble in the evening in the place agreed upon for a camp, bringing with them the opossums, lizards, eggs, honey, and whatever else they may have collected during the day.

The only result of our march was a considerable amount of honey, which we found near the top of a high tree, which from its character the natives believed to be hollow all the way down to the root. The honey would in that case have fallen to the bottom and been wasted if they had

attempted to gather it in the usual way—by cutting a hole
in the trunk.   They therefore borrowed my axe to fell the
large tree, which was more than three feet in diameter, and
of very hard wood.   They worked very industriously for an
hour and a half, taking turns at chopping down the gigantic
tree, and they did not rest till it fell.   This may serve as
an illustration of the perseverance and energy of the otherwise indolent and lazy Australian native while pursuing any
game that he has discovered.

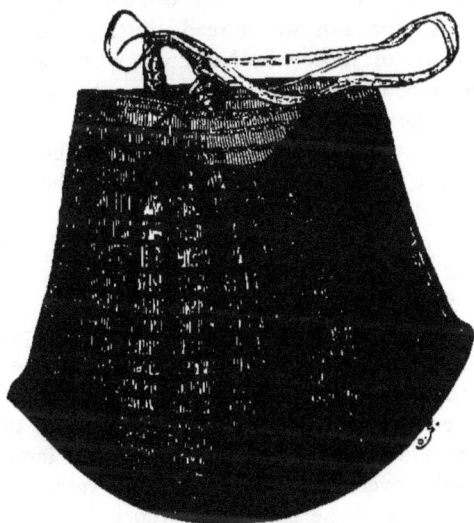

BASKET FROM HERBERT RIVER, PAINTED WITH STRIPES AND DOTS OF
HUMAN BLOOD (¼ size).

They were well rewarded for their trouble.   The great
amount of honey found in this tree astonished me, and
it had a fine flavour and in spite of the excessive heat
was solid and cool.   The natives brought the greater part
of the honey to a brook close by, and not having any trough
at hand, they mixed the old and the new honey with water
in the most primitive manner.   They laid the honey in a
hollow rock near the stream, and scooped water into it with
both hands, afterwards stirring it.   Then they all sat down
round the " flowing bowl," and with tufts of fine grass.
growing near, they soon emptied the hollow rock.

Upon our arrival at the camp the women were sitting on the green grass round a little fire. A strange tribe had come to the camp, who were friendly to my companions. All were as lazy as possible; some lying on their backs, others sitting still and gazing vacantly into space, while a few were engaged in conversation. The women had told the strange tribe about the arrival of the white man, and had of course made great boasts of the tobacco and provisions which he carried with him. They were very proud of having him with their own tribe, but had not made the slightest preparations for building huts nor even gathered palm leaves. As soon as we came the women began to bestir themselves, for the sun was already setting. The strange tribe, and many of those who had come with me, encamped on the one side of the valley, while my men and I pitched our camp on the other side.

It was an excellent locality for hunting the boongary, and not so difficult to penetrate as the scrubs in the mountains. Our semi-wild dingo was utterly useless, and I had no person with me whom it would follow; but I was now accompanied by so large a number of natives that I still looked for good results.

In the scrubs here I shot a very remarkable specimen of a phalanger, which has since been described by the name of *Pseudochirus lemuroides*, because it bears a certain resemblance to the lemurs of Madagascar; its tail is not smooth on the under side, as in the other members of this family, but is nearly entirely covered with hair. In some respects it unites the characteristics of the phalanger proper with the pseudo-chirus, and thus possibly forms a new sub-genus, *Hemibelideus*. The natives call it *yabby*. They first attempted to kill it in the usual way—by climbing the trees and throwing sticks at it. The animal is not very shy, but when disturbed it runs rapidly out upon the branches, so that it is difficult for a native to kill it unless he has one or two of his companions to hinder it escaping on to the neighbouring trees. The natives kill all phalangers in this manner. In order to end the chase the natives shouted to me and asked me to shoot it. It fell from the branch, but remained for a moment suspended by the tail before it dropped down

dead. . When they saw the animal fall from so great
a height they broke out in shouts of wonderment, and this
event was for a long time the leading subject of conversation
among them.   It proved to be a female with a remarkably
large young one, entirely covered with hair, in her pouch.   The
young one, which had also received a fatal shot, was nearly
half the size of its mother.   Although it was midsummer, the
animal had a full coat of hair on its beautiful skin.   I have
found no marsupials of this kind since, and the two above
described are the only specimens that have hitherto been
shot.   The *Pseudochirus lemuroides* is not found in the part
of the Coast Mountains lying east of Gowri Creek.   We
first meet with it in the mountains between Gowri Creek
and Herbert river, and it increases in number as we proceed
toward the north;   these two specimens were shot in a
table-land scrub.

Late one evening, after we, as usual, had encamped on
both sides of the little valley which extended down toward
the river, a shout came from the other camp that hostile
natives were heard in the grass on the other side of the river
from where our camp was situated.   My companions arose at
once and cried *Kolle! mal!*—that is, Hush! man!

I was so accustomed to the imaginary fears of the natives
in the evening that I did not pay much attention to their
alarm, but a few moments later I too thought I heard voices
in the distance.   No sooner had my men discovered my
suspicion than they called over to the other camp, " *Mami*[1]
also hears."   There was now a stillness so profound that a
leaf falling to the ground might have been heard.   For my
part I attributed the suspicious sound to the trees rubbing
against each other in the evening breeze.   My opinion was
at once reported to the other camp; but the natives there
were not to be quieted; they still heard voices, and after a
short time a number of young men, followed by children
crying with all their might, came to me: all were very
much frightened.   I was obliged to rise and fire two shots
in the pitchy darkness of the night; this quieted my men,

---

[1] *Mami*, which means a great man, is the same name as the natives give to
the officers of the native police.   Thus they gave me the highest title of which
they had any knowledge.

and they even expressed their sympathy for their comrades in the other camp, where there reigned the stillness of
death, and where an old man stood guard during the whole
night. From what I afterwards learned I am persuaded
that we had actually heard the voices of a hostile tribe, which
in all probability would have attacked us had I not frightened
them away with my shooting. How little it takes to demon-
strate the superiority of a civilised man over the savage !

I found it useless to remain here any longer. There
were but few traces of boongary to be seen, and the natives
had, during the whole time, evinced little disposition to
hunt them, partly because the animals were so scarce, and
partly because we did not have dogs. My men, however,
had much to say of a more distant " land," where they claimed
there were *komórbory* (many) boongary. They were, however,
afraid to accompany me thither, on account of strange tribes.
Nevertheless I determined to visit this "land," but as not
one of my people would admit that he was acquainted with
it, I had to try to find a guide among natives who had
friends there. This proved to be a far more difficult task than
I had supposed. I offered provisions, I offered tobacco—
but all in vain. All thought it was sheer madness to
attempt to go there, for they were afraid of the strangers
whom they had heard that night.

I tried to make a friend of the old boongary hunter, and
gave him something to eat. Before meeting me he had
tasted neither salt beef nor damper, and he had become
exceedingly fond of both. He ate with a ravenous appetite,
but stubbornly refused to accede to my wishes. After much
parleying I at length succeeded in inducing one of 'them to
go with me by giving him a shirt and the promise of much
tobacco and much food if he procured a boongary. To make
sure of him I gave the old hunter, who had considerable influence over him, a large piece of meat, and requested him
to encourage my new guide to stand by his purpose and go
with me.

The old man kept but a very small piece for himself,
and with the liberality peculiar to the Australian native,
generously distributed the rest in all directions for the purpose of enhancing his influence in the tribe. The Australian

native is by nature lavish, and when he bestows gifts he does it liberally. Thus when a civilised black man returns with his master to the station after a prolonged journey he shows great liberality to his comrades, who then gather round him. His new clothes are freely distributed, and after a few hours one black may be seen wearing his trousers, another his spurs, a third his hat, etc., while he himself frequently retains nothing but the shirt.

The black man whom I had persuaded to go with me was related to one of my men, Yanki. He was Yanki's *Otero* In the tribes the words *otĕro, gorgĕro, gorilla,* and *gorgorilla* are found, which designate various kinds of relations. Sometimes a man would be called *otero* or *gorgero* without the addition of any other name, and still everybody knew who was meant. There are similar words to designate female relatives, in which case the termination *ingan* is substituted for the final *o* or *a*, thus *oteringan, gorgeringan,* etc.

Doubtless these appellations are in some way connected with the matrimonial system of the natives, but I have never been able to get to the bottom of this subject. The natives were either unwilling or unable to give me a satisfactory explanation, while the men, contrary to what has been experienced in other places, made no objections to telling me their own or the women's names, or who was their *otero,* etc. As a rule the members of Australian communities are divided into four classes, and according to the Australian author Mr. E. M. Curr, the object of this division is to prevent the intermarriage of relatives, a thing for which the Australian natives appear to have the greatest abhorrence.

Yanki was exceedingly amiable to his *otero,* and was very happy that he was to be one of my party. Yanki was to share his bed and his tobacco with him, and they were to have a very nice time together. And now the rest of my men were willing to accompany me. Happy at the result, I gave small pieces of meat to those who were not going with me, and we parted the best of friends.

It did not escape my observation that during all these negotiations the blacks kept consulting an old woman. She took a very serious part in the discussion, and gave the most positive advice not to accompany me because *mal* had been

so near to us that night.   The reason why the natives con-
sulted her I do not know.   It may be that she was skilful in
procuring human flesh and other food.   The Australian native
has a certain respect for old women, provided the latter are
not too old to be useful.   The instinct of the blacks for
finding food seems to increase with their years, the fact being,
I suppose, that they have the advantage of experience.   Old
women usually take part in the hunting of human game, and
they even find means of supporting those of their sex who
are too old to leave the camp and seek food for themselves.
Were this not the case the men would certainly soon get
these old women out of the way ; for the Australian does
not hesitate to remove anything which is an obstacle to him.
But these old women are far from being superfluous.   I have
often seen strong young men appeal to them for food, and
their requests have been granted.

As we were proceeding across the grassy plain my men
suddenly shouted, *Boongary! boongary!* and started off after
an animal which disappeared behind a grassy hill.   They
soon returned with empty hands, but they were convinced
that they had seen a boongary.   I expressed my surprise at
its being found on the grassy plain ; but the natives assured
me that it moved about a great deal, and made long journeys
across the table-land from one scrub to the other.

CHAPTER XVI

THE season was already so far advanced that it was out of the question to get back to my headquarters before Christmas. The new "land," which we reached after a short time, presented a grand, wild, and romantic aspect. We descended from the table-land and suddenly got sight of Herbert river, flowing dark and restless far down in the depths below.

We followed the bend of the river to the east, walking on a ledge of the steep mountain nearly a thousand feet above the level of the water. Below us the mountain presented a wild, broken mass, while above it was overgrown with dense scrubs. Near the chief bend of the river we made our camp by the side of a mountain brook which plunged down over the precipice. It was no easy matter to find a place for a camp here, for it was a spot on which a person could scarcely lie in a horizontal position.

The natives had some strange superstitions in regard to this place. In the depths below dwelt a monster, *Yamina*, which ate men, and of which the natives stood in mortal fear. No one dared to sleep down there. Blacks who had attempted to do so had been eaten, and once, when a dance had been held there, some persons had been lost. I proposed to take a walk thither, but they simply shrugged their shoulders and did not answer. A gun would be of no use they said, for the monster was invulnerable.

It was *Kvingan*, their evil spirit, who chiefly haunted this spot. His voice was often heard of an evening or at

night from the abyss or from the scrubs. I made the
discovery that the strange melancholy voice which they
attributed to the spirit belonged to a bird which could be
heard at a very great distance. But I must admit that
it is the most mysterious bird's voice that I have ever
heard, and it is not strange that a people so savage as the
Australian natives should have formed superstitious notions
in regard to it. *Kvingan* is found in the most inaccessible
mountain regions, and I have heard it not only here but
also in the adjoining districts. During these moonlight
nights I tried several times to induce the natives to go
with me to shoot the bird, but it was, of course, blasphemous
to propose such a thing, and their consent was out of the
question.

At other times, when they spoke of their evil spirit, I
found that it manifested itself in a cicada. Their notions in
regard to their evil spirit appeared to be very much confused.
This insect, the cicada, produces in the summer a very shrill
sound in the tree-tops, but it is impossible to discover it by the
sound. It is this loud shrill sound, which comes from every
direction, and which is not to be traced to any particular
place, that has evidently given rise to superstitious ideas
concerning it.

In the south-eastern part of Australia the evil spirit of
the natives is called *Bunjup*, a monster which is believed to
dwell in the lakes. It has of late been supposed that this
is a mammal of considerable size that has not yet been
discovered. It may be added that the devil in various parts
of Australia is described as a monster with countless eyes
and ears, so that he is able to see and hear in all directions.
He has sharp claws, and can run so fast that it is difficult to
escape him. He is cruel, and spares no one either young or
old. The reason that the natives so frequently move their
camp is, no doubt, owing to the fact that they are anxious
to avoid the devil, who constantly discovers where they are.
At times he is supposed to reveal himself to the older
and more experienced men in the tribe, who accordingly
are highly esteemed. The natives on the Gulf of Carpentaria say that the devil's lips are fastened by a string to his
forehead.

With the exception of the instance already described,[1] I never heard of any effort being made by the natives to propitiate the wrath of this evil being. They simply have a superstitious fear of it and of the unknown generally.

We searched the scrubs in the vicinity thoroughly, and found many traces of boongary in the trees, but they were all old. The animal had been ex-terminated by the natives. It could be hunted more easily here, for the reason that the lawyer-palm is rare, and conse-quently the woods are less dense. The natives told me that their "old men" in former times

YELLOW NECKLACE WORN BY THE BLACKS AS AN EMBLEM OF MOURNING.

had killed many boongary in these woods on the table-land.

Two of my men brought to the camp a very large eel, about as thick as a man's arm and very long. They had found it dead, for the sun had dried up the puddle in which it had lived. This was enough to keep me from tasting it; but the blacks were very much excited about it. It was prepared in the same refined manner as the chief delicacies of the natives.

Several of my companions were not old enough to be permitted to enjoy the privilege of tasting it. Others wearing yellow necklaces as an emblem of sorrow were also forbidden to eat of this aristocratic food. These necklaces consist, as above stated, of short-cut pieces of yellow grass strung on a string long enough to go round the neck ten to twelve times. Sometimes they are worn as ornaments by both men and women. While in mourn-ing the Australian natives carefully abstain from certain kinds of food, and it was a surprise to me that they could maintain this fast so well as they did; but at last I found out that the reason for this was a superstitious notion that the forbidden food, if eaten, would burn up their bowels. They are very happy when the season of mourning is ended, and although they have but vague notions of time, they know precisely when they may lay

[1] Page 136.

aside their mourning dress—that is, the yellow necklace.
I have also seen the women paint their bodies with chalk
while they are in mourning. Near Rockhampton the blacks
used to cut themselves with stones or tomahawks; the
women besides paint round their eyes with white chalk.
On the Barcoo I once met two women who had their whole
head plastered over with the same kind of stuff, which they
wear for weeks.

Their sorrow for the dead is not very deep; they chant
their funeral dirge for several evenings, but this is simply
a formal respect paid the deceased. I have many times
heard these melancholy mourning tunes in the silent night.
The same strophe—for example, *Wainta, bémo, bémo, yougool
naiko ?* (Where is my brother's son, the only one I had?)
—was continually repeated. As a rule, the old women
furnished the lamentations.

In the vicinity of Coomooboolaroo in Central Queensland
an old woman exhibited her sorrow at the deathbed of her
husband in a very singular manner. Having made a series
of breakneck somersaults along the ground, she took two
pieces of wood and beat them together in despair. Her
husband died soon afterwards, and in a quarter of an hour
he was buried.

During the days of mourning the deceased is rarely
mentioned, and when the yellow necklace has been laid
aside his name is never heard again. This is doubtless
the reason why the Australian natives have no traditions.
Many of them do not even know their father, and any knowledge of earlier generations is out of the question. Strange
thoughts came to my mind as I walked the scrub paths
which the blacks had trodden with their naked feet for centuries. Here generation had succeeded generation without a
thought in regard to the past, and with no care in reference
to the future, living only for the present moment.

In the evening, after the eel had been consumed, the
natives laid themselves round the fire and enjoyed rest
after the toils of the day. It was late, and I thought my
men were sleeping. The beaming rays of the full moon
illuminated the romantic landscape. Now and then the
silence was broken by the mysterious notes of that singular

night bird, the evil spirit of the natives. Suddenly two of
the natives arose, came to my hut, and said: "We must
depart, a great water will rise here; this is not a good place
to remain in!"

I remained perfectly calm and quiet in my hut, and expressed my contempt for their silly notions. I answered that
they might go if they pleased, but that I would stay where I
was. My opinion was that they would remain with me.
But presently they all got up, and pointing with their open
hands to the two persons who had eaten the eel, they said
that these men best understood the dangers connected with
this place.

The fact was, of course, that they had become ill from
eating the eel, which had died a natural death. They now
cursed the place by spitting in all directions. The others
followed their example, and immediately thereupon they all
proceeded up the mountain slope, spitting all the time. I
hoped they would return, but in this I was disappointed.

At length I came to the conclusion that it would be
best for me to follow them, lest they should leave me
altogether. In that case my situation would be a most
deplorable one; for, although I had abundance of tobacco,
my supply of provisions was very low, and without the aid
of the natives I would be unable to get the necessaries of
life. Game is scarce in this part of the world, and the
vegetables are either uneatable or of very poor quality. All
I had in my possession was a small piece of meat and a
handful or two of flour, scarcely enough for a small damper.

I arose and climbed after them up a grassy and stony
slope extending to the top of the mountain along the scrub.
The moon shone bright and clear, so that it was not difficult
to find the path. I called to them, but they did not answer.
Finally I reached the summit, and there I caught sight of
them. They sat crouched together under a casuarina-tree,
and were utterly speechless. They had actually intended to
run away. But when they heard me calling they decided
to wait, in order that I might join them and go to the
"land" we had left. This place was evidently too full of
Kvingan.

I refused, however, to go, and threatened to return to

Herbert Vale and get the black police to deal with the matter, and they, I said, would hunt them for months and shoot them. On the other hand, I used kind words and promised them much tobacco, the only thing I had left worth mentioning. Without guides I could not, of course, continue my journey. We finally compromised the matter. I agreed that we should all sleep on the summit of the mountain, but, on the other hand, they were to go with me down to the camp to fetch our baggage. Strange to say, they made no objections to this proposition. Their main object was to avoid sleeping down in the valley.

On our return to the camp we found that the dingo had availed himself of the opportunity of stealing the small piece of meat I had left. All agreed that he should suffer for this mischief, but unfortunately he was nowhere to be found.

The next day we came into a wild region abounding in scrubs and declivities. Progress was most difficult, and it was almost impossible to find a place suitable for a camp. *Otero*, who knew the country, conducted us at last to a small flat spot near the upper edge of the scrub. Here there was a little brook, though, upon the whole, water was very scarce in this region. We remained here several days. I had never before seen so many fresh traces of boongary, and the natives did their best to secure specimens of the animal in this terrible locality ; but we had no dog, for the tribes we had visited had none, and the want of dogs was a great misfortune. Still we were not discouraged. It must, however, be admitted that the blacks did not feel perfectly safe in this region : *mal* was not very far away. We could see smoke on the mountains very distinctly, when they burned the grass to hunt the wallaby.

One day, as we were rambling through the scrubs, we heard somebody chopping with an axe in the distance. *Otero* climbed a tree in order to give a signal to the persons chopping, for he was acquainted with the tribe that owned this "land." He shouted at the top of his voice, the chopping ceased, and a shout was heard from the distance.

Otero shouted : *Ngipa ngipa Ka-au-ri !*—that is, I—I [am] Ka-au-ri !

My blacks had already comprehended the situation.

The man whom we had heard chopping was out in search of honey, and from this they at once made up their minds as to where his camp was, for the natives usually have regular places for camping. They also discovered his name, for they knew whose land it was. Where the women of the tribe were, and what they were doing, my men also seemed to know ; for it was the season for harvesting a certain kind of fruit, and they knew where this fruit grew most abundantly.

In other parts of Australia I have seen the people make signals with fires, indicating by the number of columns of smoke in what direction they intended to go, etc. It is said that they can also make themselves understood by the inflection of the words shouted.

It was Christmas Eve, and in honour of the day I had requested my men to do their best to procure me something good to eat. I had promised them twice the usual amount of tobacco if they were successful.

I was sitting all alone by my hut. A strange feeling came over me as I pondered on the fact that it was Christmas Eve, and that I was in the midst of an Australian forest and far away from the borders of civilisation. The summer sun had clad the neighbouring hills with a heavy carpet of green, the gloomy scrubs below had the appearance of a boundless sea, and the sun shone in all its effulgence on the fresh colours. On the summit of the mountain where I was sitting it was somewhat cooler than in the bottom of the valley, where the heat was oppressive. There was not a breath of air stirring, and the entire landscape presented a scene of refreshing repose. In the tree-tops the cicadas vociferously chanted the praises of the midsummer. All was light and cheerful,—if we had only had something to eat !

All I had was a piece of bread ; rather slender fare for Christmas. In the afternoon the natives returned, bringing a few pieces of a rare root called *vondo*, some honey, and a few white larvæ. But the nicest present they brought me was an animal, which I had not seen before. The natives called it *borrogo*. It is a marsupial of a brownish-yellow colour, and about the size of a small cat. My *menu* therefore was : broiled borrogo, a small piece of bread, broiled vondo, and honey mixed with water. The food was not to be complained of, the only trouble being that there was not enough for so many people as we were. I could not help thinking of all the kettles in which delicious rice porridge was now boiling in far-off Norway. What would I not have given for a plate of it!

Thus it will be seen that it is no easy matter to sustain life in the wilds of North Australia, when one has to depend upon what he can find in the woods and on the plains. The fare of the Australian native is not well adapted to the wants of the constitution of a European. The flesh of the marsupials has a sickly taste, while talegallas and pigeons, the best game to be had, are rare. Lizards are not bad, but snakes are dry and tasteless. There are only one or two kinds of fruits or roots that can be eaten with appetite. One of them is the above-mentioned vondo, which grows in sandy soil on the summit of the scrub-clad mountains, has a stem as slender as a thread, and climbs the trees; hence is difficult for any one but a native to find it. A fig called *yanki*, which is yellowish in colour and semi-transparent, has an excellent flavour, but it is so rare that I did not see it more than a single time during my whole sojourn in Northern Queensland. Another variety of fig, *veera*, grows on the grassy plains and is more common.

One evening a dingo came stealing into the camp, and we soon discovered that it was our old runaway rogue who had abused our hospitality in so shameful a manner. The natives eagerly besought me to shoot it, and although I had a faint hope that it might be of some use to me, I finally yielded to their entreaties, and to their great satisfaction made the dingo suffer the penalty of death.

On our march through the scrub I heard *Otero* tell one of his comrades, that in that very place he had once seen a boongary jump from a tree down on the ground and then disappear. He pointed out the tree. This report made me still more eager, but all our exertions were in vain. Meanwhile we secured a few other specimens of Australian fauna, and among them four little flying-squirrels (*Petaurus breviceps*), which we found lying together in a hollow tree.

It was still very difficult to secure a sufficient amount

of food ; and when *Otero* one day suddenly absconded, remaining longer was out of the question, for the others were all strangers in this "land," and hence they felt unsafe and were anxious to get home.

The one who, next after me, had the most cause to be vexed at *Otero's* flight was Yanki, his faithful relative. Yanki had on all occasions devoted himself to his *Otero*—had shared with him his food, his tobacco, and all other good things he had. Despite his innocent looks, *Otero* had now run away, and he had also taken Yanki's shirt with him. His conduct was most disgraceful, and it illustrates how little the Australian blacks are to be depended on.

I persuaded the others to remain here one day longer, and promised them to shoot a wallaby when we reached the grassy plain. But they were of but little service to me after we had lost our guide, and we were obliged to leave, to get something to eat, if for no other reason.

We had to take a zigzag course to reach the bottom of Herbert river valley, so steep was the descent. A rock-wallaby ran across our path and disappeared at once. At noon we passed the great falls of the river, and made a short halt in their vicinity. The surroundings were exceedingly wild and romantic, but I confess I was too hungry to enjoy the imposing scenery. Then we followed the course of the river, and walked as fast as we were able in the high grass. All nature seemed to be fast asleep. We did not see a sign of life as we walked along the bank of the river in the scorching heat of the sun and in the tall grass. The only sound I heard was the roar of the waterfall thundering among the mountains in the distance. It has been said that an Australian landscape breathes melancholy, and the truth of this statement is fully appreciated by a person who, on a day like this, wanders amid these sober, awe-inspiring gum-trees and acacias. One's mind cannot help being overcome by a sense of solitude and desertion.

One or two hours before sunset and early in the morning the wallabies are in the habit of coming out to feed on the grass, and at such times it is not very difficult to get within shooting range of them ; but on this particular evening they were very shy. The few that we got sight of disappeared again, thus frustrating all hopes of getting a good supper that night.

It was late and perfectly dark when we arrived at our old camp, where we had left our horses. I had been prudent enough to save a small piece of bread for myself, and I would have preferred as usual to share it with my men, but it was not enough to divide, and besides, I knew that the natives were able to endure hunger far better than I was.

As they had nothing to eat, I gave them a little tobacco, in order that they might have some comfort ; but they put it away without smoking it, and soon laid themselves down by the fire to sleep the time away—a common habit of the blacks when it, for instance in the wet season, is difficult to secure food to allay their hunger.

We had left the horses in a place enclosed by nature in such a manner that they could not get away. It would, therefore, be an easy matter to find them, provided they had not been killed by the natives during our long absence. There was reason to suspect this, and we were agreeably surprised when, in the darkness of the night, we heard the tinkling of the bell, and the next morning found them all safe and sound.

Before sunrise the next morning Ganindali and I set out to hunt the wallaby, and near the camp we discovered a large number feeding on the grass, and shot two of them. Ganindali brought one to the camp, and asked one of his comrades to fetch the other, while he and the rest began to cook the first. This produced life in the camp! Within two minutes a splendid fire was burning. One of the animals was thrown upon the burning embers, and was turned by its long tail. Ganindali acted as chief cook. When the hair was scorched off the skin, the animal was dragged out of the fire. The belly was opened with a sharp stone, and the entrails were drawn out. Four red-hot stones replaced the bowels, and the animal was placed on the cinders. As soon as it was tolerably well roasted, the blacks attacked it most greedily and tore it into pieces.

Before long they had eaten their fill of the juicy meat ; then they ran down to the river, waded a little way into the stream, and drank from the hollow of their hands. Having quenched their thirst, they returned in a leisurely way to the camp and resumed their eating. Then they sat down round the fire and began lighting their pipes. But they did not want to light their pipes with embers from the fire ; they demanded matches. I did not as a rule give them matches when we sat round a blazing fire, but now, as our journey was nearly at an end, I did not begrudge them the pleasure of lighting their pipes in the same manner as the white man does, and of hearing the crack of a match. Meanwhile I, too, had finished my supper, and the unsavoury kangaroo flesh had a most excellent flavour on this occasion.

CHAPTER XVII

ON our return to Herbert Vale after a month's absence the old keeper gave me an unusually friendly reception. He said he had repeatedly been on the point of sending some blacks to look for me, as he feared I might have been attacked by the natives.

I experienced great satisfaction in being able to sleep comfortably and safely once more.

The next day two natives came down from the mountains and reported that the blacks with two dogs "were killing and eating a lot of boongary up there." The result was that I had to be off again, and I made haste to gather men and provisions ; but the next day, just as we were ready to start, it began to rain. I feared that the rainy season had set in, and in that case it would be impossible to undertake an expedition. The rainy season usually lasts from three to four months, with slight interruptions, in Northern Queensland, generally commencing in January, and we were now at the beginning of this month. After a day or two, however, the rain ceased, and we started on our journey.

Near Herbert Vale I had the good fortune to be able to witness a marriage among the blacks. A camp of natives was just at the point of breaking up, when an old man suddenly approached a woman, seized her by the wrist of her left hand and shouted, *Yongul ngipa !*—that is, This one belongs to me (literally " one I "). She resisted with feet and hands, and cried, but he dragged her off, though she made resistance during the whole time and cried at the top of her voice.   For a mile away we could hear her shrieks. I jokingly asked some of my men if they did not want to help her, but they simply laughed at me.   There had long been gossip about this match.   What was now happening was simply the public declaration of the marriage, and there are no other wedding ceremonies.   In this instance the match was a very appropriate one.   He was a widower, she a widow.   But the women always make resistance, for they do not like to leave their tribe, and in many instances they have the best of reasons for kicking their lovers.   If a man thinks he is strong enough, he will take hold of any woman's hand and utter his *yongul ngipa*.   If a woman is good-looking, all the men want her, and the one who is most influential, or who is the strongest, is accordingly generally the victor.   Thus she may happen to change husbands many times in her life, but sometimes, despite the fact that her consent is not asked, she gets the one she loves— for a black woman can love too,—and then she is very happy.   It not infrequently happens that women elope with men whom they love.   The black women are also capable of being jealous, and they often have bitter quarrels about men whom they love and are anxious to marry.   If the husband is unfaithful, the wife frequently becomes greatly enraged.   However fond a man and his wife may be of each other, they are never known to kiss each other.

The women are more fond of a handsome face than of a good figure, though they do not despise the latter.   They take particular notice of the part of the face about the eyes, and they like to see a frank and open, or perhaps more correctly a wild, expression of the countenance.   They pay but little attention to a man's size.

That these blacks also may be greatly overcome by the sentiment of love is illustrated by the following incident.   A "civilised" black man entered a station on Georgina river and carried off a woman who belonged to a young black man at the station.   She loved her paramour and was glad to get away from the station ; but the whites desired to keep her for their black servant, as he could not be made to stay without her, and they brought her back, threatening to shoot the stranger if he came again. Heedless of the threat, he afterwards made a second attempt to elope with his beloved, but the white men pursued the couple and shot the poor fellow.

Our first camp was in a valley far up in the mountains, where we fell in with some blacks, who had just killed a very young ornithorhynchus in a brook which falls into Herbert river, and here we left our horses.

The next day as we proceeded up the valley we met two natives, who had taken part in the boongary hunt which had been reported to me. My men informed me that these two men owned one of the dogs that had been used in the chase and it was therefore of importance to secure the attendance of both the men and the dog. The one remained half concealed behind a gum-tree, but kept peeping out and laughing the whole time, while the other man stood perfectly quiet by his side. Apparently they had never before seen a white man in this part of the country, and could not comprehend what business I had there. I offered them food and tobacco, and asked if they would not take their dog and come with me. They seemed to be very anxious to do so, this being particularly the case with the one who stood behind the tree. His name was Yokkai. Although the dog was with a tribe far away, they offered to go and fetch it and join me as soon as possible, so we agreed to meet on the top of the mountain.

After a few hours' march we came to a little tribe camping near the foot of the mountain where we hoped to find the other dog. But after the hunt the tribe had scattered in various directions, and I was consequently unable to secure many men. We encamped in the evening far up in the mountain, in order to wait for the two men with the dogs. As the weather was clear, the natives put up a hut for me alone. The strangers, who were perfectly savage, looked at my baggage with the greatest curiosity, and watched every motion of mine with intense interest.

Up here I saw several nests of the beautiful king-pigeon (*Megaloprepia magnifica*). The nest is built near the outer end of a branch, and according to the habit of the pigeons, it is constructed very carelessly, consisting simply of a few sticks. I never found more than one egg in these nests. How the young keep from falling down when the wind blows is a mystery to me. The natives, who are fond of eating them, generally shake them down.

On the summit of the mountain there were also talegallas in great numbers. My men found several of their nests, and dug out a considerable number of eggs from the large mounds. While the result of my hunt was of but little consequence, the natives were perfectly happy, and burst out in shouts of joy every time they found talegalla eggs. Once or twice we stopped to rest, and then they fairly gorged themselves with these large eggs.' One man consumed fourteen of them in two hours, and yet he felt no inconvenience therefrom. It was a feast day for my men.

In the course of the day Willy procured me an unusually large specimen of mongan (*Pseudochirus herbertensis*), full grown, black as coal, with a bright white breast and white shoulders. He was proud of his conquest, and expected a fine lot of tobacco. Though I was very anxious to secure the specimen, still I told him to keep it, for I wanted to make it plain that it was boongary I was in search of.

I soon made up my mind that these big eaters were of no use to me, and I therefore resolved to go to another tribe to find men who could be of service to me. On my way I met the two natives with the dog. They had put on their best clothes. One of them strutted about in a shirt, the other wore a woman's hat. Articles of clothing are precious ornaments in the eyes of the blacks, and they pass from one tribe to another, from the more " civilised," who dwell near the settlers, to the savages who have never come in contact with the white man. Ere long the hat was borrowed by my men, and several of them sported this emblem of civilisation. One of them presented a most comical figure as he strutted before me and perspired *in puris naturalibus,* with my gun on his shoulders and the woman's hat aslant on his head. I could not help thinking of all the experiences of this hat on its long and eventful journey from its original white owner to these savages in the mountains.

When we came down to the camp of the strange tribe, Willy's game was to be prepared. It vexed me to see the beautiful skin scorched over the fire, for it deserved a better fate, but this could not be helped.

I still had difficulties in securing people to assist me. In addition to the two who owned the dog, I secured only four for the continuation of the journey. Willy, who was well acquainted with the "land" we were to visit, could not be persuaded to go with us. Another person whom I had positively counted on also failed me. He and I had gone out in the morning in order to find the horses and ride them home, but when we dismounted he declared that he was unable either to walk or ride any farther, and so refused to continue the journey. I became vexed at this ridiculous excuse, but his comrades took his side and assured me that he was wholly unable to take part in the expedition. The blacks doubtless suffer less pain from wounds or scratches than we do, but they are utterly lacking in endurance and in patience, and if one of them has a crack in the skin of his toe, he is the object of everybody's sympathy and remains at home in the camp.

By an insignificant circumstance like this I lost another man, so that there were only five of us when we started. After a journey of two days we reached the summit of our hunting district, where we made our camp. The natives were not able to find their bearings. The only exception was Mangola-Maggi, who had twice before been with me on similar expeditions. He was not, however, an ideal man, but a lazy cunning fellow, whose highest ambition was to consume my provisions. Not only, therefore, was his acquaintance with the country of no advantage to me, but on the contrary he demoralised the others, who were lazy and silent, and utterly indifferent to the things that interested me. It may be, too, that they stood in more or less fear of the white man. Nor could they understand why a man should travel so far and have so much trouble for the sake of a boongary. The dog kept faithfully in the footsteps of its master and did not care to chase the game.

It was also a source of great annoyance to me that I did not have suitable shoes. My shoes were worn out, and the soles fell off, so that I was obliged to stop several times and tie them on with bark strips of the lawyer-palm.

The next day I sent two of the blacks away to look after the poisoned pieces of meat, which I had laid in various places for the yarri. I showed them a lot of tobacco, which I said I would give them if they came back with any game. Having been assured again and again that the other dog, "Balnglan," which had been mentioned to me, was the only one fit to be used, I resolved to send two other blacks to fetch it. I gave them a lot of meat and damper, and promised them more if they brought the dog. I showed them my whole store of provisions, in order to make sure of their return.

Thus I was now left alone with only one of the blacks in the midst of the dense scrubs. It was Yokkai, the above-named owner of our dog. We spent the day in rambling about waiting for the return of the others. Yokkai gathered fruits and I shot a talegalla, but on our return in the evening the camp was still deserted, not even those who went to look after the poisoned meat having returned.

In the evening Yokkai prepared tobola, and ate with all his might. I also ate half a dozen roasted kernels, but I neglected to beat them before doing so. An hour afterwards I was sick and chilly, and felt very ill. I feared I had taken malarial fever, but Yokkai at once understood that the cause of my indisposition was the fact that I had eaten the tobola without beating it. He was right, and the next morning I was well again.

The four men did not return the next day, and so I was forced to the conclusion that they had deserted me. The atmosphere was clear and hot, but heavy and oppressive. Not a leaf was seen to stir, and the only sound that came to my ears was the monotonous, melancholy humming of the cicadas in the tree-tops, a sound that only served to increase the sense of desolation. The only rational being near me was Yokkai, but it was very difficult to make ourselves understood to each other; besides, he was still more or less timid. It surprised me that he, too, did not find an opportunity of stealing away. Evidently he was not sufficiently well acquainted with these regions.

He was a well-built man, but not strong, with something almost feminine in his looks. His forehead was very low and receding, still less so than the average foreheads of the blacks. For a black man, he had uncommonly beautiful eyes; hazel-brown and clear, with long eyelashes, but at times when the light fell on them in a certain way they had a bluish tinge. His nose had an upward tendency, and bore the marks of having once been broken. There were distinct scars on the rest of his body. He spoke a different dialect from that of the other blacks of Herbert Vale.

We waited and waited. Alone we could do nothing. I did not even dare use my gun, for Yokkai might get frightened and run away.

When it became dark I had given up all hopes of my men returning. I was left to my fate on the summit of a steep mountain difficult of access, surrounded on all sides by dense scrubs, and thus shut out from the world. The damp air, like that of a cellar, streamed in upon me in the inky darkness. The only light I had came from my camp fire, and this illuminated Yokkai's despairing face. If he, too, deserted me, I should have to climb down the rocks alone with my gun.

I went into my hut and tried to sleep. I then observed that my tomahawk was not in its place, and I asked Yokkai, who had borrowed it during the day, where he had put it. He did not know, and began to look for it. After he had searched for it everywhere, both in-doors and out-of-doors, and after I had given up all hopes of getting it back, he suddenly, to my great surprise, found it in his own hut. This was rather suspicious, and I scarcely knew what to make of it. Perhaps I misjudged Yokkai, but I feared that my provisions—a large bag of meat—were a greater temptation than he could bear, and I was well aware that the Australian natives do not hesitate to sacrifice the life of a man to satisfy their desires. Meanwhile I concealed the tomahawk, and decided to rise early the next morning and watch him so that he might not run away.

I slept quietly that night, and rose early the next morning, and then waked my companion, whereupon we at once got ready for the descent. I promised him plenty of food and tobacco if he would assist me in carrying my baggage. Strange to say, he agreed to this, and he helped me faithfully during the whole day.

During this difficult descent I discovered that Yokkai was no common black man, and before I reached my head-quarters I had formed a very high opinion of him. From that time he was my constant companion until I left Herbert river, and during these many months he was of great help and service to me ; nay, he even saved my life several times, and he was at all times faithful and devoted to me. Still I could not place full confidence even in him, and I was always obliged to be cautious in regard to him ; for he had a flighty temperament, and I was not sure but that his black companions might at any time persuade him to betray me, and find some opportunity of taking my life.

Yokkai was not so lazy as the other blacks with whom I had had to deal. Upon the whole, though active and lively, and far more frank and emotional than the other natives, he was cunning and had a perception quick as light-ning and a good understanding. When I asked him to do anything, he never grumbled, but was attentive and helpful, and frequently did things without being asked to do them.

He thought the descent proceeded rather slowly, and repeatedly urged me to quicken my steps or we would not reach the foot of the mountain before night. But the march was a severe one. I frequently had to crawl on my hands and feet and drag the baggage after me. Add to this, that my boots were in the worst possible condition. Yokkai was now and then obliged to find strips of bark with which to fasten the soles on. If we waded across a river I had at least this advantage, that the water ran out of my boots as fast as it came into them. Sometimes leeches would creep in through the holes in my socks and fasten themselves between my toes.

A short time before sunset we reached the foot of the mountain, and having rested there, we finally arrived at the station in safety.

The rainy season had set in, but much rain had not yet fallen. Meanwhile wet weather might be looked for any day. It was, therefore, impossible to think of undertaking long expeditions. We might run the risk of finding our return cut off, for the heavy rains make the rivers utterly impassable. During this season the blacks stay on the grassy plains, and are unwilling to visit the scrubs. The animals, and all nature for that matter, were now one scene of restlessness. It was evident that we were in the transition between two seasons. The birds of passage had nested, or hatched their young, and were only waiting for cooler weather to start for the north. The Torres-Strait pigeons (*Carpophaga spilorrhoa*) were now very numerous, and had nests everywhere in the trees.

During the expeditions I made in the neighbourhood of the station I succeeded in securing a number of interesting specimens for my collection. I also shot a snipe and a white kite of the same kind as that which I secured in Western Queensland (*Elanus axillaris*). The blacks brought me a fine specimen of the beautiful black and white *ngalloa* (*Dactylopsila trivirgata*), which is as fond of honey as the natives themselves. This rare animal, which also occurs in New Guinea, is not found south of Herbert river.

I gathered several beautiful beetles both in the trees and in the grass. Thus I found in the grass near Herbert river, near the end of December 1882, a beautiful beetle, a *Stigmodera* (see coloured plate), which is new to science. The head and the under side of the body are of a metallic green; the thorax is nearly a purple-blue. The wing-cases are yellow a little more than one-third from the base; the rest is dark blue with a red band about a third of the distance from the point, the band being narrowest at the centre. Underneath, the body has five yellow spots on each side. The length of the beetle is one inch. I would suggest that it be denominated *Stigmodera alternata*.

One day I observed a peculiarity of conduct, which shows what respect the natives may have for the relations of their wives. I was walking with one of my men in the scrub, when we discovered thousands of flying-foxes (*Pteropus*) hanging down in long strings from the branches. My companion urged me to shoot some of these animals for him, though I had no use for them and did not care to frighten the game I was pursuing; but he persisted in his request, and explained to me what a delicate morsel these animals would be for him, especially now, as he was so hungry. At length I yielded to his requests and shot three of the flying-foxes. On our way home we met an old man who was returning from the chase, and my companion surprised me by immediately throwing the three animals to the old man, who was exceedingly glad to get them. To my question why he did not himself keep what I had shot for him, he replied that the stranger was his wife's uncle. Though himself hungry, he wanted to show magnanimity to his uncle, from whom he had received his wife, and he was anxious to give some proof of the gratitude he owed him. This young man had not stolen his wife, nor did he have any sister or daughter to give in exchange. He must, therefore, have obtained her in some other way. I have reasons for believing that certain peculiar laws exist, known only to the blacks, according to which women even from their birth are intended for certain men. The man who has obtained a wife in this manner shows his gratitude to her relatives by gifts of food, tobacco, and other things.

The weather continued to grow more variable, and in the evenings we frequently had heavy thunderstorms. At Herbert Vale everything was quiet as usual. The only change I observed was that the natives about the station had become much more bold than they were before. They entered everywhere, stole potatoes from the garden and meat from the kitchen. They usually stole into the kitchen in the twilight of the evening, and there took what they could find.

One evening we caught in the kitchen a half-tame opossum (*Ir. vulpecula*). It made the most violent resistance, and wanted to get away from us. One of the blacks then offered to quiet it. He seized it with one hand and held it close to him, while with the other hand he gathered perspiration from his armpits and rubbed it on the nose of the opossum. This did not, however, seem to do any good, for the animal was as wild as ever. I take this opportunity of remarking that the civilised blacks have a remarkable talent for gaining the goodwill of the domestic animals of Europe, especially of horses. No matter how wild and unmanageable a horse may be, they make it so gentle that a white man will scarcely care to ride so dull a beast. More than once did I get vexed at Nelly for spoiling my dog ; for she used to take it into her lap to hunt fleas, and would keep it on her knees by the hour and eat the fleas she found.

During my sojourn at Herbert Vale a woman offered to sell me a bird, which she had deprived of the power of flight by plucking out the feathers of the wings and tail. She laughed at and was merry over the poor bird, which was unable to fly away. The natives may often appear cruel toward animals and birds, though it is not their intention to give pain to the game they capture. It amuses them to see maimed animals making desperate efforts to get away. As a rule they kill the animal at once, not for the purpose of relieving it from pain, but simply to make sure of their game. On many occasions I observed how the blacks amused themselves by watching kangaroos whose hind legs had been maimed struggling in vain to get away.

Any studied cruelty toward the white men is out of the question. They do not, like the Indians, use torture, for they are anxious to take the life of their enemies as quickly as possible.

Cicada aurora.

CHAPTER XVIII

THE blacks had for several days been talking about a dance to be held in a remote valley.

A tribe had learned a new song and new dances, and was going to make an exhibition of what it had learned to a number of people. The Herbert Vale tribe had received a special invitation to be present, and the natives assured me that there would be great fun. My action was determined by the fact that Nilgŏra, who owned the splendid dog "Balnglan," already mentioned, would be there. But I had my misgivings on account of the horses, for as we were in the midst of the rainy season, I ran some risk of not being able to bring them back again.

Early one morning we set out, a large party of men, women, and children. A short time before reaching our destination we were met by a number of natives, for they expected us that night. Some of the strangers were old acquaintances of my people, but this fact was not noticeable, for they exchanged no greetings. In fact an Australian native does not know what it is to extend a greeting. When two acquaintances meet, they act like total strangers, and do not even say " good-day " to each other. Nor do they shake hands. After they have been together for some time they show the first signs of joy over their meeting.

If a black man desires to show how glad he is to meet his old friend, he sits down, takes his friend's head into his lap, and begins to look for the countless little animals that annoy the natives, and which they are fond of eating. When the one has had his head cleaned in this manner, the two change places, and the other is treated with the same politeness. I accustomed myself to many of the habits of the natives during my sojourn among these children of nature, but this revolting operation, I confess, was a great annoyance to me. A more emphatic sign of joy at meeting again is given by uttering shrieks of lamentation on account of the arrival of strangers to the camp. I was frequently surprised at hearing shrieks of this sort in the evenings, and found upon examination that they were uttered in honour of some stranger who had arrived in the course of the day. This peculiar salutation did not last more than a few moments, but was repeated several evenings in succession during the visit of the stranger. The highest token of joy on such occasions is shown by cutting their bodies in some way or other.

Later in the afternoon we arrived in the valley where the dance was to be. Those who were to take part in the dance had already been encamped there for several days. We had also taken time by the forelock, for the festivities were not to begin before the next evening. Several new arrivals were expected in the course of the next day, among them Nilgora. A proposition was made that two men should be sent to meet him on the mountain and request him to look for boongary on the way down, and early the next morning before sunrise they actually started after being supplied with a little tobacco.

My men and I had encamped about 200 paces from the others. I made a larger and more substantial hut than was my usual custom. It did not reach higher than my chest, but the roof was made very thick and tight on account of the rain. At first the blacks were very timid, but gradually the bravest ones among them began to approach my hut. As was their wont, they examined everything with the greatest curiosity. Yokkai walked about in the most conscious manner possible, and assumed an air of knowing everything. He brought water from the brook, put the tin pail over the fire, and accompanied by one or two admirers, went down to the brook to wash the salt out of some salt beef which was to be boiled. The matches, the great amount of tobacco, my pocket handkerchief, my clothes, and my boots,—all made the deepest impression upon the savages. After unpacking, a newspaper was left on the ground. One of the natives sat down and put it over his shoulders like a shawl, examining himself to see how he looked in it; but when he noticed the flimsy nature of the material, he carelessly let it slip down upon the ground again.

My white woollen blanket provoked their greatest admiration, which they expressed by smacking with their tongues, and exclaiming in ecstasy: *Tamin, tamin!*—that is, Fat, fat! The idea of "excellent" is expressed by the natives, as in certain European languages, by the word "fat."

It is an interesting fact that, much as the civilised Australian blacks like fat, they can never be persuaded to eat pork. "There is too much devil in it," they say.

At noon I heard continuous lamentations, but as I supposed they were for some one deceased, I paid but little attention to them at first. Lamentations for the dead, however, usually take place in the evening, and so I decided to go and find out what was going on. Outside of a hut I found an old woman in the most miserable plight. She had torn and scratched her body with a sharp stone, so that the blood was running and became blended with the tears, which were flowing down her cheeks as she sobbed aloud.

Uncertain as to the cause of all this lamentation, I entered the hut, and there I found a strong young woman, lying half on her back and half on her side, playing with a child. I approached her. She turned her handsome face toward me, and showed me a pair of roguish eyes and teeth as white as snow, a very pleasing but utterly incomprehensible contrast to the pitiful scene outside. I learned that the young woman inside was a daughter of the old woman, who had not seen her child for a long time, and now gave expression to her joy in this singular manner. I expressed my surprise that the old woman's face did not beam with joy, but this seemed to be strange language to them. These children of nature must howl when they desire to express deep feeling.

Night was approaching, the sun was already setting behind the horizon, the air was very hot and oppressive, and

Q

it was evident that there would soon be a thunderstorm. The blacks sat at home in their huts or sauntered lazily from place to place, waiting until it became cool enough for the dance to begin. I had just eaten my dinner, and was enjoying the shade in my hut, while my men were lying round about smoking their pipes, when there was suddenly heard a shout from the camp of the natives. My companions rose, turned their faces toward the mountain, and shouted, *Boongary, boongary!* A few black men were seen coming out of the woods and down the green slope as fast as their legs could carry them. One of them had a large dark animal on his back.

Was it truly a boongary? I soon caught sight of the dog " Balnglan " running in advance and followed by Nilgora, a tall powerful man.

The dark animal was thrown on the ground at my feet, but none of the blacks spoke a word. They simply stood waiting for presents from me.

At last, then, I had a boongary, which I had been seeking so long. It is not necessary to describe my joy at having this animal, hitherto a stranger to science, at my feet. Of course I did not forget the natives who had brought me so great a prize. To Nilgora I gave a shirt, to the man who had carried the boongary, a handkerchief, and to all, food. Nor did I omit to distribute tobacco.

I at once began to skin the animal, but first I had to loosen the withies with which its legs had been tied for the men to carry it. The ends of these withies or bands rested against the man's forehead, while the animal hung down his back, so that, as is customary among the Australians, the whole weight rested on his head.

I at once saw that it was a tree-kangaroo (*Dendrolagus*). It was very large, but still I had expected to find a larger animal, for according to the statements of the natives, a full-grown specimen was larger than a wallaby—that is to say, about the size of a sheep. This one proved to be a young male.

The tree-kangaroo is without comparison a better proportioned animal than the common kangaroo. The fore-feet, which are nearly as perfectly developed as the hind-feet,

have large crooked claws, while the hind-feet are somewhat like those of a kangaroo, though not so powerful.   The
sole of the foot is somewhat broader and more elastic, on
account of a thick layer of fat under the skin.   In soft ground
its footprints are very similar to those of a child.   The ears
are small and erect, and the tail is as long as the body of
the animal.   The skin is tough, and the fur is very strong
and beautiful.   The colour of the male is a yellowish-brown,
that of the female and of the young is grayish, but the head,
the feet, and the under side of the tail are black.   Thus it
will be seen that this tree-kangaroo is more variegated
in colour than those species which are found in New
Guinea.

Upon the whole, the boongary is the most beautiful
mammal I have seen in Australia.   It is a marsupial, and
goes out only in the night.   During the day it sleeps in the
trees, and feeds on the leaves.   It is able to jump down
from a great height and can run fast on the ground.   So
far as my observation goes, it seems to live exclusively in
one very lofty kind of tree, which is very common on the
Coast Mountains, but of which I do not know the name.
During rainy weather the boongary prefers the young low
trees, and always frequents the most rocky and inaccessible
localities.   It always stays near the summit of the mountains, and frequently far from water, and hence the natives
assured me that it never went down to drink.

During the hot season it is much bothered with flies,
and then, in accordance with statements made to me by the
savages, it is discovered by the sound of the blow by which
it kills the fly.   In the night, they say, the boongary can be
heard walking in the trees.

I had finished skinning the animal, and so I put a lot of
arsenic on the skin and laid it away to dry in the roof of
my hut, where I thought it would be safe, and placed the
skin there in such a way that it was protected on all sides.

Meanwhile my men had gone down to witness the dance.
Happy over my day's success I too decided to go thither
and amuse myself, but before I had prepared the skin with
arsenic and could get away, darkness had already set in, and
the dancing was postponed until the moon was up.   The

natives had in the meantime retired to their camps until the dance was to begin again.

The tribe that was to give the dance had its camp farthest away, while the other tribes, who were simply spectators, had made their camps near mine. There was lively conversation among the huts. All were seated round the camp fires and had nothing to do, the women with their children in their laps, and those who had pipes smoking tobacco. I went from one group to the other and chatted with them ; they liked to talk with me, for they invariably expected me to give them tobacco. Occasions like this are valuable for obtaining information from the natives. Still, it is difficult to get any trustworthy facts, for they are great liars, not to mention their tendency to exaggerate greatly when they attempt to describe anything. Besides, they have no patience to be examined, and they do not like to be asked the same thing twice. It takes time to learn to understand whether they are telling the truth or not, and how to coax information out of them. The best way is to mention the thing you want to know in the most indifferent manner possible. The best information is secured by paying attention to their own conversations. If you ask them questions, they simply try to guess what answers you would like, and then they give such responses as they think will please you. This is the reason why so many have been deceived by the savages, and this is the source of all the absurd stories about the Australian blacks.

Among the huts the camp fires were burning, and outside of the camp it was dark as pitch, so that the figures of the natives were drawn like silhouette pictures in fantastic groups against the dark background.

It amused me to make these visits, but my thoughts were chiefly occupied with the great event of the day. In the camp there were several dingoes, and although the boongary skin was carefully put away, I did not feel perfectly safe in regard to it. I therefore returned at once to look after my treasure ; I stepped quickly into my hut, and thrust my hand in among the leaves to see whether the skin was safe ; but imagine my dismay when I found that it was gone.

I was perfectly shocked. Who could have taken the

skin? I at once called the blacks, among whom the news spread like wild-fire, and after looking for a short time one of them came running with a torn skin, which he had found outside the camp. The whole head, a part of the tail and legs, were eaten. It was my poor boongary skin that one of the dingoes had stolen and abused in this manner. I had no better place to put it, so I laid it back again in the same part of the roof, and then, sad and dejected in spirits, I sauntered down to the natives again.

Here every one tried to convince me that it was not *his* dog that was the culprit. All the dogs were produced, and each owner kept striking his dog's belly to show that it was empty, in his eagerness to prove its innocence. Finally a half-grown cur was produced. The owner laid it on its back, seized it by the belly once or twice, and exclaimed, *Ammery, ammery!*—that is, Hungry, hungry! But his abuse of the dog soon acted as an emetic, and presently a mass of skin-rags was strewed on the ground in front of it.

My first impulse was to gather them up, but they were chewed so fine that they were useless. As the skin had been thoroughly prepared with arsenic, it was of importance to me to save the life of the dog, otherwise I would never again be able to borrow another.

Besides, I had a rare opportunity of increasing the respect of the natives for me. I told them that the dog had eaten *kóla*—that is, wrath—as they called poison, and as my men had gradually learned to look at it with great awe, it would elevate me in their eyes if I could save the life of the dog. I made haste to mix tobacco and water. This I poured into the dog, and thus caused it to vomit up the remainder of the poisoned skin. The life of the dog was saved, and all joined in the loudest praises of what I had done. They promised me the loan of " Balnglan " again, and thus I had hopes of securing another boongary; of course they added as a condition that I must give them a lot of tobacco.

The next morning early I persuaded them to get ready for the chase, but they did not want me to go with them, as the dog was afraid of the white man.

Most of the blacks remained to witness the dance, for

the camp was in a festive mood, and in the morning before
daylight I was awakened by the noise.   As soon as the
weather became hot, they again gathered in groups under
the shady trees, where they chatted in idleness until it
became cool enough to dance again in the evening.   I
went from one group to the other.   They asked me to give
them European names, a request often made to me on my
journeys among the tribes.   The reason appeared to be that
the savage blacks, who had not been in contact with the
white man, were anxious to acquire this first mark of
civilisation, which they found among my men, and which
they imagined brought tobacco and other gifts.   Among
themselves these savage natives kept their own names, which,
as a rule, are taken for both men and women from animals,
birds, etc.   The father will under no circumstances give his
son his own name.

I gave them various Norwegian names.   It was difficult
for them to pronounce some of them, but such names as
Ragna, Inga, Harald, Ola, Eivind, etc., became very popular.

One of the natives came to me and asked for some salt
beef, giving as an excuse that he had a pain in his
stomach, because he had for a long time eaten nothing but
tobola, the main food of the natives during about two months
of the year.   This fruit, which grows in the scrubs on the
mountain tops, is of a bluish colour, and of the size of a plum.
The tree is very large and has long spreading branches, so
that the natives prefer waiting until the fruit falls on the
ground to climbing the trees for it.   It is gathered by the
women and brought to the camp, where it is roasted over
the fire until the flesh is entirely burnt off and the kernel is
thoroughly done.   The shell round the kernel then becomes
so brittle that it is easily peeled off.   Then the kernels are
beaten between two flat stones until they form a mass like
paste.   When they have been beaten thoroughly in this
manner, they are placed in baskets and set in the brook to
be washed out; and the day after they are fit to be eaten.
The paste, which is white as chalk and contains much water,
looks inviting, but is wellnigh tasteless.   The blacks eat this
porridge with their hands, which they half close into the form
of a spoon.   This food is certainly very unwholesome, for the

natives, who, by the way, are very fond of it, often complained
that they did not feel well after eating it for some time.
The amount of nourishment in tobola is very small, and the
natives eat a very large amount before they satisfy their
hunger, a fact which, in connection with its indigestible
character, cannot fail to produce harm. I have often wondered how they can preserve their health so well as they do,
considering all the unwholesome and indigestible vegetable
food they consume, and the great lack of variety. It is even
more surprising that they have found out that there is any
nourishment at all in the poisonous plants, which they know
how to prepare, and which at the very outset would appear
to be unfit for human food. It is also an interesting fact
that different poisonous plants, or plants not fit to be eaten
raw, are used in different parts of Australia and prepared by
one tribe in a manner of which another tribe has no knowledge.

On my visits to the huts I met Chinaman, who had
deserted me in so disgraceful a manner and ruined my whole
expedition. He now imagined that all was forgotten. After
a month the blacks think no insult is remembered, not even
a murder. Chinaman tried to be polite, but I kept him at
a respectable distance in order to show the blacks that I did
not tolerate such conduct as that of which he was guilty.

Late in the afternoon we were overtaken as usual by a
heavy thunderstorm. One flash of lightning followed the
other in rapid succession. The thunder-claps were echoed
back from the steep mountain walls, and I expected the trees
around us would be struck by lightning every moment.
The natives, however, were not afraid. At every flash of
lightning they shouted with all their might and laughed
heartily. It was a great amusement to them.

At sunset, just as the dance was to begin, Nilgora and
his companions returned from their hunt, and to my great
satisfaction they brought with them another boongary. This
was also a male, but somewhat smaller than the one I had
lost. On its back it had distinct marks of "Balnglan's"
teeth. As I have since learned, this animal is hunted in the
following manner :

The chase begins early in the morning, while the scent

of the boongary's footprints is still fresh on the ground. The dog takes his time, stops now and then, and examines the ground carefully with his nose. Its master keeps continually urging it on, and addresses it in the following manner : *Tshe'—tshe'—gangary pul—pulka—tshe', pul—tshinscherri dundun—mormango—tshe', pul—pulka !* etc.— that is, *Tshe'—tshe'—tshe'*, smell boongary—smell him—*tshe'*, smell—seize him by the legs—smart fellow—*tshe'*, smell—smell him, etc. If the dog finds the scent, it will pursue it to the tree which the animal has climbed. Then some of the natives climb the surrounding trees to keep it from escaping, while another person, armed with a stick, ascends the tree where the animal is. He either seizes the animal by the tail and crushes its head with the stick, or he compels it to jump down, where the dingo stands ready to kill it.

In the evening, when I came down to the blacks, who were waiting for the moon to give light to the dancers, my men expressed a fear that strange tribes would attack the camp in the course of the night. I ridiculed this fear, now that they were assembled in such numbers, but they replied that the strangers also were numerous, and they would not be at rest until I had fired a shot.

Thereupon a few persons came in great haste to the blacks with whom I was talking, from the camp of the dancers, who had evidently been frightened by the shot, and explained that they would like to talk with me, and asked me to go with them, so we all went to the dancers, where all was excitement ; everybody was talking at the same time, but when I came nearer I could catch in the midst of the confusion such words as *kóla* (anger), *nili* (young girl), *Kélanmi Mamigo*[1] (Kélanmi shall belong to Mami). One of my men explained to me : The blacks wish to give you a *nili*. They are afraid of the baby of the gun ! "Very well," I answered, "bring her to my hut."

The blacks had become afraid of me, having interpreted the shot I fired as a sign that I was angry, and to propitiate me they wished to give me Kélanmi, a young girl, who was

---

[1] *Go* is a suffix, which means with reference to ; thus literally, Kélanmi with reference to Mami—that is, me.

looked upon as the prettiest woman in the whole tribe.

KÉLANMI.

When I agreed to accept her they became quiet and their fears were allayed.

Evidently Kélanmi was afraid of the white man, and
was reluctant to leave her tribe ; when I went away I heard
them scold her and try to force her to go to the white man.
I learned that she was, in fact, promised to one of the blacks,
by name Kāl-Dúbbaroh, and so I asked him to go with her
to my hut.   I kindled a fire in my hut, and waited for them
to come with Kélanmi.   The moon was just rising, so that I
was able to discern the dark figures approaching me, but at
first I saw no *nili*, as she was walking behind one of the men,
who held her by the wrist.   She made no resistance, and
came willingly.   When the party reached my hut the men let
go of the girl, but said nothing, and I asked her to sit down.
She was a young and tolerably handsome girl about twelve
years old, with a good figure, and was clad in her finest attire
in honour of the dance, both her face and her whole body
being pretty well covered with red ochre.   She was very much
opposed to getting married, particularly to a white man, and
sat trembling by the fire, awaiting the orders of her new
master.   To quiet her, I at once got some bread and beef,
but she concealed it, out of fear of the bystanders, for such
delicacies are too good for a woman.   Then I gave her a
little tobacco, which she also put away.   No doubt she
intended to give it to her old adorer Kal-Dubbaroh, who
I suppose expected some compensation for his loss.   I
pitied the little embarrassed girl, and told her, to the great
surprise of the spectators, that she might go, whereupon she
immediately ran out.   This puzzled the blacks, who could
not conceive any other reason for my refusal than that I was
displeased with her, and so they offered me another girl.
But I tried to explain to them that all was well between us,
and I proposed that we should go down and dance.

They were just beginning to dance when we came down
to the camp, where I sat down among the spectators and
amused myself by witnessing the manner in which the natives
enjoyed themselves on such occasions.   To give them a proof
of my goodwill, I took a whole stick of tobacco and threw it
down among the dancers.   This liberality was a surprise to
the natives, who, of course, vied with each other in trying to
secure the tobacco.   Quick as lightning, one of the men
caught hold of the stick and ran with it to his hut.

On the way home Yokkai urged me to shoot Kal-Dub-baroh, saying: "Kal-Dubbaroh not good man." I could not quite comprehend the meaning of this. The fact was, how-ever, as I afterwards learned, owing to his so frequently troubling me with this request, that Yokkai himself was anxious to marry Kélanmi, and consequently would like to have his rival out of the way.

The next day Nilgora again consented to go out hunting, and returned with a young boongary, still smaller than the others. The day was so hot that when I undertook to pre-pare the new specimen, the feet had already begun to decay, and I was afraid the animal would spoil before I got the skin off it. I therefore took it to the coolest place I could find, and prepared the skin. I sat in the shade of a gum-tree, and had to keep continually moving out of the sun's scorching rays. The flesh, which we roasted on the coals, had a fine gamey flavour, and did not taste at all like kangaroo meat. One circumstance, however, de-tracted from the enjoyment. The boongary, like most of the Australian mammals living in the trees, is infested by a slender, round, hard worm, which lies between the muscles and the skin. There these little worms, rolled together in coils, are found in great numbers. They did not trouble the natives, who did not even take the pains to pick them out.

They grumbled, on the other hand, because they were not permitted to gnaw the bones, especially the feet, which they looked upon as the best part of the animal.

CHAPTER XIX

THE next day, before sunset, the dance began again. At one end of the little place for dancing, where the grass had already been well trampled down, sat the orchestra, consisting, as usual, of only one, or sometimes of two men. The musician was sitting on the ground with his legs crossed, and was singing the new song, accompanying himself by beating together a boomerang and a nolla-nolla.

In front of him on the little plat of level ground fourteen to sixteen men were dancing in ranks of four or five each. Near the orchestra, on the right, a woman kept dancing up and down, keeping time with the men and with the music.

On Herbert river more than one woman never takes part in the dance. This is a great honour to her, and she is envied by all the other women, who sit in rows on both sides of her and the musician. They assume their favourite position and do not, like the men, cross their legs before them or sit on one of their hams, but they rest on their legs and heels, the legs being very close together. In this position they usually play an accompaniment to the music by beating both their open hands against their laps, thus producing a loud hollow sound.

The spectators sit on both sides of the dancers all the way up to the corners occupied by the women. The arrangement is as follows:—

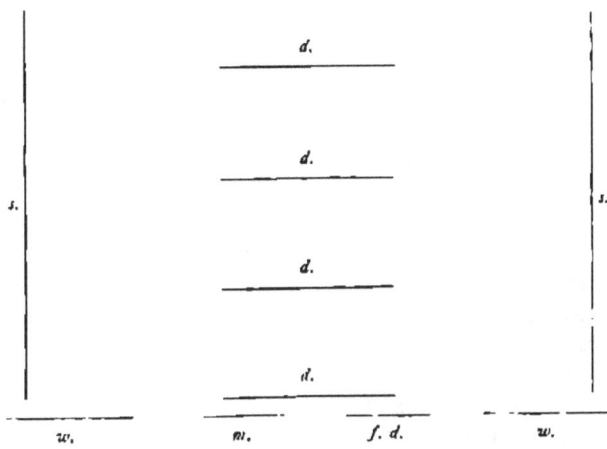

m. the music.   *f. d.* the female dancer.   *ww.* the women.   *dddd.* the dancers.
ss. the spectators.

As a rule the spectators do not decorate themselves much
for the occasion ; one may be seen here and there who has
painted himself with a little ochre borrowed from a comrade.
The dancers, on the other hand, have done all in their power
to beautify themselves.   Their bodies shine with red, yellow,

A TUFT OF TALEGALLA FEATHERS.

A SHELL USED AS AN ORNAMENT.

or white paint.   Their hair is well filled with beeswax, and
decorated with feathers, with the crests of cockatoos, and
similar ornaments.   For the purpose of giving themselves a
savage look, some of them hold in their mouths tufts either

of talegalla feathers or of yarn made from opossum hair. The latter kind of tufts or tassels the natives call *itaka*. Some of the natives have mussel-shells glued fast to their beards with wax. The Australian blacks and the Malayans are the only savages who employ this ornament in this manner.

Several of the women had painted themselves, some of them with alternating black and red bands across the face. Strange to say, the *dombi-dombi* (dancing-woman) wore no ornaments. She was middle-aged, with a pair of beauti-ful eyes, but her limbs were slender, and she had a large protruding stomach. The very uniform hopping move-ments of her lean body were not graceful. She kept her arms extended and spread the long slender fingers of her hands as far apart as possible. The sight of this woman jumping up and down in the same place, in the attitude above described, and with her large breasts dangling, was truly disgusting. But the woman seemed to enjoy herself wonderfully, and she was not relieved by any of the other women.

The chief attention centres on the male dancers, who are the heroes of the day. They start on the open side of the ground opposite the orchestra, and gradually approach the latter. Their twists and turns keep time with the music, and they continually give forth a grunting sound with accents in harmony with the music and their own movements. Near the orchestra they suddenly pause, scatter for a moment, and then begin again as before.

The music was quick and not very melancholy; the monotonous clattering, the hollow accompaniment of the women, the grunting and the heavy footfall of the men, reminded me, especially when I was some distance away from the scene, of a steam-engine at work.

While both the music and the song are an endless repetition of the same strophes, the dance has a few variations. Now and then a different figure is presented. One of those figures looked very well. Six men marched to the music in closed ranks, accompanying the rhythmical tramping of their feet with blows to the right and left with tomahawks and boomerangs. In other figures they presented a variety of comical movements. With arms akimbo, they spread their

THE NATIVES.

To face page 303.

knees as far apart as possible, and jumped and grunted in time with the music.

The dance was utterly childish, but it interested me to observe that they had a somewhat different programme for each evening. They several times produced what might be called a pantomime, but, as I did not quite comprehend it, I cannot fully describe it. On the open side of the square, opposite the music, a sort of chamber was constructed, where the chief performers made their toilets and kept themselves concealed until the performance commenced. When it was time to begin the pantomime, they rushed forth, all more ornamented than usual with ochre spots of different colours over their whole bodies, and with false beards and hair made of fibres of wood. They took their places in line with the other dancers, and with the usual twists and turns and keeping time with the music, marched up to the orchestra, where they paused for a moment. Then they formed in two long lines, opposite each other, and two of the most gaudily decorated men stepped forth from the ranks. While the others remained standing in their places, these two kept running up and down along the ranks, acting like clowns, and making all sorts of ridiculous gestures. The most important part of their acting consisted in kneeling down opposite one another and putting a stick into the ground with the right hand, at the same time bending to one another with various kinds of gestures and grimaces. Thus they kept entertaining the spectators for a long time, and it must be admitted that these two natives gave evidence by their performances of no small amount of comic talent. The closing scene was vociferously applauded, and the charmed natives asked me if I, too, did not think the acting splendid. I could not induce them to explain to me the significance of the performance, but still I managed to find out that it had some connection with the devil.

The spectators now and then indicate their approbation by laughing aloud. The women sit with smiles on their lips, and take great pleasure in witnessing the performance. The female dancer also keeps her eyes constantly on the male dancers, but the musician at her side apparently takes no interest in what is going on. He sits there beating his wooden weapons together and singing with his hoarse but powerful tenor voice. He rarely looks up, as he has already been watching the exercises for weeks, and knows them all by heart; but even he sometimes seems to be amused. Now and then he raises his eyes and looks happy as a lark at the naked figures moving backwards and forwards in the strangest contortions. He never tires of singing, and whenever he begins the strophe anew he raises his voice with a sort of enthusiasm.

These festivals, called by the civilised blacks *korroborec*, are of course evidence of friendly relations between the tribes. On this occasion the dance was given by several neighbouring tribes that were on friendly terms with each other. As a rule, however, the korroborees in Australia are given upon the settlement of wars and feuds among the tribes, and are a sort of ratification of the treaty of peace. Doubtless these festivals have, in the history of Australia, been of considerable importance in regard to the social development of the natives. The korroborees have facilitated bartering among them, and have also contributed toward promoting social intercourse among the tribes. It is a curious fact that these "ratifications of treaties of peace" frequently give rise to new feuds, on account of insults to women that are apt to occur at such festivals.

The dance always begins with the full moon and about half an hour before sunset. When the sun's last rays disappear from the horizon there is a pause until the moon rises, when the dancing begins in earnest and may last all night; but, not satisfied with the pale light of the moon, they kindle a large camp fire, the red flames of which, mingling with the white light of the moon, produce a strange fantastic effect. Toward morning they took a little rest, but before dawn I was again awakened by their monotonous song and clattering. When the sun rises it becomes too hot to dance.

The natives are wonderfully frugal in their eating at their festivals. I have never seen them eat together for pleasure or to celebrate any event. Anything like a banquet is entirely out of the question, nay, on the occasion I have described they might be said to be fasting. Those invited had taken no provisions with them, as they expected to be fed by their hosts. The latter supposed that the guests would bring food with them, and the result was that they had to subsist on almost nothing during the three days devoted to the dance. Some of them got a little tobacco. There were no other stimulants, for the blacks of Herbert river produce no intoxicating drink. They contented themselves with pleasure and water, but when the three days were gone they had to take to the scrubs and look for tobola. After gathering tobola for a few days, they renewed the dance in another place, where the same songs and the same performances were repeated, after which they again took to the woods to find means of subsistence.

In this manner the scene of the dance gradually approached Herbert Vale, and as the dancers were on a friendly footing with the blacks of that district, they gave entertainments on two evenings for their benefit. These festivities continued for nearly six weeks. On the other hand, it may take years before the blacks give another dance, for they must have new dances and new songs every time they dance, and their song-makers and dancing-masters do not care to bother their brains with too much exertion.

While the blacks went up into the mountains to gather tobola, I persuaded Nilgora and one or two others to remain with Yokkai and me. I did not like to leave a place where boongary were to be found without securing a full-grown specimen, but they preferred to go up the mountains with the others, and were tired of hunting for me day after day. The natives are fond of change, and cannot endure monotony. They repeatedly tried to convince me that there were no more boongary, but I knew this to be mere pretext. I explained to them what I would pay them, and though I offered them all I had, even the shirt I wore, if they could procure me a boongary, they still answered *Wainta boongary, wainta? maja, maja! nongarshly yongul!* (Where is boongary, where? no, no! there is but one in the woods).

Finally Nilgora and his men started early one morning to go hunting with "Balnglan." As he returned in the evening without any game, I had the next morning to renew my persuasions, and I showed him my tobacco. My provisions

R

were no temptation to Nilgora, for I had none, and as I had already given him a shirt, the one I wore was no inducement to him. My last hope was my hat, an ornament highly prized by the blacks. He finally yielded, but to no purpose, as he returned in the evening as empty-handed as the day before.

Nilgora started for the mountains to attend the dance, while Yokkai and I betook ourselves back to Herbert Vale.

Nilgora was a typical savage, and as he had never before been in contact with white men, he was more easy to manage than the others, but was reticent and reserved. I was surprised to find him always armed with a sword-bayonet, the history of which it was impossible for me to get at. He was very much afraid of the white men, and for this reason he never came down from the mountains, and hence I infer that this weapon must long have travelled from tribe to tribe before it came into his possession. The native police do not use bayonets.

What particularly attracted my attention in Nilgora's looks were his tall powerful figure and his almost Roman nose, another proof to me that the natives here are mixed with the Papuans.

On the descent to Herbert Vale, Yokkai had the important task of carrying the skins in a bag. They had to be handled with great care, a fact that my black friend did not understand. Fortunately, he was afraid of the poison with which the skins were prepared, and this made him very circumspect.

In a cheerful frame of mind I proceeded down to the grassy plain. The dark claws of the boongary protruding out of the bag reminded me of what had been accomplished during the past few days, and besides it was a source of gratification to me that Yokkai did not, on a nearer acquaintance, disappoint the good hopes I had formed in regard to him on our first meeting. I felt that I could look the future cheerfully in the face, and I had reason to hope for good results so long as he was my companion. Yokkai was well acquainted with several of the most savage tribes in the neighbourhood, and with his help it would be more easy for me to secure companions on my expeditions. By reason of

his *naïveté* and good humour, I might count on having in him
a lively and entertaining companion. Nor was he so savage
and greedy as the other blacks. A circumstance which
made him particularly devoted to me was his decided
eagerness to become a "white man." His ambition was to
eat the food of a white man, to smoke tobacco, to make
damper, to shoot, to take care of horses, to wear clothes, and
to talk English.

He told me a number of stories in regard to himself,
and gave me much interesting information about the life
and customs of the natives. Among other things, he said
that he once had stolen from a white man, but it seems that
in connection with that he acquired a great dread of the white
men and their dangerous weapons. The whites were too
angry, he said, and he assured me that he never more would
gramma—that is, steal. Together with his comrades, he had
ventured to go down to a farm near the coast, where he had
been tempted by the sight of a wash-tub containing some
clothes. On one of his shoulders he still bore the mark of
a rifle ball, by which he had been greeted on his visit to the
white man.

My plan now was to go to the table-land seventy miles to
the west, where Mr. Scott, the owner of Herbert Vale, had
his head station, the Valley of Lagoons. Up there it rains
less in the rainy season than it does at Herbert Vale, and
for this reason I decided to change my headquarters.
When I came to the station, I met a white man who was
going the same way as I, and we decided to travel together.
Yokkai remained at Herbert Vale. The next day, January
30, we proceeded toward Sea-View Range, where we
arrived the first afternoon. Here my companion wanted to
encamp for the night.

I looked back upon the scrub-clad mountains on the
other side of the valley. The air was clear, and the setting
sun caused long shadows to fall in the mountain declivities.
Far away, on the summit of a mountain, smoke was ascending.
The blacks were burning the grass and were hunting the
wallaby, free from every care and anxiety. The palms, the
ferns, the rays of the sun glistening in the waterfalls, all this
charming scenery I was now to abandon, and I was to live

at a station with the white men on the prosy plains. No, this was not possible; I longed to get back to my black friends! When I saw the sun setting amid an effulgence of crimson, and thus indicating fine weather for the morrow, my mind was made up. I decided to wait for the rain as long as possible, and this year the rainy season set in un-usually late.

I bade farewell to my travelling companion, and started back for Herbert Vale.

Early the next morning I went in search of Yokkai, whom I soon found. He and I started up the mountains to pro-cure, if possible, more people to assist us.

In a small tribe which we came to, some of the natives were found willing to go with us, and soon afterwards we had the good fortune to meet Nilgora and "Balnglan." We made our camp in the same place as before—on the old dancing-ground. Nilgora was now very accommodating. He had employed his time since we parted in eating tobola, and was now longing for the white man's food, which he had learned to like when he was with me before. During the four days we spent here we succeeded in securing a small female boongary and a young one. Thus I now had in all five males and one female, though none of them were full grown. The female (represented on the coloured plate) had a little young one in her pouch, but the black had already given it to "Balnglan," thinking it was worthless.

One day, when Yokkai and I were left alone in the camp, he suddenly broke out, "Poor fellow,—white-fellow!" Thinking that he referred to me, I, half angry, asked him what was the matter. "Poor fellow, white-fellow—Jimmy," said he, beating the back of his head, "Jimmy, white-fellow *ngallogo*"—that is, "in the water." I now understood that something was the matter, and on inquiry at last found out that the same Jimmy who had been with me before had killed a white man and thrown him into the water. The white man had been camping near a river in the middle of the day, "while the sun was big," not far from Herbert Vale. Jimmy had gone to him and offered to find fuel and build a fire, services which were accepted. The white man made his tea and sat down to eat, but Jimmy did not get any of the food, and at

once became angry, and struck the white man on the back
of the head with his tomahawk as he brought his tin cup to
his lips to drink, so that he fell down dead. Then Jimmy
robbed all that the white man had and threw his body into
the water.

The report of the murder made a deep impression on
me. Perhaps I ought to be satisfied with the results I had
already gained. If I remained longer I might meet with a
similar fate. I did not dare show Yokkai that the information
affected me, though the words did escape my lips, that the
black police would be angry with Jimmy and kill him.

When Nilgora came home in the evening, I heard
Yokkai at once informing him "that the police would kill
Jimmy." That whole evening the blacks were very reticent
and unapproachable. Doubtless my ill-advised statement
had frightened them, for they were aware that the police
paid no respect to persons, but would shoot the first native
they found, and they were also afraid that Yokkai would
have to suffer for his thoughtlessness in telling tales out of
school.

It was necessary to be equal to every emergency, for it
was in their power to hinder the news of the murder from
spreading. To avoid every danger, I resolved to be on the
alert that night—the only night I ever kept awake during
my life with the blacks. As was my custom, I fired a shot to
remind my companions that my weapon was still in existence.

The natives were lying down round the fire in front of
the opening of my hut, and from time to time they cast sly
glances at me lying with half-closed eyes in my hut. The
camp fire made it easy for us to watch each other. To
convince them that I was wide awake, I now and then
ordered them to fetch wood for the fire. I did not feel at
all safe, and not until morning did I fall asleep, exhausted
with fatigue.

When I opened my eyes the first rays of the morning
sun were shining into my hut, and it was a source of the
keenest gratification to know that I was unscathed. Never
before had the dewy tropical morning seemed so beautiful
as it did after this night.

I decided to go back to Herbert Vale for the present, and

the same day Yokkai and I started on our return. I was determined to do all in my power to secure the punishment of Jimmy. Something ought to be done to show the blacks that they could not with impunity take the life of a white man.

Jimmy had accompanied me on several expeditions, so that I knew him well. He was a brutal, despotic fellow, and very reserved. Not long before this he had also killed one of his wives. He had robbed a man of his pretty young wife, Mólle-Mólle. But she loved her first husband and could not get on well with Jimmy, the less so as he had another wife, who was very jealous and always inflamed him against Mólle-Mólle. She tried to escape to her former husband, but was recaptured by Jimmy, who cut her on the shoulder with his axe to "mark" her. Still, she soon again found an opportunity to escape, and came to Herbert Vale, where I then happened to be staying. On her shoulder was a large open wound, which did not, however, appear to give her much pain. She requested me to shoot Jimmy, for he was "not good." In spite of her beautiful, beseeching eyes and her coquettish smiles, I could make her no promise, but I urged her to make haste and go to her former husband, whom she was seeking. The same night she disappeared.

I afterwards learned that she had found the man she loved, but her joy was of short duration. Jimmy was the stronger of the two men; he recaptured her, and punishment was again inflicted. According to the statements of the natives, he had almost killed her. He had struck her with a stone on the head, so that she fell as if dead on the hot sand. There he left her, in the middle of the day, after covering her with stones. The next time I saw Mólle-Mólle she had grown very thin and pale, and had great scars on her head. She was on the point of going with Jimmy down the river to another "land." On this journey he killed her with his tomahawk, and an old man buried her. This happened only three weeks after Jimmy had slain the white man.

Yokkai was afraid that he would be killed by the blacks at Herbert Vale, because he had revealed the murder of the white man, but I quieted him with the assurance that his name should not be mentioned.

CHAPTER XX

WHEN I arrived at the station I talked with the natives about the event. They seemed to be surprised, but observing that I knew all about the matter, they found there was no use of assuming ignorance, and they began to converse with me about the murder as a matter well known to them. Thus I secured all the details in regard to this horrible affair. But they held it perfectly proper for Jimmy to kill the white man who was unwilling to share his food with him. I made them understand that this was not my view, and threatened to send for the police. This threat I would also have carried out, had not, three days later, a sergeant of the native police, with a few troopers, accidentally come and encamped at Herbert Vale. He had been in Cardwell to fetch provisions and liquor for his chief, who lived on the table-land.

When the blacks saw the police their memory again failed them. It was no longer Jimmy who had murdered the white man, but two other blacks, Kamera and Boko. In a certain sense this was true, for a year and a half previously they had actually murdered a white man. It was thought that he had been eaten by a crocodile, and now for the first time it was discovered that a murder had been committed, but this man was not Jimmy's victim. By confusing the two events, they tried to draw attention away from Jimmy. For Kamera and Boko they cared less, they being strangers, but Jimmy belonged to their own tribe and must be saved.

The boldest and most experienced of these "civilised" natives therefore sought to make friends with the police. They brought them their best women, carried wood and water for them, and tried to serve them in every way. I told the police sergeant what had happened, and requested him to arrest Jimmy, who could be found at a great borboby which was to be celebrated just at this time two or three miles from Herbert Vale.

The next day the sergeant went to the borboby to arrest him, taking with him three of the blacks at the station, and also the Kanaka, in order that they might identify Jimmy.

While he was absent, the postman came from Cardwell. When he learned what had happened, he remembered that he several times had felt a bad smell where the murder was supposed to have taken place—that is, near Dalrymple Creek.

We now hoped that the sergeant would bring the murderer in the evening, but he returned without the prisoner. Three persons called Jimmy had been shown to him, and they all denied having perpetrated the murder. The natives who had gone with the sergeant to the borboby had declared that the right Jimmy was not there. I knew this to be not true, and so I requested the sergeant to make another effort. The Kanaka told me that the right Jimmy really was there, and that it had vexed him to see that the sergeant would not arrest him. The sergeant had given all his attention to the fair sex, and had taken no interest in finding Jimmy.

As I insisted that the murderer should be arrested, the sergeant started off early the next morning, again in company with the Kanaka. He now took with him two of his own men and handcuffs for the culprit. In a few hours they returned with the prisoner, and I was sent for. It was Jimmy. He was handcuffed; his suspicious face was restless, the blood rose to his face, and if a black man can be said to blush, then Jimmy did so now.

Under the storehouse, which stood on high posts, there was a large room surrounded by a lattice. Here the court was held. The prisoner was brought in by two of the troopers, and the examination began. The persons present were the sergeant, the old keeper of the station, the postman, the Kanaka, and I. The blacks stood outside the gate and watched the whole proceeding with the greatest interest.

The sergeant, a tall powerful man, who was the representative of the law there, began the trial by snatching a throwing-stick from one of those standing outside and striking Jimmy on the head with it, in order to force him in this brutal manner to tell the truth.

" You have killed the white man," he kept repeating, and added new weight to his words by inflicting fresh blows; but the criminal denied everything, while he tried to protect himself with his fettered hands.

" You have killed your wife," shrieked the sergeant; but Jimmy made no answer to this charge, he simply tried to ward off the hard blows he was getting. Suddenly the sergeant broke the stick over Jimmy's head, which fortunately ended this inquisitorial part of the trial. The sergeant, who in the meantime had become heated by his exertions, then turned and said in a faint voice: " There is no doubt that he is the culprit, but let us now hear what the blacks have to say."

One or two of them were called in, and made the same statements as Jimmy, insisting that he had not killed the white man, but they all testified unanimously that he had murdered his wife, Mólle-Mólle. As she was a woman, they saw no peril in making this admission. Jimmy, too, confessed this crime.

" That is quite sufficient," muttered old Walters.

" Take him down to the river and wipe him out," said the sergeant to his men.

" And throw him into the water, then there will be no smell," added the postman.

In a hesitating manner the troopers began to execute the order of their stern master. One of them, David, suggested that the prisoner ought first to show the body of the dead man, a pretext for getting the matter postponed and thus saving Jimmy's life, for the police were anxious to do him and his friends a service in return for the women they had sent as a bribe.

Meanwhile the sergeant gave orders that they should bring the culprit to the camp and make short work of it.

When Jimmy discovered that the sergeant was in earnest he became literally pale, and went with them as one having no will of his own. The natives, who at first were utterly perplexed, followed slowly and silently.

The keeper of the station had during the trial suggested that the matter ought not to be reported to any white man. The fact is, the police had no authority to carry out the sergeant's severe orders. I found upon investigation that, no matter how clearly the murder is established, the English law does not permit the shooting of a criminal in this manner without a regular procedure. The prisoner had not confessed the murder, nor, as was remarked by David, had the corpse been produced. I was anxious that the proceedings should be in all respects regular and legal. I therefore at once went down to the camp and explained my doubts in the matter to the sergeant.

Here all was quiet. The police were taking things easy, and the prisoner, who had received something to eat, seemed very comfortable.

The sergeant informed me that the prisoner had now made a full confession. When he got sight of the guns he became very communicative, and had given a number of details. He had attacked the white man at Dalrymple Creek, had given him a blow with his axe on the back of the head, and had thrown his body into the water. He was also willing to show the place where he had committed the murder.

I suggested to the sergeant that Jimmy should be taken to the Cardwell police court, which was the proper court to decide this matter. On the way thither the prisoner might show the body of the dead man. The sergeant considered my suggestion to be very proper, and not thinking himself particularly qualified to make a written statement to the authorities, he left it to me to prepare the written report.

Jimmy rode a horse between David and another policeman. The handcuffs were taken off, put on his ankles, and fastened to the stirrups. All this surprised me, but I said nothing, as I supposed they knew best what was necessary. In my letter to the police magistrate in Cardwell I informed him that the prisoner had confessed the murder and was willing to go and point out the body of his victim. The police were to travel the whole night, and might be expected back in the evening of the next day.

The sergeant now relapsed into a most astonishing *dolce far niente*. He went into his tent and began to drink the rum that belonged to his chief, and for the sake of convenience he had set the jug by the side of his bed.

Early the next morning I was greatly surprised at meeting David, who handed me back the letter I had written, and told me they had had the misfortune to lose the prisoner. On their arrival at Dalrymple Creek, Jimmy had shown them the dead body in the creek, then he suddenly severed the stirrup straps and fled with the irons on his feet. The night was dark, and it was raining, so that it was easy for him to escape, although the police fired some shots after him.

This information was a great disappointment to me, but it had an opposite effect on the natives, who assured me that Jimmy would break the irons with stones and thus free himself from them. I could not help suspecting that David had been in collusion with the natives and given aid to the prisoner, and I did not conceal the fact that I was greatly displeased. Meanwhile it was impossible to discuss the matter with the sergeant. He was dead drunk in his tent, and continued in this condition for four days and nights. Now and then he became conscious, but then he would take another drink, and perhaps request some one to fan him with the tent door. Once or twice a day he would take a little walk round the tent, supporting himself on two of the troopers, who almost had to carry him. The condition of affairs kept growing worse. The troopers availed themselves of this opportunity to help themselves from the jug, and they even gave the natives grog, or "*gorrogo*," as they called it.

In this manner the sergeant maintained the law in the eyes of the natives, and in this manner he preserved discipline among his subordinates. What an impression this would leave among the blacks in regard to right and wrong! When sober, he was in the habit of saying that "the only way of civilising a black-fellow is to give him a bullet."

I sent a letter to Mr. Stafford, the sergeant's superior officer, who lived in the police barracks on the table-land. I gave him an account of what had happened, and demanded

the punishment of Jimmy for the two murders he had committed. I added that, if nothing was done in the matter, I
would make a full report to the Government.

After putting my collections away in good order at my
headquarters, I got myself ready to depart for the Valley of
Lagoons, where I intended to pass the worst part of the
rainy season. During the last days my collection was aug-
mented by the addition of two most interesting specimens of
the Australian fauna. The one was a pouched mouse
(*Sminthopsis virginiæ*), which is tolerably abundant in the

STRIPED-FACED POUCHED MOUSE (*Sminthopsis virginiæ*).

Herbert. river valley. It burrows in the earth and is dug
up by the natives, who are fond of its flesh. The specimen I secured is the only one to be found in museums.
From a complete description by De Tarragon in 1847 it is
evident that he found the same animal, but his specimen
has been lost.

Under very peculiar circumstances I also secured a young
talegalla, which the Kanaka had obtained from the blacks.
It was in fact intended for the sergeant, but he had requested
the Kanaka to keep it for him. The animal was placed
under a kettle on the bare ground in the kitchen, where it
spent six days without food. The Kanaka informed me that

the talegalla was in his keeping, and offered it to me, since its rightful owner was in no condition to take care of it. The poor creature had tried to maintain life by scratching the hard ground, where no food was to be found, and still it was in perfectly good condition. The blacks had taken it out of the nest while they were digging for eggs, and when found it was not more than one or two days old.

Near the end of February I said good-bye to Herbert Vale for a time, and was glad to get away from the annoyances I had had during the latter part of my sojourn there. My relations with the blacks had become more complicated, for they had noticed that I was the only one who insisted on the punishment of Jimmy, and they saw that my efforts were frustrated. They had for the time being lost their respect for me, but I had hopes of re-establishing my authority when Mr. Stafford came down and made them fear the agents of the law. My safety demanded that severe measures should be taken, and I therefore made up my mind to try to meet him personally. He lived not far from Mr. Scott's station, the Valley of Lagoons.

The scenery is quite different on the table-land from that in the Herbert river valley, and consists of large green grassy fields extending far and wide, sometimes covered with tall forests of gum-trees. The heat and rainfall are considerably less, but still water is abundant, especially around the Valley of Lagoons, which has its beautiful name from the numerous fresh-water lakes found in that locality. At the station, situated on a high hill, there was always a cool refreshing breeze.

There are several indications that this region is gold-bearing, and some day we may hear of the discovery of large quantities of the precious metal. Near the station is a large district covered with lava, in which are many caverns serving as hiding-places for the savages, who are constantly at war with the white population. Rock-wallabies are fond of this lava district. I there shot the beautiful little bird *Dicæum hirundinaceum.*

In Burdekin river, which is full of fish, I one day discovered an *Ornithorhynchus anatinus* swimming in the clear water.

A few days after my arrival I received a visit from Mr. Stafford, who expressed his regret that his men had acted so foolishly. As soon as he could get his horses shod, he would himself go down to Herbert Vale and "investigate the matter." He said nothing about calling the sergeant to account for his conduct, but seemed to be chiefly interested in a journey which he was about to make to Townsville.

The blacks in this vicinity were not to be trifled with. They had repeatedly surrounded the police barracks in the night, and there was constant danger of an attack. They were also dangerous enemies to Mr. Scott's cattle, and according to the statement of the overseer, they had killed thousands of them. Three blacks were servants at the station, and were therefore "civilised," but their life here had not had any visible influence on their morals. One of them, a woman, told me that her fellow-servant had given birth to three children, all of which had been killed. The mother had put an end to two of them herself, while the third had been permitted to live until it was big enough to be eaten. The one who told me the story had herself put her foot on the child's breast and crushed it to death; then both had eaten the child. This was told me as an every-day occurrence, and not at all as anything remarkable.

I remained only fourteen days at this station, and in the middle of March I was back at Herbert Vale. The keeper told me that Mr. Stafford had spent a night at the station and had proceeded to Cardwell without taking any step in regard to Jimmy. He might possibly give his attention to the matter on his return. Meanwhile the postman and a sergeant sent by the police court at Cardwell had found the body of the white man and buried it. Jimmy had grown very bold, and had made his camp only a mile and a half from Herbert Vale. Still, it would be difficult to capture him. I tried to induce the blacks to kill him, representing to them that in that event no one else would be shot, while, if they did not kill him, they might all have to suffer.

They did, in fact, seem to get frightened, and told me they would have him shot. Under all circumstances, they promised to deliver him up as soon as Mr. Stafford returned. Had the latter taken up the matter on his return, Jimmy would not have escaped his deserts. But Mr. Stafford was wholly indifferent. He spent the night at the station, and in the morning, as he was mounting his horse, he addressed a few words to one or two natives who happened to be present, and said, "You had better kill Jimmy yourselves." That was all he did in the matter.

My position was a perilous one, and my authority among the blacks had now received a new shock. The natives saw that they could take the life of a white man with impunity, and that Mr. Stafford was unwilling to pay any attention to my representations. From this they concluded that he was on their side, and that it would be safe to kill me. Even Jimmy felt secure. The next day he moved his camp nearer to Herbert Vale, and before long he visited the station itself. Still I never saw him. A few weeks later he broke into Mr. Gardiner's farm on the Lower Herbert and killed his dog.

JIMMY.

CHAPTER XXI

IT grew more and more difficult to secure serviceable men. Yokkai I could usually depend on, but all the others I suspected more or less. Several times I was nearly ready for an expedition, when it began to rain. The weather was, of course, very unreliable during the rainy season. Old Walters had gone down to Cardwell for provisions, and I was left alone at the station with the Kanaka, where time hung heavily on my hands, for I had but few books. I kept writing as long as I was able, and the rest of the day I sat in the kitchen chatting with the Kanaka and the blacks, who usually came in late in the afternoon to warm their naked bodies by the fire. Their bodies were washed clean by the rain, and the wet steamed off them in the warm kitchen. They had a hard time of it during this season. The weather was cold and wet, and the women did not find much food in the woods, so that they suffered from hunger.

We generally sat round the fire, and the blacks told stories from their everyday life. One of them, who was the most frequent visitor, was Jacky, whom I mentioned before, a cunning black man, but upon the whole a good-natured, sociable fellow, who was highly respected by his companions. We therefore looked upon him as a sort of chief. One evening he remained long, and entertained us with his stories. The conversation turned upon our flour which was nearly finished, and it was stated that we soon would have to live on the potatoes in the garden until the overseer returned. It might take weeks before he came back, as the rivers had overflowed their banks and the rain still continued. Jacky, the rogue! pitied us. The next morning the Kanaka told me that most of the potatoes were gone. Either Jacky's women had stolen them, while he kept us talking to prevent any suspicion on our part, or he must have taken them immediately after he left us.

After a week's continuous rain we again got clear weather. The only pleasure I had had during this time was bathing. Whenever the weather permitted, I would go down to the river in the misty cold air, but it was necessary to keep a sharp look-out for crocodiles and not venture too far out in the stream. In the same stream where I was in the habit of bathing, a dog had recently been caught by a crocodile, while swimming by the side of his master. Thus the dog saved the man's life, for the crocodile is particularly fond of dog's flesh. Strange to say, the natives are not afraid of swimming across a river, but I would not advise a white man to attempt it.

Whenever it was possible I made excursions with the blacks, even during this time. One day while we were out I met a black woman, who I knew had a child two weeks old. She carried a basket on her back, and I, assuming that the child was in the basket, asked her to show it to me. She at once placed the basket on the ground, thrust her hand into it, seized the child by the feet, and held it with the head down for me to look at. The child awoke and began to cry a little, but did not seem to suffer much by this treatment. The children are, upon the whole, hardy. At a station near the tropics the white people several times saw a child only a few days old lying out in the cold on a piece of bark with hoar-frost round about it; and apparently it was not injured thereby.

At another time the conversation turned on a child that had died about a month ago. One of the natives, who was aware that I collected various things, asked me whether I would like to get this child, and added: "Why have they been so stupid as to lay it in the ground? You and I will dig it up and hang it in a tree to dry." He was very eager to undertake this work for me, hoping thereby to earn some tobacco.

S

The child's mother, who had not thought of the possibility
of getting any profit out of her dead child, became from this
moment very eager to sell it.

It is not often that it is so easy to get the natives to
part with their dead. They dislike to disturb their own, and
are afraid to meddle with those of other tribes. At this
very time I was trying to secure a cranium of a full-grown
individual, and in connection with this I had some very
interesting experiences. I offered a reward of tobacco for
the head of a man of a distant tribe, who some time ago
had been killed at a borboby. From fear of the strange tribe
they could not be persuaded to procure it, so I made up
my mind to try to get it myself. I took Yokkai with me to
show me the grave, but I did not find it.

Finally I succeeded in inducing Mangola-Maggi to fetch
the head ; but the skull he brought me belonged to a young
person and not to a full-grown man. Besides, there was
a large hole in the top of it, which made it much less
desirable as a cranium. I asked him what had produced
the hole. "Dingo has eaten it," he said. Though I insisted
that this could not be true, he kept asserting that it was the
right head. As, however, he got no tobacco and as I
promised him a large amount if he would bring the right
one, he set out again in company with another native. After
he had gone, the blacks explained to me the facts concerning
this skull. Mangola-Maggi as a young man had experienced
great difficulty in getting a wife, and had therefore requested
an old man to give him one of his. But, as was natural, the
old man refused to do this. Mangola-Maggi, who was a
person of high authority on account of his ability to secure
human flesh, became angry, and decided to take revenge.
On meeting the young son of the man, he struck him on
the head with a stone and killed him, and it was the skull of
this young man that they had now brought to me and were
trying to get a reward for. The body he had eaten immediately after the murder.

The next day Mangola-Maggi and his companion brought
the right cranium and got their reward. When I reproached
Mangola-Maggi for his conduct toward the old man's son,
he simply shrugged his shoulders and smiled. I afterwards

learned that he was challenged by the father to a duel with

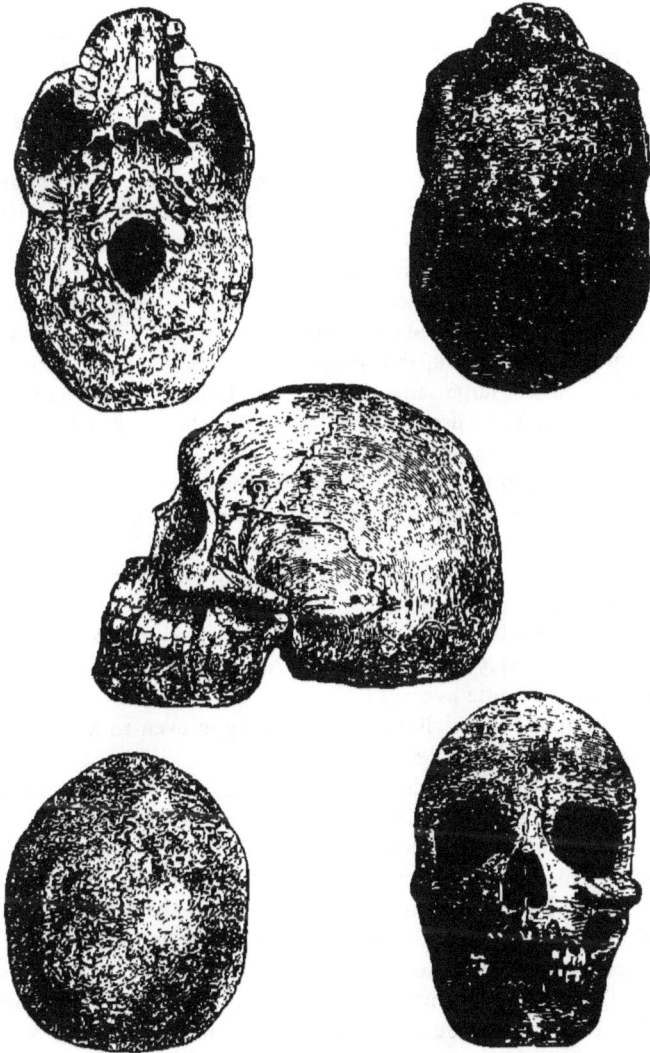

A MALE CRANIUM FROM ROCKHAMPTON, CENTRAL QUEENSLAND,
SEEN FROM FIVE SIDES.

wooden swords and shields, and that in this manner the whole
affair was settled.

It is a well-known fact that the Australian natives, according to Gustaf Retzius, belong to the prognathous dolichocephalous class. Their projecting jaws make them resemble the apes more than any other race, and their foreheads are as a rule very low and receding. The bone is thick and strong. Few crania are to be found without marks of injuries, whether they be male or female. The muscles of the face, particularly the masticatory muscles, are very fully developed ; the superciliary arches are very prominent ; the cheek-bones are high, and the temporal fossæ very deep. The skull-bones form a high arch. The orbital margin is very thick, the nasal bones are flat and broad, and the teeth large and strong, the inner molars having as many as six cusps. The hollow of the neck takes an upward and receding direction.

In the eight crania brought by me from Central and Northern Queensland the length-breadth index is 71, the length averages 180.5, and the breadth 128. The dolichocephalous character of the skull is mainly owing to the great narrowness of the cranium.

The facial angle averages 68°. *Index orbitalis* is microseme (81.5), *index nasalis* is platyrhine (53), and Daubenton's angle averages 5°.

The male crania have the savage type even to a greater degree than the female.

The above measurements, particularly the small capacity of the cranium, and the low receding forehead, which is unfavourable to a development of the frontal lobes, indicate the low plane of intellectual development of the Australian natives. The smaller the skull is the lower the race ranks in culture, but the organs of the face are all the more developed in comparison with the rest of the head.

The features distinguishing the cranium of the Australian from that of the European are, in the first place, the projecting jaws (the prognathous character), which are very rare and never marked among Europeans ; in the second place, the low forehead and the small capacity, which among Europeans would be called microcephalous, and would indicate a weak mind ; in the third place, the flat nose, which is also very rare in Europe ; and finally, the large Daubenton angle.

In course of time we got better weather, so that I was able to start on a long expedition to Cardwell to buy provisions, and thereupon to examine the country north-west of this village. Yokkai and I succeeded after much trouble in gathering a few people for this journey. We also had the dog "Balnglan." All looked fresh and green after the rain ; but it is wonderful how quickly everything dries up again, and how soon the rivers fall to their usual level. After all the rainfall the air was cool and very pleasant.

One evening I got a tangible proof, showing how important it is to clear with fire the ground on which one is going to camp for the night. Yokkai called my attention to the remains of a venomous serpent that had been in the grass. The above precaution is also important in sanitary respects, for the old grass is full of miasma, which makes the ground unhealthy.

On our way we passed the place on Dalrymple Creek where Jimmy had murdered the white man. A heap of stones marked the spot where the postman had buried him. In the pool of water hard by I found a few bones. Soon after this we crossed the ridge at a place called Dalrymple Gap. To a person looking down from the summit there is a most beautiful view on either side. The spectator is greeted by a luxuriant tropical vegetation ; palms and bananas, and a multitude of other trees of greater or lesser size, cover the ground, while across the gap hangs the telegraph wire which connects civilised Australia with Europe. It made a strange impression on me to find this emblem of civilisation after spending so long a time among the savages. A wide swath for the telegraph wire is cut through the dense forest, and continues its way northward all the way to Cape York. This opening must constantly be cleared, otherwise the rank vegetation would soon disturb the telegraph.

In these very regions a horrible murder was committed a few years ago by the blacks. The fact is well known in Northern Queensland, but except the natives, very few people are familiar with the details of the murder. The natives often talked with me concerning this event, which has not been forgotten by the white population either. The blacks did not hesitate to talk about it now, as so long a time has elapsed since it happened.

A settler named Mr. O'Connor, who had come to reside on the Lower Herbert, cultivated a farm, and employed a great many blacks to help him to clear the scrubs and to work in the fields. He paid them well, was very kind to them, and did not shoot them, as so many of the other colonists did, but was what is called "a blacks' protector." He paid them in meat, flour, and tobacco, but was too kind to them, and so the natives felt perfectly safe and had an irresistible desire to possess all his property.

They resolved to make an attack on his farm, and marched against the house armed with wooden swords and shields. O'Connor became alarmed, took his revolver, and finally had to shoot at them. But at every shot the natives ran behind the trees and shouted : "Shoot away, it will soon be our turn!" At last he had fired his six shots without hitting one of them. They had ceased to fear him to such a degree that they did not even respect his revolver, and rushing upon him, they slew him with their heavy swords, mangled his body, and plundered his house. They took the bananas in his garden and stole his chickens. His wife was dragged in an unconscious condition into the woods, where she was killed.

A police officer happened at the time to be on a tour of inspection in the neighbourhood. As O'Connor was the only settler in this district, the inspector wanted to visit him, and thus he discovered the crime that had been committed. He ordered a battue of the blacks in all directions. The troopers, who had on several occasions enjoyed the hospitality of the settler, were furiously enraged, and pursued the criminals like bloodhounds. The blacks report, however, that they did not succeed in shooting more than two of the men—an old man and a youth—but nearly all the women fell into their hands. The women, who generally are spared by the native police, were on this occasion obliged to suffer for the crimes of the men, and even the children were murdered and thrown into the flames.

This account, given me by several natives whose statements agreed, I consider perfectly reliable.

We encamped near Cardwell, a little settlement of about a hundred inhabitants on the seashore. I had great trouble in getting any of my men to go with me into the village, but finally succeeded in persuading one man to accompany me, while the others remained in the camp awaiting our return.

AN OLD MAN FROM TOWNSVILLE, NORTHERN QUEENSLAND.

Our entrance into the village attracted considerable attention. I was on horseback, and my attendant, Morbora, marched at my side in his "garments of paradise." With one hand he shouldered my gun, and with the other hand he led the pack-horse. We must have looked like travelling gypsies.

The people of the village gathered round us, and asked with the greatest curiosity how I could live among the natives without being killed. They all knew me from the postman, whose route began at Cardwell. I at once went to the "hotel"—for there is no town with twenty inhabitants without its hotel—to get my dinner, and procured for Morbora, who was sitting on the verandah and taking care of the horse, a large amount of leavings—"a black-fellow's meal," as it is called. He seemed to enjoy the food immensely, as he had never before had such a feast. He was in perfect ecstasy over all that he saw, and every trace of fear had left him. The white men entered into conversation with him, and it surprised me to see how well he used the few English words I had taught him. He felt like a lord as he sat there eating the food of the white man.

I paid a visit to the police magistrate, and talked with him about Jimmy. Then I bought provisions and returned to the camp, bringing with me woollen blankets for all my men. The Government of Queensland annually distributes blankets to the natives on the Queen's birthday, if they will but come and get them. This is the only thing the Government does for the black inhabitants. The day for distribution had not yet arrived, but I succeeded in getting blankets for my men in advance. Here, on the borders of civilisation, there are but few natives who avail themselves of this privilege, as they are too timid to approach the whites.

On our return to the camp these blankets were a source of joy and admiration. My blacks now made their first acquaintance with this sort of luxury, and they seemed to be perfectly delighted The flour and sugar I had brought made, however, the deepest impression on them. The amount was not large, but my blacks had never before seen such a lot of dainties. In their simplicity they thought all was to be eaten at once, though I tried to make them understand that it was to last a long time. I did not give them much of the sugar, as they were able to procure honey for themselves. Sugar had become an absolute necessity to me, and I was unable to swallow my food without sweetening the water. It frequently happened that I lay down in the evening

munching dry food without being able to swallow it. This
made the natives envious, for, having devoured their own
share at once, they wanted to get what I was trying to eat.

We proceeded up the Coast Mountains north-west from
Cardwell, and encamped near the summit on a grassy lawn
in the scrub, constructing our huts with more care than
usual, and digging ditches round them so that we could
keep dry. The vegetation here was remarkably luxuriant.
We had a fine view of the ocean and of the coast below us,
including a long series of scrub-clad hills toward the north.

Yokkai, whom I had educated as well as I could to
prepare the food, was very proud of being permitted to
handle the white man's things. I had taught him to wash
himself and to keep himself clean, but only insisted on
his doing this when he acted as cook, and at such times I
was always present, as he was especially fond of baking
damper. It was never necessary to ask him twice to do
this. He made no delay in procuring the bark, on which
he carefully laid the necessary amount of flour, adding
the proper amount of water, and kneaded the dough with a
skill that a baker might envy. When the dough was
kneaded, and he had shaped it, he threw it a few times
into the air, and caught it like a ball, to show us that
he understood the art perfectly. After placing the cake in
the ashes, he carefully collected all the small pieces of dough
remaining and made a little cake of them, which he baked
for his own special benefit. Besides, I gave him, as his
perquisite, a small piece of the damper when it was done.

As he gradually grew more accustomed to the baking,
I noticed that the remnants of dough on the bark kept
increasing in quantity, but as he was, upon the whole, a rather
scrupulous man, I said nothing about it. I also gave him
permission to prepare the meat. I had abandoned the tin
pail and now prepared my meat in the same manner as the
natives.

We made daily excursions into the woods, which were
unusually dense and abounded with lawyer - palms. As
usual, the leeches [1] were very numerous in 'these mountains,
and were very annoying. As you walk through the woods,

---

[1] They are not eaten by the natives.

exhausted and dripping with perspiration, you scarcely notice their bites before they have satisfied their thirst for blood, but then the blood flows freely from the wound. The ticks, however, are a far greater annoyance. All the scrubs up here are so full of these insects that a white man dreads to enter them, though the natives are not at all annoyed by them. A splendid remedy for the itching caused by these insects is lemon juice, and hence I always took lemons with me on my expeditions from Herbert Vale. I put this juice over my whole body, and thus the insects were doubtless killed, for I immediately felt relief. A larger species of tick is also found here which kills the dogs of Europeans, but, strange to say, has no effect on the dingo. They are, however, a great inconvenience to the white man, and should at once be killed by applying petroleum to them. It is useless to try to jerk them out, for a part of them will remain in the flesh and may cause bad sores. I know a man who became blind for a few minutes on account of a tick which he could not get entirely rid of, a part of it remaining in the flesh of his back.

On my wanderings here, my blacks found in a pool formed by a mountain brook a toollah (*Pseudochirus archeri*). The natives all shouted at once, *yarri*. They told me that the large yarri, which I never succeeded in securing, but of whose existence I have no doubt, subsists for a great part on this animal, which, in this instance, it had left in the cool water for future consumption. One is tempted to believe that the yarri understands the preserving quality of the water. The natives, too, preserve their meat in the water during the hot summer months, as the temperature of the water is, of course, lower than that of the air. The fact probably is, that the yarri has found the water to be a safer place for storing the meat. The toollah was put between some stones near the edge of the river. I was much pleased with what the natives told me, for it awakened in me hopes of securing a specimen of this large marsupial. Fortunately, I had strychnine with me. I poisoned the toollah and laid it on the bank. Farther up the stream I left several pieces of meat, likewise prepared with poison, a source of great aggravation to the blacks, who would have

liked to eat the meat. As we went to examine the snares
every day, I was very much afraid that our dog might eat
the poison, and I kept constantly warning the blacks.

One day, as we were returning to the camp, the natives
were to take a beat by themselves through the scrub. I
urged them particularly not to return along the river, but to
come through the woods, so as to avoid the poisoned meat.
Later in the day, as they were coming home, I heard them
talking about poison and about "Balnglan." I at once became suspicious, and asked if the dog had eaten any of
the poison. They denied it, but when I pressed them with
questions they admitted that they had returned by the way
of the river, probably because they were too lazy to go
the other way, and they also confessed that "Balnglan" had
taken the poisoned toollah in his mouth. Yokkai had at once
taken the toollah out of "Balnglan's" mouth, so that he had
not eaten any of it. No sooner had they made this statement than the dog fell into spasms. I rushed into my hut,
mixed as quickly as I could some tobacco and water to pour
down the dog's throat, while Yokkai and another man held
it, but it died at once.

Yokkai gazed at it for a moment, then turned away
and wept bitterly. He sat down and wrung his hands in
despair, while large tears rolled down his cheeks. The other
man also began to sob and cry aloud.

Though I felt the deepest sympathy for them, I could
not endure these endless lamentations. I got two large
pieces of tobacco, and offered it as a reward to them if they
would cease their sobbing. Yokkai became silent at once and
straightened himself up, while he looked at the tobacco with
his eyes full of tears. He accepted it with contentment, but
there was not a smile on his face. The other continued
sobbing until it came to be his turn to get tobacco, then his
sorrow was cured instantly.

I myself was touched by this event, for the good beast,
which lay there dead and rigid, had been of great service
to me. It was the best dog for miles round, and was
the most intelligent dingo I have ever seen. I not only
placed a high value on it, but I was also very fond of it,
though it had several times attacked my leather traps,

such as strings, shoes, and even my revolver case. I
was anxious to preserve at least its fine black skin with
white breast and yellow legs, and I suggested to Yokkai that
he should let me have it. Knowing that such a request
would be opposed, I at the same time offered tobacco as a
compensation. He at first objected, but when he saw two
whole sticks of tobacco, every scruple vanished and his eyes
beamed with satisfaction. He even assisted me in skinning
the dingo, and from this time he regained his usual good
humour. He had some suspicions that Nilgora, the owner of
the dog, would become angry when he learned of this sad
event, but he felt certain that he could satisfy him by giving
him his woollen blanket and some tobacco.

CHAPTER XXII

NATIVES ON HERBERT RIVER.

FROM this time forward I seldom visited Herbert Vale. It was easy to understand that the old overseer was anxious to get rid of me, though I had not troubled him much with my presence. He was one of those Australian hermits who had lived so long by himself that he could not brook others near him. I did all in my power to avoid any change in his old habits. But he got tired of my skins and was annoyed by my skeletons, the smell of which he could not bear, though I kept them in another building. At last I hardly knew what to do with them. He was peevish and unsociable. We never conversed unless it was absolutely necessary.

My relations with Nelly and the Kanaka had hitherto been pleasant; but things came to pass which made a change in their conduct. Nelly had an old one-eyed cur that it was dangerous to approach. When I returned from the expedition to Cardwell it was determined to hinder me from entering my room, barking the whole time and showing its angry teeth. I took a stick and gave it a severe blow, but as I was too angry to calculate the weight of the blow, the dog fell to the ground unconscious. Nelly, who meanwhile had come to the rescue, at once uttered a shriek so terrible that I could hardly conceive it as coming from a human being. It was impossible to get her to stop. She threw herself upon the dog and did not cease shrieking until it became conscious again. She thought I had killed it, but it became perfectly well again, though the pleasant relations between Nelly and myself were gone for ever.

The Kanaka did not take much interest in this matter, for he was used to hearing Nelly cry, but another incident disturbed our intercourse. I reproached him for his conduct towards a girl eleven years old, and for this he could never forgive me.

On account of these strained relations, Herbert Vale was even less attractive than before. I spent most of my time with the blacks, simply paying an occasional short visit to the station. Yokkai was still my faithful companion, and assisted me in gathering men.

One day we crossed a valley, where he told me many blacks had at one time lived of whom not a trace was now to be seen. They had gradually been killed and eaten by other tribes.

As has repeatedly been stated, the Australian tribes are constantly at war with each other. They try to exterminate one another whenever there is an opportunity. They constantly plan attacks, and in their warfare exhibit a cunning worthy of a better cause. This enmity between the tribes is attributable to the superstition that any black man can by witchcraft cause death among the members of his tribe. Hence it is of importance to kill as many strangers as possible, but as cowardice is no vice or fault among the Australians, they content themselves with hating and fearing one another, except when the opportunity of taking life is, so to speak, forced upon them. There is much talking and loud boasting, but the words seldom ripen into action. Still, it sometimes happens that they attack each other for the purpose of revenging direct insults, as for instance the stealing of women, hunting on another tribe's territory, or on account of some death, for which the strangers are of course blamed. Then they are enticed by the hope of getting more wives; but the greatest incentive to taking life is their appetite for human flesh. The blacks never wage war to conquer new territory.

On Herbert river expeditions are sometimes undertaken for the special purpose of securing *talgoro*—that is, human flesh. On such occasions a small company of the boldest and most depraved gather together, and they are, of course, persons of high standing in the tribe. They are not many in number, as a rule only three or four; for the attacks are made on small family tribes that live scattered through the district, sometimes consisting of not more than five or six individuals. The expedition travels slowly, as they have no provisions with them and must find their subsistence from day to day. It is of course necessary to proceed with the greatest caution, lest they be themselves discovered and attacked.

When they have found a small family tribe to be attacked, they try to stay near their camp in the evening. Nothing having happened to cause apprehension during the day, the family sits comparatively secure round the camp fire. Early in the morning, before sunrise, a noise is suddenly heard and the family wakes up in a fright. The black man's highly-wrought fancy always makes him imagine that his enemies are far more numerous than they are in reality. Each one tries to save his life as best he can; resistance being out of the question, there is no gallant defence of women and children. Each one has to look after himself; and it is generally worst for the old individuals, who are killed and eaten. A woman is as a rule splendid booty; if she be young her life is generally spared, but if she be old she is first ravished and then killed and eaten.

The natives of Northern Queensland and of many other parts of Australia are cannibals. My people never made any secret of this, and in the evenings it was the leading topic of their conversation, which finally both disgusted and irritated me. The greatest delicacy known to the Australian native is human flesh. The very thought of *talgoro* makes his eye sparkle. When I asked my men what part of the human body they liked best, they always struck their thighs. They never eat the head or the entrails. The most delicate morsel of all is the fat about the kidneys. By eating this they believe that they acquire a part of the slain person's strength, and so far as I could understand, this was even more true of the kidneys themselves. For according to a widespread Australian belief, the kidneys are the centre of life.

It happened years ago in Victoria that a white policeman was attacked by the blacks. They struck him with their clubs until they believed him dead, and then they took out his kidneys and ran away. The man came to his senses again for a moment and was able to relate what had happened, but a few hours afterwards he died. The natives on Herbert river are particularly fond of the fat of a dead foe, which is not only eaten as a delicacy and as a strengthening food, but is also carried as an amulet. A small piece is done up in grass and kept in a basket worn round the neck, and the effect of this is, in their opinion, success in the chase, so that they can easily approach the game. A man told me that immediately after beginning to wear a small piece of human fat, he waded across the river, and came at once to a tree where he found a large edible snake.

As a rule the Australian natives do not eat persons belonging to their own tribe. Still, I know instances to the contrary, and I have even heard of examples of mothers eating their own children. Besides the circumstance already related, it happened in 1883, about a hundred miles from Townsville, that a child which had died a natural death was eaten, and that the mother herself took part in the feast. A day or two later she too died and was eaten. In connection with this I must call attention to the fact that the killing of children rarely happens on Herbert river, for the mothers are invariably fond of their children. I know of examples of their killing their children because they were a burden to them, but such things also happen in civilised countries. Moreover, the father is the one who determines whether the child is to live or not, so that when the mother kills the child she usually obeys the orders of her husband.

Mr. White has informed me that the natives south of the Carpentarian Gulf also are cannibals to some extent. They never kill anybody for the purpose of eating him, but the women eat those who die a natural death ; near Moreton Bay the dead are also eaten, and by their own relatives.

In Western Queensland, at Westlands station on Thompson river, a woman belonging to a tribe of civilised blacks gave birth to a so-called *half-caste* child—that is, the offspring of a black mother and a white father. Such half-breeds are not as a rule much liked, and are therefore usually killed by the blacks who are in the first stages of civilisation. In this instance the blacks had indeed been in long intercourse with white people, and still the child was killed. It was permitted to live about three weeks, but one day one of the men put his hand round its neck and held it up till it was choked to death. Thereupon it was roasted on the fire and distributed among those present, and eaten most greedily. Many of the white people at the station were witnesses of this event. It is not known whether the mother in this instance ate any of the flesh of her child or not.

The blacks do not like to eat white people. When Jimmy had killed the white man near my headquarters, my question as to whether the dead man had been eaten caused great surprise. The answer was: *Kölle mah! komorbory kawan!*—that is, By no means! terrible nausea! At the same time the person pointed at his throat to indicate his disgust for the flesh of a white man. The other persons present agreed with him. I have often since heard them say that the white man's flesh is not good ; this may be owing to his constant diet of salt beef, tea, and bread, which possibly gives his flesh a different taste from that of the blacks. The black man lives on vegetables nearly all his life. I have heard it stated by "civilised" blacks that the white man's flesh has a salt taste, which the natives do not like.

This also seems to harmonise with their fondness for the flesh of the Chinese, whose food consists largely of rice and other vegetables. Farther north in Queensland it twice happened during my sojourn in Australia that the blacks killed the Chinese in great numbers. It was said that ten Chinamen were eaten at one dinner. All strangers who

travel through the land of a tribe are of course their enemies.
This is true both of the Chinese and the white men, both of
which races are looked upon as another kind of black who
come from distant lands, and are killed when the opportunity presents itself.

Human flesh, however, is not the daily food of the
Australian. On the contrary, he seldom gets a mouthful
of this delicacy. During all the time I spent on Herbert
river only two blacks were killed and eaten. One of them
was a young man who had ventured to go into the territory
of a strange tribe, where he was surprised and killed. The
other was an old man who was not able to run fast enough
when his tribe was attacked, and he was stoned to death.
His flesh was brought in baskets to Herbert Vale.

It is a mistake to suppose that the cannibals have an
uglier look than other savages. Those who go in search of
human flesh are certainly the boldest and the most cunning,
but a cannibal may look very quiet and approachable. Both
men and women take part in the feast of human flesh.

Doubtless cannibals can be found even at the present
time in other lands than Australia. There are said to be
cannibals in the interior of Africa and in Borneo, but I doubt
whether it is generally known that there is a peculiar kind
of cannibalism in certain hill districts of Burma, in regard
to which I have recently obtained interesting and reliable
information from the distinguished Burmese barrister Mr.
Chan-Toon, and I take this opportunity of relating some of
the facts gathered from him. He says that in the north-
east part of Burma there are mountain tribes who live a
savage life resembling that of the Australian blacks, and
who eat the congealed blood of their enemies. The blood
is poured into bamboo reeds, corked up, and in course of
time hardens. The filled reeds are hung under the roofs
of the huts, and when the chief of the tribe wants to treat
his friends to this kind of food the reed is broken and the
contents devoured with the greatest relish. The origin of
this custom is, according to Mr. Chan-Toon, a superstition
that the natives will thereby acquire the courage and strength
of their enemies. He thinks that at first the blood of
captives must have been drunk as soon as they were slain.

CHAPTER XXIII

ON our way home from an expedition we discovered a grave in a "white ants'" hill. The entrance was about a yard high. It was built on the side of the ant-hill, extending about half way up, and had a sloping front. In front of the opening large pieces of the bark of the tea-tree were placed, on which heavy stones were rolled in order to keep wild dogs from getting to the corpse. In a tree near the grave hung a capacious basket. This led me to think that the Australian natives probably believe in a future life, and I examined this basket to see whether provisions had been left in it, but I found it empty. I asked the natives whether there had been food in the basket, so that the deceased might have something to eat, but this was an idea which they could not comprehend.

BURIAL IN NORTHERN QUEENSLAND.

They informed me that a child was buried here. The parents were so much grieved at the loss of their child that they did not care to keep the basket in which they had carried it, and had accordingly left it beside the grave.

The Australian natives usually bury their dead, but they invariably strive to avoid letting the corpse come into direct contact with the earth, and the dead body is therefore

A LARGE BASKET FROM NORTHERN QUEENSLAND FOR CARRYING CHILDREN (⅓ size).

wrapped in bark or other materials. The graves are not very deep, and sometimes have a direction from east to west, and the foot of the grave is toward the rising sun. In some parts of Queensland two sticks, painted red and about a yard high, are erected near the grave, and on the tops of the sticks feathers of the white cockatoo are fastened. If the deceased was a prominent man, a hut is sometimes built over his grave. The entrance, which faces the east, has an opening through which a grown person may creep. In some

parts of Australia the dead body is placed in a sitting
posture, and a mound is built over it.   There are also tribes
which bury their dead in a standing position.   Near Rockhampton I saw several graves not more than a foot deep, in
which the feet were directed toward the rising sun.   Hills
are usually selected as burial-places.   At Coomooboolaroo
the dead bodies both of women and men are laid into
graves as long as the corpses, about a yard under the sod,
and wrapped in pieces of cloth or bark.   The graves are
filled with small tree-trunks up to the level of the ground,
and then a thin layer of soil is laid on the top.

East of Fitzroy river women are laid in an open trench,
the earth having been dug out with a "yam stick" and
neatly piled up all round ; the body is in this way left
quite exposed, and the legs are bent upwards.   The grass
all round for a couple of yards or more is removed, leaving
the ground quite bare ; this is probably done to protect the
grave in case of bush-fire.   After a time their relations come
and gather the bones, cut a hole in a hollow tree, and put
the bones into it.   The hole is then filled up with grass, and
twigs or sticks are laid on the top to keep the grass in.
The tree-trunk above and below the hole (around which the
bark is cut away) they paint with red or red and white
colours.

An old warrior who has been a strong man and therefore
much respected by his tribe, is after his death put on a plat-
form made with forked sticks, cross-pieces, and a sheet or two
of bark ; he is hoisted up amidst a pandemonium of noise,
howling, and wailing, besides much cutting with tomahawks
and banging of heads with nolla-nollas.   He is laid on his
back with his knees up, like the females, and the grass is
cleared away from under and all round.   The place is now
for a long time carefully avoided, till he is quite shrivelled,
whereupon his bones are taken away and put in a tree.   The
common man is buried like a woman, only that logs are
put over him and his bones are not removed.   Young
children are put bodily into the trees.

The fact that the natives bestow any care on the bodies
of the dead is doubtless owing to their fear of the spirits of
the departed.   In some places I have seen the legs drawn

up and tied fast to the bodies, in order to hinder the spirits of the dead, as it were, from getting out to frighten the living. Women and children, whose spirits are not feared, receive less attention and care after death.

In several tribes it is customary to bury the body where the person was born. I know of a case where a dying man was transported fifty miles in order to be buried in the place of his nativity. It has even happened that the natives have begun digging outside a white man's kitchen door, because they wanted to bury an old man born there. In Central Queensland I saw many burial-places on hills. Such are also said to be found in New South Wales and in Victoria. These burial-grounds have been in use for centuries, and are considered sacred.

In South Australia and in Victoria the head is not buried with the body, for the skull is preserved and used as a drinking-cup. It is a common custom to place the dead between pieces of bark and grass on a scaffold, where they remain until they are decayed, and then the bones are buried in the ground. In the northern part of Queensland I have heard people say that the natives have a custom of placing themselves under these scaffolds to let the fat drop on them, and that they believe that this puts them in possession of the strength of the dead man.

A kind of mummy, dried by the aid of fire and smoke, is also found in Australia. Male children are most frequently prepared in this manner. The corpse is then packed into a bundle, which is carried for some time by the mother. She has it with her constantly, and at night sleeps with it at her side. After about six months, when nothing but the bones remain, she buries it in the earth. Full-grown men are also sometimes carried in this manner, particularly the bodies of great warriors. This is done, for instance, in the southern part of Queensland, and a mummy of this kind may be seen in the Brisbane Museum. Mr. Finch-Hatton relates in *Advance Australia* that when an old warrior dies he is skinned with the greatest care, and after the survivors have eaten as much of him as they like, the bones are cleaned and packed into the skin, and thus the remains are carried for years.

The natives in the neighbourhood of Portland Bay, in the south-western part of South Australia, cremate their dead by placing the corpse in a hollow tree and setting fire to it. This is also done by the tribes west of Townsville.

In connection with this, I am reminded of Lucian's words : " Various people have various modes of burial. The Greeks cremated their dead ; the Persians buried them ; the Hindoos anoint them with a kind of gum ; the Scythians eat them ; and the Egyptians embalm them." Here we are given nearly all the modes of burial which have existed both among civilised people and among barbarians, and strange to say, we find all these modes represented among the savages of Australia.

The natives of Australia have this peculiarity, in common with the savages of other countries, that they never utter the names of the dead, lest their spirits should hear the voices of the living and thus discover their whereabouts.

There seems to be a widespread delief in the soul's existence independently of matter. On this point Fraser relates that the Kūlin tribe (Victoria) believes that every man and animal has a *mūrŭp* (ghost or spirit), which can pass into other bodies. A person's mūrŭp may in his lifetime leave his body and visit other people in their dreams. After death the mūrŭp is supposed to appear again, to visit the grave of its former possessor, to communicate with living persons in their dreams, to eat remnants of food lying near the camp, and to warm itself by their night fires.[1] A similar belief has been observed among the blacks of Lower Guinea. On my travels I, too, found a widespread fear of the spirits of the dead, to which the imagination of the natives attributed all sorts of remarkable qualities. The greater the man was on earth the more his departed spirit is feared. Of the spirits of those long since departed there is no dread. Upon the whole, it may be said that these children of nature are unable to conceive a human soul independent of the body, and the future life of the individual lasts no longer than his physical remains.

In the various tribes are so-called wizards, who pretend to communicate with the spirits of the dead and get informa-

[1] *Transactions of Royal Society of New South Wales*, 1882.

tion from them. They are able to produce sickness or death whenever they please, and they can produce or stop rain and many other things. Hence these wizards are greatly feared. Mr. Curr has very properly called attention to the influence of this fear of witchcraft upon the character and customs of the natives. It makes them bloodthirsty, and at the same time darkens and embitters their existence. An Australian native is unable to conceive death as natural, except as the result of an accident or of old age, while diseases and plagues are always ascribed to witchcraft and to hostile blacks.

This superstitious fear causes and maintains hatred between the tribes, and is the chief reason why the Australian blacks continue to live in small communities and are unable to rise to a higher plane of social development.

In order to be able to practise his arts against any black man, the wizard must be in possession of some article that has belonged to him—say, some of his hair or of the food left in his camp, or some similar thing. On Herbert river the natives need only to know the name of the person in question, and for this reason they rarely use their proper names in addressing or speaking of each other, but simply their class-names. The wizard is, as a rule, a man far advanced in years, but I knew a youth of only twenty who enjoyed a great reputation for his sorcery. The wizard is also the physician of the tribe, and imagines that he can cure all diseases and that he has great power over the "devil-devil."

I once met a black man who told me that he personally had been the victim of strange wizards, and that ever since that time he had been a sufferer from headache. One afternoon, many years ago, two wizards had captured him and bound him; they had taken out his entrails and put in grass instead, and had let him lie in this condition until sunrise. Then he suddenly recovered his senses and became tolerably well, a result for which he was indebted to a wizard of his own tribe, who thus proved himself more powerful than the two strangers. The blacks call an operation of this kind *kóbi*, and a man who is able to perform it, and who, as a matter of course, is very much respected and feared, is

said to be " much kóbi," a fact of which I, too, used to boast,
for the purpose of maintaining my importance in the eyes
of the blacks, and in this I was successful, at least in the
beginning. " Kóbi " was the most dreadful thing imaginable.
It usually ended in death, and although the life of the victim
might be saved, he would for ever after have a reminder in
the form of constant headache.

An old warrior in a tribe not far from Rockhampton
was taken very ill. The tribe being at the time near a
station, asked the manager, who was a friend of mine, to
give the sick man some medicine. " Holloway's pills," the
usual medicine in the bush, was accordingly supplied to him,
but without making him any better. The doctor of the
tribe had then to bring his powers into action. All the
blacks attributed his illness to some strange black-fellows
who had put some pieces of broken glass into him, and these
the doctor was now willing to take out, in order to effect
a cure. The old man was laid in front of a big fire ; all
the members of the tribe had placed themselves solemnly
round him, some of his five " gins " crying. Suddenly out of
the darkness appeared a huge black-fellow dressed up to his
eyes in paint and feathers and carrying a long spear in his
one hand, while in the other he held a small pouch made
out of a kangaroo's scrotum. Then began the most awful row
one can imagine—crocodile tears flowing in streams. The
doctor placed himself within reach of the patient, stretched
out his spear and touched him with the point, and all the
noise at once ceased ; the eager look on all the dark faces
round was something to see. Every time the doctor
raised his spear he produced a piece of broken glass from his
hair and put it into the bag, this performance being followed
by a great yell from all those assembled. He produced
altogether seven pieces of glass, and the crowd uttered a yell
for each piece. When all was over, the doctor disappeared
into the darkness, and the sick man recovered. All the
blacks believed that he had drawn these pieces up the spear
into his hair, and to try to convince them of the absurdity
of such an opinion only made them sulkily say, " White-
fellow stupid fellow."

Strange to say, many of the civilised blacks believe that

they will be changed hereafter into white men—that they will "jump up white-fellow," and it is also an interesting fact that many tribes use the same word for "spirit" and for "white man." It has frequently happened that the savages have taken white men to be their own deceased fellows, which confirms the theory prevalent in many parts of Australia that the natives believe in a future life. Near a station in Central Queensland the white population observed that a black woman repeatedly brought food to the grave of her deceased husband.

The Australian blacks do not, like many other savage tribes, attach any ideas of divinity to the sun or moon. On one of our expeditions the full moon rose large and red over the palm forest. Struck by the splendour of the scene, I pointed at the moon and asked my companions: "Who made it?" They answered: "Other blacks." Thereupon I asked: "Who made the sun?" and I got the same answer. The natives also believe that they themselves can produce rain, particularly with the help of their wizards. To produce rain they call *milka*. When on our expeditions we were overtaken by violent tropical storms my blacks always became enraged at the strangers who had caused the rain. Even my naïve friend Yokkai once boasted that he and the young Mangola-Maggi, who was a wizard, had produced rain to worry other blacks.

I never succeeded in discovering myths and legends among the blacks of Herbert river; but they are close observers of the starry heavens, and I was surprised to find that they had different names for the planets, distinguishing them by their size. In other parts of Australia the fancy of the natives makes the stars inhabited, and in this way several beautiful myths have been developed.

The southern tribes of Australia not only occupy their minds with myths and legends, but they also have definite religious notions. Some very interesting information in regard to the idea of a God cherished by these southern natives has been furnished by Mr. Manning, who in 1845 discovered among some tribes of New South Wales a doctrine of the Trinity, which bears so striking a resemblance to that of the Christian religion that we are tempted to take it to be the result of the influence of missionaries.[1] But according to the author, the missionaries did not visit these tribes until many years later. They recognise a supreme, benevolent, omnipotent Being, *Boyma*, seated far away in the north-east on an immense throne made of transparent crystal and standing in a great lake. He has an omniscient son, *Grogoragally*, who brings men to his father's throne, to be judged by the latter, and the son is the mediator. There is also a third person, half human, half divine, *Moogregally*, who is the great lawgiver to men, and who makes Boyma's will known to them. They also believe in a hell with everlasting fire, and a heaven, where the blessed dance and amuse themselves. Several other authors agree that the southern tribes of Australia believe in a supreme good Being, though they have nowhere found a religious system so perfectly developed as the one above described. Mr. Ridley's statements concerning the Kamilaroy tribe are particularly remarkable. These natives believe in a creator, *Bhaiamé*, who is to judge mankind. The word is derived from *baio*, to cut or make—thus creator,—and is distinctly identical with Manning's *Boyma*.

Others again, as for instance Mr. Mann (in New South Wales), who has made a thirty years' study of the blacks, deny that the natives have any religion whatever except fear of the " devil-devil."

It is not easy to understand this want of agreement among the authorities. If, however, the above-mentioned theory, that the south part of Australia is inhabited by a higher and more developed race than that in the north, is correct, then this supplies the solution of the problem.

As to the natives on Herbert river, it is my opinion that they do not believe in any supreme good Being, but only in a demon, and it was even difficult for them to give any definite account of this devil. On the other hand, it must be admitted that the natives are very reluctant to give any information in regard to their religious beliefs. They look upon them as secrets not to be divulged to persons not of their own race. Hence there is a possibility that they believed in a God and had more developed notions than I

[1] *Transactions of Royal Society of New South Wales*, 1882.

suspected, but I do not regard this as probable. Besides, I have evidence from various sources that the same is the case with other tribes.

Mr. George Angas[1] says of the tribes on Murray river in South Australia: "They appear to have no religious observances whatever. They acknowledge no Supreme Being, worship no idols, and believe only in the existence of a spirit, whom they consider as the author of ill, and regard with superstitious dread. They are in perpetual fear of malignant spirits, or bad men, who, they say, go abroad at night; and they seldom venture from the encampment after dusk, even to fetch water, without carrying a fire-stick in their hands, which they consider has the property of repelling these evil spirits."

In *The Fifth Continent*, p. 69, Mr. Charles Eden appears to me to use rather strong language when he says: "I verily believe that we have arrived at the sum total of their religion, if a superstitious dread of the unknown can be so designated. Their mental capacity does not admit of their grasping the higher truths of pure religion."

Mr. Curr is of the opinion that the religious ideas which people claim to have found among the Australian natives are simply the result of the influence of the white man, the ideas being modified to suit the fancy of the natives.

At all events, it is certain that neither idolatry nor sacrifices are to be found in Australia. Nor have the natives, so far as I know, ever been seen to pray.

In conclusion, I will give a brief account of a conversation which I had one evening with the Kanaka at Herbert Vale, for in my estimation it throws some light on this question. In his native home, in the far-off South Sea Islands, he had received instruction from missionaries, but had not been converted to Christianity. He said he did not like the missionaries. On this occasion—it was a mild, starlit night, such a one as can be seen only in the tropics—he asked me if it was true that we would some day go to the stars up there. I explained to him what Christianity teaches in regard to a life hereafter. "There is a much

---

[1] *Savage Life and Scenes in Australia and New Zealand.* London, 1850, vol. i. p. 88.

better place up there after death," he remarked. Some of
the natives were standing round us with their mouths wide
open. Suddenly he burst into laughter, and pointing with
one hand to the glittering stars, said : "The blacks do not
believe that there is anybody above us up there."

The objection might be made to this statement, that the
natives, particularly the older ones, had secrets which they
were unwilling to divulge to the younger members of the
tribe, with whom the Kanaka mostly associated, and that he
consequently was not acquainted with the religious ideas of
the tribe, but it appears to me that so important a matter
as the belief in a God could scarcely have escaped his
observation, for he was constantly with them both by day
and by night. He spoke their language fluently, was
married to a woman of their tribe, and had become wholly
identified with them in customs and habits of thought.

CHAPTER XXIV

My life in danger—Morbora's ingratitude—Another danger—My position grows
more precarious—The black man's fondness for imitating. ·

DURING the last part of my sojourn in Australia my
situation grew more and more perilous. In an unguarded
moment Yokkai even happened to tell me how the blacks
were constantly laying plots against me.

We were at this time about to set poison for some
animals, which I was trying to secure in Morbora's "land."
Morbora was himself one of our party, and I promised him
not only tobacco, but also a handkerchief of many colours, if
he would tell me honestly where I had better lay the poison.
There were two valleys to choose between, and I had a
strong suspicion that he from sheer laziness chose the
nearest one. I therefore assured him most positively that
if he deceived me he would get nothing, but he insisted
that the animals were usually found in the nearest valley,
which accordingly was to be preferred.

As the others declared themselves willing to go farther,
but still maintained that he was right, I was forced to believe
him. We had much work and trouble in placing poisoned
pieces of meat in various places along the river.

Here we remained for two days without catching anything, and I therefore grew impatient, and declared that he
had deceived me. To my surprise the others admitted this
with smiles in their faces: *Oito Morbora*—that is, Morbora's
jest. He accordingly received no pay from me, although he
demanded it. Still, later in the evening, I gave him a little
tobacco so that he might be able to join the others in smoking, but he was not satisfied with this. He had made up

his mind to get possession of all the tobacco I had left by
taking my life. He got Mangola-Maggi—who, by the way,
had admitted that Morbora had lied to me—to join him in
this foul plot. As the reader will remember, he was an
experienced cannibal. Together with two others he had
recently been out in search of human flesh, and had been
successful. He had no objection to give his assistance on
this occasion, the more so as the reward would be abundant
according to the standard of the blacks. Only the opportunity was wanting.

The opportunity presented itself the next morning.
They were all ready to attack me, and a part was
assigned to each one of them. Mangola-Maggi was to seize
me from behind my back, while Morbora, who was the
strongest, was to strike me on the head. I was sitting on
the ground a short distance from the hut, and had carelessly
left my revolver and my belt in my hut. They also tried to
get Yokkai into the plot, but at this time he had, fortunately
for me, been inspired to do all in his power to save my life,
and so he detained them for some time with his objections,
advising them not to attack me just at that time. Before
they had come to any definite conclusion I had got up and
gone into my hut, and so I this time escaped Morbora's
murderous plot. It was not until some time afterwards
that I learned from Yokkai the details of this intended
attack.

. Later in the day, while we were resting on the bank of
a river which we were about to cross, we met a dozen natives,
with whom Morbora at once entered into a spirited conversation. I had seated myself on the soft sand, and intended to
eat my dinner there, but I began to suspect that mischief was
brewing, for I observed that Morbora grew more and more
excited in his conversation with the strangers, and at last
became perfectly pale with rage. I therefore decided to cross
the river and eat my dinner on the other side, where I would
feel more secure. I afterwards learned from Yokkai that
he had heard Morbora propose to the strange blacks that
they should join him in killing me now that the opportunity was so favourable. It was not, therefore, strange that
Morbora did not cross the river with me. He remained

with the natives he had met, and with whom he soon
disappeared in the scrubs. After that time I never saw
him again.

I had taken more interest in the education of this man
than in that of any other; I had treated him well and
taught him, timid as he was in the beginning, to have confidence in the white man. And now my reward was that
he tried to take my life no less than twice on the same day.
It was to me a new and striking evidence of the bad character of the Australian native.

At another time the danger was even more imminent.
I had my camp near a little tribe, where there was an old
acquaintance of mine, viz. Mangoran. As will be remembered, he had accompanied me on my first expedition with
the blacks.

We had just made our camp when he put in his appearance, and my people, who were afraid of him, gave him the
greater part of the food and tobacco which they had received
from me. This was more than I could stand, and as his
laziness, moreover, had a bad influence on my people, I
requested him to remain in his own camp. On this account
Mangoran became mortally offended, and from that day I
was the object of his deadly hate. My request that he
should leave my premises was not complied with at once,
but threats to use my revolver had the desired effect. Still,
I did not care to lose sight of him, for my provisions were
never safe in his greedy propinquity.

Yokkai, too, comprehended the situation, for soon afterwards, when we were to start on an expedition, he proposed
that for safety's sake we should take Mangoran, otherwise he
would steal our provisions during our absence. Mangoran
appeared willing at once, and seemed to be pleased with
the usual reward of meat and tobacco which he would get
on our return.

The same evening I went down to the mountain stream
near the camp to take my bath. My daily intercourse with
the natives had made me less observant than caution demanded. I had left my revolver in the hut. While I was
absent a council of war was held in the camp. Mangoran,
who for several days had been looking for an opportunity,

was now eagerly urging the others to murder me, and was explaining how easy it would be to do this.

The grass all the way to the bank of the river was tall, so that they could steal down upon me unobserved. He explained to them what their reward would be—flour, meat, tobacco, and a large woollen blanket. They could take all, even my gun. The other blacks, however, hesitated. An old man who once had been shot in the leg by the native police considered the undertaking risky. Yokkai and another boy who was with me also argued against killing the white man. The end of the deliberations was that Mangoran and his wife should commit the murder. They were to steal down through the grass and attack me in the water—he armed with an axe, she with her "yam-stick." It is not difficult to see how this matter would have ended had I remained in the water as long as usual ; but as good luck would have it, the weather happened to be so cool that I could only take a short bath, and I made haste to dress myself again. Thus they did not get to the river in time to attack me in my defenceless condition, and when they saw that I was already dressed and on my way to my hut, they abandoned the project for the time.

When Yokkai, a long time afterwards, reported these facts to me, I asked him if they were not afraid of the police, to which he made the very appropriate response, "That the scrub is very large." They had been so sure that the murder would be a success that they had already in advance divided my property among themselves, and decided that my body was to be thrown into the water and not eaten. One of the horses was to be eaten, but the other, the old pack-horse, which was very lean, was to be set at liberty. Yokkai added that he had made up his mind not to allow this, but would have taken both the horses to the station, and would there have told the keeper what had happened. All this came from Yokkai's lips as naïvely and confidently as if he were talking about a person already dead and gone.

It seemed to me like reading in a newspaper about my own death and all its details, for I fully comprehended how near I had in fact been to death's door. I was surrounded by dangers on all sides, and I had no reason to look for any bettering of the circumstances, for the natives respect only those whites who shoot them, and as I did not use my gun against them, I at length came to be looked upon as "a small white man." Yokkai frequently blamed me for not being sufficiently *kóla*—that is, angry. "You do not shoot anybody," he added.

My clothes were so tattered and torn that they scarcely hung together, and this fact did not tend to raise me in the eyes of the natives, who, like children, have a keen eye for such exterior matters, and regarded my rags as evidence that I was no longer the great man they had supposed. Add to this the defeat I had suffered on account of the conduct of the police, and it is evident that my life hung by a thread.

The blacks near Herbert Vale having proved themselves lazy and useless, I never took them with me, so they got no tobacco, which made them angry. Every time I started out on an expedition they urged my people to murder me and throw my body into the water. This advice came, not only from my former friends Willy and Jacky, but even from Nelly and the Kanaka.

The greatest danger, however, threatened me from my own people, though I felt convinced that Yokkai, despite his emotional disposition, would defend me to the extent of his ability. He had himself on one occasion told me that "he did like the white man."

Despite these many difficulties, I was determined not to give up, feeling sure that I would yet be able to make new discoveries in these interesting and strange regions.

Yokkai was my only faithful friend. Once in a while he had to go to his mother to get some tobola, but he soon returned, and he stayed with me, for "he wanted to become white man."

He had also made considerable progress. He could smoke tobacco as well as anybody, was himself the owner of a clay pipe, and was able to use a few English words with more or less ease. Still, there were some gaps in his education. He was continually pestering me to teach him how to ride and shoot. His eagerness to ride was soon cured. To mount the horse he would climb up one of the forelegs, just

as if he were about to climb a tree. Not entirely pleased
with this new style of being mounted, my pack-horse, old
Kassik, put forth the remnant of his strength and made a
buck, so that Yokkai came down much quicker than he had
climbed up ; and from that time I heard no more about his
desire to ride.

As my cook he was very useful, and saved me much
trouble, but I always had to watch him. On one occasion, when he was to bake damper (he first had to wash
his hands, a trouble he did not care to take), instead of
going down to the brook he filled his mouth with water from
the pail and squirted it upon his fingers, which he thereupon
dried on the grass. He showed his hands to me to convince
me that he had washed them, but I insisted on his doing it
once more and in the proper way.

Whatever fault might be found with Yokkai, he had
become utterly indispensable to me, and besides I gained
much pleasure and entertainment from his company.

I also made him laugh many a time, and after I had
become a tolerable master of his language, and was able
to tell him things for his amusement, he laughed so
heartily that I have sometimes seen the tears stream down
his cheeks. What is comic to the blacks strikes them at
once, and makes them laugh immediately. They are very
humorous, have a decided talent for drollery, and are skilful
mimics. I once saw a young Australian receive an order
from his master, whereupon he immediately went to his
companions and imitated his master's manner of speaking
and acting, to the great amusement of the whole camp. In
their dances they imitate in a striking manner the hopping
of the kangaroo and the solemn movements of the emu,
and never fail to make the spectators laugh.

The natives like to imitate the white man's manners.
My people had observed that I rinsed my mouth every
evening ; when they had observed this for some time I
was surprised to find some of them doing the same thing.
They were also very fond of soap, not for the purpose of
washing themselves clean, but to wash some shirt or other
article of clothing which I had given them. They had
frequently seen me use soap in washing my clothes.

In spite of their respect for the gun, the clothes, and
the many good things of the white man, they still look upon
him as their inferior when they are on their own territory,
and it must be admitted that there he actually is their
inferior in many respects.

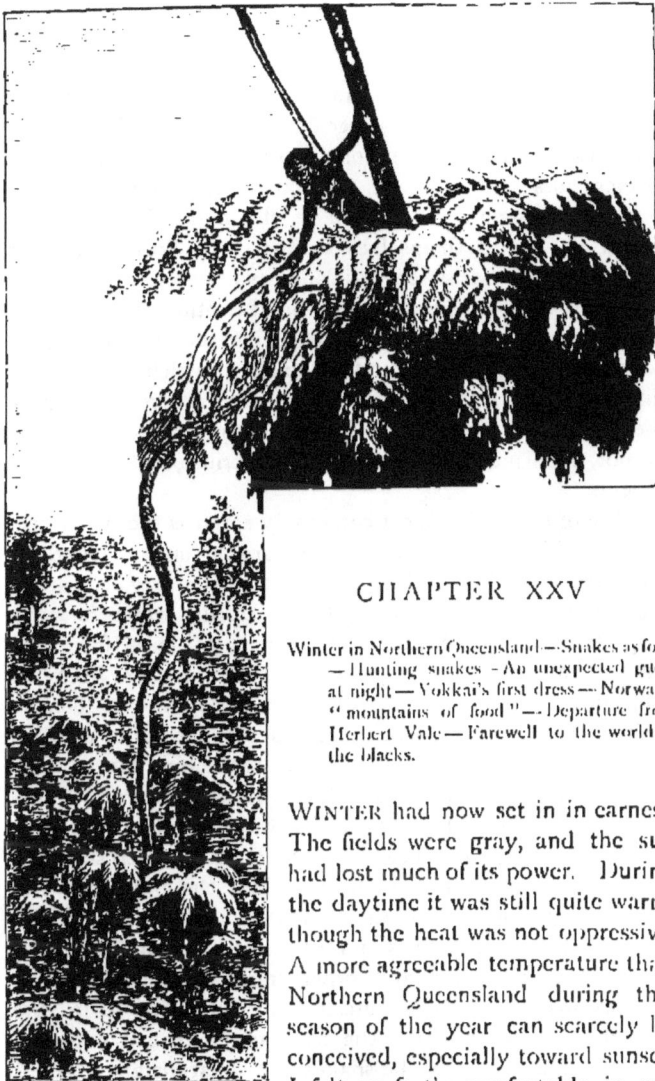

HUNTING THE PYTHON.

CHAPTER XXV

Winter in Northern Queensland—Snakes as food
—Hunting snakes—An unexpected guest
at night—Yokkai's first dress—Norway's
"mountains of food"—Departure from
Herbert Vale—Farewell to the world of
the blacks.

WINTER had now set in in earnest.
The fields were gray, and the sun
had lost much of its power. During
the daytime it was still quite warm,
though the heat was not oppressive.
A more agreeable temperature than
Northern Queensland during this
season of the year can scarcely be
conceived, especially toward sunset.
I felt perfectly comfortable in my
shirt sleeves without any vest.
During the night so much dew falls that the woollen blanket
becomes saturated if one sleeps beneath the open sky.
Walking in the grass in the morning is almost like wading

in a river. One becomes drenched to the hips. But what glorious mornings! They stimulate a person to work, and their freshness awakens all the joys of life.

The scrubs are very still in winter, and it is this stillness that gives the season its peculiar character. While the mammals and birds have donned their most beautiful and warmest furs and plumage, the natives go about as naked as in the summer. Not even in the night do they wear clothes, but warm themselves by the camp fires. Yet it is easy to procure subsistence during this season of the year. Fruits are not so abundant, but, on the other hand, animal food is easily obtained. During this season the natives are much occupied in hunting snakes, which during the winter are very sluggish, and can be slain in great numbers. The blacks are particularly fond of eating snakes, but they do not, like many of the southern tribes, eat poisonous serpents.

One of the snakes most commonly eaten is the Australian python (*Morelia variegata*), the largest snake found in Australia, which here in Northern Queensland may even attain a length of more than twenty feet. During winter it seems to prefer staying in the large clusters of ferns found on the trunks of trees. At night it seeks shelter from the cold among the leaves, but during the daytime it likes to bask in the sunshine, which enables the natives to discover and kill it with their clubs. If attacked it may bite with its many and sharp teeth, but the wound produced is not dangerous. These ferns grow in wreaths round the large trunks of trees, and look like the topsails of a ship, but they are far more numerous, and like the orchids, which grow pretty much in the same manner, are constant objects of interest to the natives, for in them they find not only snakes, but also rats and other small mammals, *Uromys*, *Sminthopsis*, *Phascologale*, etc. They therefore, as a rule, take the trouble to climb the trees to make the necessary search. They discover the snakes at a great distance, though the wreath may be fifty to sixty yards above the ground.

We were at one time travelling along one of the mountain streams, while the blacks as usual kept a sharp look-out and examined the numerous clusters of fern in the

scrub. Suddenly they discovered something lying on the
edge of one of these fern clusters, but very high in the air.
Notwithstanding their keen eyesight, they were unable to
make out whether it was a serpent or a broken branch,
so a young boy, whom I usually called Willy, climbed
up in a neighbouring tree to investigate the matter. Ere
long he called down to us, *Vindchch! vindchch!*—that is,
Snake! snake! I was very much surprised, for the object
looked to me like an old leafless limb of a tree. Willy
came down at once, and lost no time in ascending the tree
where the serpent was lying.

When he had obtained a foothold near the fern wreath,
he broke off a large branch and began striking the serpent,
which now showed signs of life. The lazy snake soon
received so many blows on the head that it fell down, and
proved to be more than ten feet long. While we were
taking a look at it we heard Willy, whom it was almost
impossible to discover so high up in the tree, call down
that he had found another snake, and this made the blacks
jubilant.

It seemed, however, to be more difficult for Willy to get
this snake down, for it was protected among the leaves, and
he was obliged to use his stick with all his might in order to
drive it out. At last it tried to make its escape, and crept
out over the edge of the wreath of ferns in order to lay
hold of the tree-trunk, but the distance was too great,
and it slipped. It could not get back, for Willy stood
there striking it, and so this serpent, which was more than
sixteen feet long, fell off; in coming down it struck the
crown of a palm-tree, which broke its fall, and quick as
lightning, it coiled itself round the trunk of the tree like a
corkscrew. Willy did not give up. He came down, and
immediately climbed up in the palm-tree to his victim, which
was, however, so tenacious of life that it did not let go its
hold until its head was crushed.

When we came to look for the former serpent we were
astonished to find it gone. We all searched carefully everywhere among the stones on the bank of the river, but it was
not to be found, and we had given up the search when Willy,
to our surprise, came dragging it behind him. He had

found it at the bottom of a hole in the river, and had dived after it.

These serpents are wonderfully tenacious of life. The one in question was apparently dead and motionless when we left it, still it had been able to crawl twenty paces, and keep itself hidden at the bottom of a hole in the river-bed.

The natives, being anxious to secure themselves against other mishaps of this sort, decided to roast the serpents at once. But, as we had not time for this, they procured a withy band from a lawyer-palm, tied the two together until we returned in the evening, and made them fast to a tree, round the trunk of which the serpents coiled themselves. When we passed the place in the afternoon there was still life in them, but they were soon despatched, put together in bundles, and carried to the camp to be roasted for supper.

As quickly as possible the camp fire was made and stones were heated ; for snakes are one of those delicacies which are prepared in the most *recherché* manner. The snakes were first laid carefully in circular form, in order that they might occupy as small a space as possible ; each forming a disc fastened together with a reed, they looked like the rope-coils made by sailors on the deck of a ship. Large serpents, and the flesh of fish, cattle, and men, are all prepared in the following interesting manner. First a hole is made in the ground about a foot deep, and in it a great fire is built. Over the fire a few stones about twice the size of a man's fist are placed. When the stones have become red-hot, they are laid aside and the rest of the fire is cleared away. Then a number of the stones are put down into the hole, and over them are laid fresh green leaves, especially of the so-called native ginger (*Alpinia cærulea*). Upon these the meat is placed, and is covered with leaves and with the rest of the hot stones ; the dug-out earth is then spread over the whole, which has the appearance of an ant-hill. If an opening is discovered letting out steam, it is immediately covered so as to keep the heat within the hill.

Now the baking is permitted to go on undisturbed. The natives know precisely when the meat is done, and they never make a mistake. The hot stones have developed an

intense heat, which gradually bakes or roasts the food
thoroughly and preserves all its flavour.

On opening the mound the outer leaves are found to be
scorched, while the inner ones are fresh and green, and give
the dish a very inviting appearance. Beef prepared in this
manner has a very fine flavour. If leaves of the ginger-
plant are used, they give the food a peculiar, piquant taste.
While I lived among the savages I adopted this manner of
preparing my salt beef, after leaving it in a brook over night
to get rid of the saltness.

No one who has never tasted meat prepared in this
manner has any conception of what an excellent flavour it
has. The principle is much the same as that applied in
France, of roasting birds in clay; and in America, of baking
clams. In my opinion, fishermen and hunters should adopt
this method of preparing their meat. Large leaves are not
necessary—common grass may be used, but it must be fresh
and green, and must be put on in thick layers.

The Australian native does not take so great pains with
common meat, but simply roasts it on the fuel or in the
hot ashes. In this manner he also prepares his larvæ,
beetles, birds, lizards, and eggs. His fish he wraps up in
leaves, and then roasts it in the ashes. The natives never
use boiling water in preparing their food, hence they have
no kettles. Food is not kept in a raw state, but is always
roasted before it is put away. There is, however, rarely
anything to save.

When the serpents were done and were taken out of
the hot leaves, they were perfectly whole as before. The
bands were loosened, and the snakes stretched out to their
full length and cut open along one side with one of their
own jaw-bones. First the fat is taken and handed in long
strings to the greedy mouths; then the heart, liver, and lungs;
finally the body itself is to be divided. As the jaw-bone
is not a sufficiently sharp tool for this purpose, they bite the
serpent into pieces with their teeth. Nothing is wasted, for
even the back-bone is crushed between the stones and
eaten, and the blacks lick and suck the small amount of
juice which drops from the meat, and enjoy themselves
hugely. But the greatest delicacy is the fat. What cannot

be eaten on the spot is put away in the hut, and in this instance they ate the leavings for four whole days, until the meat finally became putrid. When we left the camp I observed that they, strange to say, did not burn these remains of the serpents, which is their usual custom with uneaten food, in order to prevent the witchcraft of strangers.

Snake-flesh has a white colour, and does not look unappetising, but it is dry and almost tasteless. The liver, which I found excellent, tastes remarkably like game, and reminds one of the best parts of the ptarmigan. While they were being carved the serpents diffused an agreeable fragrance like that of fresh beef, and the large liver, which I obtained in exchange for tobacco, supplied me for several days with a welcome change of my monotonous fare.

The natives stand in great fear of poisonous serpents, a fact no doubt due to their helplessness against them. If they discover such a one they usually get out of its way, and if they attempt to kill it they do so by throwing at it from a distance. Accordingly the blacks were frequently surprised to see me go close to a poisonous snake and kill it with a stick. On such occasions they certainly realised the superiority of the white man. For my part, I had gradually become so accustomed to snakes that it simply amused me to see them, if they did not come into too dangerous proximity. The beauty of their forms and motions awakened my admiration, though on the other hand it must be admitted that their life and habits are not particularly interesting.

About two-thirds of the Australian serpents are poisonous, but only five varieties are said to be absolutely dangerous to man.

People who visit the tropics for the first time always fear these reptiles at first, and no doubt justly so, but in course of time they discover that their fear has been too great and that it should be overcome. When a person is bitten it is especially important to keep cool, for fear and excitement make the matter worse and may end in disaster. It is no rare thing for a bushman when bitten to be foolish enough to chop off the bitten limb.

As the serpents are so numerous in Australia, it is of course necessary to keep a sharp look-out and not get too

SNAKE FEAST IN MY CAMP.

To face page 367.

close to them. They may be met with everywhere—on the ground, in the trees, in the water, nay, even in the houses. Though most of the snakes seek their food at night, one's watchfulness should not be relaxed in the daytime. The bushman's precaution of always examining his bed before retiring to rest I deem worthy of imitation. A boy near Rockhampton was bitten by a brown snake in his bed and died.

Deaths from serpent bites are rare in Australia. In a case known to me a man died from the bite of the brown serpent (*Diemenia*) without feeling any pain to the very last, while I also know of instances where serpent bites have caused the most violent pain.

The serpents are in fact timid, and are inclined to run away from danger, and so far as I have been able to observe, they never attack men unless during the pairing season. But if we come suddenly upon them, their irritable and ugly temper makes them bite with a movement as quick as lightning.

Poisonous serpents were not so numerous here as farther south in Queensland, still they could not be called rare. One day, as we were sitting together round the fire, I was startled by the cry of the blacks, '*Vindcheh! vindchch!*—that is, Snake! snake! A serpent had appeared in my hut, but hid when it heard the shouting of the blacks. Being utterly unable to get it out of the foliage of which the wall of my hut was constructed, I assumed that it had crept back into the grass which grew outside. The same night I was awakened by some inexplicable cause; there was no sound, and in the clear light of the camp fire no suspicious object could be discerned. At the same moment I discovered a serpent, which was slowly and noiselessly creeping up my left side toward my head. I quietly allowed the snake to proceed until I saw its tail pass my cheek. After a few moments I arose, quickly changed my bed, and slept the rest of the night on the other side of the camp fire. Had I made the slightest motion the snake would doubtless have bitten me.

. . . . . .

It was near the end of June. The expeditions I had made during the last weeks were in a certain sense interesting, but they were less profitable than heretofore. I had discovered that there was not much more for me to do here. And even though I might have had a rich field to explore, I was hardly able to stand any longer the many privations and difficulties with which I had to contend.

I did not find my occupation tedious, but still I could not help longing to get away. There was here absolutely nothing of that to which I had been accustomed; for months I had lived with people who were not even able to pronounce my name. A feeling akin to home-sickness kept getting possession of me. I longed for civilisation. No matter how zealous a naturalist a man may be, he is first of all a human being, and when this feeling comes upon us we cannot conquer it, but must perforce give in.

I accordingly went back to Herbert Vale, and prepared to leave these regions and return to Central Queensland.

It was necessary to get some of the natives to go with me to assist in carrying the baggage, but it was important to be careful in the choice of men. I was unwilling to trust myself to the blacks about the station, and the others were afraid of the strange land which we had to traverse. Their speech would betray them, they said, and so they would in a short time be killed and eaten. Yokkai alone expressed a desire to accompany "Mami," still he would not dare unless he was joined by another black man, viz. Chinaman—the person I disliked most of them all. As the reader may remember, he was a great rascal who had caused me much annoyance, but as there was no other way, I had to swallow this bitter pill, for I could not go alone.

With the greatest care all my specimens were packed into large cloths which the postman had brought me from Cardwell, and which I had sewed into a kind of bag. Then all was put on the backs of the horses, and it made them look like camels. Yokkai and Chinaman carried some of the smaller bundles and led the horses, and I followed on foot.

To Yokkai I had given a whole suit of clothes as a reward for his services. I am sorry to say it was about all I was able to do for him. He was, however, exceedingly happy in his first dress and felt more secure against strange blacks, who would judge by his clothes that he was in the service of

a white man. The natives hesitate to attack a black man
who is dressed, for they are afraid they may be shot by his
master. Yokkai had of late talked much about going to Norway—across the great water in the great canoe. There he
was sure of getting all he wanted of flour and tobacco. In
Norway he would get him a wife, he said. She must be a
white woman, but one was enough ; it would not be good to
have two, he thought. I had also taught him to say Norway,
and he believed that we were now bound for that country,
with its mountains of " food and tobacco."

On the way my old pack-horse tumbled backwards down
a steep river bank, and lay on his side with my valuable
baggage under him. I got him up again, and was happy to
find that no damage had been done. With the exception of
this mishap, I arrived unscathed at Mr. Gardiner's farm at
Lower Herbert, where I met with the most friendly reception.

Great changes had been made here since I left. I could
scarcely recognise the place. Near the farm a whole sugar
plantation had grown up. Where the dense scrubs flourished
when I was there before, the fields were now covered with
sugar-cane, and there was life and bustle everywhere. On
the plantation I got some boxes, in which I packed my collection, and soon was ready to go on board a barge which
was to carry me down the river to Dungeness.

Yokkai took a deep interest in all that he saw and heard.
He lived high, stuffed himself with sugar-cane, and pretended
to be a man of great importance; in this case it certainly was
"the clothes that made the man." But everything was so
new and strange to him that he did not feel perfectly at home.
He had already given up the journey across the great water,
and he was longing to get back to his own mountains.

I had taken precautions that he should in no way suffer
in "the strange land," and I also made arrangements for
his safe return to his own tribe.

Before I went on board the boat I asked him if he would
like to go with me to Norway. He shrugged his shoulders
and answered a positive No. I shook his hand and bade him
good-bye; but I did not discover the faintest sign of emotion.
He gazed at me steadfastly with his large brown eyes beneath
his broad-brimmed hat, but did not understand the signifi-

cance of shaking hands. Thus I parted from my only
friend among the savages, and many emotions crowded upon
me as the vessel glided away, memories of the stirring days
I had passed with him, and a sense of deep gratitude for the
many services he had done me.

Upon the whole, I took leave of the country of the blacks
and my interesting life in the mountains with strange feelings
in my breast. Some of the impressions derived from this grand
phase of nature I shall never forget. When the tropical sun
with its bright dazzling rays rises in the early morning above
the dewy trees of the scrub, when the Australian bird of paradise arranges its magnificent plumage in the first sunbeams,
and when all nature awakens to a new life which can be conceived but cannot be described, it makes one sorry to be
alone to admire all this beauty. Or when the full moon
throws her pale light over the scrub-clad tops of the mountains and over the vast plains below, while the breezes play
gently with the leaves of the palm-tree, and when the
mystic voices of the night birds ring out on the still quiet
night, there is indeed melancholy, but also untold beauty,
in such a situation.

I was, however, not sorry to leave the people. I had
come to Herbert Vale full of sympathy for this race, which
the settler drives before him with the rifle, but after the
long months I had spent with them my sympathy was gone
and only my interest in them remained. Experience had
taught me that it is not only among civilised people that
men are not so good as they ought to be.

CHAPTER XXVI

A RACE so uncivilised as the Australian natives has of course no written language. Still they are able to make themselves understood by a kind of sign language. Now and then the natives send information to other tribes, and this is done by the aid of figures scratched on a " message stick " made of wood, about four to seven inches long, and one inch wide. Some of them are flat, while others are round and about as thick as a man's finger ; they often are painted in different colours. I myself saw one of these sticks which came to a native among my acquaintances on Herbert river. The man told me that he understood the inscription perfectly well, and he even prepared a similar stick, on which he wrote an answer. The message stick shown on page 304 is from Central Queensland. One side is meant to represent an enclosed piece of ground. There is a gate in the fence, and the dots mean grass and sheep. I am also fortunate in being able to give an illustration of another message stick (p. 304), with the interpretation of its inscription, which conveys a message from a black woman named Nowwanjung to her husband Carralinga of the Woongo tribe. Other message sticks are engraved with straight or circular lines in regular patterns as in embroidery ; this has caused an entirely different view of their significance, which supposes them to be merely cards to identify the messenger. This view may be correct, but it is not corroborated by my experience on Herbert river.

Nearly every tribe has its own language, or at least its own dialect, so that the members of different tribes are unable to understand each other. The reason for this is to a great extent the hostility existing between the tribes. Of course

A MESSAGE STICK FROM CENTRAL QUEENSLAND.

every tribe is familiar with the language of its nearest neighbours, and makes use of nearly the same dialect when they talk with a friendly tribe, but they treat a hostile tribe with scorn, and ridicule their language. The language, not being

REVERSE SIDE OF THE SAME.

written, is constantly undergoing change, and there is even a difference between the speech of the old people and the children. If you put the same question to a black man three or four times, his last answer will be expressed differently, though he uses the same words.

In spite of difference between the languages spoken in

Carmlinga
come here to-morrow
and take　　　　Nowwanjung.

MESSAGE STICK, WITH INTERPRETATION OF INSCRIPTION.

the various parts of the continent, an intimate relation is believed to exist between them, and it is the prevailing opinion that they spring from a common root language. At all events it is a fact that many words are the same in very large districts, even in places so far apart that they cannot possibly have influenced each other by communication. I know a case where a black man from Clermont understood the language spoken in Aramac and on Georgina river, and yet he had never been there.

This similarity of vocabulary must not be confounded with those words which are used everywhere, and which have been spread by Europeans. Many of these are not Australian in their origin. The colonist, who moves from one part of the country to another, generally takes with him some of the words of the language of the blacks, and thus these are transplanted into new soil. In this manner many words have emigrated from Victoria and New South Wales, and have taken root with the new civilisation. There are now a number of such words which are in vogue throughout the civilised part of the continent—for example, *yariman*, horse ; *dillibag*, basket ; *kabra*,[1] head ; *bingee*, belly ; *gin*, woman ; *gramma*, to steal; *bael*, not ; *boodgary*, excellent ; *korroboree*, festive dance ; *dingo*, dog, etc. We can even trace words which the Europeans have imported from the natives of other countries—for example, *picaninny*, a child. This word is said to have come originally from the negroes of Africa through white immigrants. In America the children of negroes are called *picaninny*. When the white men came to Australia, they applied this word to the children of the natives of this continent.

Such " civilised " words, however, seldom take root in the language of the blacks. They simply use them in conversation with the white man. Though a few words are carried in this manner from one district to another, this method of transplanting is not of any great importance.

A natural affinity between the languages can with certainty be pointed out. Some words are almost identical throughout the continent. An excellent illustration of this is found in the word for *eye*.

In Caledon Bay, on the Gulf of Carpentaria, it is *mail ;* Endeavour river, on the north-west coast (16° S. lat.), *meul ;* Moreton Bay (29° S. lat.), *mill ;* Port Macquarie (33° S. lat.), 68 miles south from Sydney, *me ;* Port Jackson (Sydney), *mi* or *me ;* Limestone Creek (140 miles west of Sydney), *milla ;* Yarra tribe, Victoria, *mii ;* King George Sound

[1] According to a word-list from the beginning of the century this word was used in Port Macquarie (*cahbrah*), and Port Jackson (*cabbra*).

(south-west coast, 35° S. lat.), *mil;* Herbert river (18° S. lat.), *mill.*

An equally interesting example is found in the numeral 2, which is tolerably constant throughout the continent— *bular, bulara, buloara, budelar, burla, bulla, buled, boolray, pulette, pular, pollai, bolita, bulicht, bollowin,* etc. Even in Tasmania the word is found, *pualih.* The words for 1 and 3 are, on the other hand, always different. For comparison I give the following table—

NUMERALS.

	1	2	3	4	5
Near Adelaide, South Australia	kumande	purlaitye	marnkutye	purlaitye-purlaitye	
Moreton Bay, Southern Queensland	ganar	burla	burla ganar	burla burla	korumba (much)
Boraipar, West Australia	keiarpe	pulette	pulekvia	pulette-pulette	...
Burapper, S.E. Australia, near Murray river	kiarp	bullait	bullait-kiarp	bullait bullait	
Mount Elliot, Northern Queensland, 19° S. lat.	woggin	boolray	goodjoo	munwool	murgai
Tasmania, south coast	marrava	pûalih	...	wullyava	

A common root can also be shown in the personal pronoun. *I* is called *ngaia, nganya, ngatoa, ngaii, ngai, ngie, ngan, ngu, ngipa, ngâpe,* etc. *Thou—inta, nginta, nginte, nginda, ngin, ninna, nindu, nginne,* etc.

Upon the whole, though the various languages have but little in common, there are certain peculiarities which may be regarded as characteristic of them all. They are polysyllabic, the accent is usually on the penultimate or antepenultimate, and the words are, therefore, not unpleasant to the ear. Indeed, many of them are full of euphony and harmony. The large number of vowels contributes

much to this result. Guttural sounds are particularly prominent. The *s* sound appears to be very rare. On Herbert
river I heard only two words which contained the letter *s*—
suttungo, tobacco, and *sinchen*, syphilis, and so far as I know,
s is found only in the beginning of words.

In grammar the languages also differ widely. At all
events, the authors who have sought to discuss these matters
thoroughly have arrived at very different results.

Mr. Beveridge, who has studied the languages of
Victoria, claims that the syntax is very simple, saying that
the various grammatical relations are expressed solely by
prolongations, accentuations, and changes of position of the
words. Mr. Lang, on the contrary, holds an entirely different
opinion. He supports the popular theory that the Australian
natives have in the past occupied a much higher plane of
civilisation than at present, and thinks he is able to find
traces of a decayed civilisation in the languages of the tribes,
which in his opinion are very perfect.

As a striking example he mentions the inflections of the
verbs. At Moreton Bay the verbs have far more inflections
than the verbs in the Hebrew language. They can be conjugated reflexively, reciprocally, frequentatively, causatively,
and permissively. They have not only indicative, imperative,
and subjunctive, past, present, and future, expressed by definite inflectional endings, but each one of these endings may
assume distinct shades of meaning expressed by different
inflections. The imperfect of the verb to speak (*goal*) has
not only a form which means "spoke," but forms which
mean "spoke to-day," "spoke yesterday," "spoke some days
ago," etc. The same is the case with the future. There are
three imperatives : (1) speak ; (2) thou shalt speak (emphatic) ; (3) speak if you can, or if you dare (ironical). The
nouns are regularly inflected by suffixes ; *ngu* means of, *go*
to, *da* in, *di*·from, *kunda* with, etc. The pronouns have both
dual and plural form : *ngaia* I, *ngulle* we two, you and I ;
ngullina (comp. Herbert river, *allingpa*) we two, he and I, etc.
This complicated syntax is found in many tribes, though
they may have widely different languages.

Mr. E. M. Curr, of Melbourne, has recently in a great
and very meritorious work, *The Australian Race*, pointed out

a most striking resemblance between the languages of the Australian blacks and those of the African negroes. His opinion is that the Australian natives are descended from the African negroes by a cross with some other race. He admits that the Australian blacks look quite different from the natives of Africa, but he shows that the customs, the superstitions, and above all the languages, agree in many respects in a most remarkable manner. He points out the striking fact that while the Papuan and the Australian languages are almost totally different, still many of the words used by the Australian blacks are almost identical with those employed by the negroes of Africa.

The language of the natives on Herbert river is imperative and brief. A single word frequently expresses a whole sentence. "Will you go with me?" is expressed simply by the interrogation *nginta?* (thou?), and the answer, "I will stay where I am," by *karri ngipa* (I remain). "I will go home," *ngipa mittago* (literally, I in respect to the hut).

The suffix *go* literally means "with regard to," and is usually added to nouns to give them a verbal meaning, but it is also sometimes added to verbs. The question *Wainta Morbora?*—that is, "Where is Morbora?"—can be answered by saying only *tityengo* (he has gone hunting *tityen*) (wallaby), (literally, with respect to wallaby); or, for example, *mittago* he is at home (literally, with regard to the hut). *Mottaigo* means 'he is eating" (literally, with regard to eating). "Throw him into the water," is expressed simply by *ngallogo*. As is evident, this is a very convenient suffix, as it saves a number of moods and tenses. It may also be used to express the genitive—for example, *toolgil tomobrogo*, the bones of the ox.

There frequently is no difference between nouns, verbs, and adjectives. *Kola* means wrath, angry, and to get angry. *Poka* means smell, to smell, and rotten ; *oito* means a jest, and to jest.

"It is noon," is *vi ōrupi* (sun big). "It is early in the morning," is *vi naklam* (sun little). "It is near sunset," is *vi molle mongan. Kolle* is a very common word. It is, in fact, used to call attention to a strange or remarkable sound, and means "hush!" *Kolle mal!* "Hush, there is a strange

man!" *Kölk* is also used to express indignation or a protest,
"far from it." A superlative of an adjective is expressed
by repetition—for example, *krally-krally*, "very old."

The vocabulary is small. The language is rich in words
describing phenomena that attract the attention of the
savage, but it lacks words for abstract notions. The natives,
being utterly unable to generalise, have no words for kinds
or classes of things, as tree, bird, fish, etc. But each
variety of these things has its own name. Strange to say,
there are words not only for the animals and plants which
the natives themselves use, but also for such as they have
no use for or interest in whatever. On Georgina river the
natives have a special word for sweetheart.

On Herbert river I found, to my surprise, various names
for flame and coals. *Vákkun* meant camp fire, coals, or the
burning stick of wood, while the flame was called *koyilla.*

Of numerals the Australian natives have no comprehen-
sion. Many tribes have only two numerals, viz. 1 and 2, and
by combining these they can count to five, thus—1 *keiarpe,*
2 *pulette,* 3 *pulette-keiarpe,* 4 *pulette-pulette,* 5 *pulette-pulette-
keiarpe.* Several tribes have three numerals, as, for instance,
Herbert Vale tribe—1 *yóngul,* 2 *yákkan,* 3 *kárbo,* 4, etc.,
is usually expressed by *taggin* (many). Occasionally a tribe
may be found which has a word for 10. The word literally
means two hands (*bolita murrung*), a remarkable parallel
existing in many other languages (from the Sandwich
Island to Madagascar) in which the word *lima* means both
hand and five.

The dialects of the natives abound in proper nouns.
Every locality has its name, every mountain, every brook,
every opening in the woods. Many of these names are
remarkable for their euphony. As a curiosity I quote the
following stanza—

> "I like the native names as *Paramatta*
> And *Illawarra* and *Woolloomoollo.*
> *Toongabbe, Mittagong,* and *Coolingatta,*
> And *Yurumbon,* and *Coodgiegang, Meroo,*
> *Euranarina, Jackwa, Bulkomatta,*
> *Nandowra, Tumbarumba, Woogaroo;*
> The *Wollondilly* and the *Wingycarribbee,*
> The *Warragumby, Daby, Bungarribee.*"

It is a strange fact that the dialects in a great part of the country are named after their respective negatives. *Wiraiaroi* is a dialect in which *wirai* means "no," and *Wailwun* is one in which *wail* means "no." Thus *Kamilaroi*, *Wolaroi*, etc. *Pikumbul* is an exception. In this dialect *piku* means "yes." One cannot help thinking of the French *Langue d'Oc* and *Langue d'Oyl*.

COMPARATIVE VIEW OF SOME AUSTRALIAN DIALECTS.

	Endeavour river, York peninsula.	Herbert river, Northern Queensland.	Mount Elliot, Northern Queensland, 19° S. lat.	Moreton Bay, Southern Queensland.	Goulbourn river, New South Wales.	Port Jackson, New South Wales.	Yarra tribe, Victoria.	Near Adelaide, South Australia.	Doraipar, West Australia.
Man	bama	mal	munyah	malar	goleen	mulla	kolin	(pl.) meyu	(pl.) wootawolli
Woman	mootjel	dombi-dombi	younngoorah	jundal	badyuroo	din	bajor	ngammaitya	liu
Kangaroo	kangooroo	...	oodra bourgoola	kurruman	marram	wallibah	mirrm	nanto wauwe	...
Stone	walbah	faringa	...	mulla	moid yerre	keba¹ giber	mojerr	pure	...
Water	poorai"	ngallo	doongalla	dabil	parn	badoo	paen	kauwe	wolpool
Sun	gallan	vee	ingin	beeké	nummi	goona	ngumi	tindo	nauwingy
Moon	...	ballan	wurboonbura	kihbom	ninnun	yennadah	meenean	piki	miiyah
Head	wageegee	mogil	coode	magul	kowanoo	coblra²	kuvang	makarta	poorpai
Hair	morye	pocka	weir	kapui	kowung	kewarra	yarré	yoka	...
Hand	marigal	mallan	(pl.) cabankabun	marra	munangoo	tammirra	marnong	pemarra	mannangy
Foot	(pl.) edamal	bingan	(pl.) deenah	sidney (ichidna)	tinnanoo	manoe	jenong	(pl.) tidna	(pl.) tchinnangy
Nose	bonjo poteer	wooroo	...	muloo	garknoo	nogro	ká-ang	mudla	cheen-je
Belly	nelmal	vomba	booloo	gunmung	bendé	barrong	...	...	...
Excrements	...	kona	...	koodna	kournong	...	conong	kudna	...
Fire	menanang	(flame) koyilla	ejugabah	kuddum	wein	gweeyong	ween	gadla	wanappe

¹ See the Gospel of St. John i. 42, "Thou art Simon the son of Jona : thou shalt be called Cephas, which is by interpretation, A stone."   ² Spanish : *cobra*.

Arabic : *ka-aba* or *giber* (Gibraltar).

Allínkpa, we two.
Ámmery, hungry.
Ámnion, breast.
Átta [Moreton Bay and Rock-hampton : atta], I.

Bággoro, sword, serpent-liver.
Bállan, moon.
Bámbo, egg.
Bámpa, distant.
Bátta, take.
Bémo, brother's son.
Bínghan, foot, footprint.
Bínna, ear.
Boongary, *Dendrolagus lumholtzii*.
Bórboby, battle, duels.
Bórrogo, a variety of *Pseudochirus*.

Deerbera, to-morrow.
Dómbi-dómbi, woman.

Era, teeth.
Etaka, tuft.
Evin, *Calamus australis*.

Farínga, stone, rock.

Gangítta, handkerchief.
Gilg/a [the *l* to be pronounced with thick palatal sound], casso-wary.
G'rauan, *Megapodius tumulus* (bird, egg, nest).
-Go [suffix, Moreton Bay : -co], in regard to.
Gómbian, *Echidna*.
Góri, blood.

Hánka, whence ?

Káddera, opossum (*Trichosurus vulpecula*).
Kádjera, *Cycas media*.
Kainno, to-day.
Kainno-kainno, well, sound.
Kakavagó, go.
Kalló, come on !
Kámin, climbing implement.

Kámo, water.
Kárbo, 3.
Kárri, remain.
Kawan, nausea.
Káwri, axe.
Kedool, cold.
Kelán, old man, sir [word of ad-dress].
Kóbi, arts of witchcraft.
Kóla [subst. and adj.], anger, angry.
Kólle, hush !
Komórbory, many, large multi-tude.
Kóna, excrements.
Kónka, unharmed, raw, not roasted.
Kóntagan, nice weather.
Kontáhberan, dark, dark night.
Koonduno, thunder.
Koráddan, a kind of fruit.
Koyílla, flame.
Králly, old.
Kuroonguy, thirsty.
Kootjary, *Talegalla lathami*.
Kvíkkal, *Perameles nasuta*.
Kvíngan, evil spirit, devil.

Mah, } not, no.
Maja, }
Mal [Moreton Bay: malar. Yelta : mallé], man, especially of a strange and hostile tribe.
Mállan, hand.
Mally, good, excellent.
Mami, master.
Mánta, *membrum virile*.
Manta korán, an oath of uncertain meaning, also a word of abuse.
Márbo, louse.
Márgin, gun.
Máwa, crawfish.
Mílka [verb], produce rain.
Míll, eye.
Minná [cf. Moreton Bay : menäh], how ?
Minná-minnana-gó, how in the world ?

Mítta, hut.
Mogil [Moreton Bay: magul], head.
Mólle, near.
Móngan, mountain.
Móngan, *Pseudochirus herbertensis*.
Móttai [verb and subst.], eat, food.
Móyo, *anus*.

Nahyee, no.
Naiko [verb], own.
Naklam [the *l* to be pronounced with thick palatal sound], little.
Ngallo, water.
Ngalloa, *Dactylopsila trivirgata*.
Nginta, you.
Ngipa, I.
Nongáshly, only.
Nili, girl.

Oito, jest.
Oonda, see.
Ōrupi, large.

Peera [subst. and adj.], fear, afraid.
Pipo [from the English], pipe.
Póka, hair ; smell [Echuca: boka].
Pókkan, grass-land, grass.
Pul [verb], smell.
Púlli, flea.

Sinchen, rash, syphilis.
Suttúngo, tobacco.

Tággin, many, much, also the numeral 4.
Takólgoro [a word of exclamation], poor fellow !
Tálgoro, human flesh.
Tállan, tongue.
Tamin, fat.

Tchígga, sit.
Tītyen, wallaby.
Tobola, a kind of fruit.
Tomóbero, cattle, meat.
Toollah, *Pseudochirus archeri*.
Toolgil, bone, bones.
Toolgin, scrub.
Toongna, drink.
Toongu, sweet.
Towdala, *Orthonyx spaldingii*.

Vákkun, coals.
Vaneera, hot.
Vee, sun.
Veera, a kind of fig which grows on grass-land.
Vikku, bad.
Víndchch, snake.
Vómba, belly.
Vóndo, an edible root of a climbing plant.
Vooly [adj.], dead.
Vooroo, nose.
Vótel, sleep.
Vukka, thigh.

Wainta, where ?

Yábby, *Pseudochirus lemuroides*.
Yákkan, 2.
Yálla, remain.
Yamina, a monster (p. 201).
Yanky, a kind of fig.
Yárri, *Dasyurus*.
Yári, honey.
Yeergilíngera, star.
Yókkan, fog, rain.
Yóngul, 1.
Yópolo, *Hypsiprymnodon moschatus*.

NAMES OF MEN.

Eergon.	Kawri.	Mórborn.	Póko.
Ganindály.	Mángola-Mággi.	Nángo-Maddal.	Yánky.
Góngola.	Mangóran.	Nílgora.	Yáwra.
Kāl-Dúbbaroh.	Mawa.	Píngaro.	Yókkai.

NAMES OF WOMEN.

Gónbaro.	Kélanmi.	Mólle-Mólle.	Olánga.

CHAPTER XXVII

AFTER a voyage of a few days I arrived in safety at Grace-mere. On the journey from Herbert river down the coast you

THE FREEZING ESTABLISHMENT, LAKES CREEK, NEAR ROCKHAMPTON.

pass two establishments for freezing meat for export, viz. Bowen and Rockhampton. This comparatively new industry in Australia has recently been largely developed, and is no doubt destined to become of great importance to the country, which will in this manner be able to dispose of its great surplus of meat. The largest amount is exported from New Zealand.

Gracemere was now in its winter dress. How poor Central Queensland looks to a person coming from the charming tropics of Northern Queensland! But here in the south the genuine Australian landscape is found, the characteristic feature of which is the fantastical and the gloomy; solemn gum-trees, which lose their white bark in winter just as European trees shed their leaves, stiff grass-trees, solemn-looking acacias, can hardly give any charm to a landscape. And yet I have seen beautiful landscapes outside Northern Queensland, as for instance the fern-tree gully in Victoria, where the most splendid tree-ferns grow at the feet of the highest trees in the world. The views from the heights in the rear of the capital of South Australia across the wide Adelaide plains are very imposing, as are also those obtained on a journey across the Blue Mountains in New South Wales, especially where the windings of the Paramatta river are seen in the distance.

Though I enjoyed in a high degree the pleasure attendant upon a return to the comforts of civilisation, I soon began to make expeditions northward along the coast.

On one occasion I was invited to take part in hunting the dugong (*Halicore dugong*). I set out in the latter part of August in a carriole (*karjol*), which the Archers many years ago had imported from Norway, and which probably is the only one of the kind in all Australia. A carriole requires a good road, for it easily upsets, on account of the short distance between the two wheels, but in the open woodlands of Australia it is possible to drive almost anywhere, if there are no fences, brooks, or other obstacles.

After a journey of four days I arrived at Torilla, where preparations were at once made for the hunt. The first need was a boat. My host had only a small sailing boat given to him by some French Communists who had escaped from their confinement in New Caledonia and landed on his premises. One of these fugitives had been employed on the farm, and was an excellent carpenter. He undertook to repair the old rotten hulk, which had been lying on the bank of the river for a long time exposed to the sun and rain. It was a well-built boat with new sails and good masts, but in other respects it had seen its best days. The Frenchman went to work industriously, encouraged by the lady of the house, who promised him that he should be permitted to take part in the hunt, which in her mind was a guarantee that he would repair the boat properly. And after he had spent eight days in calking, rigging, and pitching the craft, he declared her seaworthy, and we at length put to sea. The crew consisted of my host, my English friend the squatter, the Frenchman, and myself. We were to take turns in baling.

After a pleasant sail we reached an island late in the evening, and there we made our camp on the shore. We had taken drinking water with us. The old mangrove stems made an excellent fire, and the soft sand a pleasant bed. We also set fire to some tall grass, in order to give the signal to some blacks who had agreed to join us here.

Early the next morning two natives, who were to assist us in hunting, came rowing in a canoe from the mainland. One of them paddled the canoe, while the other one kept baling out water with a large shell.

The canoe of the natives here is made of three pieces of bark, one forming the bottom and two the sides. The pieces are sewed together with wood fibres, and there is nothing, by way of ribs, to keep the pieces of bark together ; simply a small cross-piece to support the sides, nor are there rowlocks or rudder. There is only room for two, and as the water continually pours in, one man is occupied in baling, while the other paddles on the two sides alternately with a stick about two yards long.

We took both the blacks and their canoe on board and started with full sail for Saltwater Bay. The difference between ebb and flood was here about twenty-eight feet. In Broad Sound, which lies a little farther to the north, the difference is said to be greater than anywhere else in the world—that is, about thirty-three feet.

Saltwater Bay is very shallow, and the large fields of mud that become visible at ebb-tide are covered with submarine Algæ. Here the dugong, the strange Australian sea-cow, seeks its food when the tide rises. In the innermost part of the bay we found a place for a camp ; we rose early

the next morning, and as soon as the water was deep enough
rowed out.   The blacks brought the implements to be used.
The harpoon consists of two parts, the handle and spear, of
which I give an illustration below.   The point or spear
is a piece of wire about eleven inches long, sharpened at one
end, the other being enclosed in grass and wood fibre, forming
a sort of knot which fits exactly into a hole in the handle so

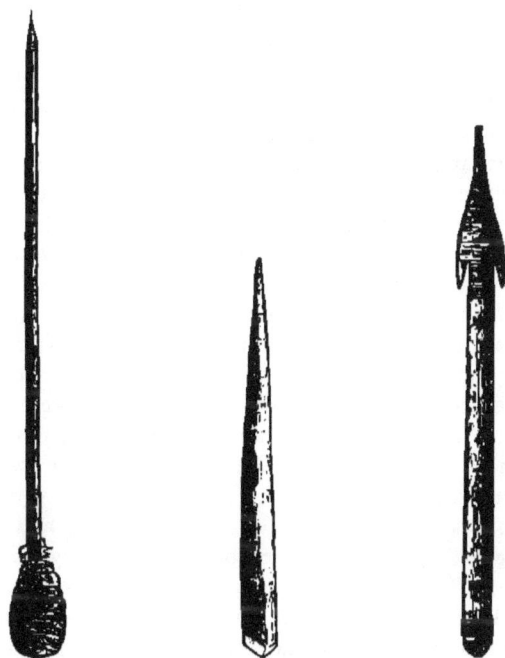

A WIRE HARPOON POINT.   A WOODEN PLUG.   A WOODEN HARPOON POINT.

as to be held firmly in its place.   To this knot a line is
fastened.   When the harpoon is thrown the point enters the
animal, and at the same time the handle is set free and floats
about on the water.   This handle is a heavy wooden rod
about three yards long.

Although the point is without barbs, still it sticks fast
in the dugong's thick skin, as if the latter were made of
gutta-percha.   The point of the harpoon is bent into a
hook the moment the animal starts away, and when, from

tugging at the canoe, it has become sufficiently exhausted, it is finally towed up to the boat and its nostrils adroitly closed with wooden plugs, and thus it is choked. Before the natives in this part of Australia had come in contact with Europeans and had learned the value of iron, they used barbed harpoon points made of wood. The manner in which the natives catch the dugong shows more thought and reflection than we would expect from savages so low in the scale of development as the Australian aborigines. The fact that the black man, lazy as he is by nature, will submit to all the toil necessary to capture the animal is proof of the great value he puts upon its flesh and fat.

As we sailed across the bay before a light breeze our natives did not fail to discover a large amount of loose grass floating on the water, positive evidence that the dugong was not far away. Nor did many moments pass before the man keeping watch in the stern of the boat called out : *Parábela, parábela !*—that is, Dugong, dugong ! We sent the blacks out in their own canoe. One of them seized the baling-shell, while the other put his long spear and his lines in order, and so they rowed softly out among the animals, which kept coming nearer and nearer. We remained as quiet as possible in the distance and witnessed the scene before us with the deepest interest.

More than fifty dugongs were approaching, and one or two came within a few yards of our boat. They frequently raised their heads above the water to get breath ; making a heavy loud expiration, and then, with a quick inspiration, they again disappeared in the deep.

The blacks kept rowing among them in order to select a suitable victim. At length the spear leaves the unerring hand of the black hunter. A great splash in the water shows that the harpoon has not missed its aim. The animal is pierced by a second harpoon and starts off with two lines. After half an hour it is so exhausted that it can be brought up to the canoe, where its nostrils are plugged.

By uniting our efforts we at length succeeded in bringing the animal into our boat. Although it was a mere calf, it was no easy matter to get it on board.

We took the blacks into our boat and set sail so as to reach

our camp at the head of the bay before the water became too
shallow.   It was a touching sight to see the mother of the
slain animal following us for a long time, swimming to and
fro near the boat for half an hour and then going away.

We brought our game safe ashore, and at once began to
skin it.   In the meantime the blacks were cooking a gray
mullet (*Mugil*), which has an excellent flavour.   They fried
it in fat from the dugong, and this, accompanied by a glass
of whisky, formed an excellent meal.   The successful hunt
put us in the best of spirits.   The squatter jokingly proposed
that we, like the blacks, should anoint our bodies with dugong

THE DUGONG, OR AUSTRALIAN SEA-COW (*Halicore dugong*).

oil and dance a korroboree all night through.   The Frenchman, our cook, was as happy as a lark, and was quite in his
element when some of the most tender parts of the dugong
were placed over the coals to roast.

The meat had an exceedingly delicate flavour, and tasted
like something midway between veal and pork, but far better
than either.   The squatter imagined himself in Paris, and was
reminded of the Hôtel du Louvre, where he had spent many
a day of his earlier life.

My host and myself were busy preparing the skin.   The
blacks were in the best of spirits.   They fried and ate as
much of the meat as they pleased, and thereupon an unlimited

supply of tobacco was placed at their disposal. When night set in, our camp presented a most picturesque appearance. Three large camp fires blazed among the gum-trees, the columns of smoke ascended in the calm evening, and the stars glittered over a company as wide apart in tastes and interests as in nationality, but all gay and happy: one Englishman, a white Australian, a Frenchman, a Norseman, and two Australian blacks.

The dugong has become widely known on account of its fat, which even several years ago was found to be an excellent remedy for consumption and nervous prostration. A physician in Brisbane found, it difficult to procure cod-liver oil from Europe for his patients, and so he determined to try the fat of the dugong. He boiled it into an oil, of which the medicinal qualities were found to be most remarkable. Near Brisbane a dugong-fishing establishment was started and a number of black harpoonists were employed. Dugong oil fetched a high price, but unfortunately it soon became adulterated with shark-liver oil and similar fats. Its reputation fell, and the market was destroyed. There was also a large demand for skeletons to supply all the museums of the world.

The fat used for medicinal purposes is taken from the sides, and the oil, which is almost as clear as water, is absolutely tasteless. As the animals have become very scarce, and as they, moreover, are very shy, the oil is naturally very expensive. This fact is greatly to be deplored, for its nourishing and nerve-invigorating qualities can scarcely be over-estimated. There are most remarkable instances on record of its having cured nervousness, and according to the report of Dr. Hobbs it must be credited with being in all respects superior to cod-liver oil. I am familiar by experience with the excellent effect of both on the nervous system, and although I greatly prefer the dugong oil, still, as we have in cod-liver oil so good a subsitute for it, I cannot but regret that the value of this kind of food is not appreciated more than it is. Is it not possible that we here have a cure for the overworked nerves of our time? Unfortunately most people have a dislike to cod-liver oil, which is in part attributable to the poor preparation of former times and in part to the fact that it is rarely obtained fresh. Nowadays conscientious manufacturers produce an article having, when in good condition, the flavour of fresh cod-liver oil, which by the majority of people is looked upon as a delicacy. It now only remains to find some way of preserving that flavour of the oil.

At present there are two dugong-fishing establishments in Queensland, both on the east coast, but they are not managed with sufficient energy, and the result is that cod-liver oil is used more extensively than dugong oil. The fact that the animals move from one place to another, and have to be followed by the fishermen, makes the capture of the dugong very difficult. The fishing is carried on mainly by very strong nets, in which the animals are caught when they return, with the ebb-tide, from their pasture grounds on the shoals to deep water. The dugong is not found south of Moreton Bay, but is plentiful everywhere north of it, particularly in the Gulf of Carpentaria. It is also found in the Mozambique Channel and in the Indian Ocean, and the Malayans are said to be skilful in harpooning it. Besides the oil, the skin of the dugong, which is an inch thick, is also very valuable, as it is made into a gelatine or into strong leather. The bones, which are very heavy, may be used as a substitute for ivory.

It is said that the dugong mother constantly holds fast to her young with her pectorals, and in ancient times this gave rise to the traditions about sirens or mermaids. The Dutchman called the dugong *baardmaenetje*, *i.e.* the little bearded man.

The next morning, while I was putting the finishing touches to the preparation of my skin, I heard the squatter cry out, " Here! the boat is sinking! " We all ran to see what was the matter, and we discovered our boat on the point of being swallowed by the waves, and my two bottles of alcohol floating in the water. There was no actual danger of the boat being lost, for the water was shallow, but the tide was now rising with the force of a river, so that it was not long before only the masts of our boat were visible. As there were traces of crocodiles to be seen everywhere on the strand, one of us took a rifle in order to keep guard, while

Y

the rest tried to save the boat, which after wading in mud up to our waists, we finally succeeded in doing.

It was impossible to secure a full-grown dugong, for our lines were not strong enough, and we therefore started on our journey home again.   The next night we made our camp on an island, and the squatter at once went out to shoot rabbits with his rifle.   The rabbits had been placed on this island a few years previously, and although there was no fresh water excepting when it rained, still they throve very well, and had greatly increased in numbers.   Strange to say, these rabbits are said to be poisonous, doubtless on account of the food on which they are obliged to subsist.   The squatter informed me that a year ago he had visited this island and shot some of these animals, which were roasted and eaten, but had made both him and his companions ill.

A large number of Australian plum-trees were found on this island.   We shot a mound-builder and several pigeons. The next morning the blacks left us, and we continued our sail home.   On the coast we saw large numbers of rock-oysters.   It happened to be ebb-tide and there were three large peninsulas, like a yellow-brown mass, entirely covered with these fine-flavoured shell-fish.

I remained a few days longer with my most amiable hosts at Torilla.   The lady of the house was a very intelligent woman.   Her parents had taught her Greek and Hebrew in order to enable her to read both the Old and the New Testament in the original tongue.   Though she was well versed in both languages, she was no blue-stocking, but a very practical woman.   She gave her daughter the very prudent advice, " Never you marry a bad breakfastman." The first thing she noticed in a man was his teeth.   If these were sound, the rest of the body was sure to be right —a sound mind in a healthy body.   Like the majority of Australian ladies, the daughter was natural and free from affectation.   She took a deep interest in zoology, and was an industrious collector of specimens.   On her solitary excursions she did not hesitate to climb trees after birds' eggs, and she complained bitterly that the men were too lazy to help her.   The ladies who are brought up in the Australian bush have, upon the whole, a peculiar frankness and in-

dependence, for from their very childhood they have to
rely on themselves. Another " bush girl " of my acquaintance
rode thirty miles to try on a dress.

The whole family at Torilla were excellent riders, and
had the reputation of being the best in Queensland. An
unmanageable horse at the station had thrown both his
master and mistress, nearly killing them, but they nevertheless continued to care for the animal with the greatest
tenderness, a proof of the great sympathy an Australian
feels for his horse.

On my way back to Gracemere I saw a large number of
wading birds in the lagoons. I took special notice of the
splendid Australian jabiru (*Mycteria australis*), and I had
the good fortune to shoot on the wing a specimen of this
beautiful variety of the stork family with swan shot at a
distance of no less than 127 paces.

I passed the oldest gold mine in Queensland, called
Canoona Diggings, but the place was now almost entirely
abandoned. Here I met a Dane, who was very kind to
me. He had been in the gold mines since their discovery,
about thirty years ago, and in spite of the fact that both
he and his family had to work hard for a living, they looked
healthy and contented.

It is a great mistake to suppose that digging gold is
easy work. As everybody knows, "nuggets of gold" are
scarce. Most of the gold is found as fine grains, and requires
great labour to separate it from the gravel, which in this case
had to be hauled a great distance to the only place where
water was to be found in the whole region. Here the water
was pumped up from a deep well by horse power. This is
the so-called alluvial gold. Gold in quartz has to be worked
by mining and by costly crushing machines, in the construction of which a fortune must be spent before any pure
ore can be secured. Most of the gold is now produced in
the latter manner in Australia.

I watered my horse at the pump of the gold digger, said
good-bye to the kind people, and continued my journey down
along Fitzroy river.

The country along the lower part of this river is very
rich in gold. Farther east, near Rockhampton, a whole

gold-bearing mountain was discovered in 1884—Mount Morgan, which at present is the richest gold bed in the whole world, and has made Queensland the first gold-producing colony of Australia. It is also a remarkable fact that the gold here appears in an entirely new form. Mount Morgan, which is about 300 feet high, has been produced in the tertiary period by a hot spring, which may have resembled the geysers of Iceland or the hot springs of Yellowstone Park. It is formed of siliceous sinter, with some limonite and clayey substances, and the gold is distributed throughout the rocky mass. This discovery has made the owners immensely rich; the value of some of the original shares exceeding one and a half million pounds. One of my friends who bought a share for £1000 has now made out of this an income of more than £2000 a year. By boring it has been demonstrated that the gold increases in quantity with the depth, so that there seems to be no end of this fabulous wealth. No wonder that it has attracted the attention of speculators in every part of the world.

At the present time the weekly output of ore is 1500 tons. The average yield is 6 ounces per ton, and accordingly £36,000 of pure gold is produced per week.

This great find of gold is interesting, both from a theoretical and from a practical point of view. It shows that gold-bearing siliceous sinter can be the result of volcanic agencies, and that there is a hope that gold may yet be found in formations that have hitherto been regarded as worthless.

Nephrurus asper.

CHAPTER XXVIII

A family of zoologists—Flesh-eating kangaroos — How the ant-eater propagates—Civilised natives—Weapons and implements — Civilisation and demoralisation.

SOME time afterwards I made a journey to the west to a station owned by Mr. Barnard, and bearing the strange name Coomooboolaroo. The family of the squatter was particularly interested in natural history, an interest I had observed in several places, but rarely so marked as here. Mr. Barnard himself was a very able entomologist, and possessed a fine collection of insects, which he was constantly increasing. His wife was a great help to him, and made excellent drawings of the specimens. Their four sons had a similar taste, and they added to the family museum many valuable specimens. Upon the whole, these boys were the most skilful collectors I have ever met. They accompanied me on many excursions into the woods, when we camped together, and on such occasions I had the best opportunity of witnessing their matchless skill.

They climbed the trees as easily as any black man. When they had their tomahawks in their hands no tree was too high for them. Like the blacks, they cut niches in the bark for the support of their toes, and in this way they were able to secure insects found only in the highest tree-tops.

They were always barefooted, in order to get about more
easily, and the stones and uneven ground gave them no
trouble on our excursions, as they planted their supple and
sure feet in the most difficult places.   Ever on the alert,
nothing escaped their attention.   Even when they stood ready
to fire their guns, they would suddenly start off to catch an
insect flying by ; and in the woods they were able to seize
with their hands, while running, one beetle after the other
that came flying past.

Their keen faculty of observation astonished me again
and again.   They studied the life and habits of animals,
and gave me much valuable information, for they knew the
fauna of the locality perfectly.   They did not confine themselves to the neighbourhood of the station.   Their father
sometimes sent them on long expeditions, and they invariably returned with large collections.

There were many brush-turkeys (*Talegalla lathami*) in
this region.   So far as I am aware, it has not hitherto been
known how the young of this bird work their way out of
the peculiar mound in which the eggs are laid to be hatched
by artificial heat, after the custom of the megapodidæ.   Mr.
Barnard thinks he has found this out.   His sons had at
one time brought home some eggs from such a mound
made of earth and decayed plants.   Two of them were
laid under a hen, but rotted away.   One egg he placed in a
heap of goats' manure near his house.   When a few days
later he went to look after the egg, and carefully removed
the covering, he at once discovered the fact that a little
bird was lying on its back and trying to work its way out
of the heap of manure.   It had already reached to within
two inches of the surface.

His sons had also, in digging for talegalla eggs, observed
young birds lying on their backs and trying to work their
way out with their feet.   The material of the mound seems
to be more loosely put together at the bottom than at the
top, where it is made of coarser stuff.

At a station in the neighbourhood there was a tame
male talegalla which lived with the hens.   It was in the habit
of chasing them together into a little grove near the house,
and the proprietor of the station was convinced that the

bird in this manner was trying to compel the hens to build a mound. When the hens, not understanding what was expected of them, ran away, the talegalla would chase them back into the grove, and at last he became so troublesome that it was found necessary to shoot him.

Near Fairfield, close to the station, my young assistants found, in the month of September, nests belonging to the beautiful Australian parrot *Platycercus pulcherrimus*. Usually the nests were several miles apart. The eggs were partly hatched. The strange fact about these nests is that they are built in the hills of "the white ants." There is an irregular entrance about two inches in diameter and about a foot above the ground. In the interior the parrot makes an opening about a foot high and two or three feet in diameter. None of the building material is carried away, but all the cells and canals are trampled down, so that there remains simply a wall one or two inches thick around the whole nest. Here the female lays five white eggs.

In this locality there were countless kangaroos. Though these animals are really harmless, still the colonists keep at a respectful distance from an old kangaroo which has been driven to a tree by the dogs. This is not surprising, when we learn that in a sitting posture it may attain a height of six to seven feet. A specimen measuring eight feet has been shot. It is said that the male marsupials, particularly kangaroos, continue to grow as long as they live. The kangaroos never make an attack, but I know of instances when this animal has given proof not only of its strength but also of its fearlessness.

Mr. Barnard informed me that his dogs were one day chasing an old kangaroo when an ox-driver happened to be passing with his waggon. At the sight of the animal the man ran behind his waggon to avoid the kangaroo, which was advancing toward him, but when it came near the ox-driver it made a jump sideways, seized him, and carried him about twelve paces, until the dogs compelled the powerful animal to let go of its victim.

A stalwart Highland shepherd was on his way home one evening with his dog, when suddenly he discovered a large object in front of him. Having lately come to Australia he had scarcely seen one of these animals before, and being very superstitious, he thought it was the devil himself. Meanwhile his dog attacked the monster, but instead of taking flight it assumed the form of a great kangaroo, came up to the shepherd, put its large arms around him, and hopped away with him. The dog pursued the bold robber until the latter let go of its victim, after having carried him ten to twelve paces.

On another occasion, when Mr. Barnard was out riding with some of his friends, he met an "old man kangaroo." One of the company galloped after it and struck it several times with his whip, so as to compel it to sit down and thus be more easily subdued; but suddenly the kangaroo turned, clasped its arms round the neck of the horse, so that it was hanging with its breast against the head of the horse. In this position the kangaroo made desperate efforts to rip the horse's belly open with its large claw, while the horse, on the other hand, leapt about frantically to get rid of its unwelcome embraces. That it was difficult for the rider to keep his place in the saddle it is not necessary to state. The scene was so comical that his companions were hardly able to give him the necessary assistance as soon as they ought to have done.

When a kangaroo with a big young one in its pouch is pursued, it will throw it out of the pouch in order to make its escape easier. This done, the mother runs in a zigzag direction, probably to draw the attention of the pursuer away from the young, which lies perfectly still where it is dropped. A kangaroo never carries different broods in its pouch; but a well-grown one may often be seen following its mother while she is carrying a little one in her pouch.

I am able to relate, as a most remarkable fact, that a wallaroo, a peculiar kind of kangaroo (*Macropus robustus*), which was kept tame at a station, showed a marked fondness for animal food, particularly for boiled salt beef. A dove had been its companion, and these two animals were the best of friends for half a year, when the wallaroo one day killed its companion and partly ate it. This wallaroo had been captured while young, and had been brought up on milk, bread, and fresh grass. As an analogous circumstance I may mention that rabbits which have been brought up together with chickens have killed the latter and eaten some of their flesh.

I brought many interesting things from my sojourn at Coomooboolaroo, among others a fine collection of *Buprestidæ*. The strange-looking lizard at the beginning of this chapter, *Nephrurus asper*, and the *Bolboceras rhinoceros*, given on a separate plate, are also from this locality. In the evenings a number of insects usually came flying into the house, attracted by the light, and in this manner I caught this rare beetle and many other specimens. On the ground near the station there were large flocks of cockatoos. With their powerful beaks they dug up roots of a grass (*Panicum semialatum*) of which they are very fond. It interested me to observe that among the many kinds of grass, so similar in appearance that a superficial observer would take them to be identical, the cockatoos never failed to find at once the one they wanted. One day the rare hawk variety *Astur radiatus* was shot near the station while it was consuming a white cockatoo it had caught. The nest, found close by in the top of a high Moreton Bay ash, resembled the nests of other hawks, and contained two eggs, of a dirty white colour, with a few irregular light brown marks (length $2\frac{6}{10}$ inches, breadth $1\frac{3}{4}$ inch).

One of my chief occupations during these days was the study of the spiny ant-eaters' mode of propagation. One of my young friends at the station and a black man had found a spiny ant-eater (*Echidna*), from whose pouch they took an egg which, according to their description, was not quite half the size of a hen's egg, and the shell of which was like leather and resembled that of an "iguana" egg. This egg, however, had been destroyed, and so I resolved to do all in my power to investigate the matter, and had a large number of ant-eaters examined. My investigations extended from the beginning of February to the middle of March, and I made the observation that the ovaries were constantly growing in size during this time. As I had to leave Australia at the end of March, I unfortunately was unable to continue my observations to the end of the development, but still I came to the conclusion that the reports I had received from the blacks corresponded with the facts, as has since been demonstrated in other quarters. According to the statements of the blacks, the ant-eaters were to have young in April or May. The nearly mature eggs, lying in the ovaries and taken from a full-grown specimen, in the beginning of March measured about $\frac{1}{9}$ of an inch[1] in diameter. The *mammæ* of the same individual were large and swollen, and contained much milk. The ovaries are very much like those

NATIVES FROM THE VICINITY OF ROCKHAMPTON.

of birds in appearance, but are distinguished from the latter by the fact that the right and left ovary are of the same size, while in birds only one ovary is usually developed.

In August of the same year the English naturalist Mr. Caldwell established the fact that the spiny ant-eater actually lays eggs, and he has shown that the same is the case with the ornithorhynchus. The egg, which was found at the same time by Mr. Haacke in Adelaide, was $\frac{3}{4}$ of an inch in diameter,

[1] Prof. G. A. Guldberg : *Beiträge zur Kenntniss der Eierstockeier bei Echidna.* Jena, 1885.

and had a shell like parchment, which was broken by a slight
pressure of the finger. As is well known, turtles and other
reptiles have eggs of this kind. By this important discovery it is therefore established that the ant-eater and the
ornithorhynchus nurse their young with milk as do other
mammals, but that they lay eggs like birds and reptiles.

The natives occasionally came to Gracemere either to fish
in the lagoon or to gather the roots of the blue water-lily,
which they use as food. It is claimed that the blacks of this
part of Australia are familiar with the use of stimulants.   If
the leaves of *Erythroxylon australis*, which is common in the
scrubs near Rockhampton, possess stimulating qualities similar
to those of South America's *Erythroxylon coca* ("cocaine"), then
we may presume that the blacks are aware of it.

At the lower part of Fitzroy river the natives used
to catch mullets with their hand-nets in the winter season ;
they knew by the appearance of a certain star, which they
called "Nia," that the mullet was coming down the river to
spawn, and they always caught a great number of this fish
that were full of roe.

The Australian natives are very skilful in various kinds
of handiwork, but their talent manifests itself in different
ways.   One may excel in making baskets, another in produc-

BROW-BAND FROM CENTRAL QUEENSLAND (⅓ size).

ing the best fishing-nets, a third the best weapons, etc.   I
purchased a number of articles from the natives of Central
Queensland.   Near the coast I secured several bands for the
forehead, remarkable for their solidity and beauty.   The
little bags, which they plait with great skill, are also very
strong and pretty.   Some of these things are made from

cotton thread, but the most common material is the so-called
opossum yarn—that is, hairs pulled out of the opossum
skin (*Trichosurus vulpecula*) and twisted into threads
between the flat hand and the thigh.   From this
yarn the blacks make a little apron, worn about the
waist in this part of Australia.   Opossum yarn is
also worn in bunches on various parts of the body,
for instance round the loins or over one shoulder.
Sometimes a " band " of this sort is thrown over each
shoulder, in such a way that they form a cross on
the breast and on the back.   I have even seen civilised
blacks wearing these bands under their clothes, but their
purpose I do not know.   The natives are very willing
to part with them.   Frequently five or six threads of
opossum yarn are twisted together to form a plain
ornament about the wrist or neck.   Opossum skins
are also sewed together and used partly as articles
of clothing, partly as mats.

OPOSSUM
THREAD
(⅓ size).

Their shields are small, and as a rule are made
of the light cork-tree (*Erythrina vespertilio*).   The
front side is rather curved, while the reverse is flat
and furnished with a little handle cut out of the shield
itself.   Like most of the weapons of the natives, the shield
is carved and then usually painted with white and red.

APRON MADE FROM OPOSSUM YARN, CENTRAL QUEENSLAND (⅓ size).

Wooden swords are rare, and differ from those of
Northern Queensland, being more curved, not so broad, and
usually coloured with cross-bars of chalk.   A weapon even
more rare is the so-called *bendi*.   It resembles a small
pickaxe, and is made of the *Eucalyptus exserata*, called by

the natives bendo. The bend or curve forms a right angle, and ends in a point, the wood itself giving the weapon this form. Bendi is not a javelin, but a weapon to strike with, and with it the natives try to hit the kidneys of their opponents ; for these they regard as the seat of life.

The spears of these natives are thrown by the hand alone, without the aid of any other implement. Near the

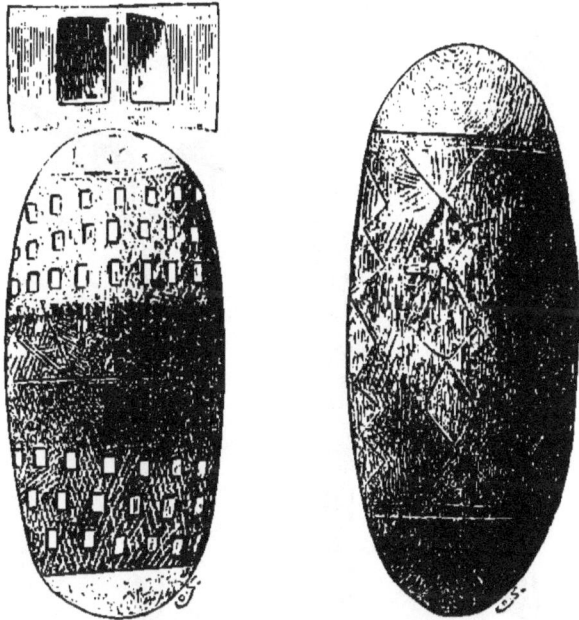

SHIELDS FROM CENTRAL QUEENSLAND (½ size).
Showing a part of the inner side with the handle.

point the spear has two to four enlargements resembling rings, and as the latter are rifled, they form a sort of barb.

The most important weapon of the Australian native is the tomahawk, which is made of basalt, greenstone, or some other hard stone, sometimes even of phonolite. The natives have been known to travel great distances in order to secure, by barter from foreign tribes, the best material, and thus trading centres sprang up in some districts. The stone is either cut into the proper shape, or one is used which is naturally of the correct form, and the edge is generally made

sharp by whetting. The handle is invariably made by bending a piece of vine stalk round the stone, and then tying
the ends of the stalk together with withies as close under
the stone as possible; gum is also put on to make the
joint more firm. Axes with holes through them have not

WOODEN SWORD (¹⁄₁₀ size). BENDI FROM COOMOOBOOLAROO, CENTRAL QUEENSLAND.

been found. The Australian makes most of his weapons
with the tomahawk, which also serves as his most important
weapon for the chase, and which he is never without. All
kinds of fine work are performed with the aid of pieces of
hard stone, which he usually fastens to a handle and uses as
a chisel. For carving he uses implements of stone or of bone.

An idea of the culture of the Australian is easily gained by examining his weapons and implements. They are made mostly of wood, and bows and arrows are unknown. On Herbert river the natives employ javelins almost exclusively for hunting, but when in the dense scrubs they are as a rule unarmed. If they discover an animal they break branches off the trees, and try to kill it with these. They are generally successful, for most of the animals frequent the trees, and

CRYSTALLINE AXE FROM PEAK DOWNS IN CENTRAL QUEENSLAND (½ size).

escape is therefore difficult when the natives make an attack from all sides and surround them. When an animal has been slain and is to be prepared for food, the belly is opened by the first stone or piece of wood found suitable for the purpose. The game is divided for distribution either with a stone or with the teeth, which are also largely used for breaking off limbs of trees and for making implements. The knives used by the natives of Australia are either pieces of hard stone accidentally found ready for use, or are secured by breaking pieces off the rock, but not much additional labour is bestowed on them, though they are sometimes shaped or fastened with glue to a kind of wooden handle. On the other hand, the natives understand how to polish their tomahawks; and when tribes have been found who had only roughly worked ones, the reason is not ignorance in polishing, but that the hardness of the material made the tomahawks quite sharp enough without it. Still, it will be seen that the aboriginal Australian has not advanced very far in the stone age.

When the natives become "civilised" they at once exchange their stone weapons for the white man's weapons of iron. They are particularly fond of his

A SPEAR FROM THE COAST OF CENTRAL QUEENSLAND (⅓ size).

tomahawk. Even on Herbert river the stone axe had given place to the latter tool, which however was so rare in some parts that a whole tribe sometimes had to be satisfied with one or two implements of this kind. Blacks who have never seen a white man occasionally get iron implements by bartering with other tribes. After becoming civilised the Australian native begins to make tomahawks from broken horse-shoes or from some other piece of iron, and to stud his club with nails. There are instances on record where the natives have cut down the telegraph poles and used the wire for spear points and fish-hooks. After becoming acquainted with the use of iron, the black man makes but little use of his wooden weapons and implements, and strange to say, does not make them so nicely as formerly, when his tools were inferior. He also takes less pains with all kinds of carving.

The natives of Central Queensland have, as a matter of course, obtained that kind of civilisation which necessarily results from a prolonged intercourse with the white population. They have long since recognised the superiority of Europeans, and the new condition of things is leading them to give up their former occupations. The most capable ones become servants at the stations, partly as cooks, partly as stock-men and shepherds, and they are of considerable use to the white population ; but the great mass of them prefer to enjoy their liberty, while at the same time contact with the white man gives their life and habits a new character. The settlers are on account of their flocks obliged to encroach on the hunting-grounds of the black, and the natives, who have no thought of the future or of posterity, are satisfied with the advantages obtained in exchange for the loss of their hunting-grounds—that is, they get the leavings from the kitchen and the slaughter-house, milk, old clothes, tobacco, etc. Sometimes the squatter appoints the best native near his station a "king," and as a mark of this dignity he gives him a piece of brass containing his civilised name to wear on his breast. In return for food, tobacco, woollen blankets, and similar things, the "king" promises to watch his tribe, and keep them from doing damage to the white man's property. Every native is anxious to become "king," for the brass plate, which is considered a great ornament, also secures the bearer many a meal. At first, while the natives are more or less dangerous, a chief of this kind may be very valuable to a squatter, who may in this way be

"KING BILLY OF GRACEMERE" WITH HIS "GIN" (WIFE).

warned of attacks from hostile tribes, but after the natives have become quiet and peaceable the institution is of value only to the bearer of the brass plate, who continues to demand his pay.

The degeneration and demoralisation of the natives, which

are an inevitable result of the march of civilisation, are already far advanced even in this part of Australia. The natives become more indolent, and they lose their former self-reliance and independence after they acquire the habit of relying on what they can get from the white man. They spend most of their time near the stations and villages, where they are able to obtain liquor and opium, for which the Chinese immigrants soon give them a taste. I cannot conceive a more disgusting sight than a camp of such ragged, impudent blacks marked by all the vices of civilisation. To me, coming from Northern Queensland, where the natives still were in their pristine vigour, the picture was an exceedingly sad one, when I considered the future awaiting the friends I had left there.

Shortly before my return to Europe I visited a camp of "civilised" blacks near Rockhampton. Even before reaching the camp I felt the smell of opium, and on coming nearer I was the witness of a most disgusting scene. Around the camp fires sat natives pale as death itself. The opium-pipe was constantly in their mouths and their eyes stared out bewildered from their deep hollow sockets. I approached the man whom I wanted to see. He had lost his flesh, and his skin had become yellow and sickly. It was all he could do to stammer forth a request for money to buy more opium. A month ago I had seen him strong and well, now he was a mere skeleton and presumably on the brink of the grave.

I turned my face away from this horrible scene and mounted my horse, sad to think that this was to be my last impression of the world of the blacks.

CHAPTER XXIX

A NATIVE who had been brought up by the white men was visiting the tribes near Peak Downs, where I stopped for a time. He was able to read and write, and on Sundays he sometimes sent word to the station and asked to borrow a Prayer-book, from which he would read passages aloud to the other blacks in the tribe, who looked with wonderment upon his superiority over them. He also frequently read chapters from the Bible to them, but apparently he did not himself understand much of what he read. Once, when an old woman of the tribe died, he asked to borrow the Prayer-book, in order "to read" over the dead as he had seen the whites do. Finally a Prayer-book was presented to him. He read its title, *Book of Common Prayer*, whereupon he handed it back, saying he did not want anything that was "common."

It is a well-known fact that the Australian natives are almost wholly devoid of religious susceptibilities, and that missionaries seldom succeed in imparting to them more than the outward appearance of Christianity. Upon the whole, there are but few missionaries in Australia, and the natives come but little in contact with Christianity. Missionary efforts have been made, especially in the southern part of the continent, but with poor success. The lack of the receptive faculty on the part of the blacks and the ill-will of a portion of the white population are great hindrances in the way of missionary work ; rough colonists will not abandon the practice of prostitution, from which the blacks derive some pecuniary advantage. The fact that the missionaries see but little fruit from their labours does not therefore allow us to draw the conclusion that the Australian race is quite unsusceptible to religious influence.

In my opinion, an Australian native cannot be christianised unless he is brought up outside his own tribe from infancy. In such circumstances he has been found to be capable of considerable mental development. Many of the natives have learned reading, writing, arithmetic, singing, etc. It is even claimed that they acquire these accomplishments more rapidly than white children, but that they also more quickly forget them again. They are also able to play cards, even "euchre," a game requiring considerable thought. A squatter in the far west informed me that when he forgot what day in the week it was he only needed to ask his black boy, who never failed to know.

The highest degree of civilisation attainable by the blacks is skill in the work to be done at a station. Women are usually employed in the house, and at each station two or three find work. They make good waiters, but poor cooks. As stock-men and shepherds the blacks are excellent, in this work sometimes even surpassing the whites. They are superb riders, and have a wonderful talent for mastering an unruly horse. On the other hand, they are unable to break a horse properly, and as a rule have very heavy hands.

Among the sheep and cattle the blacks are wellnigh indispensable at every station. They know every animal, and give it much better care than it can get from a white man. A black boy whom I knew was able to distinguish the footprints of the various horses belonging to the station. Some of them have great skill in making whips and bridles, in carving whip handles, and in doing other handiwork.

These civilised blacks soon try to acquire the white man's manners; they like to wear clothes, and they like to have their clothes fit nicely. Some even shave and wash themselves, use towels, and are perfect bush dandies. They soon acquire a very high opinion of themselves, of their ability, and of their importance. They look upon themselves not only as equally good, but as better than the white men. No man on earth is more proud than a black man on horse-

back, with good clothes on, his clay pipe lit, and his
pocket full of tobacco and matches.

This "civilisation," which is quickly assumed through

CIVILISED GIRLS FROM THE VICINITY OF TOWNSVILLE.

intercourse with the white man, does not, however, strike
deep root, and the good nature which often accompanies
their brutal qualities rarely wholly overcomes the latter.
However comfortable they may be with the white man,

they still long to get back to their forests. As a rule they must have an annual vacation, when they visit their tribe and take part in the hunting and in other amusements. There is no use in refusing this, for then they would become sulky and unwilling to work. Their love of change makes them constantly give up one situation for another, though they may have no reason to be dissatisfied with the one they abandon. In some few cases a black man will become very much devoted to his master, and will occasionally serve the same one a long time if he only gets his annual vacation. I may mention that a black boy who had been with his master for many years nursed him during a severe illness, nay, even prevented him from committing suicide in a moment of desperation.

A black man twenty-three years old, who from childhood had been educated at a station in Victoria, where he had lived nearly all his life and had been treated almost as a member of the family, one day suddenly disappeared. He was found in the camp of the blacks as naked as he was born, but later on he returned to the station, where he resumed his former work. Sometimes this kind of civilised native becomes so fond of savage life that he never returns to the stations.

It frequently happens that a black-fellow makes a journey abroad when the squatter goes to visit his native country. It would be reasonable to suppose that the great cities of the old world would make some, if not a very deep, impression, on this child of nature, but such is not the case. The Australian native is not surprised, because he lacks the faculty of appreciating. A locomotive flying past him for the first time does not astonish him very much. When, after a long journey, he returns to his tribe he sees the difference, but he has no words with which to explain himself, although his fellows get the general impression that their comrade has had wonderful experiences. He is naturally very proud of his achievements, and wears an air of superiority over both white and black men. A colonist who was trying to give a black man a grand impression of Sydney, received the startling answer: " I like London better."

Though the language used by the colonists in conversation with the blacks, which the latter gradually learn, is a disconnected jargon, still some of the natives learn to speak English very well. These more talented blacks, mostly from Victoria and New South Wales, become literally angry when addressed in the common jabber-jabber English. A white man who was out hunting emus asked a black of the above kind: *You been see 'im tshukki-tshukki big fellow?* The latter indignantly replied: "I suppose you mean an emu."

Though the Australian native is thus able to acquire some of the fruits of civilisation, it still remains a characteristic fact that he never gets so far as to occupy an independent position. As a subordinate he may serve to the complete satisfaction of his master, but he never saves anything, and does not comprehend the value of money. He never learns enough to become a tradesman, and all that he gets he at once spends. In his natural condition he has a decided distaste for agriculture, and this aversion clings to him when he becomes civilised. Cattle-raising is an easy way of making money, but not even this can teach him to make money on his own account.

"A living sheep is an impossibility in the camp of the blacks," most truly writes Mr. Finch-Hatton, and the gold of Australia is nothing but a common stone to him, even when he sees the greedy digger getting rich by seeking the precious metal. A strong tendency to communism hinders social development among the tribes. Natives employed on a farm invariably share their earnings with their relatives and friends, who live in their camp near the station. When a black man has regular employment at a station he frequently gets five shillings a week besides board and tobacco, but all this he divides with his comrades in the camp. The latter do not care to hunt, but live on what he or their women earn from the squatter. No sooner has one of them saved a pound than he and his friends go to town and buy brandy and opium with the money.

As a rule the relation between the whites and the blacks is not at first a friendly one. It has occasionally happened that the natives have received the whites kindly the first time they met them; they have even given assistance to people who have been shipwrecked, but in most instances a war soon breaks out between the two races. Sheep and cattle begin to feed on the grounds that have belonged to the blacks, and the latter are prohibited from going where

"THE LONELY OLD PEOPLE," NATIVES FROM THE NEIGHBOURHOOD
OF TOWNSVILLE.

they please; because the herds are disturbed by the black men's hunting, nay even by the smell of the savages. As a matter of course, the natives therefore try to resist the strangers who interfere with their inherited rights.

The rough settler, who never sees a woman of his own

race, soon begins to associate with the black women. A friendly relation between the two races is made impossible ; the white men shoot the black men, and the black men kill the white men when they can, and spear their sheep and cattle.

Both parties, however, gradually learn to take advantage of each other. The colonist avails himself of the cheap labour furnished by the blacks, and the natives acquire a taste for what the white man has to offer, though it is of course mainly limited to tobacco, food, and clothes. Of this change of condition the colonist reaps the whole advantage, for the invariable result to the black man is both mental and physical degradation and retrogression. Unfortunately the first white men with whom the blacks on the frontiers of civilisation come in contact are frequently rough and brutal, and hence we cannot expect any marked improvement on the part of the natives from their new acquaintances. Their keen sense of observation enables them to discover quickly the bad qualities in the white man's character, and these they are not slow to imitate ; but they have no eye for the good qualities. There is not much to be said of the morals of the blacks, for I am sorry to say they have none. Still, their moral condition has a somewhat better aspect before they come in contact with the white man. It cannot be denied that the young black women originally had a certain amount of modesty. In some parts of the country they assume the position of a Venus of Milo, or they hide behind the older women to take a peep at the white man, whom they see for the first time. It has been observed that the savages who wear an apron are more modest than those who are naked. I have also heard that the women in some tribes take their baths by themselves. It should also be remarked that the natives never represent obscene ideas in their rude drawings, and though it cannot be denied that the husband, in return for certain advantages, will part with his wife, yet he jealously protects her as his most valuable and dearest possession. On the other hand, as soon as the white man comes, immorality knows no bounds, and the black race hasten on to the inevitable ruin awaiting them. Sometimes the most brutal settlers even make use of the revolver to compel the natives to surrender their women ; sometimes they actually kill the black man if he makes resistance. At length threats become unnecessary, for the blacks do not need to remain long under the influence of "civilisation" before they offer their wares for a little tobacco, or when the "civilisation" has struck deeper roots, for a shilling. The murder of infants increases, syphilitic diseases become common, and the women having become prostitutes, cease to bear children.

The settlers also reduce the numbers of the natives in a more direct way, and the latter have often been slaughtered in the most unmerciful manner. At times there may possibly be some excuse for this. The white man's friendship may be rewarded with ingratitude. The blacks frequently punish the innocent for the guilty, and they spare no white man. I know of instances where the blacks have persisted in killing cattle, in spite of the fact that the owner has been extravagant enough in his friendship to give them cattle for slaughter. In such circumstances the blacks do not care if some of their comrades are shot ; but at last their ranks become so reduced that they have to yield. They may dog a white man secretly for days, with no less energy than they exhibit in pursuing their game for food, and on the first favourable opportunity take his life. In North Australia no traveller is safe, and many a lonely wanderer who has disappeared in these remote regions has been slain by the spear of the black man. They rarely attack a man on horseback.[1] Still, they watch him and lie in ambush for him, in case he should dismount to look for water to drink, or to rest for the night. In some instances the blacks have attacked a station and killed all the inhabitants. Thus it is necessary for the white man to defend himself, but there is no doubt that in this respect he has gone further than necessity demanded. The settling of Australia is stained with more than one shocking story of this sort. There are instances where the young men of the station have employed the Sunday in hunting the blacks, not only for some definite purpose, but also for the sake of the sport ; the blacks have even been killed with

[1] A white man on foot is always regarded as a "little" white man.

poison. A squatter at Long Lagoon, in the interior of Queensland, achieved notoriety by laying strychnine in the way of the blacks, and thus taking the life of a large number of them in a single day.

Similar acts of brutality occur even at the present time. A farmer whom I met at Lower Herbert boasted that he had cremated some blacks whom he had shot. He looked upon this as a most excellent precautionary measure, for it made proof against him impossible. The life of a native has but little value, particularly in the northern part of Australia, and once or twice colonists offered to shoot blacks for me so that I might get their skulls. On the borders of civilisation men would think as little of shooting a black man as a dog. The law imposes death by hanging as the penalty for murdering a black man, but people live so far apart in these uncivilised regions that a white man may in fact do what he pleases with the blacks.

In Northern Queensland I often heard this remark : " The only treatment proper for the blacks is to shoot them all." A squatter in that part of the country acted on this principle. He found it severe, but necessary. He shot all the men he discovered on his run, because they were cattle killers ; the women, because they gave birth to cattle killers ; and the children, because they would in time become cattle killers. " They are unwilling to work," I have heard colonists say, " and hence they are not fit to live."

The result of this is that in the frontier districts there is still being waged a war of extermination between the two races. Any savage discovered by the white men runs the risk of being shot. Poison was laid in the way of the blacks once while I was in Queensland. I also take the liberty of reporting the following shocking event, though without giving the names of any of the parties concerned.

A cedar-cutter in Northern Queensland had one day left one of his white workmen in charge of the camp, while he and his other labourers went to the woods to work. In districts where the blacks are dangerous it is always necessary to leave a man on guard in the camp. In the course of the day two blacks came to the guard, and as the latter had no ill-will to the natives, he treated them in a friendly manner

and gave them tobacco. When the master returned in the
evening he became very angry on account of what had
happened, and the next day he set a Kanaka to watch the
camp. The natives of course thought the white man was
friendly, as he had given them tobacco, and so they did not
hesitate to visit the camp again the next day; but they
soon found out their mistake. One of the blacks who tried
to make his escape was wounded in the leg, while the other
one was captured and tied to a tree. This done, the
wounded man was seized and killed with a butcher's knife.
When the Kanaka came back to the camp the master had
returned, and the latter at once ordered, in cold blood, that
the prisoner who was tied to the tree should also be killed.
They did not even waste a bullet on the poor fellow, who
was pierced with a knife.

That inhuman institution, the native police, has also
been an important factor in the destruction of the natives.
They have not only slain a large number of this unhappy
people, but also contributed largely to their demoralisation.

In the courts the blacks are defenceless, for their
testimony is not accepted. The jury is not likely to declare
a white man guilty of murdering a black man. On the
other hand, if a white man happens to be killed by the
blacks, a cry is heard throughout the whole colony.

There are, however, persons who look upon the blacks
as human beings with a right to live in the land which is in
fact their own. "Were I a black man, I would kill all the
whites," an Australian gentleman once said to me. One
of these protectors of the blacks writes to me—

"If I thought that anything I might say on the treatment of the aborigines would in any way tend to ameliorate
their present wretched condition, I would not for a moment
grudge my lost health, and would plead their cause to my
last breath. But alas! it were vain to hope for any improvement in their condition; for it is an immutable law of nature
that the strong will prey upon the weak. I always look
upon the condition of the lower order of 'whites' as a fearful
satire on Christianity. The English nation is continually
casting stones at other nations for the treatment of con-

NATIVE POLICE DISPERSING THE BLACKS.
Sketch after a description given to me on the spot.

To face page 348.

quered races, but nothing could be more barbarous than their own treatment of the aborigines of Australia."

It must be admitted that the colonists in several places have tried to protect the blacks by giving them reservations and means of existence.   In Victoria there are six stations, where the natives raise crops and cattle, and receive instruction.

All this, however, is of no avail. It only gives the doomed race a short respite.   It is supposed that there were 9000 blacks in Victoria when the colony was founded.   There now remain scarcely 800, and many of these are *half-castes*, who are but little superior to the pure blacks in intelligence, while they have an even less favourable appearance.

"When civilised nations come into contact with barbarians, the struggle is but short, excepting where a dangerous climate helps the native race," says Darwin, and history corroborates his statement.   In 1872 the last Tasmanian died.   His ancestors succumbed, not only because they were weaker than the invading race, but also because they were abused by the invaders.   The same fate as that which overtook their brothers in Tasmania is in store for the natives of Australia.   They have proved themselves almost incapable of receiving either culture or Christianity, and they have not the power to resist the onward march of civilisation. They are therefore without a future, without a home, without a hope,—a doomed race.   The two races cannot exist together. If the Australian attacks the whites or their herds, he is shot ; if he tries to secure the friendship of the white men, his ruin is no less certain.   He is unwilling to abandon his habits of life, and for this reason the settlement of the country robs him of his means of existence, while European culture at the same time causes his moral and physical degradation.

The philanthropist is filled with sadness when he sees the original inhabitants of this strange land succumbing according to the inexorable law of degeneration.   Invading civilisation has not brought development and progress to the Australian native ; after a few generations his race will have disappeared from the face of the earth.

APPENDIX

AN OUTLINE OF AUSTRALIAN HISTORY

THE history of Australia illustrates in broad outlines how a continent inhabited by a most primitive race of men becomes known to the Europeans, how the latter colonise the country and drive the natives before them, and how the new community is organised and developed. Thus the subject may be divided into three chapters— (1) The condition before the discovery; (2) the story of the discovery; and (3) the story of the colonisation.

THE CONDITION BEFORE THE EUROPEAN DISCOVERY

The degree of culture attained by the Australian aborigines when they first came in contact with the Europeans was not a high one. We find a race living in small tribes, without any social organisation, always moving from one place to another, living in huts hurriedly made of leaves or bark; almost naked; destitute of implements of metal, destitute of perforated stone implements, destitute of bows and arrows; having miserable boats, or none at all; having no other domestic animals than the semi-wild dingo, and having no knowledge of agriculture. The development which preceded this stage of civilisation must be looked for in the very infancy of human culture, where we have but little light to show the way. Nor is any special value to be attached to peculiar customs which this people may have in common with other races similarly situated. Circumcision, tattooing, exogamy, and sorcery are found in every part of the globe, but for none of these have we been able to show a common origin. Nor has the science of philology hitherto been able to connect the prehistoric ages of Australia with the culture of the rest of the world, though efforts have been made to show linguistic resemblances both with the Dekkan races and more recently with the negroes of Africa. The archæological investigations are confined to enormous "middens" or refuse heaps. One science remains, viz. comparative anthropology; but even this is not able to give a satisfactory answer, for the Australian aborigines form a group by themselves without any marked similarity to any other races. A few anthropological correspondences have led to comparisons with the Papuans, who geographically are their nearest neighbours.

There are in like manner faint traces pointing to the north and north-east, when we seek the source of the earliest culture of Australia. A later current from north-east to south-west has been suggested, but cannot be made to serve as the basis of any reliable hypothesis. It has been shown that weapons (the bow), and boats, and houses, and physical development reveal progress as the York peninsula is approached, and the influence of Malays and Papuans can be definitely pointed out. But all this bears the stamp of modern times, and must be the result of communications in a very recent period. The one thing certain is that the Australian race must have originated ages ago.

Investigation, which shows how completely Australia has been cut off from external influence, gives the best answer to the question why the development of the blacks has made so little progress, for the development of the world is found to be dependent on the intercourse between different races, on the conflicts between them, and on the struggle for existence thus caused.

The very nature of the country has helped to keep the people from making progress. In the first place there are but few inlets of the sea, and in the next place there are two other circumstances which only need to be pointed out to be appreciated. There are no ruminating animals, and grain is very rare. The transition from the most primitive life to that of the herdsman was therefore impossible, and this common door to a higher culture was closed. On the other hand, there was but little inducement to become agricultural, though the wild rice found in the northern part of South Australia has been used as food. Besides the climatic conditions, the long droughts— sometimes lasting for years in the interior of the country—were a decided obstacle to agriculture, even if there had been grain that could bear them better than rice. Finally, it should be added that the natural products are usually so abundant that it is comparatively easy to subsist without labour.

The fact is, at all events, that the great discovery on which all higher civilisation is based, viz. agriculture, had not been made in Australia at the time when it was colonised by Europeans.

There could be no doubt about the result when the aborigines and the Europeans met. The difference was so great that assimilation was impossible. The only vocations open to the aborigines in the new Australian community were those of the herdsman and policeman. The latter of these was of no advantage to the natives. The first English colonists were mainly banished criminals, reckless people a fact that gave the conflict between the two races the character of a war of extermination from the very outset, and in this warfare the native police has contributed much toward the destruction of the aborigines.

It is difficult to estimate the number of aborigines in Australia at the time when the European colonisation began. Natives, or traces of them, were met everywhere. Sturt relates that he met about 4000 in the course of a few days. We probably are not wide of the mark when we assume that fifty years ago there were about 200,000 natives in Australia ; their number is now estimated at about 60,000.

The world is familiar with the systematic cruelty with which the Tasmanians were exterminated. In 1872 occurred the death of the last representative of a people which numbered about 5000 souls at the time of the founding of the colony in 1803. Many were killed in wars, many were even hunted out of the woods and destroyed. A large number of them were transported to the islands in Bass Strait, where death and ruin soon overtook them. The regular hunting and shooting of the natives in the early days of Queensland suggests the question, whether the coming of the new settlers deserved the name of the "advent of civilisation."

HISTORY OF THE DISCOVERY

Australia was the last continent discovered by the European, a fact easily explained by its situation. In the age of the great discoveries, navigators were seeking a way to India, and whether they chose to go by the way of the Cape of Good Hope or by the Straits of Magellan, in either case the route was far to the north of Australia. The navigators also seem to have kept as far to the north as possible. Still, a very long time cannot have passed ere sailors came in sight of the Australian coast. Strange to say, it is not known with certainty who was the first discoverer of this great continent. Some old maps seem to show that the Portuguese were aware of the existence of a large country south of Java before the year 1545, viz. "Great Java." On these maps are found coral reefs, rivers, promontories, etc., and a number of names. It is, however, difficult to determine how far these maps may be based on the old purely theoretical assumption that there was a large *terra australis incognita*, to give equilibrium to the earth and balance the northern hemisphere.

Ere long the Spanish, the chief rivals of the Portuguese, also presented their claims. By the decision of Pope Alexander II, who acted as arbitrator, the Spanish were permitted to develop their sway only westward of Europe, while all to the east was left to the Portuguese. The conflict which then arose in regard to the Moluccas may explain why both parties were silent in regard to the great country they may have discovered south of the boundary.

At all events, the first Australian discoveries of which we have perfectly reliable accounts were not made before the beginning of the seventeenth century. We first come across the Dutch, who

COOK'S MONUMENT IN SYDNEY.

during their war of independence attempted to conquer the rich colonies of their enemies—the Spanish and the Portuguese. In connection with this we obtain the following reliable dates: in 1601 the Portuguese De Eridia landed on the north-west coast from the west; in 1606 the Spaniard Torres passed from the east through the straits named after him; and subsequently a Dutch ship called *Duyfhen* sailed along the coast toward Cape York. From this time the Dutch carry on nearly all the explorations. It would take us beyond our present limits to present the details of this gradual discovery, from the Dutch headquarters in Java, or on their route to East India, a route which they had to lay south of that of the Portuguese. In 1627 Peter Nuyts entered the great Australian bay from the west. In 1642 Tasman gained the south point of that country, which he called Van Diemen's Land. It is not easy now to decide whether his reasons for regarding the latter as the southern point of a large continent were based on old theories or on more recent observations.

The English, the nation which was destined to control the development of Australia, did not make their appearance before 1688, when the freebooter Dampier explored the west coast. This happened one hundred years before the first colonies—the centenary of which has been recently celebrated—were planted, in 1788.

It was a long time before anybody made any decided effort to take possession of the country, and for this delay there were many reasons. The power of the Spanish was exhausted, and so was that of Portugal, while the victorious Dutch were fully occupied with their new rich provinces. To this must be added that all descriptions of Australia represented the continent as barren and without water to drink, and its natives as poor and savage. Nor did the coasts that had been seen present any very inviting aspect. There are but few harbours on the west and south coasts, and on the northeast side are dangerous coral reefs. The wrong side of Australia had been seen, and it was absurd to prefer this country to the Spice Island or America.

It is interesting to note that it was a scientific expedition which first led to the colonisation of the country. In 1768 Captain Cook carried an astronomer and one or two other scientists to Tahiti to observe the transit of Venus, and to make some other researches on their home voyage. This was the beginning of the present phase of scientific expeditions. In 1770 he touched Australia at Botany Bay, and made a chart of the coast to the north as far as Torres Straits, the importance of which he was the first to point out.

At this time England was greatly puzzled as to what it should do with all such criminals as it had heretofore sent to America. The declaration of independence on the part of the United States had put an end to the transportation of criminals to that country, and the favourable report made by Cook in regard to Botany Bay led Sydney to make up his mind to try Australia. The first transportation was made in 1788, but the colony was soon moved to the magnificent harbour of Port Jackson, where the city of Sydney was gradually built up.

The opening up of the continent was continued with this solitary colony as the base of exploration. Flinders and Bass commenced their expeditions in the year 1795 in a small open boat to both sides of the coast. In 1797 Bass called attention to the strait between Tasmania and the continent, and the next year he circumnavigated the island with Flinders. At the expense of the Government Flinders made charts of a large part of the coast of Australia, and this coast survey was continued from time to time almost to the present day.

During the most recent years attention has been chiefly given to the exploration of the interior.

How difficult it must have been to penetrate the Blue Mountains separating Sydney from the plains in the interior is evident from the fact that men like Bass attempted it in vain. It took twenty-five years to advance the first fifty miles, and thus to find a way between the steep rocks to the open country beyond. The first passage was effected in 1813, and from that time the explorations have progressed rapidly. Oxley, Cunningham, Mitchell, Sturt, and others explored the whole country along the rivers toward Victoria. The German naturalist Dr. L. Leichhardt began his explorations along the Gulf of Carpentaria in 1835, and made most valuable reports. In 1847 he undertook his last expedition, a bold attempt to penetrate to the west coast. Not a word was heard of him after April 3, 1848.

From Adelaide, settled about the same time, a series of attempts were begun in 1839 to penetrate the country from the south to the north. Heroic efforts were made in this direction by Eyre, who afterwards suffered untold hardships in travelling 1200 miles along the coast to King George's Sound. O'Hara Burke and Wills were the first to reach the north coast in 1861, but both perished from hunger on their way back. The following year M'Donald Stuart, after having made two abortive attempts, succeeded in getting through, and from that time onwards the route was open. In 1872 a telegraph line was laid, amid great difficulties, across the whole continent. It followed Stuart's route, and this enterprise became the basis of a series of explorations all the way to the west coast, and thus the main features of the geography of Australia have become established. Prominent names in connection with this are Giles, Forrest, Warburton, and Gregory.

Most of these expeditions into the interior have been undertaken amid the greatest privations, such as a constant lack of water and terrible heat, even up to 127° F., so that it has at times been necessary to bury one's self in the ground in order to endure it. Add to this the almost impassable spinifex-scrubs, the salt lakes, the sand-storms, etc., and we can form some idea of what the explorer had to suffer. The bright sunlight destroyed Sturt's eyes, and many a life has been lost in the conflict with these similar impediments. But a large territory has been opened to civilisation by these martyrs.

History of the Colonies

On January 26, 1788, Captain Arthur Phillip landed at Sydney with his first company of prisoners, and in a solemn manner took possession of a whole continent in the name of the inhabitants of a small island on the opposite side of the globe. Had the French expedition under La Perouse come earlier than it did to this place, the whole development of Australia might have taken a different direction. As it was, the ruling power of the British nation got an opportunity of expanding, and a new world was added to the dominion of the Anglo-Saxon race.

The beginning was made by about 1000 deported criminals, about one-fourth part of these being women. Now, one hundred years later, the population of the Australian colonies, leaving New Zealand out of consideration, is nearly 3,000,000. The first means of sub-sistence had to be produced by agriculture, but as few of the new settlers had any knowledge of this art, there was much suffering in the beginning, and in order to escape death from starvation, the domestic animals which had been brought had to be slaughtered. One hundred years later Australia contains 80,000,000 sheep and almost 8,000,000 head of cattle, and it sends annually to the mother country beef, mutton, wool, tallow, wheat, and metals to the value of about £40,000,000 sterling. A most remarkable progress!

The story of the early days of the colonies is chiefly a history of the deportation of criminals. The first colony received, from 1788 until the importation was stopped in 1839 by the energetic protest of the "free immigrants," in all 60,000 criminals. The next colony of criminals was Tasmania, or as the island was then called, Van Diemen's Land (1803). The deportation of criminals to the latter place ceased in 1853, when 68,000 prisoners had been sent there. What the condition was during the early days of these colonies, guarded by rough soldiers, we can judge from the fact that there occurred in 1835 in New South Wales, among 28,000 prisoners, 22,000 disciplinary punishments (3000 floggings) and 100 executions. In Tasmania, with a population of 37,000, about 15,000 were punished in 1834, including one-seventh part of the free citizens arrested for intemperance.

The last colony to which convicts were regularly deported was West Australia, founded in 1839. In 1849 this colony sent a petition to the Government asking for criminals to be sent thither, in order to promote the development of the colony. Under pressure from the other colonies, which finally on their own account resisted by force the landing of such immigrants, West Australia had to abandon this traffic in 1868, having then received about 10,000.

Thus it will be seen that this transportation introduced great numbers of people to Australia, and at the same time the voluntary immigration kept increasing. Two of the present colonies were not started as convict settlements. There was an attempt to send convicts to Melbourne in 1803, but the plan was soon abandoned, and the colony of Port Phillip, as Victoria was then called, was founded in 1834 by free citizens from Tasmania. South Australia was colonised directly by an English company, who received the land for nothing on condition that they should encourage immigration. In 1841 this settlement contained 23,000 inhabitants, chiefly freemen.

The growth of the colonies depended on the development of trade and industries. In the beginning all labour was confined to agriculture, and but little progress was made, till during the first decades of this century MacArthur advocated the raising of sheep with great energy, and after a passage through the Blue Mountains had been found by Macquarie, a new impetus was given to the development of Australia. The manner in which the country became settled may be described as follows—

In the first place, an explorer makes his way into unknown regions. Close on his heels follows the squatter or shepherd, and slowly in his track comes the selector, the permanent agricultural settler. The original huntsman, the shepherd, and the farmer follow each other in rapid succession—it is the history of civilisation in a nutshell.

The economical politics of Australia have long been wrestling with the question of the proper *modus vivendi* between the squatter and the selector, whose interests are conflicting. Many experiments have been made in the various colonies, but this troublesome question has not yet been solved.

In the midst of the development of sheep-raising and agriculture a third factor, gold, was added, which gave Australia an immense advantage, even though it at the same time interfered with the above-mentioned industries.

. . . . .

The year 1851 marks an epoch in the history of Australia. It was literally the beginning of a golden age for the continent, for in that year the great gold mines of Victoria were discovered.

It had long been believed that gold must be found in Australia ; among the deported criminals there were all sorts of reports about finds said to have been made in the Blue Mountains; but the Government paid no attention to these strange rumours and the result was that the matter was not properly investigated.

But in 1851 the greatest excitement was created when the

Government purchased from a Californian gold digger, for a large sum of money, some rich gold fields which he had discovered in the Blue Mountains. When the Government by this step had given its public sanction to the question, the colony became wild with excitement. The most extravagant reports concerning the immense wealth of the gold fields were circulated, and were accepted as gospel truth. From all quarters people assembled to the new fountains of wealth, where they expected to find the pure gold in such quantities that it was only necessary to stoop down and fill their pockets with the precious ore. The disappointment when they arrived in the promised land and learned from experience that there was need of months—nay, of years—of hard and persistent labour to attain the wealth they were seeking, was as great as the expectation which had previously been formed. The larger part of the army of adventurers who had flocked together to the gold mines to secure all of a sudden a wealth which they had neither the strength nor the endurance to acquire under ordinary circumstances, returned discouraged to Sydney, after having spent a month in idleness in the gold fields. In their wrath on account of the deception, as they called it, they nearly took the life of the Californian who had discovered the fields.

A number of gold diggers, however, gradually congregated in the Blue Mountains from the various colonies. When the work proved to be very profitable the rush was so great that one of the earlier colonies, the little Victoria, which had recently been founded, was on the point of being entirely deserted. To prevent the colony from perishing altogether, the leading men in Melbourne offered a large reward to any person who succeeded in discovering gold in Victoria. Before long, specimens of gold were found on the Yarra river, a few miles from Melbourne; in the course of a short time the famous gold mines of Ballarat and Bendigo were discovered.

At first gold was found in Ballarat in the usual manner—that is, in the bed of a river; but this was soon exhausted. A thick layer of clay was struck below the sand, and the work was abandoned in order to search for new fields. Fortunately one of the gold diggers, who had made up his mind to stay some time longer, got the idea of working through the clay, and by so doing he reached enormous quantities of gold in the old bed of the river. For centuries the streams had carried gold down from the mountains and deposited it here in "pockets" in the bed of the river. A single "pocket" of this kind would sometimes contain thousands of pounds' worth of gold. Within a month Ballarat became the richest gold field in the whole world.

The gold fever grew into a perfect rage. Melbourne was almost deserted. People of every class and from every part of the world left their work, their situations, and their homes to seek their fortunes.

In Melbourne policemen left their posts of duty, officials threw up their offices, and sailors deserted their ships.

In spite of the fact that everybody rushed to the gold mines, thus preventing a normal development of the country, Australia got full compensation in the new impetus given to immigration. The year after the discovery of gold more than 100,000 immigrants arrived in Victoria. Thus the population was doubled in a single year, and during the following five years it increased fivefold. While in 1830 there were less than 4000 inhabitants, in 1860 their number had increased to 1,300,000. The quantity of gold found was also sufficiently large to explain this increase of population. During the next ten years £100,000,000 were produced in Victoria alone.

As a matter of course, money had but little value in such circumstances. During he first years after the discovery of the gold fields sovereigns passed as freely as copper pennies. A barber would get £1 for cutting a gold digger's hair; the idea of giving change back was never thought of.

Many characteristic stories are told of this golden age of the fortune-seekers. A gold digger took a holiday, and went into a restaurant where he demanded a breakfast for £10. The hostess looked at him, smiled, and answered that she was not able to furnish so expensive a breakfast at present. Her highest price was five shillings. "Well," said the customer, "give me the best you have." The hostess did her best, and served every hot and cold dish she could devise. The gold digger seated himself at the table, looked at the various dishes with the air of an epicure, but at length turned up his nose and declared that there was nothing fit for him to eat. Then he took a large roll of bank-notes out of his pocket, selected a £10 note, laid it between two pieces of bread and butter, ate it, and washed it down with champagne. "That's what I call a ten-pound breakfast," he added, and paid his bill and walked out.

Two Irishmen came into an inn to rest while the coachman was changing horses. The Irishmen were gold diggers who had reaped an abundant harvest, and they were now on their way home to the Emerald Isle with their pockets full of gold.

They learned that the innkeeper also was an Irishman, and this fact aroused their patriotism; so they resolved to drink a toast to old Ireland in champagne. Fifty bottles of this choice beverage were demanded for the honour of Ireland. But no sooner had they paid the £50 and opened the first two bottles than the coachman shouts, "All ready!" The Irishmen climb into their places in the coach and proceed on their journey, leaving the host to finish the remaining forty-eight bottles.

The average individual gains were, however, not so large, and the digging for gold was gradually reduced to systematic methods.

The work by degrees became a link in that mining industry which embraced copper, coal, and tin. Copper and coal were discovered in Australia long before gold—as was also tin, which in its importance to the colonies may in time equal the others. New discoveries of gold have attracted adventurers to the north of Australia, and opened new avenues for immigration; but the continent is, upon the whole, pastoral and agricultural.

The Chinese have forced their way into all the islands of the Indian Ocean, and this new current of immigration has given the development of Australia, particularly of tropical Queensland, a peculiar character.

Efforts have been made to check in an effective manner this influx of Chinese labourers, who supplant the white workmen. Here, as in America, an "import duty" and similar obstacles have been tried in order to stop the stream, but still the Chinese kept coming. A treaty with China, making immigration therefrom almost impossible, last year failed to be ratified by the Chinese Government. It is still an open question whether there is any way of stopping this influx, or whether the Chinese stream of immigration will continue to form an undercurrent to that from Europe. It does not seem possible that the Chinese will ever become the predominating element.

The Kanakas being better able to endure the heat than the white population, it is probable that here, as in America, a class of Anglo-Saxon plantation-owners dependent on coloured labour may be developed.

The nature of the country has given its industries their peculiar character. The raising of sheep requires immense pastures, and agriculture assumes wide dimensions on the new and fertile soil. The result is that local centres are created with great difficulty in the midst of this industry spread over so large a domain. The points of colonisation first chosen thus obtain a great advantage and monopolise the trade. They become centres of knowledge and of pleasure, and they absorb all that stream of immigrants who are not suited to agriculture and do not acquire land but settle wherever they can earn a bare living. The fact that a population of less than 3,000,000 scattered over an immense territory has two cities, Melbourne and Sydney, of nearly 400,000 inhabitants each, and that one-third of the population of Australia lives in five of the largest cities, is unique and is explained by what has been stated above.

The political separation of the different colonies is intimately connected with the uneven distribution of the population. The independent development of the two chief centres, Melbourne and Sydney, could not fail to break the old New South Wales into two colonies (1851). Tasmania obtained its own seat of government in 1825 in Hobart Town. With Brisbane's development came Queensland's separation in 1859 as an independent colony, which doubled its population in the subsequent six years. There is a constantly growing desire for emancipation, and at the present time strenuous efforts are being made to make the north part of Queensland into a separate colony.

At the same time as this work of separation is progressing there are also centralising elements at work, and the latter will no doubt lead to favourable results in the near future. Efforts are being made to unite the various colonies into a confederation. There also prevails a strong common sentiment in regard to the efforts of all other nations to establish colonies in the neighbouring countries (the Germans in New Guinea and the French in New Caledonia), and an arrangement for a common defence of their interests against these rivals has already been begun. National pride is very marked in Australia.

The bond of union between Australia and the mother country has not been loosened in the midst of this development toward independence. On the contrary, the Australians cling to it with increasing tenacity, and with even more enthusiasm than Englishmen themselves. The best proof of this is the fact that Australia sent a special contingent to take part in England's last war at Suakim. The form of the proposed imperial federation has, however, not yet been worked out.

A similar effort for political emancipation from British control has been going on within the separate colonies. In the first convict settlements of course martial law was administered by their governors, but in the political conflict—carried on chiefly in the mother colony, New South Wales—home rule became fully established. At first the governor chose his own ministers; but in course of time (1824) the ministry became dependent on the general elections, as in England. At length in 1851, the critical year in the annals of Australia, the colonies secured a perfectly independent constitution providing for two legislative houses. In the various colonies members of the upper house were chosen either by the Government or by the wealthy classes of the community. A certain property qualification was also originally necessary for members of the lower house, though this is now merely nominal.

The English system of jurisprudence and of municipal rule prevails everywhere. The schools are free and unsectarian, and attendance is compulsory. The colonies which originally consisted of criminals have developed a remarkable interest in the cause of education. As in the United States, universities and academies are largely the product of private munificence.

Relying on their rapid development and on their large natural resources, the colonies have been induced to incur an enormous public debt, amounting to about £20,000,000, and we must bear in mind that the population is only about 3,000,000. The above debt includes, however, local expenditures, and much of it has been created for building railroads, which were very much needed in this large country. But the Government owns 1,400,000,000 acres of unsold land, and though a part of this is almost worthless, still the revenue which will come in from its sale may justify the incurring of such a debt.

The history of the colonisation reveals a community which still possesses the vigour of youth, and whose culture is wholly European, and these results, wonderful as they are, have been achieved in two generations. If we could visit Australia two generations hence we would probably find a country where not only European flora—grain, grass, etc.—and European fauna—the sheep, horse, cow, rabbit, sparrow, etc.—will have invaded and conquered the large districts which have been cut off from the rest of the world since the tertiary period, but where every trace of the original population will have disappeared. Instead of a stagnation of thousands of years in the first stages of the stone age, we shall have a vigorous development parallel with the culture of Europe and America.

In the whole history of man's development a more sudden revolution is not known than that which has happened in Australia during this century.

At the centennial festival celebrated last year in Australia it was prophesied that one hundred years hence Australia will be a federal republic with 50,000,000 English-speaking inhabitants, who, sprung from the same race as that which gave birth to the Americans, will have developed into a new but easily recognisable type, resembling but yet differing from their Yankee cousins. The motto of the Australians is "Advance Australia!" They have proved that they have been able to carry out this maxim in the past and they will not fail to do so in the future.

GEOLOGY

AUSTRALIA may be compared to a gigantic plate. The interior part is flat, moderately high (300 to 2150 feet), and the elevation increases toward the edges. The raised edge of this plate is in the south-east, where we find the highest summit in Australia, Mount Townsend, in Kosciuszko Range, which is 7059 feet high. The edge of the plate has a very marked character on the east coast, where a continuous though not very high chain of mountains stretches from Victoria through the eastern part of New South Wales and Queensland to the York peninsula, which bounds on the east the great Gulf of Carpentaria. This whole mountain chain is embraced by the Australian geographers (e.g. G. Sutherland) in the term "The Great Dividing Range," the separate parts of which have separate names. In the boundary between Victoria and New South Wales it is called the Australian Alps, and west of Sydney the Blue Mountains.

Round the lower part of the Gulf of Carpentaria and in a part of the south coast of Australia the "plate" has no edge, and low and flat country stretches here from the sea far into the interior. On the other hand an elevation is found in the "bottom of the plate" in Central Australia, but this elevation nowhere reaches 3000 feet.

Australia has no streams to be compared with the great rivers of other countries, a fact due to the scarcity of rain. The largest stream is Murray river, which empties itself into the sea on the south coast. With its tributaries it drains a country as large as the triangle formed by North Cape, Christiania, and St. Petersburg. During the rainy season the lower part of Murray river is navigable.

Australia consists of primitive rock, granite, gneiss, and silurian rock—that is to say, very old formations, and nearly identical with those of the Scandinavian peninsula.

There are many coal-bearing strata in Queensland and in the north-eastern part of New South Wales; thus Australia, in addition to its other mineral wealth, also possesses "black diamonds." In many places strata from the mesozoic period of the earth's history have been found.

The shell given below, of which I found a large number lying in sandstone near Minnie Downs 400 miles west from Rockhampton, is a gigantic *Inoceramus* from the cretaceous period. I gave this fossil to the mineralogical cabinet in Christiania

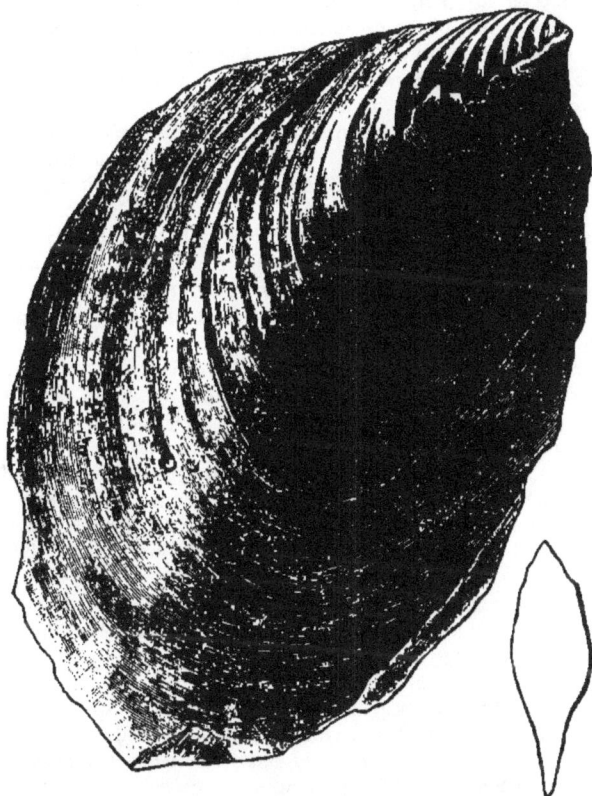

A LARGE FOSSIL SEA-SHELL FROM WESTERN QUEENSLAND (*Inoceramus maximus*)
(length 12¾ inches, breadth 7¼ inches).

University, and it has been described by the Swedish Professor Bernh. Lundgren, who is an authority in this field of science.

The remains of animal and vegetable life found in the older strata agree, as a whole, with those found in other parts of the globe of the same periods. At some time in the mesozoic age the Australian continent must have been separated and have become a continent by itself. This plainly appears in the tertiary period, during which the greater part of Australia seems to have remained an independent dry country. This was also the case during the quaternary period.

Australia has had no ice period. At least but uncertain traces of glacial actions are to be found.

In the tertiary period we must look for the oldest ancestors of the present fauna, in the quaternary for the immediate progenitors, which resemble the present animals, and many of them are remarkable for their size. There has been a kangaroo one-third larger than the present species, there has also been a gigantic animal related to the kangaroo and living on vegetables, the *Diprotodon*, which was about as large as an elephant. The remains of this animal are so widespread and so numerous as to make it evident that it must have existed wellnigh throughout Australia.

At the time when the country became inhabited by man there still lived one of the great animals of the palæozoic times, namely a bird resembling the ostrich and much larger than the emu. Its bones have been found in the middens of the savages, and the joints show marks of their flint knives.

Among the more recent geological formations is the so-called "desert sandstone," which is found scattered through a great part of the interior. It contains no sea-shells, and but few remains of plants and of fresh-water shells. There are various opinions in regard to its origin. Some think it was deposited in large lakes, which are supposed to have been very numerous in a remote age. A more probable theory is, however, that the substratum has been disintegrated into sand and stone dust and blown about by the wind.

Australia has no active volcanoes, but extinct ones are numerous. Some of those found in Victoria are believed to have been active in a late prehistoric age.

Among the mineral products of Australia gold is the most important. It had its seat originally in veins of quartz in the oldest rocks. By the disintegration of the rocks during the long geological ages much alluvial gold has been deposited among the sand and the gravel. The running water carries stony substances with it more rapidly than gold, which lags behind on account of its weight. The result is that the deposits increase in quantity as we approach the original seat of the gold, and when circumstances are favourable the gold digger may be handsomely rewarded for his labours.

FLORA

Scarcely a flora is to be found with so many peculiarities as the Australian. Still this does not imply that the things which appear so remarkable to the traveller are of equal interest to the botanist, though often they are more so. It is often stated as a curiosity that the Australian "cherry-trees" have the stone outside of the berry, and not inside, as with us in Europe. As a matter of fact this is nothing remarkable, the explanation being simply that what we call the fruit is merely an enlarged berry-like stalk, while the fruit proper is an unsavoury nut, hard as stone, growing at the extreme end of this stalk. Hence the tree is called *Exocarpus* ("outside fruit"). Similar phenomena are found in other parts of the world.[1] The Australian "pear" grows with the large end nearest the stalk; but it is not a pear, just an inedible fruit, hard as wood, of a Proteacea called *Xylomelum pyriforme*.

This is not uncommon near Port Jackson. Another species of the same genus inhabits Queensland, and two others Western Australia; all bearing similar woody fruits or seed-vessels.

The arboreous and shrubby vegetation of Australia is almost exclusively evergreen, or rather one might say the leaves are persistent, for the beautiful shades of green characterising the forests and fields of the northern hemisphere are wanting, and are replaced by a monotony of olive-green or bluish-green. On the other hand, brilliantly coloured flowers abound, the natural orders *Leguminosæ*, *Myrtaceæ*, and *Proteaceæ* being especially numerous, diversified, and generally dispersed over the whole country.

Although large areas in the interior have not been botanically explored, the flora of the country is almost as well known as that of Europe, not in its minutest details, but in general character and composition. Robert Brown the eminent English botanist, *facile princeps* among botanists of his time, was the first real investigator

[1] In the West Indies there is a similar fruit, *Anacardium*, growing at the extremity of the enlarged stalk.

of the exceedingly rich Australian flora. He accompanied Flinders on his voyage of discovery in Australian seas during the first years of the present century, and made very extensive collections of dried plants, which he elaborated after his return home. Noteworthy among subsequent botanists who have turned their attention to the vegetation of that part of the world are Sir Joseph Hooker, Sir Ferdinand von Mueller, and the late Mr. George Bentham. Assisted by the extensive collections and notes accumulated by Mueller, combined with the numerous earlier collections preserved in England, Bentham wrote a descriptive account of all the plants known to inhabit Australia. This work is in English, and it is a monument of industry and learning, consisting of seven octavo volumes with an aggregate of 4000 pages.

Sir Ferdinand von Mueller has since largely supplemented this work, besides publishing a number of highly important, fully illustrated monographs of the more important genera, such as *Eucalyptus* and *Acacia*. According to Mueller's latest census of the flora, the number of species of flowering plants and ferns known to inhabit the country at the end of 1888 was 8909, belonging to 1394 genera and 149 natural orders.

These are large numbers, but, what is more remarkable, something like 7700 of these species are endemic, or peculiar to Australia. The endemic element in a flora is nowhere in the world higher, if even so high, in so large an area, as in Western Australia, where eighty-five per cent of the species are peculiar, and of the remaining fifteen per cent few species extend beyond Australia.

LEAVES, FLOWERS, AND FRUIT OF
Eucalyptus amygdalina.

Several genera are very numerous in species, notably *Acacia*, of which there are upwards of 300, and *Eucalyptus*, of which there are 150; and *Grevillea* (*Proteaceæ*) is represented by 150, and *Melaleuca* (*Myrtaceæ*) by 100 species.

Foremost in utility and most prominent in the scenery all over Australia are the species of *Eucalyptus*, locally named blue gum, green gum, iron-bark, stringy-bark, etc. etc. They vary in stature from dwarf bushes to the tallest tree in the world, one species, *E. amygdalina* (p. 370), considerably overtopping the "big trees" (*Wellingtonia*) of California. In some parts of Victoria there are groves of this tree averaging upwards of 300 feet in height, and several, as recorded in Mueller's useful *Eucalyptographia*, have been found to measure more than 400 feet, and the tallest of all 471 feet.

In addition to being the largest and most durable timber of the country, the gum-trees yield a variety of useful products. Most of them exude a valuable gum resin; the bark of others is employed in tanning, and the oil of *Eucalyptus* is now extracted to the extent of 2000 gallons annually in one factory. Several of them periodically shed their barks in large sheets, after the manner of our planes and birches, but more thoroughly. The leaves, like those of many other Australian trees, are vertical instead of horizontal, so that they afford comparatively little shade. Unlike our forest trees, too, they have more or less conspicuous flowers—some of the western species especially large and highly coloured flowers, followed by woody seed-vessels varying in different species from less than a quarter of an inch to three inches in diameter, and containing numerous very small seeds.

The genus *Eucalyptus* belongs to a tribe of the *Myrtaceæ* characterised by having a dry instead of a fleshy fruit. To the same group belongs the large genus *Melaleuca*, which is likewise almost peculiar to Australia and spread all over it. Conspicuous among the species of *Melaleuca* is *M. Leucadendron*, which inhabits all except the south-eastern region. It is called tea-tree, paper-bark tree, and milkwood in the different colonies. The wood of this tree is very beautiful and durable, and valuable for shipbuilding and other purposes; and the papery bark is said to be impervious to water and remains sound after the wood has decayed. The accompanying woodcut (p. 373) will give an idea of the aspect of the tree.

Next to the *Eucalypti*, the *Proteaceæ* and *Acaciæ* are almost everywhere prominent features in the landscape. The numerous species of *Banksia*, honeysuckles of the colonists, are generally dispersed, and easily recognised by their large dense heads of showy flowers, succeeded by large, gaping, woody seed-vessels.

With few exceptions, the species of *Acacia* differ from those of other parts of the world (except two or three in the Mascarene and Sandwich Islands) in the feathery pinnate leaves being reduced to vertically flattened, rounded, and variously shaped organs corresponding to the leaf-stalk, and termed phyllodes. Occasionally, and especially in young seedling-plants, the ordinary pinnate blade is born at the end of the phyllode, thus giving a clue to its true nature.

True cone-bearing trees are rare in Australia, but the allied slender-branched weeping species of *Frenela* (*Callitris*) and the very similar *Casuarinae* (the she-oak, river oak, forest oak, etc.) are almost inseparable from Australian scenery. In Queensland and northern New South Wales there are, however, two remarkable true

AN AUSTRALIAN SPRUCE (*Araucaria Bidwillii*).

cone-bearing trees: namely, the bunya-bunya (*Araucaria Bidwillii*) and the Moreton Bay pine (*A. Cunninghamii*). There are other species of *Araucaria* in Norfolk Island, New Caledonia, and South America. The Australian species both afford a valuable timber, but it is not permitted to fell the bunya-bunya on the Crown lands, owing to its seeds being a valuable article of food to the aborigines.

Even so slight a sketch as this of the vegetation of Australia

THE TEA-TREE (*Melaleuca Leucadendron*).

would be singularly imperfect without some reference to the highly peculiar grass-trees (*Xanthorrhœa*), which form so striking a feature in the scenery, especially in West Australia. The larger species have stout trunks surmounted by a tuft of long narrow recurved leaves, from the centre of which rise the tall, slender, shaft-like inflorescences.

Few persons knowing anything ot botany have not heard of the gigantic African baobab; yet fewer probably have heard of the Australian baobab, found on the sandy plains and stony ridges from the Glenelg river to Arnhem's Land. It is equally remarkable for the great size of its trunk, which is sometimes as much as eighty feet in circumference.

Tree-ferns are abundant and exceedingly fine in some parts of the eastern side of Australia, and there are some handsome palms in Queensland and New South Wales; but neither of these groups is represented in West Australia, unless it be quite in the north.

One more prominent feature in Australian vegetation are the large expanses of the so-called "scrub" of the colonists. This is a dense covering of low bushes, varying in composition in different districts, and named according to the predominating element.

The nearest botanical affinities of the Australian flora are with that of South Africa, though the characteristic genera, as well as the species, are invariably different in the two countries.

I am indebted to Dr. F. Kiær for the following brief note on the Australian mosses :—

The moss flora of Queensland has hitherto been comparatively but little studied. The number of varieties of foliaceous mosses known does not reach 200, while there doubtless are three or four times as many. Among those who have collected mosses in Queensland may be mentioned Miss Hellen Scott and Mrs. Amalie Dietrich, and more recently Mr. F. M. Bailey. Some of the mosses found belong to genera scattered throughout the world, *e.g.*, *Sphagnum*, *Dicranum*, *Barbula*, *Bryum*, *Neckera*, *Thuidium*, *Hypnum*, etc. On the other hand genera are found that are peculiar to Australia, and finally there are forms which are characteristic of the tropical and sub-tropical zone.

As peculiar to Australia, we must first mention among the mosses bearing top-fruit the genus *Dawsonia*, which has not hitherto been found outside of this continent. This genus, of which there are three known species in Queensland, is one of the most beautiful and the largest of all mosses. It resembles a *Polytrichum* in appearance, and, like the latter, has a hairy cap, but around the opening its fruit is studded with a bunch of threadlike hairs, the latter attaining a number of five hundred and over.

Among other genera hitherto found only in Australia we may mention among mosses having side-fruit the *Euptychium*, remarkable for its leaves, which are folded very compactly, and the short-leaved *Bescherellea*, which abounds in Queensland. The latter genus is known in New Caledonia, and resembles a *Cyrtopus*, but has only a single row of teeth around the mouth.

The genus *Spiridens*, found in many species on the Australian islands, and also on the Sunda Isles, on the Moluccas, and on the Philippine Islands, is not represented at all in Queensland.

Among Australian forms we should also mention one or two species of *Endotrichella*, *Orthorrhynchium*, the beautiful *Braithwaitea*, three species of the handsome *Thamniella*, and a few species of the tree-like branched *Hypnodendron*. The *Ptychomnium aciculare* (*Brid.*), common in the southern hemisphere, is also found in Queensland.

In addition to *Octoblepharum albidum* and *Rhizogonium spiniforme*, found everywhere in the tropics, there are in Queensland several species of the last-named genus.

The genus *Macromitrium* has many representatives in Queensland (more than ten species). Furthermore, we may here mention several species of the genera *Papillaria*, *Hypopterygium*, and *Rhacopilum*.

The moss flora of Queensland, little as it is known, already presents a type widely differing from the European, and the future will doubtless bring forth many interesting discoveries in this extensive colony.

Of liverworts but few (eighteen) have yet been found in Queensland, but there is a prospect that our knowledge of this interesting group in this country will be supplemented before many years.

IV

FAUNA

Chlamydosaurus kingii.

IT is evident that Australia is the country which has been least changed in the later geological time, being now in the main as it was in the early part of the tertiary period. It has also been called a land forgotten in the cretaceous period by the development of the earth. This "land of the dawning" reveals to us a corresponding primitive and peculiar animal life, as well as flora with its proteaceæ, leafless casuarinas, and acacias, which remind us of the vanished vegetation of the elder tertiary period. The major part of Australia's mammals consists of the remarkable marsupials, which belong to the very oldest and lowest organisation of all known mammals, and which have, without doubt, survived from an earlier geological period, during which they were also found in Europe. Among birds the country has some remarkable species (*Megapodidæ*), the only ones in the world that do not hatch their eggs themselves but, like reptiles, bury them in earth-mounds, whose elements of fermentation produce heat and thus hatch the eggs. The two coursers, the emu and the cassowary, when we except the kiwi-kiwi of New Zealand, have more rudimentary wings than any now existing ostrich.

In the tertiary period Australia is supposed to have been much larger than it now is. It is thought to have included New Guinea and Tasmania, and possibly to have extended eastward to the Fiji Islands. According to the celebrated naturalist Mr. A. R. Wallace, this hypothesis is absolutely necessary in order to explain certain facts connected with the Australian fauna. As already stated, remains of remarkable gigantic marsupials have been found. They lived chiefly on grass, and are not supposed to have had a higher organisation than those now existing. Placental [1] beasts of prey that could disturb the existence of these giants not having been found among the fossils, Wallace is of opinion that the latter became extinct on account of physico-geographical, and particularly climatic, changes taking place at the same time as the ice period appeared in the rest of the world. As a remarkable fact it may be mentioned that remains have recently been found of the gigantic moa (*Dinornis*), a genus hitherto supposed to have been found only in New Zealand.

Among the six zoological regions into which Wallace and Sclater divide the *terra firma* of the globe, one of the best marked and certainly the most peculiar one is the Australian. Australia and New Guinea are the largest countries in this region, which, in addition to New Zealand and the islands of the Pacific, includes the Indian Archipelago east of Borneo, Java, and Bali. The latter islands, all of which belong to the Indian-Malay region, are separated from the Australian by a belt of very deep water, where Wallace's well-known line is found on the map. The water is shallow between all the islands south-east of this belt—Celebes, Timor, Amboina, Banda, and New Guinea—which evidently all lie on a submarine bank, and have at one time been united with Australia. There are the most striking differences between the fauna on each side of the belt. Apes, rhinoceroses, tapirs, tigers, leopards, and similar Indian and Malay animals disappear, and we enter an entirely new region, the Australian, the chief characteristic of which is that it lacks nearly all the groups of mammals found elsewhere in the world. Instead we either find the peculiar marsupials, or the mammals are entirely

---

[1] Placental mammals are those having a placenta to nourish the fœtus, as is the case with all mammals except the marsupials and monotremes.

wanting, as is the case on most of the South Sea Islands. In ornithology the honey-eaters are especially remarkable, then we have the birds of paradise, the cassowary, and finally the kiwi-kiwi of New Zealand.

The zoological character of the region is most marked in Australia, which is rich in peculiar animal forms. As an island-continent extending from 39° to 11° S. lat., and which consequently is several times as large as the islands of the other regions added together, the country naturally has very various climates. In the southern part there is a climate like that of the countries along the Mediterranean ; in the northern there is a regular season of rain ; while the centre is more hot and more arid than any other part of the earth. Still, strange to say, the climatic differences are not attended by corresponding variations of the fauna, which is strikingly uniform throughout the country. Many important species are found everywhere in the continent. Generally speaking, Australia is a hot and dry country, and its flora and fauna have been developed in harmony with its physico-geographical conditions. This explains, for instance, why the tropical North Australia has not so luxurious and varied vegetations as the adjacent New Guinea, with its more humid climate. Many of the Australian mammals can subsist without water for a long time. Gould is even of opinion that the large kingfishers, whose food consists mainly of lizards and insects, never drink.

The fauna of Australia has many special forms, and occupies a peculiar, isolated position. This is most apparent among the mammals, which give to the Australian fauna its most marked feature. Imagine a continent about the size of Europe with no other mammals than marsupials, a few bats, rats, and mice. There are no apes, no beasts of prey, no hoofed animals. None of those groups are found from which our domestic animals have been developed. The only exception is the dingo, the Australian dog, but although fossil specimens have been found, it is generally supposed that the dingo was introduced by man ; it does not differ much from the wild dogs of other lands. The fact that Australia at present has so many large land animals, which at one time were represented by kindred forms in Europe, shows that the country in some way or other has been united with Asia, just as Great Britain must at some time have been connected with the European continent. But the present remarkable isolation of the Australian mammals from the land fauna of the rest of the world is, as Wallace remarks, the best evidence that Australia and Asia were not united throughout the tertiary period, and it is a most characteristic fact that the only mammals which Australia has in common with the rest of the world are the flying-bats and such small mammals as could most easily be carried on floating logs, roots, and similar objects to foreign coasts. Marsupials are also found in America; but, with this exception, they now exist only in Australia and in the adjacent islands New Guinea and Tasmania, which is evidence that the latter islands were at one time united with Australia.

The marsupials are so called from their having a pouch (*marsupium*) for carrying the immature young. The young are born without much development, and they are at once transferred to the pouch, where they continue to grow until they are able to take care of themselves. The pouch is supported by the marsupial bones, which are equally developed in both sexes. There are also many other peculiarities in the structure of these animals, distinguishing them from the higher mammals, *e.g.* their teeth being quite different from those of other animals.

The large kangaroo bears a young "no larger than the little finger of a human baby, and not unlike it in form." This helpless, naked, blind, and deaf being the mother puts in an almost inexplicable manner into the pouch with her mouth, and places it on one of the long, slender, milk-giving strings found in the pouch. Here the young remains hanging for weeks, and grows very rapidly. The mother possesses a peculiar muscle with which it is able to press milk into the mouth of the helpless little one, and the larynx of the young has a peculiar structure, so that it can breathe while it sucks, and consequently is not choked. Gradually it assumes the form of its parents, and when big enough it begins to make excursions from the pouch, which continues to enlarge with the growth of the young. These excursions become longer as the young grows larger, and thus this pouch serves both as a second womb and as a nest and home. All marsupials are propagated in this manner, but the number of young may vary from one to fourteen.

The brain of the marsupial is small and has but few convolutions, indicative of small mental development. They are the most stupid of all mammals, and indifferent in regard to all things save the wants of their stomachs. Brehm calls attention to the fact that no marsupial mother plays with her young or makes any effort to teach them.

The marsupials may differ widely in appearance, structure, and habits; they may be as large as a stag and as small as a mouse. Some move on the hindfeet alone, others on all fours; some live on the ground, others in trees, others again are able to fly. Most of them feed on grass, but some of them live on fruits, roots, and leaves; others again on meat and insects; while there are also marsupials that eat honey.

Ever since Captain Cook's sailors in 1770 came and told him that they had seen the very devil hopping away on his hind-legs in the form of an animal, the kangaroo has been inseparably associated with our ideas of Australia, the land of the kangaroo. The kangaroo (*Macropus*) is also the largest and most remarkable of all marsupials, and is represented by many species throughout Australia. The largest one is reddish (*Macropus rufus*), and is found in the interior. Of the smaller kinds we may mention the wallabies, kangaroo-rats, which are about the size of a rabbit, and the pademelon, which is easily recognised by the fact that when it runs it lets one arm drop as if it were broken. During recent years kangaroos have greatly increased in number, one of the causes being the systematic extermination of the dingoes and the decrease of the number of natives. Thus kangaroos, like their smaller relatives the wallabies and the kangaroo-rats, have become noxious animals that destroy the pastures, and the colonists are making great efforts to exterminate them. In Queensland the Government pays a premium for every such animal killed, and in this way the number of marsupials was reduced in the years 1880-1885 by six millions.

The tree-kangaroos (*Dendrolagus*), living in the dense scrubs of Northern Queensland, are very remarkable and very different from the other members of the family.

The phalangers (*Phalangeridæ*) are a large family found everywhere in Australia. They inhabit the trees, and like most of the marsupials, seek their food at night. They are usually called opossums, but are very different from the genuine opossum of America. Just as the latter are the most perfect and most intelligent of all marsupials, so the Australian opossums are the most perfectly organised of all Australian marsupials. They are, so to speak, the apes of the marsupials, in that they feed on fruit, but are able to live on insects and birds' eggs; have a prehensile tail and a movable thumb, which almost converts their feet into hands.

Closely related to the latter are the flying-squirrels (*Petaurus*), which are strikingly like those in India. The smallest one of this family, the beautiful *Acrobates pygmæus*, is a perfect wonder of elegance and graceful movement. Though not larger than a little mouse, still it flies through the air as skilfully as the larger species. It frequently becomes the prey of domestic cats.

A transition between the kangaroos and the phalangers is found in the marsupial bear (*Phascolarctus*), while the rodents are represented by the large, plump wombat (*Phascolomys*).

The family *Dasyuridæ* are carnivorous. The colonist usually names them after animals of the old world, "marsupial cat," "marsupial tiger," "marsupial wolf," etc. All these marsupial beasts of prey are very rapacious, and one or two of them are quite equal to the martens and weasels in this respect. The marsupial wolf (*Thylacinus*) and the marsupial devil (*Sarcophilus*) in Tasmania are the most ferocious and most powerful of all the Australian animals, and do great damage among the sheep. The former is, however, well-nigh exterminated. Native cats (*Dasyurus geoffroyi*) are numerous everywhere, and are hated by the colonists, because they attack the poultry. Near Mount Elephant, in Victoria, five hundred of them were killed in one night by two poisoned sheep carcasses. There had long been a drought, so that the animals had congregated in the only place where water was to be found.

We now come to the *Monotremata*, the lowest group of all mammals. They have the marsupial bones, but no pouch, and they are destitute of teeth. Of this remarkable family there are only two genera, the duck-billed platypus and the spiny ant-eater.

The duck-billed platypus (*Ornithorhynchus anatinus*) is easily recognised by its horny jaws, which have a striking resemblance to the bill of a duck. The animal is about fifteen inches long, and the body, which is covered with close brown hair, is broad, flat, and somewhat like that of a reptile. The feet are short and the toes are webbed. During the daytime the ornithorhynchus sleeps in deep burrows dug in the banks of rivers. It is common in the southern and eastern part of Australia, and is also found in Tasmania.

The spiny ant-eater (*Echidna*) resembles our porcupine in appearance and size, has quills like it, and can roll itself into a ball. The toes are not webbed, but the animal is a very good swimmer. It feeds on ants and insects, and, like other ant-eaters, has a long, slender tongue, which has a secretion of a sticky substance. It is a most powerful animal, and can disappear so rapidly in loose earth or sand that it seems to sink into the ground. Its flesh is very fat, and is considered a great delicacy by the blacks. On Herbert river, where the ant-eater is called gombian, the natives hunt it with the help of tamed dingoes.

These mammals, the two most remarkable ones on the globe, reveal a wonderful relationship to the lower vertebrates, reptiles and birds. Thus we find that the front extremities are fastened to the breast-bone by a highly developed coracoid and an epicoracoid, as in the case of lizards. This does not occur in any other mammal. Their skulls, like those of birds, have no visible sutures whatever.

The most remarkable fact, however, is that these animals do not bear living young, but lay eggs. The latter contain a large yolk, and when hatched the young are suckled by the mother.

The stages of development of the eggs are different from those of all other mammals, and resemble to a great extent those of reptiles and birds. As the eggs are *meroblastic*,[1] these animals seem to be even more closely related to birds and reptiles than to the mammals.

The eggs lying in the ovaries are $\frac{1}{8}$ of an inch in diameter, possibly even more, and they certainly are the largest eggs produced by mammals. In a human being and in the higher mammals the egg averages $\frac{1}{125}$ of an inch in diameter.

---

[1] Where only a small part of the yolk goes to form the foetus, while the greater part is used to nourish it, as is the case with birds, the egg is called *meroblastic*. With mammals, all the yolk is used to form the foetus (*holoblastic eggs*).

The young seem to require a long time to arrive at maturity. They are hatched small, blind, and naked, and their mouths have not at first the form of a beak, but are thick, round, soft, and well adapted to receive the milk, which is strained through the lacteal glands, for there are no nipples. As these animals have no pouch (the ant-eater has a rudimentary one in the form of a crease in the skin while it nurses its young), the young remain in the nest, where the mother suckles them.

Though the ornithology of Australia is not so isolated in its character as the mammals are, still its birds are very remarkable, and have almost as many points of interest. We here find eagles, hawks, thrushes, swallows, fly-catchers, sea-gulls, ducks, etc., though of other species than those to which we are accustomed ; but we are astonished that vultures and woodpeckers, which exist in all other parts of the world, are wholly wanting.

The honey-eaters (*Meliphagidæ*), so well adapted to the circumstances of the country, are very remarkable. As the trees and bushes of Australia have a great wealth of flowers, but are wanting in juicy fruits, many of its birds find their food in the flowers, inhabiting the trees and bushes, particularly gum-trees and banksias, and rarely coming down on the ground to seek food. These characteristic birds, of which there are no less than 200 species, remind us by their mode of life of the American humming-birds ; still they are very different from the latter. The largest are of the size of a small dove, but much more slender. They are strong lively birds, which with their powerful feet cling fast to the branches, almost like titmice, while they suck the flowers, and their tongue ends in a brush, so that they can easily lick up the honey and the honey-eating insects. Even some of the parrots, the so-called brush-tongued (*Trichoglossidæ*), live on honey and pollen, and are peculiar to Australia.

The strange habits of many of the Australian birds have already been described, *e.g.* the play-houses built by the æsthetic bower-birds, and the three species which do not themselves hatch their eggs, like the reptiles, but leave the hatching to be done by artificial heat. The latter belong to the family of *Megapodidæ*, a group which receives its name from the fact that their feet and claws are very large and powerful, and consequently well adapted to building the large mounds in which the eggs are laid.

It is a strange fact that the kingfishers found everywhere in the world, and the equally cosmopolitan pigeons, should be so numerous in Australia. Among the former are the wonderful laughing jackasses (*Dacelo*), whose voice is unlike that of any other bird. In Australia the pigeons attain the highest development both as to wealth of species and brilliancy of plumage. Some of them even have a crest on the top of the head, a very rare ornament for this

WILD GEESE FROM NORTH QUEENSLAND (*Anseranas melanoleuca*). Photograph from nature. *To face page 383.*

family. The extraordinary development of these defenceless birds indicates that they have but few enemies in Australia. Wallace gives as the reason for their great numbers the total absence of apes, cats, weasels, and other animals that live in trees and that eat the eggs and the young of birds, while the very green colour of these birds conceals them from birds of prey, their only foes. On the plains in the interior of Queensland countless numbers of pigeons are seen, but of modest-coloured plumage, to protect them in this open country.

Many of the Australian birds are distinguished for their brilliant plumage, and in this respect they easily rank with the humming-birds of America and with the trogons and parrots of India. Thus we have the elegant little wrens whose leading colours are azure-blue and scarlet-red; the yellow and velvety black regent-bird (*Sericulus melinus*); and the metallic glittering rifle-bird (*Ptilorhis victoriæ*); and finally, the finches, that have a combination of colours the like of which is to be found only in butterflies. Among the many parrots, which include such strange forms as the white and the black cockatoos, there are some which are unique in the beauty of their colours. So remarkable a decoration as the tail of the lyre-bird (*Menura*) is found nowhere else in the world of birds.

The stately emu, which together with the cassowary represents the ostrich family in Australia, is still numerous in the open country. The cassowary, on the other hand, which is found only in the north-eastern tropical part, is rare, and will doubtless soon become extinct as civilisation gradually advances and clears the scrubs.

Ducks, geese, and other swimming birds are numerous, and afford excellent sport, but as they are much sought by sportsmen, the colonies have passed laws to protect them during a certain season of the year. Among the geese which have only half-webbed toes, the most common is the "black and white" (*Anseranas melanoleuca*). These beautiful birds gather in large flocks, but as civilisation advances they are gradually decreasing in number. At present they are numerous only in Northern Queensland, where the flocks are so large and dense that the natives can easily kill them with their spears. They were of great value to Leichhardt on his overland expedition to the Gulf of Carpentaria.

It is a remarkable fact that some species of Australian birds without any apparent reason suddenly leave the district where they have had their habitat for years, and settle somewhere else, to disappear again after a few years. Gould gives several examples of this. A squatter whom I knew told me that the pelicans several years ago quite unexpectedly made their appearance on Darling river in New South Wales, 400 miles from the coast. Neither the whites nor the blacks had ever seen them there before. They settled down near a lake called Dry Lagoon and bred there. Meanwhile the lagoon dried up as usual, and the pelicans were obliged to bring fish for their young from a lake two miles away. As soon as the young became large enough they were transferred to the latter lake, the whole colony requiring three weeks for the journey. As a rule the pelicans build their nests on islands near the coast.

Australia has no less than 700 species of birds; of these probably 600 are found in Queensland alone, and this must be said to be a great wealth of species. Europe, which is somewhat larger and has been incomparably much more thoroughly explored, has only about 500 species.

Reptiles, amphibious animals, and fishes are well represented in Australia, and among them are some of great interest.

Lizards are found everywhere, but it is a strange fact that, as in the case of plants, some species are found in West Australia that are peculiar to this district and have never been observed outside of it. That characteristic forms are not wanting is shown by the frilled-lizard (*Chlamydosaurus kingii*) represented at the beginning of this chapter. Around its neck it has a large, loose skin which it is able to raise into a Queen Elizabeth ruff. Unlike all other lizards, this animal assumes in sitting the same posture as a kangaroo, and when startled it makes, like them, long jumps five to six feet high before it begins to run.

Although *Viperidæ* and *Crotalidæ*, which elsewhere are the most venomous families of snakes, are not found in Australia, still scarcely any other part of the globe has so many venomous serpents in comparison with the number of those that are harmless. Here, as elsewhere, the number of snakes increase with the heat of the climate, so that Tasmania has only three species, while Queensland can show fifty, and among the latter several large harmless pythons, which the natives are fond of eating. Water-snakes abound along the coasts of tropical Australia, and are all venomous.

Amphibious animals with tails (salamanders) are not found. On the other hand, frogs are plentiful. They have a remarkable faculty for accommodating themselves to all the dry climatic conditions of the country. In South Australia a drought once lasted for twenty-six months. The country was transformed into a desert, and life was not to be seen. Sheep and cattle had perished, and so had the marsupials. Suddenly rain poured down. The long drought was at an end; and six hours after the storm had begun the rain was welcomed by the powerful voices of the frogs. Flies afterward came in great numbers, and then bats appeared in countless swarms. On my travels in Western Queensland I heard the people on Diamantina river speak of a species of large frog which after rain buried themselves about six inches down in the ground, and remained there during the dry season. These frogs contain much water, a fact known to the natives, who dig them up in the dry season and quench their thirst by squeezing the water out of them. The white population also sometimes resort to these frogs for water. They know the little mounds, which resemble mole-hills, under which the frogs lie hid, and dig them out. According to report, such a frog contains about a wine-glassful of "clear, sweet water."

The colonists of Australia have a fondness for giving familiar names to Australian animals. Thus they have called a large fish found in some of the rivers of Central Queensland burnett salmon. This fish, which the natives call barramunda, is, however, no salmon, for both salmon and carp are entirely wanting in Australia. But its size and its fat and delicate-tasting flesh reminded the people of the salmon, and it had long been eagerly sought as food both by whites and blacks, when in 1870 the scientific world became acquainted with it, and discovered in it a remarkable survival of the prehistoric past. Fossil teeth of this fish, now known as *Ceratodus forsteri*, had long ago been found in the Trias and Jura formations in Europe, India, and America, but the animal was of course thought to be extinct, like the *Iguanodon* or *Dinotherium*. Like the *Protopterus* from Africa and the *Lepidosiren* from the Amazon river, it belongs to the very ancient and remarkable lung-fish (*Dipnoi*), which, as the name indicates, has both gills and lungs. *Ceratodus forsteri* has only one lung, and can breathe with it alone, or with the gills alone, or with both at the same time, and therefore it leaves the water in the night and goes ashore, where it eats grass and leaves, while in the daytime it may be seen sunning itself on logs lying out of the water. This "living fossil," which attains a length of six feet, thus forms a remarkable connecting link between fishes and reptiles.

While Australia is poor in regard to butterflies, it has many beautiful beetles, e.g. the family *Buprestidæ*. The lower animal life is peculiar, but still comparatively little known.

. . . . .

Professor G. O. Sars, of Christiania, has made some exceedingly interesting experiments, whereby he has succeeded in hatching artificially and domesticating in his aquarium various Australian fresh-water *Entomostraca*. The materials for these experiments consisted of small quantities of mud taken from the bottom of lakes and small fresh-water ponds near Rockhampton. After being thoroughly dried, I forwarded this mud to Christiania. The specimens sent looked on their arrival like small masses of rock, and were so hard that they could scarcely be broken with a hammer. Nevertheless they contained living germs in the form of eggs, which had been deposited by entomostraca living in the waters in question. In most cases these eggs proved to be encased in peculiar capsules, which frequently bore a startling resemblance to bean-pods, and in some of the specimens they were found in great numbers. By softening the mud and by a suitable preparation in aquaria,

Professor Sars succeeded not only in producing perfectly developed individuals, but also in getting them to propagate in the aquaria, and thus it became possible to make very exhaustive investigations

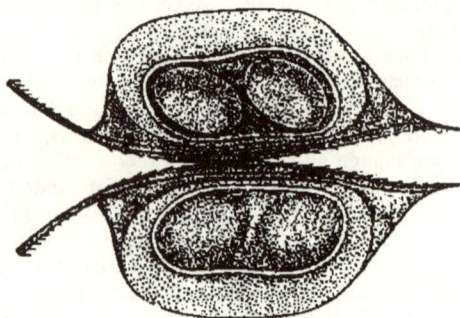

EGG OF *Daphnia lumholtzii.*

in regard to a portion of Australia's fauna hitherto almost entirely unknown.   One of the most striking forms hatched in this manner is the little *Daphnia* called *D. lumholtzii.*

Daphnia lumholtzii.

   In addition to this, nine others have been described by Professor Sars in two treatises: "On some Australian Cladocera raised from dried mud," *Christiania Videnskabs-selskabs Forhandlinger,* 1885; and "Additional Notes on Australian Cladocera," *Christiania Videnskabs-selskabs Forhandlinger,* 1888.   On the same subject he has recently published a treatise: "On *Cyclestheria hislopi* (Baird), a new generic type of bivalve Phyllopoda, *Christiania Videnskabs-selskabs Forhandlinger,* 1887," in which he has described a most interesting animal form, which the author hatched in the same manner, and observed through several generations.   This

animal has been noted heretofore in specimens from India and
Ceylon, but very imperfectly, and hence mistakes have been made
in regard to its systematic position, and no knowledge was
obtained as to its interesting habits and life.   It belongs to
the so-called shell-covered phyllopoda, of which only a limited
number of species have hitherto been known.   One of its chief

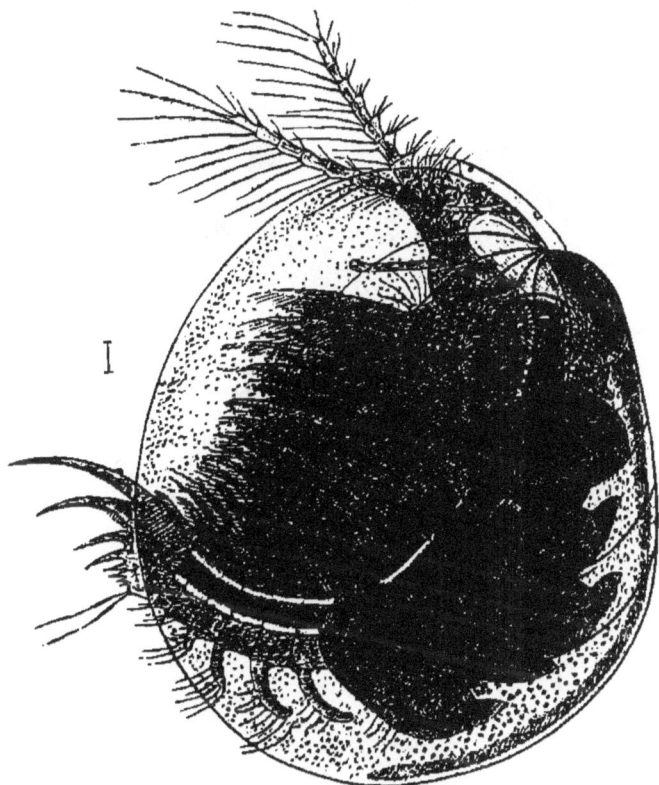

Cyclestheria hislopi.

characteristics is the fact that it is enclosed in a transparent
double shell, which has a deceptive likeness to a clam-shell   The
anatomical examination of the animal has demonstrated that it
cannot be classified with any of the known genera, but forms the
type for a new one, to which the name cyclestheria has been affixed.
In regard to propagation and development, this form differs widely
from all the phyllopoda heretofore known.   Contrary to the general

rule, the eggs are developed within the shell of the mother animal, and this development is direct, not through any metamorphosis, as is the case with the other known *Phyllopoda*. In his treatise Professor Sars has given the whole history of the development of this animal, which abounds in interesting facts.

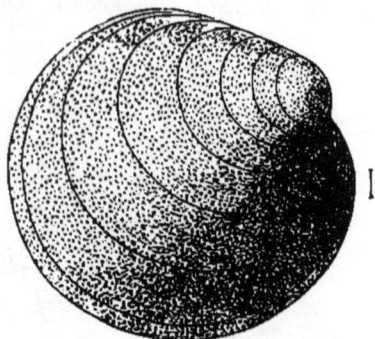

SHELL OF A *Cyclestheria hislopi.*

Finally, I may add that the results obtained by these hatchings are already so important that they supply materials for many future treatises, and that many lower fresh-water animals, not only entomostraca, but also forms belonging to totally different departments of zoology, *e.g. Bryozoæ*, have in this way been thoroughly examined and studied in a living condition.

INDEX

FINIS

www.ingramcontent.com/pod-product-compliance
Lightning Source LLC
Chambersburg PA
CBHW031819270326
41932CB00008B/472